he Wiley Marketing Series

LIAM LAZER, Advisory Editor *Michigan State Univesity*

PSYCHOLOGICAL EXP

IN CONSUMER

T

WIL

MAR

ROB
ROB
T
E

GE

EI

J

S

Psychological Experiments in Consumer Behavior

Edited By

Steuart Henderson Britt

Ph. D. in Psychology
Professor of Marketing in the Graduate School of Management
and
Professor of Advertising in the Medill School of Journalism
Northwestern University
Evanston, Illinois 60201

JOHN WILEY & SONS, INC.
NEW YORK · LONDON · SYDNEY · TORONTO

Library of Congress Catalogue Card Number: 71-127659

ISBN 0-471-10481-7

Printed in the United States of America

10 9 8 7 6 5 4 3 2 1

DEDICATED *to* P.Y.E.

Preface

The 33 articles reproduced here, in their entirety, are significant examples of psychological experiments in each of the following major areas of consumer behavior.

    I. Foundations of Consumer Behavior
   II. Cultural Influences
  III. Individual Influences
  IV. Group Influences
   V. Economic Influences
  VI. The Business Firm and the Consumer
 VII. Product Attributes and the Consumer
VIII. Promotion and the Consumer
  IX. Decision-Making by Consumers

These nine topics are exactly the same as the topics in my *Consumer Behavior and the Behavioral Sciences* (Wiley, 1966) and in my new book *Consumer Behavior in Theory and in Action* (Wiley, 1970). The three books complement each other, and thus can be used together for an overall view of consumer behavior.

The criteria used in selecting the 33 readings in the present book were that every article must:

1. Deal with a *special area* of consumer behavior.
2. Be *scientific* in method.
3. Report *empirical* studies (that is, experiments, observations, or analyses of data, or a combination of these).
4. Consist of *original investigations.*
5. Involve *actual research* rather than "library research."
6. Deal with studies of *realistic situations.*

Northwestern University
Evanston, Illinois, October, 1970

Steuart Henderson Britt, Ph. D.

Acknowledgments

The opportunity to reproduce articles from the following journals is gratefully acknowledged.

Journal	Number of Articles
Admap	1
American Marketing Association (Conference Proceedings)	8
Journalism Quarterly	2
Journal of Advertising Research	2
Journal of Applied Psychology	2
Journal of Marketing	3
Journal of Marketing Research	12
Journal of Social Psychology	1
Public Opinion Quarterly	2
Total	33

I thank David A. Woodworth (now Product Development Department, Continental Illinois National Bank & Trust Company of Chicago) who, during his senior year in the Medill School of Journalism of Northwestern University, worked with me in analyzing hundreds of articles that were possibilities for reproduction in the present volume. Discussions with Jeffrey Manning, graduate student in the Medill School of Journalism (now account executive with Grey Advertising, Inc., New York), and with James L. Lubawski, graduate student in the Graduate School of Management (currently instructor in marketing, University of Northern Iowa), helped materially in making the final selection of materials.

I feel a deep sense of appreciation for the assistance on this book from my superb secretary, Mrs. Irene E. Peach.

S.H.B.

Contents

PART VIII   PROMOTION AND THE CONSUMER

PART IX   DECISION MAKING BY CONSUMERS

FOUNDATIONS OF CONSUMER BEHAVIOR

1. The Consumer in Society

"The Automobile Buyer After the Purchase," Gerald D. Bell (Marketing Educator), *Journal of Marketing,* Vol. 31 (July, 1967), pp. 12-16.

2. Behavioral Sciences and the Consumer

"Reisman's Theory of Social Character Applied to Consumer-Goods Advertising," Patricia Roe Morton (Advertising Researcher), ©*Journalism Quarterly,* Vol. 44 (Summer, 1967), pp. 337-340.

3. Fact-finding About Consumers

"Sales Effects of a New Counter Display," Peter J. McClure (Marketing Educator) and E. James West (Marketing Executive), *Journal of Advertising Research,* Vol. 9 (March, 1969), pp. 29-34.

It is through an understanding of certain material from the behavioral sciences that we can gain insights into the "whys" of consumer behavior. And we can best utilize these insights by having some background about fact-finding techniques. Three different fact-finding studies are reported in Part I.

1 The Consumer in Society

The Automobile Buyer After the Purchase

GERALD D. BELL *(Marketing Educator)*

Customer satisfaction after the purchase is a key factor in brand loyalty. Marketing managers are becoming keenly interested in how a new purchaser feels after buying.

In this study, an analysis is made of how a new car buyer feels about his purchase after it is completed. What factors determine the reactions of a customer when he begins living with his new car?

This article explores the effect of customers' personalities in relation to salesmen's persuasion attempts upon consumers' post-purchase satisfaction.

Consumers differ markedly in their susceptibility to persuasion attempts. A growing body of research tries to explain why some individuals are more persuasible than others. However, there is a dearth of information concerning how the consumer feels *after being persuaded* to purchase a product. In this article, we analyze how a customer feels *after buying* a new car. That is, we examine the consequences of being influenced upon a buyer's cognitive dissonance, or, as automobile salesmen refer to it, "buyer's remorse" after the purchase.[1]

Research suggests that a consumer's self-confidence has an unusual effect on his persuasibility.[2] Those most confident and those least confident in their car-buying

Source: Gerald D. Bell, "The Automobile Buyer After the Purchase," *Journal of Marketing,* Vol. 31 (July, 1967), pp. 12-16.

[1] Parts of this paper were presented to the Symposium on Consumer Behavior, April 17-20, 1966, at the University of Texas, Austin, Texas. The author is grateful for financial assistance provided for this investigation by the Business Foundation of the University of North Carolina, School of Business Administration, and to the University of North Carolina Research Council. Helpful comments were provided by Donald F. Cox and Rollie Tillman.
[2] See Gerald D. Bell, "Self-Confidence and Persuasibility Among Car Buyers," *Journal of Marketing Research* (February, 1967), pp. 46-52; and Donald F. Cox and Raymond A. Bauer, "Self Confidence and Persuasibility in Women," *Public Opinion Quarterly,* Vol. 28 (Fall, 1964), pp. 453-466.

ability are most difficult to persuade. However, those moderately confident are most easily persuaded. Customers high in self-confidence are difficult to influence because they have had much experience in making acceptable decisions, and consequently have faith in their own judgment. Individuals low in self-confidence are difficult to influence because their precariously-held self-esteem causes them to react defensively against influence attempts. Those with moderate self-confidence are neither secure with their own judgment nor highly defensive. Consequently, they are the most persuasible.

PERSUASIBILITY AND COGNITIVE DISSONANCE

We were interested in what effects the above associations between self-confidence and persuasibility had upon a customer's psychological reactions after he has purchased an automobile. Do individuals who have been persuaded most easily suffer the most cognitive dissonance after the purchase? Before we attempt to answer this question, let us examine the concept of cognitive dissonance more closely.

Research Design

The study was conducted in a large urban area in the western part of the United States. One Chevrolet dealership was chosen as the source for finding customers who had just purchased new cars. This dealership had a good reputation within the region and with General Motors Corporation.

Data were collected during the summer months of 1965. During this period 289 new cars were sold at the agency under study. We attempted to interview all of these buyers and succeeded with 234 persons, which represented an 81% completion rate. Respondents were predominantly Protestant, between the ages of 26 and 45, high school graduates, and earned between $8,600 and $12,500 per year.

Personal interviews were conducted by the investigator from one to eight days after the purchase. We waited at least one day after the purchase to allow buyers time to reflect on their decisions. The reason for not allowing more than eight days to elapse before the interview was to attempt to gain a more accurate measure of the dissonance subjects were experiencing, before they distorted this state by their attempts at dissonance reduction. Fifty customers were interviewed between one to four days before they made their final purchase so we could check for the validity of our measures. Comparisons between these fifty individuals and the remaining respondents suggest that there is very little difference in answers respondents give to the measures of the above variables in a before- or after-purchase situation.

MAJOR CONCEPTS AND DEFINITIONS

We measured *cognitive dissonance* by asking questions that would reveal the respondent's feelings about his purchase. For example, we asked for his reactions to the following types of questions: "How do you feel about your new car?"

"After a person buys a new car he usually feels a little uneasy about it; do you think you got a good deal?" "To what extent do you wonder whether or not you made the right decision?" "Would most people expect to get the same kind of deal you got?"

Persuasibility was defined by first asking respondents to what extent they were influenced by the salesmen on the price, payments, particular car (color, style, size, and so forth), accessories, delivery, and service. Secondly, immediately following the sale, we asked the salesman to rank the customer on how easy he was to persuade on the above items. We then combined these two measures and ranked respondents into five categories on persuasibility.

The perceived quality of service customers received was measured by asking a respondent how he felt about the way the salesmen and agency representatives had treated him, what condition his car was in upon delivery, the way in which plans were made for future service, and what extra accessories were given or sold to him at reduced rates. Respondents were ranked into five categories on the summated scores on favorableness of service they had received.

The Findings

PERSUASIBILITY AND COGNITIVE DISSONANCE

We are now ready to ask, "What are the effects of the relationships between self-confidence and persuasibility upon customers' post-purchase dissonance?" Past research suggests that those who are most easily persuaded will be highly dissonant after the purchase.[3] Those who have been talked into deals may begin to realize they bought cars they did not like, for prices they did not want to pay. Consequently, we expected that those who were most persuasible would have the most cognitive dissonance.

TABLE 1   PERSUASIBILITY AND COGNITIVE DISSONANCE

| | | Persuasibility (in percent) | | | |
		High	Medium	Low	Ns
	High	46	26	28	78
Cognitive Dissonance	Medium	51	23	27	91
	Low	43	25	32	65

$$\chi^2 = 1.17, P < .45$$

The findings reported in Table 1, however, do not support this hypothesis, for there is no association between persuasibility and dissonance. The explanation for this unexpected finding appears to be that the customer's self-confidence influences

[3] James F. Engel, "Are Automobile Purchasers Dissonant Consumers?" *Journal of Marketing,* Vol. 27 (April, 1963), pp. 55-58.

his persuasibility as well as his dissonance. When we control for the self-confidence of the customer, we find significant relationships between persuasibility and cognitive dissonance.

CUSTOMERS WITH HIGH SELF-CONFIDENCE

The data in Table 2 point out that customers who are *high on self-confidence,* were high on dissonance if they were easily persuaded in buying their new cars. Evidently, for those who are high on self-esteem, being persuaded is inconsistent with their usual behavior.

TABLE 2   PERSUASIBILITY AND DISSONANCE FOR THOSE HIGH ON SELF-CONFIDENCE

| | | Persuasibility (in percent) | | | |
		High	Medium	Low	Ns
	High	56	31	13	36
Cognitive Dissonance	Medium	21	33	46	43
	Low	14	29	57	28

$$x^2 = 17.23, P < .001$$

107

On the other hand (see Table 2), those who are *high on self-confidence* had very little dissonance if they were not easily persuaded. They made their decisions, accepted them, and were happy.

CUSTOMERS WITH LOW SELF-CONFIDENCE

We find quite a different relationship, however, for those who had little self-confidence. The findings presented in Table 3 suggest that those *low on self-confidence* had little dissonance if they were easily persuaded. They were convinced by the salesmen that they had made very good deals, and their confidence was bolstered by the salesmen's persuasion attempts.

On the other hand, those with little confidence were highly dissonant if they resisted influence attempts of salesmen and were not easily persuaded. Perhaps their self-doubts began to influence their attitudes after they completed their purchases. They wondered whether or not they had made the proper deals much more than did those low on self-confidence who had been persuaded. They had not been convinced by the salesmen that they had made wise choices and therefore were uneasy about their decisions.

QUALITY OF SERVICE AND COGNITIVE DISSONANCE

A potential cause of a customer's dissonance after the purchase is the quality of service he receives. This, however, was not considered in the studies reviewed

TABLE 3   PERSUASIBILITY AND DISSONANCE FOR THOSE LOW ON
SELF-CONFIDENCE

		Persuasibility (in percent)			
---	---	High	Medium	Low	Ns
Cognitive Dissonance	High	45	24	31	42
	Medium	60	25	15	48
	Low	86	8	8	37
					127

$$x^2 = 54.05, P < .001$$

TABLE 4   QUALITY OF SERVICE AND COGNITIVE DISSONANCE

		Quality of Service (in percent)			
---	---	High	Medium	Low	Ns
Cognitive Dissonance	High	14	28	58	78
	Medium	22	41	37	91
	Low	63	25	12	65

$$x^2 = 54.05, P < .001$$

earlier by Ehrlich and others, and by Engel.[4] They assumed that most people who
purchase new automobiles will be dissonant, regardless of quality of service received. However, it would seem that if a person feels he has received poor service
he would quickly develop some inconsistencies in his expectations as to how he
should be treated as compared to how he is being treated.

All one needs to do to understand this process is to look at the face of a customer who proudly drives away from the dealership in his brand new $3,000 car
and suddenly runs out of gas, and while he is getting out of his car has a flat tire.
This actually happened to one customer interviewed. The icing for the cake was
that after the dealership helped the customer get some gasoline and fixed his tire
they billed him (by mistake) for their service.

The relationships between respondents' cognitive dissonance and the perceived
quality of service supports the above ideas (See Table 4). The better the quality
of service, the lower the buyers' dissonance.

PERSUASIBILITY AND QUALITY OF SERVICE

We next looked for factors which might influence the quality of service an individual receives. A rather surprising finding occurred. By relating persuasibility
to quality of service the data in Table 5 suggest a slight curvilinear relationship

[4]D. Ehrlich, T., Guttman, P. Schonbach, and J. Mills, "Post-Decision Exposure to Relevant Information," *Journal of Abnormal and Social Psychology,* Vol. 54 (1957), pp. 98-102. Also see
Engel, *loc. cit.*

TABLE 5   QUALITY OF SERVICE AND PERSUASIBILITY

| | | Quality of Service (in percent) | | | |
		High	Medium	Low	Ns
	High	41	32	27	111
Cognitive Dissonance	Medium	5	28	67	57
	Low	36	36	28	66

$$x^2 = 34.16, P < .001$$

between these two factors. Those who are low on persuasibility received quite good service. These individuals were not only difficult to persuade, but, in fact, often wore the salesmen down. The salesmen refer to these customers as "grinders." This term is a vivid reference to the vigorous effort these individuals put forth to obtain a good deal. The grinders, then, ended up with a very high quality service, usually at good prices.

On the other end of the persuasibility continuum were those who were quite easily persuaded in their car purchases. Salesmen call these customers "flakes." Salesmen seem to have an ambivalent attitude toward flakes. On one hand they make jokes about them and kid each other when they are dealing with them; yet they seem to feel sorry for these individuals and are much more likely to give them free accessories, services, and special care upon delivery. Part of the reason flakes get quite good service, however, is that they pay slightly more for their cars than do the grinders.

The surprising finding is that those medium on persuasibility get the worst service. They grind enough to put the salesmen on guard and into the game of trying to outmaneuver the customer. Yet, the customer strives to only a moderate degree to acquire top service. Consequently, the salesmen do not feel sympathetic toward the customer and do not give him top quality service. And the customer does not have the talent or desire to wear down the salesman until he does obtain good service. This customer, for whom the salesmen have no name, ends up with the worst service.

The above analysis suggests, then, that persuasibility acts as an indirect cause of buyers' dissonance. Those who are moderately persuasible receive the worst service, and those who receive poor service tend to be the highest on cognitive dissonance.

Conclusion

In sum, the findings of this investigation suggest the effect of a customer's self-confidence, his persuasibility, and the quality of service he receives upon his cognitive dissonance. All customers are not cognitively dissonant, as is suggested by past researchers. Rather, the type of personality an individual brings to the dealership and the experiences he has while purchasing his new car determine the extent of his dissatisfaction with the metallic object sitting in his driveway. Undoubtedly, the more unhappy a customer is with his purchase, the less likely he will be to return to the brand and/or dealer. These findings further suggest that the automobile industry might well increase the amount of promotion allocated to post-purchase reselling. Indeed, the feelings of the customer after the purchase are the pillars of profitability in any company's future. Two groups of customers stand out as deserving special attention in after-sale promotion. These are the buyers who were most easily persuaded and those who received the worst service. These are the groups most likely to switch brands, and consequently those who deserve the most attention from the advertising dollar.

2 Behavioral Sciences and the Consumer

Riesman's Theory of Social Character Applied to Consumer-Goods Advertising

PATRICIA ROE MORTON *(Advertising Researcher)*

What are the implications of an *other-directed* society? Is the U.S. society becoming more other-directed? Can Riesman's "theory of social character" be applied to consumer-goods advertising?

This study involves examination of the advertising content of several prominent women's magazines over a 51-year period, in order to evaluate other-directedness.

*In 1950 David Riesman in *The Lonely Crowd,* presented an impressive theory of social character that made a great impact upon the social sciences. Basically, he hypothesized that there are three types of social character, each of which enforces conformity in a definably different way:

1) The tradition-directed society insures conformity by instilling a strong tendency to follow tradition.

2) The inner-directed society insures conformity by instilling early in life a strong tendency to follow an internalized set of goals.

3) The other-directed society insures conformity by instilling a sensitivity to the expectations and preferences of others (the peer-group).

Riesman stated that the United States was moving from being an inner-directed society to becoming an other-directed society. He indicated that this change would first be noticeable in the upper middle class.

Source: Patricia Roe Morton, "Riesman's Theory of Social Character Applied to Consumer-Goods Advertising," © *Journalism Quarterly,* Vol. 44 (Summer, 1967), pp. 337-340.

*This article is based on Mrs. Morton's M.S. thesis in advertising at the University of Illinois, written under the direction of Dr. Arnold Barban.

Several studies based on Riesman's theories have been done, including those of W. M. Kassarjian, H. H. Kassarjian, Richard Centers and Walter Gruen.[1] However, only Dornbusch and Hickman have done an historical study to see if inner- or other-directedness is gaining strength in American society.[2] The study discussed here updated and elaborated the Dornbusch and Hickman effort, and attempted to validate or refute its findings.

Thus, the purpose of this study was to see if indeed other-directedness was growing in the United States. Specifically, the objectives were:

1) To record the relative number of other-directed advertisements for specific periods in history and over time.

2) To record the relative number of other-directed advertisements by product type.

3) To record the relative number of other-directed advertisements by medium used.

Advertising served as a reflection of society's values. Also, an attempt was made to see how valuable Riesman's theory of other-directedness is to advertisers.

Method

This study is similar to Dornbusch and Hickman in that it utilized a content analysis of advertisements in women's magazines and shares in the belief, "that a shift in the verbal themes of consumer-goods advertising is likely to reflect a corresponding change in the values of the audience for that advertising."[3]

In addition to the *Ladies' Home Journal,* used by Dornbusch and Hickman, *McCall's* and *Good Housekeeping* were studied after being judged as having basically the same social level audience as the *Ladies' Home Journal.* It was believed that this would make the study more truly representative of a class of magazines rather than using the audience of only one magazine.

It was hypothesized that product category might influence the degree of other-directedness shown in advertising. Product categories were drawn from the *Life Study of Consumer Expenditures* to cover items advertised in women's magazines. The 13 categories used were: Men's clothing and footwear, Children's clothing and

---

[1]W. M. Kassarjian, "A Study of Riesman's Theory of Social Character," *Sociometry,* 25:213-30 (September 1962); Richard Centers, "An Examination of the Riesman Social Character Typology: A Metropolitan Survey," *Sociometry,* 25:231-40 (September 1962); H. H. Kassarjian, "Social Character and Differential Preference for Mass Communications," *Journal of Marketing Research,* 2:146-53 (May 1965); Walter Gruen, "Preference for New Products and Its Relationship to Different Measures of Conformity," *Journal of Applied Psychology,* 24:361-4 (December 1960).

[2]Sanford M. Dornbusch and Lauren C. Hickman, "Other-Directedness in Consumer-Goods Advertising: A Test of Riesman's Historical Theory," *Social Forces,* 38:99-102 (December 1959).

[3]*Ibid.*

footwear, Women's clothing and footwear, Infant supplies, Food, Medical supplies, Cosmetics, Personal hygiene, Home operation, Home furnishings and appliances, Automotive, Recreation and "Etc." — smoking accessories, transportation, travel, professional services.

Five time periods were chosen: 1913-14, 1923-24, 1938-39, 1955-56, 1963-64. An attempt was made to choose relatively normal historical periods. A random method was used to determine which of the three magazines was to be studied for each month of the five two-year periods. The random selection method was structured so that four issues of each magazine were studied for each year in the sample. This was felt essential since comparisons between magazines were an integral part of the analysis. Advertisements of one-half page or larger were studied.

Some issues of *McCall's* were not available in the facilities used by the researcher, and thus this serves as a limitation of the sample.

Indices of other-directedness were devised by studying earlier work done on Riesman's theory and by careful reading of *The Lonely Crowd.* The following indices were used (the first five are the same used by Dornbusch and Hickman):

1) Testimonal.
2) Collective endorsement ("All housewives like product X").
3) Quantitative endorsement ("25 million people like product X").
4) Positive interpersonal ("He'll love you if you use product X").
5) Both positive and negative interpersonal ("A person is unloved until he uses product X").
6) Interpersonal activities showing the involvement of several people.
7) There is a direct bid for approval shown.
8) "Follow-the-herdism" is emphasized.
9) Social, rather than task-oriented, activities are shown.
10) Quality is determined by the peer-group.
11) There is a use of "modern, new, up-to-date" as an appeal.
12) Heroes, symbols of culture, are shown as personal, informal.

The entire advertisement was used as the study unit. Thus, if either illustration or copy was other-directed, the advertisement was classified as other-directed.

RESULTS AND DISCUSSION

Figure 1 illustrates the main finding of the study. An increase in other-directedness was found until the 1938-39 period, after which other-directedness began to decline and continued to decline during the 1963-64 period. Overall, other-directedness proved to be about 10% higher in 1963-64 than in 1913-14. However, the downward slope of the curve indicates that this difference could disappear in the near future. This graph substantially sums up the results of the study. The three magazines all yielded basically the same curve, although *Good Housekeeping* was somewhat less other-directed than the *Ladies' Home Journal* or *McCall's.* The latter two ran close together, with the *Ladies' Home Journal* a percentage point or two ahead of *McCall's* in the amount of other-directed advertising. Thus, editorial

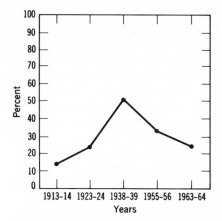

Figure 1. Percentage of other-directed advertisements for all products in three women's magazines, selected years.

differences and other factors did not, to any great degree, affect the amount of other-directed advertisements.

Product categories yielded slightly different results. Some products, as could be expected, tended to be more other-directed than others. Cosmetics and personal hygiene scored very high in other-directedness; but interestingly enough only *one* category − cosmetics − defied the general trend away from other-directedness that began after 1938-39. Personal hygiene and women's clothing, two categories that "logically" seem important in winning the approval of others, follow the general trend and do decline in other-directedness.

Explanations were sought. By going to the raw data it was discovered that cosmetic advertising did not develop until the mid-twenties; thus, its main growth occurred during a period of growing other-directedness. Clothing and personal hygiene had been strongly advertised in the periods before the mid-twenties and had a heritage of inner-directed advertising. Inertia alone may account for a slower rise in their tendency toward other-directedness.

The "control group" was meant to be the "Etc." category composed of items and services not inherently feminine. It was assumed that this category would develop somewhat later than the others, as women became less stereotyped as "wives and mothers," and would grow in the period that Riesman stated was becoming other-directed. Thus, it would tend to be more other-directed than the more traditionally "feminine" categories. In fact, the hypothesis was proved out, though not as dramatically as expected. "Etc." did, from 1913-14 to 1963-64, increase over 30% in other-directed advertisements; the other categories gained from 6 to 10%. This, then, increases support for the hypothesis that advertisements having their growth period in a period of other-directedness tend to be far more other-directed than advertisements that have had the benefit of longer and more varied experience.

A second hypothesis was suggested: as advertising moves into a period when other-directedness wanes, the percentage of other-directed advertisements also wanes. This was true for every product category except cosmetics, and suggests that cosmetic advertisers today may be using an inefficient strategy and overdoing the other-directed appeal. Actually, inner-directed advertisements that appeal to success or personal pride might be more effective. In fact, this study predicts that cosmetics will soon become less other-directed in their advertising appeals. This decline has been thwarted by the type of product and the time when the product was introduced.

Other-directedness has probably declined under the ascendance of two very powerful forces — education and cosmopolitanism. Riesman stated that the Korean conflict, and Sputnik in 1957, changed the emphasis of American education by making work and discipline far more valuable than consummatory talents. At the same time, due to the increased intimacy of communications, the whole world is more available to each individual; housewives no longer identify only with the woman down the block. This greatly loosens the power of the peer group. At the same time, the cold war, automation, the new theology, the much discussed vastness of space all tend to make the individual feel entirely alone. He sees himself as isolated in the world, dependent upon his own powers, own training, his own superiority to achieve what he wishes.

Riesman recognized the power of these forces. In a letter he wrote to Dornbusch and Hickman, he said he had no doubt education was forcing the advertiser to be more subtle in his other-directed advertising. And Riesman once wrote that, "there is a general tendency to enlarge empathy beyond one's class, one's country — more people are peers, in immediate circles or vicariously through the mass media."[4]

Conclusions

Other-directedness, as reflected in advertising, is declining in the United States. This is contrary to Riesman's hypothesis that it would grow in the 1950s and 1960s. All three magazines studied here show this decline. All product categories but one also show this decline. Cosmetics, due to its inherently other-directed character and its time of development and growth, still shows an upward movement toward other-directedness. Cosmetic advertisers may be somewhat misperceptive to the true state of other-directedness in American society, but it is suggested that this will change in the near future.

This study agrees with an earlier study by Dornbusch and Hickman; it elaborated and updated their study and came to their conclusion that the research results are "certainly contradictory to [Riesman's] expectations of a continual increase in other-directedness in recent years."[5]

[4]David Riesman and Norman Glazer, *"The Lonely Crowd:* A Reconsideration in 1960," *Culture and Social Character,* ed. Seymour M. Lipsot and Leo Lowenthal (The Free Press of Glencoe, Inc., 1961), p. 432.
[5]Dornbusch and Hickman, *op. cit.,* p. 100.

3 Fact-finding About Consumers

Sales Effects of a New Counter Display

PETER J. McCLURE* *(Marketing Educator)* AND E. JAMES WEST† *(Marketing Executive)*

Can a direct link be made between in-store promotion and cash-register receipts? More specifically, can significant increases in sales be associated with and attributed to a new counter display? This study examines these areas in a controlled random sample of stores in the Boston area.

The objective of the experiments discussed here was to determine whether significant increases in sales were associated with the use of a new counter display. Although the objective was straightforward and the experiments were uncomplicated, a discussion of the design, execution and especially the interpretation of the resulting data, may give useful insights to others considering the use of controlled experiments in marketing decision-making.

Source: Peter J. McClure and E. James West, "Sales Effects of a New Counter Display," *Journal of Advertising Research,* Vol. 9 (March, 1969), pp. 29-34.

*Peter J. McClure is an associate professor of marketing at Boston University's College of Business Administration. At present he is teaching marketing in Germany with the Boston University Overseas Graduate Program. He received his B.S.M.E. in 1958 from Purdue University and subsequently his M.B.A. (1959) and D.B.A. (1966) from Indiana University. Dr. McClure is a consultant to firms in the Boston area. His current research interests are browsing behavior and determinants of advertising readership. His article, "Differences Between Retailers' and Consumers' Perception" (with J. K. Ryans) appeared in the *Journal of Marketing Research.*

†E. James West is specialty sales manager with USM Corporation, Hoague-Sprague Division, Lynn, Mass. At the time of this research he was a product manager with the Carter's Ink Company where he was responsible for marketing a line of coloring and marking products through mass market outlets. After leaving Carter's Mr. West was manager of market development for Rust Craft Greeting Cards. He received his B.A. in English in 1955 from Williams College, Williamstown, Mass. Following his work with Professor McClure, he was awarded an M.B.A. from Boston University. **15**

BACKGROUND

Among the products manufactured by Carter's Ink Company, Cambridge, Massachusetts, is a line of dacron felt tip markers which are available in a variety of bright colors under the trade name, *Draws-A-Lot*. The product is generally packaged as a shrink-fit carded item in sets ranging from one to fourteen colors and retails between 33¢ and 39¢ per marker depending on the size of the set. The markers are sold through the company's nation-wide sales organization to drug, stationery, variety and other types of stores. Negligible consumer advertising has been employed; consequently, sales are highly dependent on packaging, price, and point-of-purchase displays.

The product line has generally been displayed in counter-top racks provided by the manufacturer or in the retailer's eye-level gondola displays or in binning glass on the open counter. An intergrated eye-catching display of the product line has seldom been achieved. The new display being tested was a counter-top 16-prong wire carrousel holding merchandise worth $50 at retail value. Visible display of a large portion of the product line in a small space was considered the chief advantage of the new display.

If the experiments yielded favorable results two actions would be taken. Existing displays would gradually be replaced with the new carrousel display, and the results of the experiments would be integrated into promotional materials designed to persuade more retailers to accept the new display in favorable store locations. Of course neither action would be taken if the results were unfavorable.

Method

The data were generated in controlled experiments of the randomized block design (Banks, 1965) executed during a six-week period beginning Friday, February 3, 1967. One experiment was conducted in four drug stores and the other in four stationery stores. The procedures for each experiment were identical.

The four stores in each experiment were drawn from a list of active accounts in the Boston metropolitan area. Conformity with a predesignated set of matching criteria, summarized in Table 1, was the basis for individual store selection. The previous year's sales to the retailer of the felt tip markers were used as the measure of store size for purposes of the experiment. The remaining criteria were evaluated by inspecting the stores visually. Once an acceptable list was developed a low pressure approach was used to solicit the store managers' cooperation in order not to stimulate unusual interest in the execution of the experiments.

Two stores selected at random from each of the four drug and four stationery stores were designated as the experimental group. The others comprised the control groups. The existing displays in all stores were filled, and ample stock was provided in under-counter locations. Managers were instructed to service the displays in their usual manner.

TABLE 1   MATCHING CRITERIA FOR STORE SELECTION

	Store Type	
Criterion	Drug Stores	Stationery Stores
Store size	Equal to other drug stores	Equal to other stationery stores
Store location	Suburban	Suburban
Service	Self-service	Self-service
Display location	Stationery section	Stationery section
Counter type	Gondola	Open or gondola
Facings	Few	Many
Stockouts	Many	Few
Neatness	Neat	Neat
Seasonal effects	None	None

On Fridays for the first three weeks, the pre-test period, a company representative visited the stores and recorded the week's dollar sales of the product line. On the third Friday the new carrousel display was set up in the two experimental drug and two experimental stationery stores. Sales were recorded in all stores on the following three Fridays. At no time during the six-week period did the company representatives disturb or restock the displays with the exception of setting up the carrousel displays in the experimental stores at the beginning of the test period. The resulting data, disguised for purposes of publication as a matter of company policy, are summarized in Tables 2 and 3 in a format which demonstrates the design of the experiments. These data were later re-coded to simplify calculations in the t test and two-way analysis of variance used to analyze the data. Disguising or coding the original data by adding or multiplying by constants does not affect the statistical analysis.

Results

The purpose of the experiments was to determine whether significant increases in sales were associated with the introduction of the new carrousel display in two of the manufacturer's most common types of retail accounts. The drug and stationery store experiments were analyzed separately by testing the hypothesis that the mean sales increase of the experimental group was less than or equal to the mean sales increase of the control group. (Data for the tests are shown in the average increase (decrease) column of Tables 2 and 3 respectively.

Results of the one sided t test indicated that the hypothesis could be rejected in the drug store experiment at less than the 0.005 probability level and at less than the 0.025 probability level in the stationery store experiment. (The t value in the drug store experiment was 21.2 compared to $t_{.005}$ (2) of 9.9. The t value in the

TABLE 2   WEEKLY SALES OF THE FELT TIP

Group	Pre-Test Period			Pre-Test Period Average
	Week 1	Week 2	Week 3	
Experimental				
Store A	$49.14	$53.82	$46.80	$49.92
Store B	44.46	47.97	43.29	45.24
Average				47.58
Control				
Store C	$39.78	$42.90	$38.61	$40.43
Store D	24.96	27.30	23.79	25.35
Average				32.89

TABLE 3   WEEKLY SALES OF THE FELT TIP

Group	Pre-Test Period			Pre-Test Period Average
	Week 1	Week 2	Week 3	
Experimental				
Store E	$31.59	$33.93	$29.25	$31.91
Store F	30.03	32.76	26.34	29.71
Average				30.65
Control				
Store G	$26.74	$29.07	$22.24	$26.02
Store H	35.10	38.61	32.76	35.49
Average				30.76

stationery store experiment was 5.0 compared to $t_{.025}$ (2) of 4.3.)

However, differences among either the three weeks of the pre-test period or the three weeks of the test period or differences among the stores relative to sales volume may have affected mean sales increases of the respective experimental and control groups. These effects cannot be identified in the t tests just described. Therefore, the fixed-effects model two-way analysis of variance was used to analyze the drug store pre-test period and the test period and the stationery store pre-test and the test period. The results of these four analyses are summarized in Table 4. In each analysis the "group/week interaction" was not significant; consequently, the error mean square was used as the denominator in calculating the "between groups" and "among weeks" F ratios. The F ratio representing the "among weeks" variation was not significant in any of the four analyses.

COLORING MARKERS IN DRUG STORES

Test Period			Test Period Average	Average Increase (decrease)	Per Cent Increase (decrease)
Week 4	Week 5	Week 6			
$58.56	$56.16	$56.94	$57.22	$7.30	
53.82	51.48	54.60	53.30	8.06	
			55.26	7.68	16.1%
$41.34	$37.05	$37.44	$38.61	($1.82)	
27.91	20.89	24.57	24.46	(0.89)	
			31.53	(1.36)	(4.1%)

COLORING MARKERS IN STATIONERY STORES

Test Period			Test Period Average	Average Increase (decrease)	Per Cent Increase (decrease)
Week 4	Week 5	Week 6			
$37.91	$32.76	$34.32	$35.00	$3.41	
36.01	33.67	38.35	36.01	6.30	
			35.50	4.85	15.8%
$25.96	$26.34	$24.87	$25.72	($0.29)	
37.44	30.03	32.37	33.28	(2.21)	
			29.50	(1.26)	(4.1%)

The F ratios representing "between groups" variation revealed mixed results. While the difference between the drug store experimental and control groups was significant at the 0.005 probability level for the test period, the difference between the same groups during the pre-test period was significant at the 0.025 probability level. The "between groups" F ratio for the stationery store experiment was not significant in the pre-test period; therefore, the null hypothesis was not rejected. In the stationery store test period the null hypothesis that there was no difference between experimental groups and control groups could be rejected at the 0.10 probability level.

Discussion

Several problems common to a variety of marketing experiments can be raised with regard to the research presented here.

Levels of Significance. The probability levels at which the various statistical tests can be considered significant have been noted in the preceding section. It is up to the marketer, however, to decide what level of significance is meaningful for the decision under consideration.

Company policy dictated that a display would be furnished to each new account and old displays would be replaced periodically free of charge. Since the new displays required no increased cost per unit and the inventory of old displays was small, the principal risk was whether the new display would affect sales adversely.

Proper wording of the t test hypothesis simplified the problem. By framing the hypothesis for a one-sided t test to state that the mean increase in the experimental group sales was less than or equal to the mean increase in the control group sales, the decision-maker could consider whether the probability of rejecting a true hypothesis was too great. In terms of the test results the probability is less than five in 1000 for the drug store experiment and less than 25 in 1000 for the stationery store experiment that the mean increase in the experimental group sales could have been less than or equal to the mean increase in the control group sales by chance alone. Such odds, when compared to the decision under consideration, make the introduction of the new display highly desirable.

The function of the two-way analysis of variance, summarized in Table 4, was to check for the presence of certain sources of sales variation not directly identifiable in the t test. The t statistic determines the confidence the decision-maker will have in adopting or rejecting the new display. Therefore, any source of variation in sales affecting the t statistic, but not attributable to the new display, should be investigated.

While the introduction of the new display seems quite reasonable, the presence of a strong upward or downward sales trend in one or more of the stores could inflate or deflate the t statistic and lead to an erroneous conclusion. The F ratio for the "among weeks" variation was not significant in any of the four analyses. This was desirable as it indicates that there was no important change in weekly sales during either weeks one through three of the pre-test period or weeks four through six of the test period in either the drug store or stationery store experiment. Consequently, it is safe to conclude that there was no important trend effect operative during the six weeks of either experiment.

The "between groups" F ratio in each of the four analyses was used to test the null hypothesis that there was no difference between the mean sales of the experimental group and the mean sales of the control group. In the test period this hypothesis can be rejected at the 0.005 probability level for the drug store experiment and the 0.10 probability level for the stationery store experiment. While they appear similar to the results of the t tests, it is well to note that neither the data nor the hypotheses are the same. The "between groups" F ratio for the test period

TABLE 4   ANALYSIS OF VARIANCE OF PRE-TEST AND TEST PERIOD
SALES

	Degrees of Freedom	Sum of Squares	Mean Square	F Ratio
Drug Stores (pre-test period)				
Between groups	1	6,473,883	6,473,883	10.3**
Among weeks	2	500,662	250,331	.4
Group/week interaction	2	20,026	10,013	.02
Error	6	3,755,349	625,892	
Total	11	10,749,921		
Drug Stores (test period)				
Between groups	1	16,888,641	16,888,641	30.8*
Among weeks	2	322,008	161,004	.3
Group/week interaction	2	70,128	35,064	.06
Error	6	3,284,965	547,494	
Total	11	20,565,743		
Stationery Stores (pre-test period)				
Between groups	1	320	320	.001
Among weeks	2	708,461	354,231	1.5
Group/week interaction	2	3,121	1,561	.007
Error	6	1,419,211	236,535	
Total	11	2,131,114		
Stationery Stores (test period)				
Between groups	1	1,080,600	1,080,600	5.8***
Among weeks	2	263,576	131,788	.7
Group/week interaction	2	44,297	22,149	.1
Error	6	1,111,678	185,280	
Total	11	2,500,150		

*   Significant at .005
** Significant at .025
***Significant at .10

indicates there is a low probability that the difference between means could have occurred by chance alone in either experiment. This suggests that the difference between mean sales of the experimental and control groups was attributable to the new display. However, it does not yield any information as to whether the four stores were equal prior to the introduction of the new display in the experimental stores.

Visual inspection of Table 2 reveals that the most important size discrepancy in the pre-test period can be attributed to Store D of the drug store experiment.

Sales of this store were approximately 45 per cent lower than the other drug stores throughout the pre-test period. The "between groups" F ratio of the pre-test period is useful to determine whether this resulted in a significant difference between the stores of the experimental and control groups. The difference between mean sales of the experimental and control groups was significant at the 0.025 probability level in the drug store experiment, leaving little doubt that it had not been adequately controlled on the variable of store size. The difference was not significant in the stationery store experiment.

In on-going business situations, such as the present, the press of time, budget limitations, or competitive considerations typically make it unrealistic to re-select new test units and start the experiment over. Therefore, the decision-maker must analyze what effect the differences in store size had on the t statistic, since this source of variation in sales is not related to the presence or absence of the new display.

A satisfactory non-statistical interpretation can be achieved by considering the effect proportionally larger sales in Store D would have had on the t statistic. Although it cannot be assumed that a larger store would exhibit the same pattern of sales as Store D throughout the six weeks, it does indicate the likely direction of change in the t statistic.

If the sales of Store D had been proportionally larger (e.g., an 80 per cent increase in the weekly sales of Store D would approximately equate the drug stores in the pre-test period), the effect would be to increase the significance of the t test, since the average decrease in the control group sales would have been enlarged, thereby enlarging the numerator of the t statistic. Furthermore, the pooled standard deviation in the denominator of the t statistic would be decreased. Therefore, it is reasonably safe to assume that the t test has been interpreted somewhat conservatively.

At this point it is interesting to note the relation between the two experiments as observed in the per cent increase (decrease) columns of Tables 2 and 3, and the levels of significance of the respective t tests. The difference between the percentage change in average sales of the experimental and control group stores was 20.2 per cent for the drug stores and 19.9 per cent for the stationery stores. While the difference between these figures is relatively small, the difference between the levels of significance revealed in the t tests (even when the smaller size of Store D is taken into consideration) is considerably greater. This is largely attributable to the greater differences among stores within the experimental and control groups of the stationery store experiment. It underscores the possible misinterpreation that can arise when the marketer relies on average percentage changes in sales without subjecting them to appropriate statistical tests.

INTERPRETATION OF EXPERIMENTAL DATA

The results of the tests have statistical meaning only within the context of the respective drug and stationery store experiments. No statement of a statistical nature can be made concerning the effects of the new carrousel display on sales of other stores or even for the same stores at another period of time. The marketing decision-maker must rely on his own experience in judging whether the new display would be as effective at some future period in time in other stores which will not necessarily conform to the matching criteria used for store selection in this experiment. This can be understood by briefly noting the principal qualitative factors which were considered prior to reaching the final decision.

Sales deterioration was not tested in the experiments. This raises at least two possibilities. First, there is a possibility that the increase in sales presumably attributable to the new display merely borrowed from future sales and that annual sales would not be noticeably increased. This is not probable. It is known that repeat sales for this product are not large; therefore, the increased sales more likely came from customers who had not previously been exposed to the product. It is likely, however, that the new display would be more effective in stores which have a higher percentage of new customers from one year to the next.

Second, the principal explanation for the increased sales is the high visual exposure of a large portion of the product line made possible by the new display. There is a possibility that the store managers of the experimental group stores did service the new display more than was normal. If so, the sales increases are erroneously inflated and could be expected to fall off as the retailer permitted stockouts to increase to a normal level. Nevertheless, if the display performs at a significantly higher level when it is first introduced to an account, there is more of a chance that the retailer will not allow as many stockouts as before.

A holiday and four severe snowstorms closing schools and some businesses occurred during the six-week period. The experimental design was capable of compensating for these uncontrollable events, since they were assumed to affect the experimental and control group stores equally. However, the experiment does not reflect the effects of the other seasons. It is known that there have been no strong seasonal cycles except minor increases during the back-to-school and Christmas seasons. Therefore, it was concluded that the new display would not be affected by, nor accentuate any seasonal sales variations.

Conclusion

Controlled experiments formally test relationships that otherwise are left to the judgment of the decision-maker. However, judgment is not eliminated from the decision-making process when experiments are utilized. If anything, the design and interpretation of experiments require more of the decision-maker. For example, would the display be as effective in Atlanta as Boston or in a large variety store as compared with either a drug or stationery store? Although it is not realistic to expect the display to be equally effective in all situations not specifically tested in the experiments, the decision-maker is probably safe in concluding in view of the highly significant test results that the new display will rarely affect sales adversely and will generally have a positive effect.

Use of the present experiments has required decisions as to the experimental design, store-selection criteria, evaluation of the levels of significance indicated in the various statistical tests, and interpretation of the experimental data in the context of the types of stores and geographic locations making up the market for felt tip markers. Without the experiment the decision-maker would have to make only one judgment as to the probable effectiveness of the proposed display. Nevertheless, many marketers believe the use of controlled experiments, even as small and inexpensive as the one reported here, are worthwhile not only for the resulting experimental data but also for the disciplined examination of assumptions that might otherwise pass unnoticed.

References

Banks, Seymour. *Experimentation in Marketing.* New York: McGraw-Hill Book Company, 1965, Chapter 4.

Dixon, Wilfrid J. and Frank J. Massey, Jr. *Introduction to Statistical Analysis,* 2d ed. New York: McGraw-Hill Book Company, 1957, Chapter 9.

Duncan, Acheson J. *Quality Control and Industrial Statistics,* revised ed. Homewood, Ill.: Richard D. Irwin, Inc. 1959, p. 520.

PART

II

CULTURAL INFLUENCES

4. Norms of Behavior

"Experimental Study of Consumer Behavior Conformity and Independence," M. Venkatesan (Marketing Educator), *Journal of Marketing Research,* Vol. 3 (November, 1966), pp. 384-387.

5. Socialization

"Social Character and Differential Preference for Mass Communication," Harold H. Kassarjian (Psychologist), *Journal of Marketing Research,* Vol. 2 (May, 1965), pp. 146-153.

Man never exists apart from his environment. And man's environment is comprised, by and large, by the *culture* of that environment. The various norms of behavior serve as guides not only for actions but also for the thoughts preceding and following these actions. And it is through socialization that norms are imposed, affecting the usefulness of mass communications intended for the consumer. Part II involves two different studies of cultural influences.

25

4 Norms of Behavior

Experimental Study of Consumer Behavior Conformity and Independence

M. VENKATESAN* (Marketing Educator)

Results of a laboratory experiment indicate that in consumer decision making, in the absence of any objective standard, individuals tended to conform to the group norm. However, when the group pressure was to "go along" with the group, resulting in restriction of choices, the individuals tended to resist the group pressure.

Although group influence is one of the important factors in the attention directing stage of the purchase process, "very little empirical work has been carried out" on this stage of the decision process [4, p. 51]. Attempts have been made to relate the findings on group influence from small group studies to consumer behavior [2]. While the investigations of group influence in consumer behavior are relatively recent, social psychology has long focused on the small group and its influence on the perceptions, opinions, and attitudes of its members.

Now there is a sizable body of social psychology literature on the experimental study of social influence. A number of experiments have demonstrated that with sufficient group pressure it is possible to influence what the individual believes he perceives. Other experiments suggested that in the absence of objective standards, an individual turns to other people for judgment and evaluation.

Source: M. Venkatesan, "Experimental Study of Consumer Behavior Conformity and Independence," Journal of Marketing Research, Vol. 3 (November, 1966), pp. 384-387.

*M. Venkatesan is assistant professor of business administration, Whittemore School of Business and Economics, University of New Hampshire. This article is based on his doctoral dissertation at the University of Minnesota. He is grateful to Robert S. Hancock and Robert J. Holloway, both of the University of Minnesota, and to Elliot Aronson, presently at the University of Texas, for their help.

The Conformity Studies of Asch [1] and the Social Judgment Experiments of Sherif [8] are best known and most representative. In the Asch experiment the task was to state which of the three lines on a card was equal in length to a comparison line. The critical subjects were exposed to the contrary-to-fact opinion of a unanimous majority (three or more confederates). The confederates had been instructed to give the same incorrect answer. Asch found that 76 percent of the critical subjects also gave the same incorrect response despite the fact that the majority response was obviously incorrect. In the autokinetic experiment of Sherif the subjects individually and in groups estimated the range of movement of a light which, in fact, was stationary. He demonstrated that in an unstructured situation the subjects, in making their decisions, were entirely dependent on the group for the norm and range.

Generally, laboratory studies of social influence demonstrated that individuals are highly susceptible to group pressure. A majority of the individuals conform to a *group norm*.[1] When objective standards were absent, more individuals tended to conform to a group norm than when the objective standards were present. The small group studies were not concerned with group influence in buying situations. Assessing their relevance to buyer behavior after an exhaustive search of the social psychological literature, Howard [5, p. 136] concluded:

Other people seem to be important influence on the individual's perception. There are two hypotheses in this connection. *First,* a number of experiments suggest that, in the presence of a sufficient amount of group pressure, it is possible to influence what the individual believes he perceives. The *second* hypothesis is that, in the absence of objective standards or accepted authority, an individual will turn to other people for judgments and evaluations. To whom he turns depends upon the circumstances.

From these hypotheses he speculated about marketing situations.

Although knowledge about conformity to group norms in the marketplace is slight, common sense would lead us to conclude that consumer decision making takes place in an environment where conformity is a major force. However, the operation of group norms in many buying situations needs to be empirically established and the social influence of groups on consumer behavior needs to be investigated systematically.

Although group influence in the consumer decision-making process is recognized, generally the attempts to influence are thought of as "pressures toward conformity." This view probably results from lack of attention to the phenomenon of independence in the social psychological literature. Little attention has been given

---

[1] A norm has been defined in two ways: (1) as role expectations, and (2) as modal patterns of behavior. Thus, in the experimental studies, group norm has been defined as the modal patterns of behavior or modal response of the group. For purposes of this study the unanimous majority judgment of an *ad hoc* group will be taken to be the norm of this group.

to conditions under which independence occurs. Jahoda pointed out that "there is ample evidence for the existence of independence not only in common-sense observations but also in every single experiment which rejects the null-hypotheses of independence on statistically impressive levels of confidence" [6, p. 99].

Many buying actions come from a desire to identify with a membership or reference group. The influence exerted by given groups, such as neighborhood groups, bridge clubs, on its members is informal and subtle. Moreover, group norms establish a range of tolerable behavior or a frame of reference. Ferber [4, p. 49] divided the consumer decision-making process into three distinct stages: (1) attention directing stage; (2) deliberation among alternative forms of action; and (3) the actual choice. Awareness, therefore, of a group norm and any tendency to conform to that norm relate to the attention-directing stage of consumer decision making.

Few individuals would care to be complete conformists in their consumption patterns. In many buying situations, an acceptable range of alternatives is available within a given norm. We all know cases where individuals conformed to the group norm by buying a product, but each individual purchased a different color, brand, etc., thus maintaining a feeling of independence. Any attempt to force compliance[2] in a buying situation would tend to restrict the consumer's choices and consequently his independence. Therefore, to study the phenomenon of independence in consumer decision making, one would have to study the effect of restriction or usurpation of choices by group pressure on the consumer decision-making process.

In a recent theoretical paper by Brehm [3], the motivational state which impels an individual to establish his freedom has been called "reactance."[3] Reactance is viewed as dissonant with compliance. Any attempt by the inducing agent, in our case the group influence, which threatens the freedom of the individual, according to this theory, would lead to a tendency for the individual to avoid compliance. Brehm [3], in an exploratory experiment, found that in a dyadic situation, the attempted influence by the confederate tended to make the subject do the opposite of what was suggested. Generally, other exploratory studies in this area supported the view that if an inducing force threatens the individual's freedom, the individual tends to oppose the inducement.

---

[2]Many authors have made it clear that distinctions between the processes of social influence are necessary for understanding the different meanings of conformity behavior. Kelman [7, p. 62] distinguishes three processes of social influences, all of which have generally been termed as "conformity" by others: compliance, identification, and internalization. "Compliance can be said to occur when an individual accepts influence from another person or from a group because he hopes to achieve a favorable reaction from the other. He may be interested in attaining certain specific rewards or in avoiding certain specific punishments that the influencing agent controls."

[3]"Reactance is a motivational state which impels the individual to resist further reduction in his set of free behaviors, and which also impels him to restore the potential behaviors lost, or eliminate any jeopardy to them" [3, p. 21].

The Study

The two main objectives of this study were: (1) to gain insight into this phenomenon—conformity to group pressure in the consumer decision-making process; and (2) to study the effects of choice restriction by group pressure in the consumer decision-making process. Based on the theoretical discussion so far, the following two hypotheses were derived:

1. In a consumer decision-making situation where no objective standards are present, individuals who are exposed to a group norm will tend to conform to that group norm.
2. In a consumer decision-making situation where no objective standards are present, individuals who are exposed to a group norm, and are induced to comply, will show less tendency to conform to the group judgment.

Research Plan

Since this study is exploratory, what we learn in the laboratory can help in understanding the effect of group pressure on the consumer decision-making process. Therefore, a controlled laboratory experiment was used to evaluate the above hypotheses.

In most instances the laboratory studies of group influence created artificial situations unlike those found in everyday buying. For this study a laboratory situation was devised in which the consumer decision-making process would come close to an actual buying situation. Since the subjects for this study were male college students, a buying situation was chosen that would reflect their familiarity with the buying process for that product.

PROCEDURE

Subjects were 144 college juniors and seniors who were drawn from a pool of the basic students in the School of Business Administration, University of Minnesota.

The task required the subjects to evaluate and choose the *best* suit among three identical men's suits labeled A, B, and C. The three suits were of the same style, color, and size. All other means of identification were removed from the suits. The positional arrangements were varied in Latin square design so that each suit was displayed in each position with equal frequency. The subjects were told: (1) that the three suits were from three different manufacturers, (2) that there were quality differences, (3) that the previous studies conducted at the Center for Experimental Studies in Business had indicated that experienced clothiers and tailors were able to pick the *best* one, and (4) that the present study was to find out whether consumers would be able to pick the *best* one.

Three experimental conditions were created for the experiment: *Condition I* was a *Control Condition;* in *Conditions II* and *III*, which will be called *Conformity Condition* and *Reactance Condition*, respectively, group pressure (independent variable, was manipulated.

The task remained the same for all three conditions. In each condition, the subjects were allowed two minutes each to physically examine the suits to help them arrive at their choices. In the *Control Condition,* after the subject had been seated, the experimenter read aloud the instructions. After examining the suits for two minutes, the subject returned to his seat and indicated his choice on a form provided for this purpose. Thus, in the *Control Condition* the subjects evaluated the suits individually in the absence of any group influence.

In *Conditions II* and *III* the suits were evaluated and the choices were made in a face-to-face group consisting of four individuals, three confederates of the experimenter, and one subject. The confederates had been told to choose B as the *best* suit. In addition, the confederates had been instructed earlier about seating arrangements. In these two conditions, after the subjects were seated around a table, the experimenter read instructions explaining the task. They were told that after they each examined the suits, they were to publicly announce their choices of the best suit. After examination of the suits, the subjects returned to their seats. Then the experimenter asked each person to announce his choice. Because of the seating and the prior instructions to the confederates, the first confederate was the first to be asked and to respond; then it was the turn of the second and the third confederates respectively. The naive subject was always last to respond.

In the *Conformity Condition* the unanimous majority judgment of Suit B was communicated by each confederate enunciating his choice clearly and unmistakably. The naive subject was faced with a unanimous majority opinion (group norm).

The manipulation of group pressure in the *Reactance Condition* was similar to that in the *Conformity Condition.* The task, the instructions, and the procedures were the same, but the response pattern of the confederates was changed. The responses were as follows:

Confederate 1: I am not sure if there is a difference—it is not great; but if I have to choose, then B is the *best* suit.
Confederate 2: (Looking at Confederate 1) You say B . . . . Well, I cannot see any difference either—I will *"go along with you"*—B is the *best* suit for me.
Confederate 3: Well, you guys chose B. Although I am not sure, I am *just going along* to be a good guy. I choose B too.

Then it was subject's turn to announce his choice. As in the above condition, group pressure was aimed at restricting the individual's choice.

Forty-eight subjects were run in the Control Condition and 48 subjects in each of the other conditions. Confederates came from the "subjects pool" and from the subjects who had been through the *Control Condition.*

The situation permitted a quantitative measure of yielding. The proportion of choices for B was taken to be the measure of yielding and the proportion of choices for A or C was taken to be the measure of nonyielding. The experimenter casually recorded the choices while the subjects were filling out a questionnaire in Phase II. The responses had not been recorded during the public announcements of the choices to avoid creating suspicion about the sequence used in the interrogation.

After the post-experimental interview, the subject was debriefed and was requested not to disclose the nature and method of the experiment to any other student until results were officially announced in class by his instructor.

Results and Discussion

The distribution of choices obtained for the three conditions are shown in Table 1.[4]

TABLE 1   DISTRIBUTION OF CHOICES OF BEST SUIT

Condition	Choice			
	A	B	C	N
Control	17	10	20	47
Conformity	11	22	9	42
Reactance	14	14	19	47

The choices made in the *Control Condition* provided the base rate for evaluating the effectiveness of group influence in the experimental conditions. The results of the *Control Condition* indicated that in the absence of any social influence, the distribution of choices did not deviate significantly from a chance distribution (x^2 = 3.4, d.f·2). Thus, in the absence of any group influence, each suit was equally likely to have been selected as the *best* suit.

Analysis of the proportion of choices obtained for choice B in the *Conformity Condition* indicated that it was significantly greater than one-third ($Z = 2.5$, $p < .01$). Therefore, by rejecting the null hypothesis it was concluded that group pressure was effective and that individuals tended to conform to the group norm. The results supported Hypothesis 1.

Hypothesis 2 was also supported by the results obtained for the *Reactance Condition*. Analysis of the proportion of choices for choice B in this condition indicated that it was not significantly different than one-third. The null hypothesis cannot be rejected for this condition ($Z = -0.63$, NS). Therefore, it was concluded that in this condition, where acceptance of group pressure would have restricted the choices available, the subjects tended either to be indifferent or to deliberately make a choice that would negate the effect of group pressure.

Implications for Marketing

Implications from this study for consumer decision-making processes are limited because study was exploratory and was set in the laboratory. However, the find-

[4] The results are based on the N shown in the table. The data for the remaining were discarded because of the subjects' familiarity with the experimental procedure.

ings support other small group studies on conformity to group pressure and the preliminary findings of the studies based on the theory of reactance.

The acceptance of social influence, as shown in the *Conformity Condition,* implies that consumers accept information provided by their peer groups on the quality of a product, of a style, etc., which is hard to evaluate objectively. More generally, the group norm or the prevailing group standard directs attention of its members to a new style or a product. It provides a frame of reference which is the first stage in the consumer decision-making process. In many buying situations there exists no objective standard independent of others' opinions. For those situations the implications are clear. The findings also imply that peer groups, friends, and acquaintances may be a major source of influence and information in the attention-directing stage of the buying process for major items.

The findings that group pressure for compliant behavior is ineffective implies that any attempt to restrict independent choice behavior in the consumer decision-making process may be resisted *under certain conditions.* In the marketplace we can observe that individuals purchase a product or adopt a new style, but reserve the right to choose different brands or variations. In this way, it seems the feeling of independence in the consumer decision-making process is maintained. The theory of reactance is undergoing extensive empirical testing. However, our findings are supported by Whyte's study [9] of the effectiveness of personal interaction in influencing the purchase of air conditioners. His analysis indicated that an "individual may sell his neighbor on the *idea* of a (air) conditioner; *he does not necessarily sell him on a particular brand or a particular store;* where you see a row of adjacent (air) conditioners, only a few of them will be of the same make, and only a few from the same store" [9, p. 117].

References

1. S. E. Asch, "Effects of Group Pressure Upon the Modification and Distortion of Judgments," in Harold Geutzkow, ed., *Groups, Leadership and Men,* Pittsburgh, Pa.: Carnegie Press, 1951.

2. E. S. Bourne, "Group Influences in Marketing and Public Relations," in Rensis Likert and S. P. Hayes, Jr., eds., *Some Applications of Behavioral Research,* New York: UNESCO, 1957.

3. J. W. Brehm, "A Theory of Psychological Reactance," Unpublished paper, Duke University, Durham, N.C., 1965.

4. Robert Ferber, "Research on Household Behavior," *American Economic Review,* 52 (March 1962), 19-36.

5. J. A. Howard, *Marketing: Executive and Buyer Behavior,* New York: Columbia University Press, 1963.

6. Marie Jahoda, "Conformity and Independence: A Psychological Analysis," *Human Relations,* 12 (May 1959), 99-199.

7. H. C. Kelman, "Processes of Opinion Change," *Public Opinion Quarterly,* 25 (Spring 1961), 57-78.

8. Mazafer Sherif, *The Psychology of Social Norms,* New York: Harper & Row, Publishers, 1963.
9. W. H. Whyte, Jr., "The Web of Word of Mouth," in L. H. Clark, ed., *Consumer Behavior: The Life Cycle and Consumer Behavior,* New York: New York University Press, 1955.

5 Socialization

Social Character and Differential Preference for Mass Communication

HAROLD H. KASSARJIAN* *(Psychologist)*

The basic hypothesis of this study is that a meaningful typology of consumer behavior may be segmented along the lines of social character delineated by David Riesman. Under experimental conditions, inner- and other-directed subjects indicated a differential preference for specially created advertisements developed to appeal to these two character types. Further, the study analyzed differential exposure to mass media and differential preference for mass media content.

Such fields as persuasion, mass communication, and marketing have long had an axiom that it is meaningless and unrealistic to speak of a general public or homogeneous market. It rather has to be assumed that there are as many publics as there are issues or sub-groups; for instance, in the field of advertising one hears of the Negro market, teen-age market, suburban market, *etc.*

Attempts at appealing to specific target groups have led to divisions along numerous variables, such as demographic characteristics, reference group membership, attitudes and values, involvement in particular issues, and personality. Riesman in his book, *The Lonely Crowd* [11], suggested still another possible categorization—social character—theorizing that the social character of people can be subdivided into three groups, tradition-directed, inner-directed, and other-directed. Depending

Source: Harold H. Kassarjian, "Social Character and Differential Preference for Mass Communication," *Journal of Marketing Research,* Vol. 2 (May, 1965), pp. 146-153.

*Harold H. Kassarjian is an assistant professor of business administration at the University of California, Los Angeles. Appreciation is gratefully acknowledged to Miss Ewa A. Thieberg, both for her conceptual contributions and the monumental clerical duties she performed, and to Waltraud M. Kassarjian for her guidance and aid in most portions of this study. Financial assistance came from the UCLA Bureau of Business and Economic Research.

upon economic, demographic, and various cultural factors, a society can generally be considered to be predominantly made up of one or two of the above categories. Furthermore, a person can be found in any one of these types or, as W. M. Kassarjian indicates in an empirical study [7, 8], somewhere along a hypothesized continuum between two of the types.

According to Riesman, tradition-directed people—seldom encountered in present-day United States—are oriented in the traditional ways of their forefathers. Their societies are characterized by a general slowness of change, a dependence on family and kin organization, a very low degree of social mobility, and a tight web of values. Inner-directed people turn to their own inner values and standards for guidance of their behavior in a rapidly changing society brought about by industrialization and subsequent increasing division of labor, greater stratification of society, and less security for the individual. Other-directed persons depend upon the people around them to give direction to their actions. Continued industrialization leads to an age of servo-mechanisms, electronic computers, and other highly automated machinery which divert the attention away from production to the consumer. Thus, in such a society the individual's personality and the reaction of other people to him become the focal point of interest.

Since contemporary United States is considered populated almost exclusively by the latter two types of people, this project is limited to the study of inner- and other-directed individuals.

In previous studies W. M. Kassarjian [8] found that foreign-born individuals and those reared in small towns tend to be inner-directed, while subjects from metropolitan areas tend to be other-directed. Her results further indicate that students with majors in the natural sciences and with occupational goals in the natural sciences are significantly more inner-directed than students preparing for public school teaching positions or business administration. Furthermore, both Kassarjian [8] and Centers [1] substantiated the trend toward other-direction claimed by the theory, showing that younger individuals are significantly more other-directed than older persons. In a study comparing occupational preferences as measured by the Strong Vocational Interest Blank with inner-other-direction, Kassarjian and Kassarjian [9] indicate that inner-directed subjects show a significantly greater preference for such inner-directed occupations as architect, artist, chemist, librarian, mathematician and physicist. Other-directed subjects, on the other hand, seemed to have interests similar to people in other-directed occupations such as elementary school teacher, life insurance salesman, business education teacher, home economics teacher, stenographer-secretary, sales manager, and office worker. In addition, the study [6, 9] indicated that on the Allport-Vernon-Lindzey Scale of Values, the inner-directed groups were significantly higher than the other-directed on the theoretical and aesthetic values while other-directed subjects scored significantly higher on economic and political values.

Centers and Horowitz [2] found that other-directed subjects were more susceptible to social influence in an experimental setting than were inner-directed subjects, while Linton and Graham [10] indicate that the inner-directed persons are less easily persuaded than other-directed persons. Walter Gruen [5] found no relationship between preference for new or older products and inner-other direction. However, Dornbush and Hickman [3] noted a clear trend from inner-direction to other-direction in consumer goods advertising over the past decades. These previous studies, however, did not specifically test preference for appeals directly created to influence these two character types. From Riesman's theoretical orientation it can be expected that inner-directed and other-directed persons would tend to show differential preference and possibly differential susceptibility to communication appeals. Hence, it was hypothesized that

(a) Inner- and other-directed individuals would show differential preference for advertisements specially created to appeal to these social character types.

(b) Other-directed people, those who tend to draw their values and opinions from other people, would believe that people-in-general would be most influenced by ads that other-directed persons themselves preferred or felt would be most influential on themselves. No predictions were made for inner-directed persons since their need-value system is not dependent upon the peer group and hence their reactions could not be theoretically predicted.

(c) Other-directed people would expose themselves more to the mass media—the voice of the peer group—than would inner-directed individuals.

Method

DEVELOPMENT OF THE APPEALS

A series of pairs of advertisements was created consisting of a slogan and an illustration by cutting and pasting pictures and background material taken from magazines. Each pair was made up of an inner-directed appeal and an other-directed appeal based on differences between these two character types taken from Riesman's writings—each pair offering the same product or service. A theoretical statement that an inner-directed person is interested in individual sports while an other-directed person is interested in group sports, for example, might lead to an ad for tennis shoes which extolls the virtues of a brand of tennis shoes with an illustration of either a group sport or an individual sport. An inner-directed ad for a Book of the Month Club would contain pictures of book jackets about great people or adventures while an other-directed ad would contain pictures of books about everyday people, best-sellers, and books on personality improvement. With some imagination, somewhat over three dozen pairs of ads were prepared, some in black and white and some in color. In some cases the slogan was kept constant between the pairs while the illustration varied, while in other pairs, both the slogan and the illustration varied. Examples of the ads are presented in Figures 1 through 4.

To provide evidence that each of the ads in the pair was equally attractive to a population of subjects similar to those in the final sample, the slogans and illustra-

Figure 1. Oregon, a must for those who appreciate natural beauty.

Figure 2. Make new friends—enjoy care-free, "crowded with fun" weeks at Oregon.

Figure 3. Excellent craftmanship, best materials—made to last a lifetime.

Figure 4. The modern, up-to-date car for active people.

tions were separated and presented in pairs to a group of business students at UCLA. Subjects selected from each pair that slogan or illustration they felt would be most effective or influential on themselves, and rated it on a five-point scale, from "most prefer Ad A" to "most prefer Ad B." Then the slogans and illustrations were presented together for whatever Gestalt effect there might be and the subjects again were asked to rate each pair of ads. Finally, each student was asked to state reasons why he made the choice he did. From the original pilot study, it was possible to choose those pairs of ads which had more or less equal desirability and in some cases to make changes so that within any given pair each of the two ads would be approximately equally often chosen.

In order to prove that in fact these pairs of ads did have a differential content appeal, three judges were used—each an expert on David Riesman's topic of Social Character, and each holding a doctorate in the social sciences. The task for the judges was to rate each ad on a five-point scale ranging from "clearly having an inner-directed appeal" to "clearly having an other-directed appeal." The criterion for acceptance of each ad for the final study was unanimous agreement from all three judges in direction but not necessarily degree, yielding 27 pairs for use in the actual study. Table 1 presents the slogans and a description of the illustrations.

THE FINAL STUDY

The final study sample consisted of 200 students in business administration courses. The subjects were first presented with the I–O Social Preference Scale developed by W. M. Kassarjian [8] to measure inner-other-direction. The instrument has a test-retest reliability coefficient of .85 and a number of previous studies

TABLE 1   DESCRIPTIONS OF APPEALS IN THE FINAL STUDY

Product	Inner-Directed Appeal		Other-Directed Appeal	
	Slogan	Illustration	Slogan	Illustration
Telephone company	Just dial—It's so easy, fast, and dependable	Attractive girl holding telephone and staring into space	The personal touch for every occasion	Five separate pictures of young ladies in a variety of situations talking on the telephone
High-fidelity turntable	Accurate, dependable, quality high-fidelity equipment	Record player, AM-FM radio in quality cabinet	In selecting components use the latest high-fidelity equipment	Turntable in foreground with homemade but attractive cabinet in back
Ralph's Market	Ralph's—Known for the finest quality at the right price	Food presented on extremely expensive silver serving piece	Ralph's—The supermarket with the greatest choice	Paper plates, supper napkins, many types of food in a buffet setting
Sea & Ski	For proper sun protection—Sea & Ski	Beach scene with three unrelated couples	For a desirable vacation glow—Sea & Ski	Two men and three women water skiing from the same boat
IBM Typewriter	You save time and money when you buy IBM Typewriters	Typist in foreground with boss giving orders in background	Your IBM Typewriter is part of the team in progressive management	Typewriter in foreground. Man and woman in background smiling and looking at some papers
Bayer Aspirin	Don't spoil your leisure time—Bayer Aspirin	Man working in "do it yourself" workshop	Don't spoil your leisure time—Bayer Aspirin	Two men holding drinks, talking at cocktail party

Kodak	For a lasting record	Man photographing London Bridge	Share your experiences with friends at home	Man photographing women in front of building. European travel posters in foreground
Fairchild's Restaurant	The height of sophistication	Waiter in tuxedo	Good food, reasonable price, gay atmosphere	People being served in fancy restaurant
Oregon Chamber of Commerce	Oregon, a must for those who appreciate natural beauty	Single man fishing for trout	Make new friends—enjoy carefree, "crowded with fun" weeks at Oregon	Four people camping at a lake. Two power boats in foreground
Community organization	Take an active part in community life—do your part for your country.	Older man in foreground. Seven men sitting around a table in background	Know what is going on—join a community project	Seven men in a room drinking in background. Man holding papers in foreground
Books	Improve yourself. Read and learn	Dozen books including: "My Life in Court," "The Outline of History," "The Valiant Years," "Conversations with Stalin"	Improve yourself; be confident in any crowd.	Illustrations of 11 books including: "Lose Weight and Live," "Women and Fatigue," "Ship of Fools," *etc.*
New house	A house that makes others stop, timeless, superb construction, designed apart	Suburban house	Contemporary style, nice neighborhood, close to schools	Suburban house
Tennis shoes	Heels reinforced, arch support—the built-in heels for sportsmen	Girl standing on deck of ship	Feel happier, comfortable in fashion	Girl dressed in tennis attire

TABLE 1   DESCRIPTIONS OF APPEALS IN THE FINAL STUDY (Continued)

| Product | Inner-Directed Appeal | | Other-Directed Appeal | |
	Slogan	Illustration	Slogan	Illustration
Swedish glass	You make your party unique with Swedish glass	Formal dining table set with wine glasses	You entertain in style when you serve on Swedish glass	Canapes, potato chips and dips on a counter
Umbrella	The smart sophisticated umbrella, timeless and attractive	Man and woman walking in rain, arm in arm	The choice of popular young women—in all color ranges and sizes	Four women carrying different umbrellas
Chrysler	Excellent craftmanship, best materials—made to last a lifetime	Chrysler auto—no background	The modern, up-to-date car for active people	Chrysler auto parked in front of nightclub
Swiss watches	The watch that is dependable	Watch pictured on wrist of man	The watch that is dependable	Watches in foreground. Two boys and a girl drinking in background
Anthony Squire Clothes	Feel smart and look smart	Young man walking in hallway	Clothing for the rising young executive	Young man and older man talking
Columbia Record Club	Select your favorite Columbia record	Illustrations of 18 albums ranging from popular to classical music	Share happy moments listening and dancing to recorded music	Two men and two women listening to records
All-State Insurance	For the finishing touch—All-State Insurance	Young man fixing motor on car	For the finishing touch—All-State Insurance	Father and son washing family car
Squibb Toothbrush Co.	For the busy man on the go. Squibb's Electric Toothbrush	Man with pleasant smile	For a natural friendly smile—Squibb's Electric Toothbrush	Man and woman smiling

Tishman Realty Co.	Maximum efficiency with a minimum of upkeep in a modern office. Tishman Realty Co.	Secretary working hard at desk	Happy employees and pleasant working conditions in a modern office. Tishman Realty Co.	Two men in an office
Horton and Converse Vitamins	For individual all around development—Horton and Converse Vitamins	Six separate illustrations of individual sports	For outstanding achievement in your group	Illustrations of basketball, golf and bowling
RCA Television	RCA Television	Man watching television	RCA Television	Two men and two women watching television
School bonds	Your child needs the best education there is. Vote Yes on school bonds	Children and teacher in classroom	Your child wants to be part of it. Vote Yes on school bonds	Four illustrations of children in school and playground
Metropolitan Life Insurance Co.	Leave some time for relaxation. Metropolitan Life Insurance Co.	Man watching television	Leave some time for relaxation. Metropolitan Life Insurance Co.	Two couples at cocktail party.
Body by Fisher	Body by Fisher	Car parked at lake. Couple in foreground	Body by Fisher	Car parked in front of house. Guests being greeted by hostess

have established this instrument's adequate validity [1, 2, 4, 6, 7, 8, 9]. The scale itself consists of 36 forced choice items scored along a five-point continuum. Here is a sample item:

> I respect the person most who
>   (a) is considerate of others and is concerned
>   that they think well of him.
>   (b) lives up to his ideals and principles.

Upon completion of the I–O Questionnaire, subjects were presented by means of an opaque overhead projector with the 27 pairs of advertisements in random order and using a randomized left-right position of the inner- and other-directed ads. The pairs of ads were to be rated on a five-point scale from most prefer inner-directed appeal (*e.g.,* Ad "A") to most prefer other-directed appeal (*e.g.,* Ad "B"). The instructions requested the student to select first the ad that "would be most effective for you, yourself—the one that would tend to influence you the most." Next the subject was requested on the same scale to select the ad "you feel would be most effective for a majority of other people—the one that would tend to influence other-people-in-general the most." Results from previous pilot studies indicated that the presentation order of the two sets of instructions would not significantly affect the results.

Following the presentation of the ads, the subjects were administered a questionnaire requesting such information as number of hours spent reading magazines and the newspapers, which magazines and newspapers they read, their exposure to shopping newspapers and advertising circulars, and which sections of the newspapers they usually read. In addition, they were asked questions on number of hours spent watching television, listening to the radio, and their favorite type of programming and favorite programs.

Results

ADVERTISING APPEALS

Each subject's evaluation of the pairs of ads was scored on the aforementioned five-point scale, minus two points if the subject felt the other-directed appeal was most effective and plus two points if the inner-directed appeal was most effective. To avoid dealing with negative scores, a constant of 50 points was added to each subject's score. Hence, each individual was assigned a total advertising preference score so that the higher the score the greater the preference for inner-directed advertisements.

Turning to the Kassarjian I–O Scale, the theoretical range of scores on the instrument is from 0 to 144 points with a theoretical mean of 72. In this study of 200 subjects, the range on the scale was from 37 to 118 with a mean of 76.5 and a standard deviation of 14.1. Statistically, this leaves no reason to suspect that these particular subjects significantly differed in their inner-other-direction scores from the population on which the instrument was originally validated [1, 7, 8].

For the statistical analysis, the subjects were divided into quartiles based on their scores on the I–O Scale–the first quartile being the most inner-directed group and the fourth quartile the most other-directed.

The first hypothesis of the study–that inner-directed individuals tend to prefer inner-directed appeals and other-directed persons prefer other-directed appeals–was confirmed by the results of a one-way analysis of variance on the four groups or quartiles (F = 6.100, df = 3/199, p < .001). Table 2 presents the means and standard deviations for the groups in the first five columns.

A t-test computed between the means of the first and fourth quartiles produced a statistic of 4.387, df = 98; p < .001. A t-test between the groups when divided at the median yielded a t of 3.686, 198 df, p < .001, further confirming the hypothesis. Supplementary evidence that preference of types of advertising and social character are related can be seen in a Pearson correlation coefficient of .30 between the inner-other-directed scores and the advertising preference score. A correlation of this magnitude is significant beyond the .001 level of confidence for this sample. Apparently other-directed people tended to prefer other-directed advertisements; that is, they felt that other-directed advertisements would be more effective on themselves, while inner-directed subjects tended to prefer inner-directed ads.

Based on the Riesman thesis that other-directed persons depend upon the people around them for guidance with respect to their actions and draw their values and opinions from them, the second hypothesis stated that other-directed subjects would tend to believe that people-in-general would be more influenced by or would prefer the ads that they themselves preferred. In other words, it was hypothesized that other-directed people would score people-in-general similar to their own score. No prediction was made for the inner-directed person. Table 2 presents the results of this phase of study in its last four columns.

The empirical data indicates that both the inner- and other-directed subjects felt that people-in-general would be more influenced by other-directed ads than by inner-directed ads (p < .001). However, differences between the inner- and other-directed groups were not statistically significant. If one may generalize beyond the data, both inner- and other-directed individuals seem to feel that people besides themselves are generally other-directed.

However, the hypothesis implied that the difference score, that is, the self-preference advertising score minus the people-in-general score, is not significantly different from zero or the other-directed group. Thus it was an unexpected finding to obtain a mean difference score for the fourth quartile or most other-directed group which is significantly different from zero. (The t-test yielded a statistic of 3.499, 48 df, p < .001.) When the data were processed by dividing the groups at the median, the other-directed half of the subjects had a mean difference score of 5.45, again significant at the .001 level (t = 6.987; 98 df). The hypothesis that other-directed individuals would score people-in-general similar to themselves was

TABLE 2 ADVERTISING PREFERENCE SCORES BY INNER-OTHER DIRECTION

Quartile	Character	N	Advertising Preference Score					
			Self		Other-people-in-general		Difference (Self Minus Other)	
			Mean	Standard Deviation	Mean	Standard Deviation	Mean	Standard Deviation
I	Inner	50	51.80	8.30	39.30	7.87	12.50	11.40
II	Inner	50	50.38	8.34	41.60	8.18	8.78	9.76
III	Other	50	48.70	8.51	41.10	8.54	7.60	10.50
IV	Other	50	44.78	7.92	41.48	8.49	3.30	6.74

rejected but gratifyingly in the direction that these individuals felt that people other than themselves are even more influenced by the other-directed appeals than they are themselves.

Further, the data indicate that the phenomenon of projection—persons in general expecting others to react as they themselves react—was not observed, since both the inner- and other-directed groups expected people-in-general to react in an other-directed fashion and not necessarily as they themselves responded.

EXPOSURE TO MASS MEDIA

The second phase of the study concerned differential exposure to the mass media. Riesman's writings clearly lead to the conclusion that other-directed persons will expose themselves more to the various mass media than inner-directed individuals. Table 3 presents the mean number of hours that subjects in each quartile (group) stated they spent reading or listening to mass media during an average week.

TABLE 3   MEAN HOURS OF EXPOSURE PER WEEK TO MASS MEDIA*

Quartile	I	II	III	IV
Character	Inner	Inner	Other	Other
Media				
Newspapers	4.18	3.52	3.80	4.50
AM radio	7.08	5.26	6.74	7.50
FM radio	3.46	3.36	2.22	2.38
Television	4.44	4.92	5.12	4.94
Magazines	3.20	2.94	2.36	3.40
Total exposure	22.36	20.00	20.24	22.72

*N is 50 for each catagory.

Analysis of variance indicates that neither the total amount of exposure nor the exposure to any one of the specific media are significant at the .05 level. Before interpreting these results as detrimental to the Riesman thesis, it is necessary to consider the source of the data. First, college students are not representative of the general population in their media habits. The demands of university work combined with the social activities revolving around the educational process may severely restrict students' free time available for the popular media, irrespective of whatever pressures their particular social character may exert. Furthermore, an overwhelming number of the subjects stated they live in a dormitory, fraternity, sorority or at home with their parents, while only a very small number live in their own apartments. This fact may further act to restrict their potential exposure to the media. For example, few if any students living in a fraternity subscribe to a newspaper or magazine, and television exposure may be limited to certain hours or limited by what is available in the living quarters. Interviews with several of the subjects lend considerable credence to this point of view, and is further supported by the fact that the mean exposure time is 21 hours per week—undoubtedly considerably less than for the general population.

It is of interest, however, to see if even with this limited exposure to the media there is a differential selection of types of programming, sections of a newspaper or particular magazines, that inner- and other-directed subjects tend to prefer.

The subjects were asked a series of questions concerned with favorite radio and television programs and type of programming, and magazines, newspapers and sections of newspapers they regularly read. The statistical analysis was carried out by dividing the subjects at the median into inner- and other-directed groups and chi square analyses were performed. Inner-directed subjects appeared to prefer and be exposed more to classical and light classical music on radio, more often read *TIME* magazine and the editorial, syndicated columnist and comic sections of the newspapers than their other-directed counterparts. Other-directed students, on the other hand, tended to prefer the sports sections and local news portions of the newspaper, rock and roll and popular music on radio and the television type of dramatic fare.

The results of the last phase of the study are not as clear cut as might be hoped. From Riesman's writings it was expected that other-directed subjects would clearly expose themselves to a much greater extent to the mass media and undoubtedly would show a differential preference to particular media content—those which would either increase a person's scope of contact with others or allow the individual to be an "inside dopester." In the sample used in this study the results did not indicate a differential exposure to the mass media among the two groups of subjects and only very few types of media content indicated significant differences between inner- and other-directed students. Most categories were not significant and even the few that were may have been statistical artifacts. The most likely explanation for these negative results again revolves around the particular character of the sample—primarily juniors in business administration at a major university. It may have been too much to expect that an individual's social character would be a powerful enough vector to overcome curricular and extracurricular demands on this quite otherwise homogeneous group of subjects. A study among a more representative sample of the population is required.

Summary and Conclusions

The hypotheses of this study were that inner- and other-directed individuals would show differential preference for advertisements created to appeal to these character types; that other-directed individuals would believe that people-in-general would prefer the advertisements that they themselves preferred; and that other-directed subjects would expose themselves to a greater degree to the mass media. Two hundred undergraduate students who had been administered the I–O Scale to measure social character were presented with 28 pairs of advertisements, one of which had an inner-directed appeal and the other an other-directed appeal, and a questionnaire tapping exposure to the mass media. The results indicated that other-directed persons tended to prefer the other-directed advertisements while the inner-directed showed a preference for the inner-directed communications. Both the inner- and other-directed groups of subjects, however, felt that people-in-general would be most influenced by the other-directed content. These results were significant even though the sample was homogeneous in nature. Differential exposure to the mass media and differential preference for media content were, on the whole, not significant.

The results, in general, confirmed the hypotheses and may be interpreted as further empirical evidence for several of the Riesman hypotheses concerning social character. A social character typology may well be a meaningful variable in communication and persuasion processes.

References

1. Richard Centers, "An Examination of the Riesman Social Character Typology: A Metropolitan Survey," *Sociometry,* 25 (September 1962), 231-240.

2. ——————— and Miriam Horowitz, "Social Character and Conformity: A Differential Susceptibility to Social Influence," *Journal of Social Psychology,* 60 (July 1963), 343-349.

3. Sanford M. Dornbush and Lauren C. Hickman, "Other-Directedness in Consumer Goods Advertising: A Test of Riesman's Historical Theory," *Social Forces,* 38, No. 2 (December 1959), 99-102.

4. William P. Gellermann, *A Field Study of Process Variables in Interpersonal Relations,* unpublished Ph.D. dissertation, University of California, Los Angeles, 1964.

5. Walter Gruen, "Preference for New Products and Its Relationship to Different Measures of Conformity," *Journal of Applied Psychology,* 44 (December 1960), 361-364.

6. Harold H. Kassarjian and Waltraud M. Kassarjian, *Social Values Associated with Riesman's Inner-Other Directed Typology,* paper presented at the 1963 annual meeting of the Western Psychological Association.

7. Waltraud M. Kassarjian, *A Study of Riesman's Theory of Social Character,* unpublished Ph.D. dissertation, University of California, Los Angeles, 1960.

8. ——————— , "A Study of Riesman's Theory of Social Character," *Sociometry,* 25 (September 1962), 213-230.

9. ——————— and Harold H. Kassarjian, "Occupational Interests, Social Values, and Social Character," *Journal of Counseling Psychology,* 12, No. 1 (Spring 1965), 48-54.

10. Harriet Linton and Elaine Graham, "Personality Correlates of Persuasability," in Irving L. Janis, *et al., Personality and Persuasability.* New Have: Yale University Press, 1959, 69-101.

11. David Riesman, Nathan Glazer and Reuel Denney, *The Lonely Crowd,* New Haven: Yale University Press, Abridged Edition, 1961.

INDIVIDUAL INFLUENCES

6. Motivation

"An Experimental Study of Customer Effort, Expectation, and Satisfaction," Richard N. Cardozo (Marketing Educator), *Journal of Marketing Research,* Vol. 2 (August, 1965), pp. 244-249.

7. Emotions

"An Experiment on Consumer Dissonance," Robert J. Holloway (Marketing Educator), *Journal of Marketing,* Vol. 31 (January, 1967), pp. 39-43.

8. Learning and Remembering

"Consumer Brand Choice as a Learning Process," Alfred A. Kuehn (Marketing Educator), *Journal of Advertising Research,* Vol. 2, (December, 1962), pp. 10-17.

9. Rational and Nonrational Thinking

(a) "Projective Techniques in Marketing Research," Mason Haire (Psychologist), *Journal of Marketing,* Vol. 14 (April, 1950), pp. 649-656.

(b) "Haire's Classic Instant Coffee Study—18 Years Later," Conrad R. Hill (Marketing Educator), *Journalism Quarterly,* Vol. 45, (August, 1968), pp. 466-472.

10. Personality and Personality Differences

"Personality and Product Use," W. T. Tucker (Marketing Educator) and John J. Painter (Marketing Educator), *Journal of Applied Psychology,* Vol. 45 (October, 1961), pp. 325-329.

11. The Self

"Perception of Self, Generalized Stereotypes, and Brand Selection," Edward L. Grubb (Marketing Educator) and Gregg Hupp (Marketing Executive), *Journal of Marketing Research,* Vol. 5 (February, 1968), pp. 58-63.

12. Individual Differences

"Differences Between Retailers' and Consumers' Perceptions," Peter J. McClure (Marketing Educator) and John K. Ryans, Jr. (Marketing Educator), *Journal of Marketing Research,* Vol. 5 (February, 1968), pp. 35-40.

A series of intricate and dynamic variables intermingle to form the *psychological* foundations of consumer behavior. And an understanding of these variables is essential in analyzing and explaining consumer behavior.

This means especially personality factors as related to the marketplace, exemplified by the eight experimental studies given in Part III.

6 Motivation

An Experimental Study of Customer Effort, Expectation, and Satisfaction

RICHARD N. CARDOZO* *(Marketing Educator)*

Results of a laboratory experiment indicate that customer satisfaction with a product is influenced by the effort expended to acquire the product, and the expectations concerning the product.

Specifically, the experiment suggests that satisfaction with the product may be higher when customers expend considerable effort to obtain the product than when they use only modest effort.

This finding is opposed to usual notions of marketing efficiency and customer convenience. The research also suggests that customer satisfaction is lower when the product does not come up to expectations than when the product meets expectations.

Customer satisfaction with a product presumably leads to repeat purchases, acceptance of other products in the same product line, and favorable word-of-mouth publicity. If this assumption is correct, then knowledge about factors affecting customer satisfaction is essential to marketers [3].

Knowledge about customer effort and expectation is important because these factors are major components of customer behavior, and because management can, within limits, influence the amount of effort customers expend and their expectations. Customer effort includes the physical, mental, and financial resources ex-

Source: Richard N. Cardozo, "An Experimental Study of Customer Effort, Expectation, and Satisfaction," *Journal of Marketing Research,* Vol. 2 (August, 1965), pp. 244-249.

*Richard N. Cardozo is assistant professor of business administration, Harvard University. This article is based on the author's doctoral dissertation at the University of Minnesota. The author is grateful to Raymond A. Bauer, Harvard University, and Robert J. Holloway, University of Minnesota, for their help in preparing this manuscript.

pended to obtain a product. One way to alter the amount of effort customers expend is to make the purchase decision more or less difficult by varying the amount of information supplied to the customer. If very little information is supplied, the customer may have to expend effort to gather additional information; if a great deal of detailed information is supplied, the customer may have to expend considerable effort to process the information. The expectations customers have regarding a product depend upon information gathered from a variety of sources. Within limits, customer expectations may be influenced by advertising, or other sales promotion methods.

Research Plan

Since the literature of marketing and economics provided neither exact definitions nor rigorous discussions of customer effort and expectation, it was felt that a fairly precise investigation of these factors might be useful. This precision could be obtained, however, only by severely limiting the range and scope of the investigation. Several considerations pointed to the use of a laboratory experiment for such a study:

(1) Controlled laboratory experiments had been successfully employed in other fields for limited investigations.

(2) A laboratory setting would permit study of the factors in relatively pure form, and such study might provide useful analytical information despite its limited nature and would provide a basis for further research.

(3) A laboratory experiment would allow maximum utilization of psychological theory, itself based upon laboratory findings.

In fact, two branches of psychological theory ("contrast" theory and "dissonance" theory) provided the basis for making specific statements about the relationships among effort, expectation, and evaluation. Contrast theory implies that a customer who receives a product less valuable than he expected will magnify the difference between the product received and the product expected. Even if this original expectation were to change, he would still be free to compare unfavorably the product received with better ones [5]. For example, suppose a customer goes to a restaurant which he expects to be good, and is confronted with an unappetizing meal. He might say that the restaurant was one of the worst he had ever been in and that the food was unfit for human consumption, *etc.*

A study by Spector [6] supports this argument. Spector found that subjects whose expectations were negatively disconfirmed evaluated a reward less favorably than did subjects who expected and received the same reward. In other words, disappointed subjects magnified the difference between the presumably more desirable reward and the one they received.

On the other hand, Festinger's theory of cognitive dissonance [4] might lead one to predict the opposite effect. Dissonance theory would imply that a person who expected a high-value product and received a low-value product would recognize the disparity and experience cognitive dissonance. (Dissonance is aroused in this case because receiving a low-value product is not consistent with having expected a high-value product.) The existence of dissonance should produce pressures for its reduction, which could be accomplished by adjusting the perceived disparity. One possible method to reconcile the difference between expectation and product would be to raise the evaluation of the product received.

In terms of the restaurant situation, the customer might say that the food was not really as bad as it appeared, that he really liked overcooked meat, *etc.* The work of Brehm [1] and Brehm and Cohen [2] indicates that people may raise their evaluations of those products which they have chosen from an array of products, when the cost to the individual of the chosen product is high.

Some reconciliation of the conflicting predictions made by contrast theory and dissonance theory is possible by introducing the concept of effort. If an individual expends effort in a situation, it is likely that the outcome of the experience has some importance for him. For instance, if our diner had made elaborate plans, driven a long distance, and paid a high price for his meal, he would probably have been much more concerned about enjoying his meal than a person who had merely stopped by the restaurant because it was convenient. Even if the outcome of this dining experience had not had initial importance, the investment of effort would have led our diner to attribute importance to it.

Thus, when a customer expends considerable effort, the prediction from dissonance theory might be expected to hold, since the consequences of that situation are important to the customer. However, when little effort is expended, the result predicted by contrast theory might be expected to occur, since the outcome of the situation is not so important. In other words, when a customer has expended little effort and receives a product less valuable than expected, he might evaluate that product less favorably than would a customer who expected, and did obtain, the identical product. However, as a customer expends greater effort, the situation becomes more important, and some dissonance is aroused when disappointed. Dissonance may be reduced by decreasing the perceived disparity between expectation and reward, but it cannot be reduced by magnifying the disparity. Thus, under conditions of high effort, dissonance reduction processes would tend to decrease the differences in product evaluation between customers who were disappointed and those who were not.

The expenditure of effort itself may produce a perceived disparity between effort expended and product received, whether customers obtained what they expected or less than they expected. If customers who expend little effort receive a product they consider appropriate for that amount of effort, those who invest considerable effort and obtain the same product are likely to perceive a disparity between effort and reward. Since magnifying this disparity would increase the dissonance aroused in this situation, customers are not likely to contrast effort and reward. Rather, they are likely to raise their evaluations of the product (or to deny the effort) relative to customers who have expended little effort to obtain the same product. This analysis presumes that the disparity is not so great that the individual withdraws from the situation altogether.

The reasoning expressed above leads to the following hypotheses, which were evaluated in a laboratory setting.

HYPOTHESES

(1) When customers expend little effort to obtain a product, those who receive a product less valuable than they expected will rate that product lower than will those who expected to receive, and do receive, the same product.

(2) As effort expended increases, this effect decreases.

(3) When customers obtain a product less valuable than they expected, those who expended high effort to obtain the product will rate it higher than will those who expended little effort.

(4) When customers obtain a product about as valuable as they expected, those who expended high effort to obtain the product will rate it higher than will those who expended little effort.

Procedure

The hypotheses were evaluated in a catalog shopping situation. Each of the independent variables, effort and expectation, appeared at two levels. The design was a two-by-two factorial, as shown in the following tabulation:

	Expectation (X)	
Effort (F)	*low((l)*	*high (h)*
Low *(l)*	A	B
High *(h)*	C	D

Subjects were 107 college juniors and seniors in the School of Business Administration, University of Minnesota.

Expectation was manipulated by the use of two 31-item catalogs in the study. Both contained descriptions and prices of ballpoint pens of the type usually purchased by the subjects. The high expectation catalog contained products whose median price was about $1.95. The products shown in the low expectation catalog were priced between 29¢ and 59¢; the average price was about 39¢. All subjects received the same 39¢ pen, ostensibly chosen by lot from the samples provided by the manufacturers whose products were shown in the catalog. Thus, the rational expecation of a student who saw the high expectation catalog was a $1.95 writing instrument; of a student who used the low expectation catalog, a 39¢ pen.

Effort was manipulated by a simulated shopping task. The task required low effort subjects to look through one of the catalogs as if shopping, and to write down one feature which impressed them for half of the items shown. This minimum effort procedure took about 15 minutes. High effort subjects worked about an hour in uncomfortable surroundings. They were asked to comb one catalog carefully, and to record five different features about each of the 31 items. The purpose of their task was to force them to invest considerable shopping effort.

The dependent measure was a questionnaire on which the product and shopping situation were rated, each on several scales. Subjects evaluated both the pen they received and the simulated shopping experience immediately after receiving the product. Subjects indicated their evaluations by placing an "X" along each of several 100 millimeter lines. For example, an individual who felt that the product he received was about the same as others in the catalog might have placed an X in the middle of the line shown below:

Compared to the products shown in the catalog, this product is:

Very inferior	Rather inferior	Somewhat superior	Vastly superior
(0) _____ X _____ (100)			

Questionnaires were scored by measuring the distance in millimeters from the zero end of the line to the point where the X crossed the line.

Results and Discussion

The results[1] of the experiment indicated that effort and expectation did influence evaluation of the product. Table 1 shows an index of product evaluation, based on an unweighted combination of responses on the "product desirability" and "comparison-to-catalog" questions. Responses on the remaining four product evaluation questions (product usefulness, price, comparative quality, comparative value), and indexes based on them yielded substantially the same results as those presented in the table. In some cases the differences among treatment combinations were more dramatic; in others, they were less so.

HYPOTHESIS 1

The results supported the first hypothesis: when subjects expended little effort, those who received a product less valuable than they expected rated it much less favorably than did subjects who expected to receive and did receive, the identical product. The same result occurred within the high effort treatment: subjects who received less than they expected rated the product less favorably than did those

---

[1] The results presented are based on data from 88 of the 107 students who participated. The remaining 19 were suspicious of the procedure. Excluding data from these 19 subjects slightly altered the size of some of the differences among treatment combinations, but did not affect the direction of any differences.

TABLE 1   INDEX OF MEAN PRODUCT EVALUATION SCORES*

Effort (F)	Expectation (X)	
	Low (l)	High (h)
Low (l)	51	35
High (h)	54	44

Comparisons among scores

Individual treatment combinations		Level of significance
Low effort:	$X_l - X_h = 16$	.01
High effort:	$X_l - X_h = 10$	.05
Low expectation:	$F_h - F_l = 3$	.20
High expectation:	$F_h - F_l = 9$	.05

Main effects and interaction

Expectation treatments combined:	$F_h - F_l = 6$	.05
Effort treatments combined:	$X_l - X_h = 13$	.01
Interaction $(X_l - X_h)F_l - (X_l - X_h)F_h = 6$		.05

*Maximum score = 100.

who received about what they expected. When the effort treatments were combined, the same phenomenon was observed—subjects who shopped the high expectation catalog and received the low-priced pen rated it less favorably than did subjects who shopped the low expectation catalog and received the identical low-priced pen.

If the experimental procedure succeeded in creating, and then confirming or disconfirming expectations, one may say that the effect of negative disconfirmation of expectation was to produce a *less favorable* evaluation of the product. Even if the procedure employed did not create firm expectations, it may be said that the perceived disparity between the product received and the products in the high expectation catalog apparently operated to produce a less favorable evaluation of the product received. In any event, it appears that the catalogs provided standards for the evaluation of the product subjects received.

HYPOTHESIS 2

The results supported Hypothesis Two: as effort increased, the difference between high and low expectation subjects' ratings of the product would decrease. Specifically, the hypothesis predicted a difference between differences, or an interaction:

$$(X_l - X_h)F_l > (X_l - X_h)F_h.$$

Table 1 shows that product evaluations were only slightly higher in the high effort, low expectation condition than they were in the low effort, low expectation condition. On the other hand, evaluation scores in the high effort, high expectation condition (while lower than those in the high effort, low expectation condition, were considerably higher than those in the low effort, high expectation condition. These observations indicated that expenditure of greater effort moderated the effect of negative disconfirmation of expectation. In order to understand this phenomenon, it may be useful to analyze each of the high expectation conditions in greater detail.

In the low effort, high expectation condition, subjects invested little time and energy, and had only limited knowledge on which to base their expectations. Consequently, the outcome of the experiment mattered little to them, and it was relatively easy to deny that they had expected a product more valuable than that received. Subjects in this condition were quite free to contrast the product unfavorably with those in the catalog, and to rate it as relatively undesirable.

In terms of dissonance theory, one may say that little dissonance would have been aroused in this condition, because the modest investment of effort minimized individual commitment to, or involvement in, the situation. Any dissonance which might have been aroused by the disparity between expecting a high value product and receiving a low value one could have been reduced by denying the expectation. Such denial would also have reduced any dissonance aroused by the disparity between expecting a valuable product and expending little effort.

On the other hand, subjects in the high effort, high expectation treatment had invested considerable time and energy before obtaining the product. This investment made the outcome of the experiment important to them, and provided substantial basis for firm expectations of receiving a high value product. In this situation, the disparity between expectation of a high value product and receipt of a low value product aroused some dissonance, which could have been reduced only by lowering or denying the rather firm expectation, or by raising the evaluation of the product. An unfavorable evaluation of the product could only have increased dissonance, whereas a more favorable evaluation of the product would have operated to reduce it.

A favorable evaluation would also have been consistent with subjects' knowledge that they had expended considerable effort to obtain the product: "If I've had to work to get it, the product must be pretty good." However, evaluation scores in this condition could not exceed the midpoint of any scale unless subjects felt that the 39¢ pen they received was superior to the $1.95 products in the high expectation catalog. Thus the "dissonance reduction" processes operating to produce a favorable rating could not entirely overcome the perceived disparity between the products in the catalog and the product received.

In summary: subjects in the low effort, high expectation condition had no reason to reduce the disparity between the expensive products they saw in the catalog and the inexpensive product they received; in fact, they were free to magnify the disparity. The result of their contrasting the product received with those in the catalog was to produce a much lower evaluation of the product in the low effort,

TABLE 2   TYPICAL SHOPPING TASK EVALUATION SCALE AND SCORES: MEAN SCORES ON "PLEASANT" SCALE*

Effort (F)	Expectation (X)	
	Low (l)	High (h)
Low (l)	59	54
High (h)	43	49

Comparisons among scores

Individual treatment combinations		Level of significance
Low effort:	$X_l - X_h = 5$	.10
High effort:	$X_h - X_l = 6$	.10
Low expectation:	$F_l - F_h = 16$	.10
High expectation:	$F_l - F_h = 5$	.10

Main effects and interaction

Expectation treatments combined:	$F_l - F_h = 11$	.01
Effort treatments combined:	$F_h - F_l = 1$	.50
Interaction $(X - X_h)F_l - (X_l - X_h)F_h = 11$		.01

*The task itself was:

Very pleasant	Rather pleasant	Rather unpleasant	Extremely unpleasant

(100) _____ (0)

high expectation condition than in the low effort, low expectation condition (where the product received was similar to those in the catalog). In the high effort, high expectation condition, this contrast phenomenon was partially blocked. As a result, higher product evaluation scores were obtained in the high effort, high expectation condition than in the low effort, high expectation condition. But, because some disparity was still perceived between products in the catalog and the product received, product evaluation scores in the high effort, high expectation condition remained somewhat lower than those in the high effort, low expectation condition.

HYPOTHESIS 3

The results supported Hypothesis Three which asserted that, within the high expectation treatment, subjects who expended considerable effort would rate the product more favorably than would those who had put forth little effort. As discussed previously, evaluations of the products were lower in the low effort, high expectation condition than in the high effort, high expectation condition because contrast processes (leading to lower evaluations) were free to operate in the former condition, but were partially blocked in the latter.

HYPOTHESIS 4

The results were in the direction predicted by Hypothesis Four, but they were not statistically significant ($p = .20$, t-test). One reason for this small difference observed between high and low effort conditions within the low expectation treatment may have been that most subjects found it difficult to rate the product received higher than 60 on any scale. Consequently, the mean rating of 54 in the high effort, low expectation condition may approach the upper limit of the range within which subjects felt the product could reasonably be evaluated. This upper limit on evaluation may have prevented individuals from adjusting completely the disparity perceived between expending considerable effort and receiving an inexpensive product.

When expectation treatments were combined, the results showed that subjects in the high effort treatments evaluated the product more favorably than did those in the low effort treatments. The investment of greater effort apparently produced a more favorable evaluation of the product.

The expenditure of high effort provided subjects both more information and a greater opportunity for commitment than did the low effort treatment. In order to see whether subjects evaluated the product differently simply because they knew more about disposable ballpoint pens, the following procedure was employed. Treatment combinations were ranked according to (1) number of products similar to the one received to which subjects were exposed in each catalog, and (2) number of product features of similar products which subjects had to record. Each of these rankings was compared to rankings of treatment combinations on both mean and median evaluations of the product. The comparison was made for the "product evaluation" scale group as a whole, as well as for each scale within the group.

Correlations between each of the rank-orders mentioned did not differ significantly from zero. Although the data do not permit the inference that an "information hypothesis" may be rejected, it does appear that an explanation of the data in terms of effort and expectation may be more fruitful. The latter explanation does, for example, account for the observed interaction, which an information hypothesis would not have predicted.

An interesting sidelight to the analysis of the effect of information is that those who recorded five features for each of 31 products (high effort) rated the products in the catalogs as "less clearly described" than did those who recorded only one feature for each of 16 products ($p < .05$, t-test). It may be that exposure to too much information makes discrimination among products *more*, rather than less, difficult.

EVALUATION OF THE SHOPPING TASK

Not surprisingly, subjects in the high effort treatments found the task less pleasant, more fatiguing and more frustrating, than did subjects in the low effort treatments. Within each effort treatment, however, some interesting reversals appeared. Within the low effort treatment, high expectation subjects found the shopping task significantly less pleasant and less rewarding than did low expectation subjects. The reverse was true within the high effort treatment, where high expectation subjects rated the shopping task more favorably than did low expectation subjects.

These results may be seen more clearly by examining a scale typical of those on which the shopping task was evaluated. Of the 12 scales, all but three showed differences in the same directions as those on the "pleasant" scale. For all three scales on which the direction was different from that shown on the pleasant scale, differences were well within the range of sampling error.

It appears that subjects in the low effort, high expectation condition generalized their unfavorable rating of the product to the shopping experience. On the other hand, subjects in the high effort, high expectation condition found some extra rewards in the shopping experience, compared to those in the high effort, low expectation condition.

This phenomenon may be interpreted from the point of view of dissonance theory. Subjects in the low effort, high expectation treatment were free to generalize their unfavorable reactions from the product to the shopping situation, for no dissonance was introduced by so doing. On the other hand, revaluating the shopping task in a more favorable light worked in the direction of reducing dissonance for subjects in the high effort, high expectation condition. They could narrow the perceived disparity between high effort and expectation, on the one hand, and low reward, on the other hand, by finding supplementary rewards in the shopping task.

Implications for Marketing

The results of this experiment showed that, under certain conditions, effort and expectation affected the evaluation of both a product and a shopping experience. When expectations were negatively disconfirmed, subjects rated both product and shopping experience unfavorably. The expenditure of high effort moderated that effect and, for the shopping experience, partially reversed it. It is obvious that one should think twice about what we can assert from results obtained under limited conditions. Nevertheless, the results lead to some interesting implications for marketing.

EFFORT

Expenditure of higher effort produced a more favorable initial evaluation of the product. Thus, a simple notion of "efficiency" cannot prevail. The effort invested in shopping may, under specifiable conditions, contribute to the evaluation of the product. Although consumers often expend more effort to obtain products they value, expenditure of high effort follows favorable evaluation in such cases. This experiment shows that a favorable evaluation may indeed follow the expenditure of high effort.

If a more favorable evaluation of a product is assumed to lead to a higher probability of repeat purchasing, one is led to the rather surprising conclusion that, within limits, greater shopping effort may lead to more repeat purchases. Although the logic of such an assertion is not unassailable, it does suggest that the notion of convenience (lack of effort) ought to be re-examined.

EXPECTATION

Under certain conditions, subjects used their expectations as guidelines against which they evaluated the product. Either their expectations, or an array of products with which they have had previous experience, may form such guidelines. What is new in the findings of this experiment is that failure of a product to measure up to these guidelines may result in no initial sale, no repeat sale, and possibly unfavorable word-of-mouth publicity. Such reactions should be expected particularly when little shopping effort has been invested.

If this interpretation is correct, marketers should endeavor to make their offerings consistent with customer guidelines, or standards. One way of achieving this goal is to manipulate expectations through sales promotion. An important corollary is that marketers should know what customer standards of evaluation are, and act accordingly.

SATISFACTION

Since both effort and confirmation or disconfirmation of expectation affect evaluation, customer satisfaction may depend not only upon the product itself, but also upon the experience surrounding acquisition of the product. Customer satisfaction, then, may be more a global concept than simply product evaluation. Satisfaction may involve evaluation of an entire product bundle or offering.

Since the shopping experience and the product are, under some conditions, evaluated differently, the definition and measurement of total satisfaction pose a complex problem. Besides evaluation of the product and shopping experience as described here, there may be still other elements of satisfaction which have not been identified, and whose impact remains to be examined.

References

1. Jack W. Brehm, "Postdecision Changes in the Desirability of Alternatives," *Journal of Abnormal and Social Psychology*, 52 (1956), 384-9.
2. ———— and Arthur R. Cohen, *Explorations in Cognitive Dissonance*, New York: John Wiley & Sons, Inc., 1962.
3. Richard N. Cardozo, "Customer Satisfaction: Laboratory Study and Marketing Action," *Proceedings, Educators Conference*, American Marketing Association, 1964.
4. Leon Festinger, *A Theory of Cognitive Dissonance*, Stanford, Calif.: Stanford University Press, 1957.
5. Harry Helson, "Current Trends and Issues in Adaptation-Level Theory," *American Psychologist*, 19 (January 1964) 26-38.
6. Aaron J. Spector, "Expectations, Fulfillment, and Morale," *Journal of Abnormal and Social Psychology*, 52 (January 1956), 51-6.

7 Emotions

An Experiment on Consumer Dissonance

ROBERT J. HOLLOWAY* *(Marketing Educator)*

> In this article the author describes a consumer-decision experiment which involved four *dissonant-producing factors* simultaneously.
>
> Even though the study is limited to only one product, an automobile battery, the findings provide useful insights that might be applicable to various product categories.

How can the theory of cognitive dissonance be applied or used by marketing practitioners? The theory itself is fairly well known—that there may exist dissonant or "nonfitting" relations among cognitive elements.[1]

But how is this idea relevant to the field of marketing? Three articles dealing with cognitive dissonance have appeared in the *Journal of Marketing;*[2] but even so, substantial research remains to be carried out before marketers can be sure of the value of the theory to marketing.

Consumers continually are receiving various kinds of information about products from friends, advertisements, and salesmen. These pieces of information are *cognitions* which, according to the theory of cognitive dissonance, consumers like to have consistent with one another. The theory is that if cognitions are inconsistent, consumers try to reduce the inconsistency, that is, to reduce dissonance, and that consumers try to reduce dissonance *after* making a buying decision.

Source: Robert J. Holloway, "An Experiment on Consumer Dissonance," *Journal of Marketing,* Vol. 31 (January, 1967), pp. 39-43.

[1] Leon Festinger, *A Theory of Cognitive Dissonance* (Evanston, Illinois: Row, Peterson and Company, 1957).

[2] James F. Engel, "Are Automobile Purchasers Dissonant Consumers?" *Journal of Marketing,* Vol. 27 (April, 1963), pp. 55-58; Bruce C. Straits, "The Pursuit of the Dissonant Consumer," *Journal of Marketing,* Vol. 28 (July, 1964), pp. 62-66; James F. Engel, "Further Pursuit of the Dissonant Consumer: A Comment," *Journal of Marketing,* Vol. 29 (April, 1965), p. 34.

Thus, a buyer who selects Brand A over other brands might experience dissonance because he is aware of attractive features of the rejected brand and unattractive features of chosen Brand A. One way for him to reduce dissonance would be to read advertisements of Brand A that would reinforce his buying decision.

However, an analysis of consumer behavior involves many interacting forces, and the post-decision emphasis of dissonance theory represents only one facet of the multi-facet problem. Even so, the theory may be useful.

Consider such questions as the following. Does dissonance relate to brand loyalty? Can marketers improve their position by helping consumers reduce any dissonance they might have developed? How does a salesman handle anticipated dissonance on the part of a potential customer? What can a salesman do in the pre-decision conflict period? How similar should alternatives be for the buyer? How many alternatives should be presented? Are impulse purchases apt to be dissonance-producing? Does planning on the part of the buyer aid the process of dissonance reduction?

Post-decision dissonance is caused by a number of factors identified by psychologists in experiments, and most of these factors relate to buying decisions. Table 1 represents an attempt to place these dissonance-arousing factors in a buying context.

As indicated in Table 1, dissonance may operate in one buying situation and not in another. Further, several factors may operate simultaneously: one may be dissonance-producing and two others may not be. Subsequently, the aroused dissonance may be reduced in a variety of ways. The buyer may change his evaluations, select supporting information, ignore conflicting information, distort his perceptions, or even return the item to the seller.

Description of the Dissonance Experiment

It was decided to carry out an experiment in which several dissonance-producing factors could be manipulated: (1) inducement to buy, (2) anticipated dissonance, (3) information, and (4) cognitive overlap.

Each of these four conditions had two levels—one with high-producing dissonance features and one with low. A factorial design was used, and 80 persons were randomly assigned to the 16 experimental conditions—as shown in Figure 1.

*ABOUT THE AUTHOR. Robert J. Holloway is Professor of Marketing at the Univeristy of Minnesota. He is also associated with the Center for Experimental Studies in Business at Minnesota, an informal organization created to encourage the use of experimental techniques in business.

The research reported was made possible by a grant from the Ford Foundation. From the beginning, the author worked closely with David Ehlen, David Garner, Donald Popielarz, Charles Stoerzinger, James Taylor, and M. Venkatesan.

TABLE 1   DISSONANCE AND BUYING SITUATIONS

Factors Affecting Dissonance	Buying Situation	Conditions with High Dissonance Expectation	Conditions with Low Dissonance Expectation
1. Attractiveness of rejected alternative	A high-school graduate decides which of several pictures to order.	Three of the proofs have both attractive and desirable features.	One of the proofs clearly is superior to the rest.
2. Negative factors in chosen alternative	A man chooses between two suits of clothing.	The chosen suit has the color the man wanted but not the style.	The chosen suit has both the color and style the man wanted.
3. Number of alternatives	A teacher shops for a tape-recorder.	There are eight recorders from which to choose.	There are only two recorders from which to choose.
4. Cognitive overlap	A housewife shops for a vacuum sweeper.	A salesman offers two similarly priced tank types.	A salesman offers a tank type and an upright cleaner.
5. Importance of cognitions involved	A child buys a present for her sister.	The sister has definite preferences for certain kinds of music.	The sister has no strong tastes for certain records.

6. Positive inducement	Parents decide to buy a photo-enlarger for their son.	The son already has hobby equipment and does not need the enlarger.	The son never has had a true hobby and needs something to keep him occupied.
7. Discrepant or negative action	A man purchases an expensive watch.	The man had never before paid more than $35 for a watch.	Fairly expensive watches had been important gift items in the man's family.
8. Information available	Housewife buys a detergent.	The housewife has no experience with the brand purchased—it is a new variety.	The housewife has read and heard a good deal about the product, and has confidence in the manufacturer.
9. Anticipated dissonance	A small boy buys a model airplane.	The boy anticipates trouble at home because of the cost of the model.	The boy expects no trouble at home relative to the purchase.
10. Familiarity and knowledge	A family buys a floor polisher.	The item was purchased without much thought.	The item was purchased after a careful selection process.

Inducement	High								Low							
Anticipated dissonance	High				Low				High				Low			
Additional information	Yes		None		Yes		None		Yes		None		Yes		None	
Cognitive overlap	High	Low	High	Low	High	Low	High	Low	High	Low	High	Low	High	Low	High	Low
	(1)	(2)	(3)	(4)	(5)	(6)	(7)	(8)	(9)	(10)	(11)	(12)	(13)	(14)	(15)	(16)

Figure 1. The experimental design. An example of 1 of the 16 conditions is: high inducement, low anticipated dissonance, no additional information, high cognitive overlap.

HYPOTHESES

The following hypotheses were developed relative to the four main conditions.

1. *Individuals with low inducement to buy will have more dissonance than those who have high inducement to buy.* As an example, a person who needs a new pair of shoes (high inducement) should experience less dissonance than one who buys an extra pair (low inducement).

2. *Individuals exposed to a condition of high anticipated dissonance will reflect greater dissonance than those in the low anticipated dissonance condition.* For instance, a buyer of a sports car, who wonders what comments his colleagues will make, should experience more dissonance than when he buys a traditional type of car which would likely not draw criticism (anticipated dissonance).

3. *Individuals to whom additional positive information is provided to aid their decision-making will experience less dissonance than those to whom no additional positive information is provided.* In other words, additional positive information concerning a purchased item should make a buyer more confident and less dissonant than when he was not given that additional information.

4. *The high cognitive overlap condition will create more dissonance than the low cognitive overlap condition.*

Hypotheses based on interactions among the four factors were not developed because we did not know what to anticipate. However, the following procedure was carried out.

PROCEDURE

Male college students of the University of Minnesota were asked to play the role of buyers of automobile batteries. They were given class credit for participating, plus a chance of receiving a new automobile battery in the several drawings that were held. The four graduate students who conducted the experiments were systematically rotated over all 16 conditions.

Twelve brands of batteries were used in the experiment:

Allstate	Goodrich	Penneys
Atlas	Goodyear	Pure
Delco	Gould	Riverside
Fisk Ambassador	National	Wizard

Each participant in the experiment was asked to complete a rating form, indicaing how favorable he considered each of the 12 brands. This rating form was actually the prerating score, later to be compared with an identical postrating score, so that the difference in the two rating scores would be a measure of the amount of dissonance reduction experienced.

After completing the form, each person was taken to another room for three minutes. On the walls of the room were diagrams of the electrical system of the automobile, annual sales figures for the battery industry, and a list of battery brands sold in Minneapolis and St. Paul. These materials were expected to help the person become involved in the study without biasing him in any way.

The person was next greeted with the purchase-decision situation which contained (1a) a *high-inducement* factor or (1b) a *low-inducement* factor, and (2a) a *high-anticipated dissonance* condition or (2b) a *low-anticipated dissonance* condition.

(1)   *Inducement*
    a. High Inducement

    You have been in northern Minnesota for the weekend and are driving back to the Twin Cities. After a stop for coffee, you find that you cannot start the engine of your car. You return to the cafe and locate the phone number of a nearby garage. The attendant arrives in a few minutes, checks your car, and reports that your battery probably has a leaky cell which is shorting out.

    The attendant tows your car into his garage and determines that your battery is dead and cannot be recharged. The long winter has apparently taken its toll.

    b. Low Inducement

    You were planning on running several errands today. After the first stop, however, your car will not start. After several attempts to start it, you give up and call the nearest garage. The attendent arrives in a few minutes and starts your car with the aid of his booster battery.

    You follow him to his garage where he checks over your engine and battery. He believes that you may have a leaky cell in the battery and that, with a little luck, it may be possible for you to get along for a few weeks.

(2)   *Anticipated Dissonance*
    a. High-anticipated Dissonance

    As the attendant checks your car, you notice the brand of the battery and you reflect that it has done a pretty good job. You also recall that your regular service station dealer is quite proud of his brands of batteries, and the thought runs through your mind that he will notice a new battery in your car the first time he checks under the hood.

    b. Low-anticipated Dissonance

    As the attendant checks your car, you notice that the battery is so encased and hidden that you cannot even see what brand of battery you now have. Since you normally trade at several stations and purchase several brands of automobile products, you cannot even guess what brand of battery it is.

Each person was then told orally:

    "At this point the garage attendant where you are now suggests that you look at several of the new batteries he has in stock."

The experimenter then stepped out of the room and wheeled in a battery-display cart on which were three batteries—the batteries available in the hypothetical situation. The three brands shown the person were selected according to a decision rule in which brands rated very high or very low in the pretest were excluded.

(3) The manipulation of the positive *information* factor occurred at this time; that is, half the subjects received no additional information, and the other half were given a card on which appeared the following:

The batteries displayed here are conventional 12-volt batteries. They are heavy duty with plenty of reserve power. Specifications range around the 75-Ampere Hour Rating, which means the amount of power stored for normal driving needs. Their Zero Start Ratings range around 6.6 minutes—the number of minutes a battery will crank in zero cold without dying out.

(4) The condition of *cognitive overlap* was handled by placing cards beside each of the batteries on the display rack. See Table 2.

TABLE 2   CARDS ON DISPLAY RACK

Battery	High Overlap		Low Overlap	
	Price	Warranty	Price	Warranty
A	$22.88	30 months	$36.88	48 months
B	22.29	30 months	27.77	36 months
C	22.49	30 months	23.49	39 months

The experimenter then said:

Now look at these three batteries. We would like you to decide which one of these batteries you would buy under the conditions you are in, that is, in the garage talking to the attendant. Think about it carefully now and then tell me which one you would select. Take your time and make what you think would be your real decision.

As soon as the person decided, the experimenter thanked him and reminded him that he had chosen Brand A, for example. The person was then asked for a "little more information," which meant that he filled out the postrating form.

Following this the experimenter discussed the study with the individual, in an effort to determine his reactions, battery knowledge, and buying experience.

Results

Reduction of dissonance was measured by comparing the prerating and postrating scores. A higher postrating score for the chosen battery or a lower postrating score for the rejected batteries, or both, indicated dissonance reduction.

The overall mean change was 2.51, a statistically significant change, which indicated that dissonance had been experienced by the participants. The mean changes for each of the 16 conditions shown in Figure 1 ranged from a low of 0.8 to a high of 4.8.

MAIN EFFECTS

Dissonance reduction was measured for each of the four independent variables. Three of the four results were in the direction predicted, although none of them was statistically significant.

However, the results concerning *anticipated dissonance* were *contrary to expectations,* and contrary to preliminary results.

INTERACTION

As to the results on interaction, two of the interactions were significantly different from the mean change and support two of the hypotheses.

In the first significant interaction, when *high inducement* interacted with the two levels of information, a significantly different amount of dissonance was measured. Thus, hypothesis 3 was in part confirmed, as the amount of positive information did affect dissonance somewhat.

When there was *low inducement,* the information effect was not apparent. The explanation probably is that because low inducement by itself produced substantial dissonance, a manipulation of information had no further effect.

In the second case, with *low anticipated dissonance combined with cognitive overlap,* a significant effect was measured. Thus, hypothesis 4 was in part confirmed, as the interaction showed the effect of high versus low cognitive overlap.

With *high anticipated dissonance,* however, the overlap manipulation produced no additional dissonance.

Several other results were in the anticipated direction but not statistically significant. As an example, the condition expected to produce the least amount of dissonance (high inducement—low anticipated dissonance—additional information—low cognitive overlap), yielded a change score of only 0.8, the lowest of all conditions anc considerably below the 2.5 overall mean.

Generalizing from the experiment, there appears to be more possibility of dissonance when buyers purchase without need and without sufficient information, and when alternatives are similar to the point of making the decision difficult.

IMPLICATIONS

Although the results of the experiment were not as positive as anticipated, they did provide a number of *tentative findings* about dissonance and buying behavior:

1. Consumers who buy when they have *strong inducement* should experience *less dissonance* than those who buy without inducement.

2. Consumers who obtain *adequate information* probably will have *less dissonance* than those who buy without sufficient information.

3. Product alternatives with very *similar attributes* may cause *greater consumer dissonance* than dissimilar alternatives.

4. *Interaction effects* occur when *various dissonance-arousing factors* are combined in one buying situation.

8 Learning and Remembering

Consumer Brand Choice
as a Learning Process

ALFRED A. KUEHN* *(Marketing Educator)*

This study examines the following questions in the light of available empirical data and a model that appears to describe them:

- What do we know about brand choice?
- What behaviorial mechanisms appear to underlie this phenomenon?
- Is such behavior habitual?
- Is learning involved?
- Does repeat purchase of a brand reinforce the brand choice response?
- What is the relationship between consumer purchase frequencies and brand shifting behavior?

We find that brand shares may be predicted from the sequence, rhythm, and frequency of consumers' past purchases.

Source: Alfred A. Kuehn, "Consumer Brand Choice as a Learning Process," *Journal of Advertising Research,* Vol. 2 (December, 1962), pp. 10-17.

[1]The research underlying this paper has been supported by grants from the Graduate School of Industrial Administration and the Market Research Corporation of America. The paper is based in part on lectures presented at the Ford Foundation Faculty Seminar in Marketing, conducted by the University of Chicago at Williamstown, Mass., in August 1961.
*Alfred A. Kuehn is an assistant professor in the Graduate School of Industrial Administration at the Carnegie Institute of Technology, as well as a consultant to the Market Research Corporation of America and to major merchandisers of packaged grocery and drug products. He received a B.S. in 1952, an M.S. in 1954, and a Ph.D. in 1960, all from Carnegie Tech. The present article appears in a book coedited by Dr. Kuehn (with Ronald E. Frank and William F. Massy), *Quantitative Techniques in Marketing Analysis,* published by Richard D. Irwin. His article, "How Advertising Performance Depends on Other Marketing Factors" appeared in the March 1962 issue of this *Journal.*

The phenomenon of consumer brand shifting is a central element underlying the dynamics of the marketplace. To understand and describe market trends adequately, we must first establish the nature of the influences on consumer choice with respect to products and brands. Research directed at establishing the conditions under which consumers will shift from one brand to another offers hope of providing a framework within which to evaluate the influence of price, advertising, distribution and shelf space, and various types of sales promotion.

What do we know about brand choice? What behavioral mechanisms appear to underlie this phenomenon? Is such behavior habitual? Is learning involved? Does repeated purchasing of a brand reinforce the brand choice response? What is the relationship between consumer purchase frequencies and brand shifting behavior? These questions will be discussed in the light of available empirical data and a model which appears to describe them.

A Model of Consumer Brand Shifting

A model equivalent to a generalized form of the Estes (1954) and Bush-Mosteller (1955) stochastic (probabilistic) learning models appears to describe consumer brand shifting quite well. To illustrate how this brand shifting model describes changes in the consumer's probability of purchasing any given brand as a result of his purchases of that brand (e.g., Brand A) and competing brands (e.g., Brand X), let us examine the effect of the four-purchase sequence XAAX on a consumer with initial probability $P_{A,1}$ (see Figure 1).

The model is described or defined in terms of four parameters, namely, the intercepts and slopes of the two lines referred to in Figure 1 as the Purchase Operator and the Rejection Operator. If the brand in question is purchased by the consumer on a given buying occasion, the consumer's probability of again buying the same brand the next time that type of product is purchased is read from the Purchase Operator. If the brand is rejected by the consumer on a given buying occasion, the consumer's probability of buying that brand when he next buys that type of product is read from the Rejection Operator. Thus, in Figure 1 our hypothetical consumer begins on trial 1 with the probability of $P_{A,1}$ of buying Brand A. The consumer chooses some other brand (X) on trial 1, however, and thus his probability of buying Brand A on trial 2 ($P_{A,2}$) is obtained from the Rejection Operator, resulting in a slight reduction in the probability of purchasing A on the next trial. On trial 2, however, the consumer does purchase Brand A and thus increases the likelihood of his again buying the brand on the next occasion (trial 3) to $P_{A,3}$. Continuing in this fashion, the consumer again buys A on trial 3, thereby increasing his probability of purchasing Brand A on trial 4 to $P_{A,4}$. He again rejects A on trial 4, however, decreasing his probability of buying A on trial 5 to $P_{A,5}$.

Two characteristics of the model should be noted: 1) the probability $P_{A,t}$ approaches but never exceeds the upper limit U_A with repeated purchasing of the brand, and 2) the probability $P_{A,t}$ approaches but never drops below the lower

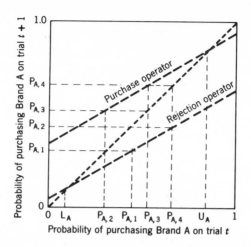

Figure 1. Stochastic (probabilistic) brand shifting model.

limit L_A with continued rejection of the brand. Using Bush and Mosteller's terminology, this would be referred to as an incomplete learning, incomplete extinction model insofar as U_A is less than one and L_A is greater than zero. This is equivalent to saying that consumers will generally not develop such strong brand loyalties (or buying habits) as to insure either the rejection or purchase of a given brand.

It should also be pointed out that the Purchase and Rejection Operators are functions of the time elapsed between the consumer's tth and $t + 1$st purchases and of the merchandising activities of competitors. The time effect can be illustrated by the three sets of operators shown for high, medium, and very low frequency purchasers of a rapidly consumed, nondurable consumer product (see Figure 2). Note that the Purchase and Rejection Operators decrease in slope and that the upper and lower limits approach each other as the time between purchases increases.

At the one limit (time between purchases approaching zero) the Purchase and Rejection Operators approach the diagonal, L approaches zero, and U approaches one. At the other limit (time between purchases approaching infinity), L and U approach each other and the Purchase and Rejection Operators approach a slope equal to zero.

The main problem that remains in making use of the model is then the estimation of the four parameters defining the Purchase and Rejection Operators as a function of the time between purchases. If this could be done a priori, the model might be of value to marketing management for use in forecasting. At present,

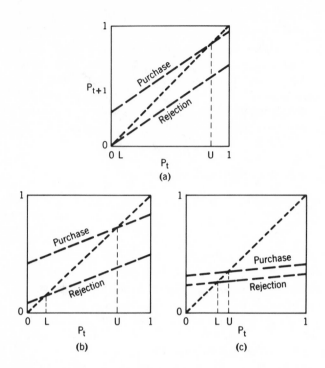

Figure 2. Effect of time between purchases upon purchase and rejection operators (a = high − frequency purchasers; b = medium − frequency purchasers; and
c = low − frequency purchasers).

however, the model's primary use is in evaluating the effects of past and current
competitive marketing activity. Thus, the parameters of the model are estimated
for short time periods and related to the actions of all competitors in the market.
Since the path of aggregate consumer purchasing behavior could be established for
any given set of parameter values, it follows that the parameter estimates obtained
from fitting the model can provide a means for evaluating the influence of the
market conditions prevailing during the period that the sequential purchase data
were collected.

An efficient method has been developed to estimate these brand shifting parameters (maximum likelihood estimates) on the basis of sequences of two to four
purchases. The method makes it feasible to relate this model to consumer purchasing behavior observed during relatively short periods of time. This is a must if the
technique is to be useful, since merchandising conditions do not remain constant
for long periods of time—products are modified, advertising themes and budgets

are altered, special promotions are generally temporary in nature, and price levels may change from time to time. The technique used to estimate the brand shifting parameters is outlined as a working paper in the Research in Marketing Project series of the Graduate School of Industrial Administration, Carnegie Institute of Technology. The Bush-Mosteller approach to estimating the parameters of their stochastic learning model cannot, in its current state of development, be applied to the brand shifting model since 1) techniques have not been developed to estimate simultaneously the four basic parameters of the model, and 2) the methods outlined require a long history or record of trials (and, therefore, data collected over a long period of time during which there is stability in merchandising activity) from which to develop parameter estimates.

Empirical Brand Shifting Research

What evidence is there in support of the model? Three types of empirical studies have led to the formulation and continued development of the above model:

1. analysis of three-, four-, five-, and six-purchase sequences of consumer brand purchases (Kuehn, 1958),
2. analysis of effects of time between consumer purchases on a consumer's probability of purchasing individual brands of product (Kuehn, 1958), and
3. simulation of consumer brand choice behavior.

Each of these three studies is discussed briefly below.

ANALYSIS OF BRAND PURCHASE SEQUENCES

Sequential purchase data can provide some insight into consumer brand switching. The data analyzed below represent the frozen orange juice purchases of approximately 600 Chicago families in the three years 1950 to 1952, covering more than 15,000 individual purchases collected in monthly diaries by the Chicago Tribune Consumer Panel. The data were analyzed as sequences of five purchases by means of a factorial analysis to determine the influence of the consumer's first four sequential brand choices on his choice of a brand on the fifth buying occasion. The data and analysis prepared for Snow Crop brand are summarized in Table 1.

In column 1, the letter "S" is used to represent a purchase of the Snow Crop brand, the letter "O" to represent the purchase of any *other* brand of frozen orange juice. Thus SSSS indicates a sequence of four purchases of Snow Crop. The sequence OSSS represents one purchase of some other brand followed by three purchases of Snow Crop.

Column 2 tabulates the sample sizes from which were calculated the observed and predicted probabilities of purchasing Snow Crop on the subsequent (fifth) purchase in the sequence.

Column 3 is computed on the basis of the observed frequencies of the five-purchase sequences. Thus, there were 296 sequences exhibiting the pattern SSSO in

TABLE 1   COMPARISON OF OBSERVED AND PREDICTED PROBABILITY
OF PURCHASING SNOW CROP GIVEN THE FOUR PREVIOUS
BRAND PURCHASES

Previous Purchase Pattern (1)	Sample Size (2)	Observed Probability of Purchase (3)	Predicted Probability of Purchase* (4)	Deviation of Predictions (5)
SSSS	1,047	.806	.832	+.026
OSSS	277	.690	.691	+.001
SOSS	206	.665	.705	+.040
SSOS	222	.595	.634	+.039
SSSO	296	.486	.511	+.025
OOSS	248	.552	.564	+.012
SOOS	138	.565	.507	−.058
OSOS	149	.497	.493	−.004
SOSO	163	.405	.384	−.021
OSSO	181	.414	.370	−.044
SSOO	256	.305	.313	+.008
OOOS	500	.330	.366	+.033
OOSO	404	.191	.243	+.052
OSOO	433	.129	.172	+.043
SOOO	557	.154	.186	+.032
OOOO	8,442	.048	.045	−.003

*To illustrate the computation of the values in column 4, the probability of a Snow Crop purchase given the history SOOO is .045 (the probability of purchase given OOOO) plus .141, or .186; the probability given SOOS is .045 + .141 + .321 = .507; and the predicted probability given OSSS is .045 + .127 + .198 + .321 = .691.

the first four positions of the sequence. Snow Crop was purchased on the fifth buying occasion in 144 of these sequences. The best estimate of the observed probability of buying Snow Crop given the past purchase record of SSSO is therefore 144/296 = .486.

The predicted column is based on the results of the factorial analysis of past purchase effects. Each of the four past brand purchases was examined with respect to its individual (primary) effect and the effect of its interactions with the other purchases. The individual effects of the past four purchase positions were highly significant but the interaction effects were not significantly different from zero at the five per cent level of significance; that is, there was greater than five per cent probability of results as extreme as those observed arising by chance if there were in fact no interaction effects.

There is close agreement between the observed and predicted probabilities, in view of the limited sample size. The predicted values, however, appear to deviate systematically on the high side when Snow Crop is purchased either one or three times on the last four buying occasions; also, predictions are generally low given two purchases.

Subsequent analysis indicated that these systematic deviations were reduced or eliminated when a record of the fifth past brand purchase was included in the analysis.

Casual inspection of Table 1 suggests that the most recent purchase of the consumer is not the only one influencing his brand choice. This finding raises some question about the uses currently being made of purchase-to-purchase Markov chain analyses which assume that only the most recent purchase of the consumer is influential. The analysis of "primary" effects referred to above showed that the purchase of Snow Crop on the most recent buying occasion added .321 to the probability of the consumer's buying Snow Crop on his next purchase. Similarly, the second most recent purchase added .198, the third .127, and the fourth .141 (see footnote, Table 1).

Note that the first three purchase effects decline roughly exponentially. That is, the ratio of the importance of the first purchase to that of the second is approximately equal to the ratio of the second to the third. The fourth, however, increases rather than decreases! This reversal occurs because past purchases beyond the fourth most recent purchase were excluded from the analysis. The increased importance attached to the fourth most recent purchase for prediction purposes reflects its high correlation with the fifth and earlier past purchases not incorporated in the study. When these same data were reanalyzed using six-purchase sequences, the exponential relationship of declining primary purchase effects fits the first through fourth past purchases. As would be expected, however, the fifth past purchase effect was larger than the fourth because of its higher correlation with the consumer's sixth and even earlier past purchases.

Observation of the exponentially declining effects of past purchases led to the testing of the brand shifting model outlined in Figure 1, since that model has the characteristic of weighting the influence of past brand choices exponentially when the slopes of the Purchase and Rejection Operators are identical. Subsequent research with products other than frozen orange juice has tended to confirm the predictive value of exponential weighting of past brand purchases by consumers. The exponential weights vary substantially, however, among product classes. Products such as toilet soaps, cereals, and toothpaste were found to have substantially lower rates of decline in weights as one goes back into the purchase history, as a result of the tendency of purchasing families to use some mix of brands on a routine basis so as to satisfy different uses, desires for variety, and differences in preference of individual family members. To be sure, this brand-mix effect is operative even in the case of frozen orange juice, but for quite a different reason. Many families use a mix of brands of frozen orange juice because of the unavailability of specific brands in all the stores among which the consumer shifts in the course of his week-to-week shopping trips.

EFFECT OF CONSUMER PURCHASE FREQUENCIES

Let us consider the effect of time between purchases on the consumer's probability of repurchasing the same brand. In Figure 3 we observe that the probability

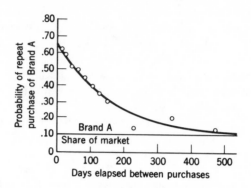

Figure 3. The probability of a consumer's buying the same brand on two consecutive purchases of frozen orange juice decreases exponentially with an increase in time between those purchases.

of a consumer's buying the same brand on two consecutive purchases of the product decreases to that brand's share of market as time between purchases increases. Whenever a great amount of time has elapsed since the consumer's last purchase of the product, the brand he last bought has little influence on his choice of a brand—the probability of his buying any given brand in this case is approximately equal to the share of market of that brand. Note that the probability of repurchase decreases at a constant rate with the passing of time; this characteristic, which we shall refer to as the "time rate of decay of purchase probability," provides a simple framework for incorporating the effects of time into a procedure for forecasting consumer purchase probabilities.

Let us now expand our view of the effects of time on repurchase probability in terms of the time period required for the consumer to make N individual purchases of frozen orange juice concentrate. Note that the curve in Figure 4 labelled N = 1 is the same curve as in Figure 3. Observe also that the probability of repurchasing the same brand at any given time in the future, without regard to the brands chosen in the interim, increases as we go up from N = 1 to N = 3, N = 10, and N = 50. Thus, on the average, a consumer who makes his fiftieth purchase of frozen orange juice 300 days after some arbitrary purchase of a given brand has a much higher probability of again choosing that brand than does the consumer who makes only 1, 3, or 10 purchases in that interval of time.

Figure 5 illustrates the relationship between the rates of decay of purchase probability associated with the curves in Figure 4 and the average time elapsed between purchases. The rate of decay of N = 1 in Figure 4 is .01298 per day. The rate of decay of N = 50 is .00282. Here again we find a relationship which, because of

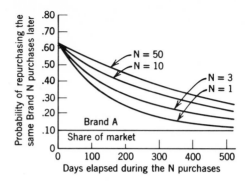

Figure 4. Consumers buying frozen orange juice with greatest frequency have the highest probability of continuing to buy the same brand.

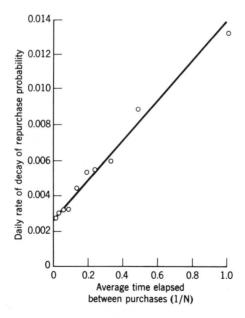

Figure 5. Relationship of decay rates to time between purchases.

its simplicity, can after some manipulation be conveniently incorporated into a model forecasting consumer brand choice probabilities. The rate of decay increases linearly with an increase in the average time between purchases. The data points plotted in Figure 5 represent the rates of decay computed for ten values of N, four of which were illustrated by the curves in Figure 4.

SIMULATION OF CONSUMER BRAND CHOICE

The brand shifting model outlined in Figure 1 has been tested by computing the predicted purchase probabilities of consumers on each of approximately 13,000 occasions of purchase of frozen orange juice, and comparing aggregates of these predictions with recorded brand purchases. The procedure followed was first to divide the probability space, zero to one, into 76 probability ranges. Then, whenever the computer-programed model predicted a certain probability of a given family's buying a particular brand on a given buying occasion, the results of that purchase were recorded in the computer storage location representing the corresponding probability range. Thus it was possible within each of the 76 probability cells to compare the average predicted probability of purchasing individual brands with the observed proportion of trials on which the brand was in fact purchased. The predicted probabilities and observed proportions of purchases were then compared individually and simultaneously for all 76 cells with respect to the binomial and chi square distributions that would be expected if the model were perfect. The 76 normal deviates, referred to here by "t," computed for the individual cells with respect to the Snow Crop predictions, were approximately normally distributed, 50 lying within one standard deviation, 71 lying within two standard deviations, and 76 falling within three standard deviations. The chi square value indicated no significant deviation at the 10 per cent level. Similar results were obtained in an analysis of predictions for the Minute Maid brand, 53 "t" values lying within one standard deviation, 70 lying within two standard deviations, and all 76 cases falling within three standard deviations.

The above results suggest that the model offers promise for use in describing consumer behavior in probabilistic terms. The model was not tested with respect to individual families, the number of purchases made by most individual families providing too small a sample to yield a reasonably powerful test of the predictions from the model. In other words, since rejection is unlikely with a small sample size per family, acceptance does not carry much weight with respect to an evaluation of the model. In the aggregate, the model stood up surprisingly well, given the overall test sample size of approximately 13,000 purchase predictions. Of course, if the sample size were to be increased substantially, significant deviations would be obtained, since the model is not a perfect representation of the brand purchase sequences of consumers.

The predictions of the model were also used to obtain a frequency distribution of consumers throughout the three year time period according to their probability of buying specific brands of product. Figure 6 provides a comparison of the

Figure 6. Probability of purchasing specific brands.

smoothed profiles for Libby and Minute Maid frozen orange juice. As might be expected, most consumers have a low probability of buying any specific brand. Those consumers who have a high probability of buying one brand must necessarily have a low probability of buying several other brands. Minute Maid was in the enviable position of having a small group of customers with a very high probability of buying the brand. Libby did not have such a following. Minute Maid developed frozen orange juice and was the first brand available to consumers; these facts probably helped develop the group of loyal (or habitual) customers, a sizable portion of whom were retained in the face of growing competition. As the innovator of frozen orange juice, Minute Maid also developed a pre-eminent market position in terms of retail availability, a factor which undoubtedly helped the firm maintain a sales advantage relative to competition.

Adaptive Behavior or Spurious Results?

In a paper titled "Brand Choice as a Probability Process," Ronald Frank (1962) reported that certain results concerning repeat purchase probabilities as a function of a brand's run length appear similar to what would be expected with associative learning under conditions of reward. He then observed in a footnote that my data (Kuehn, 1961) also seem to suggest this interpretation, a point on which there is agreement. The balance of Frank's article is then directed at demonstrating that:

1. purchase sequence data generated by families for a given brand using a Monte Carlo approach, on the assumption that each family's probability of purchasing the brand remained constant throughout the time period, produced repeat purchase probabilities as a function of run length which closely approximated in the aggregate the actual observed probabilities, and

2. the number of runs observed for *most* families is consistent with what might be expected under the assumption that each family's probability of purchasing any given brand remained constant throughout the time period.

As a result of his success in generating a relationship that has the appearance of actual data, Frank states , "These results cast suspicion on the use of a 'learning' model to describe the observations." In view of this statement, which bears directly on the work outlined here, in my thesis, and elsewhere, some defense appears to be in order.

Frank's observations in no way invalidate the findings outlined earlier in this paper. He has shown that it is inappropriate to attribute to learning *all* the increase in repeat purchase probability associated with increases in run length, an error probably made by more than a few researchers. This, however, is not the approach outlined here or in my thesis. The approach used in my thesis could be applied to Frank's coffee data to test whether the probabilities are in fact constant and, if this is not the case, to estimate the appropriate weightings. If consumers were to have a constant probability of brand choice from trial to trial, the most recent purchase positions would not have a greater primary effect on the predicted purchase probabilities than would any other purchase position—all the primary effects would be identical except for sampling variations. Similarly, if the probabilities of brand choice were constant from trial to trial, the Purchase and Rejection Operators in the adaptive brand shifting model would be superimposed on the diagonal (see Figure 1). In other words, the special case considered by Frank can be treated successfully by both of the analytic techniques used in my studies and discussed in this paper. Frank is correct when he states that much of what might appear to be a learning effect on the basis of repeat purchase probabilities as a function of run length is due to the aggregation of consumers with different probabilities (at the start of the run). But this is no problem when one takes into account the effect of all past purchases which have a significant impact on the consumer's purchase probability; such an approach does not disregard the information contained in purchases prior to the current run—an important consideration when the run is very short. Since past purchases will, except in highly unusual cases, have decreasing effects (as one goes back in time) on the consumer's subsequent purchase probability, taking into account all significant past purchases does not generally require the availability of an unduly long record of the consumer's purchase history.

The second point that Frank makes—namely, that most consumers behave as though they had constant purchase probabilities—would appear to represent a misinterpretation of statistical results. Frank sets up his hypothesis, tests it at some level of significance for each of a large number of cases (families), and then interprets the results as though all cases not shown to deviate statistically on an individual basis are consistent with the hypothesis. Actually, the hypothesis was that consumers have a constant probability of purchase, and the results indicated that a larger number of the individual cases tested lay outside the confidence limits than is consistent with the hypothesis, thereby rejecting the hypothesis *in toto*!

To be sure, the hypothesis of constant probability is, in effect, a straw man. It is generally recognized that consumers do change their buying behavior over time. Whether such behavior is called adjustment, adaptation, or learning is unimportant. It should be noted, however, that even though the overall market for coffee was quite stable in the period studied by Frank, and the sample sizes were limited to 14 months of purchase by each family, the hypothesis was in fact rejected on an overall basis, the only appropriate way in which to interpret the results of the test. Perhaps, as Frank suggests, some consumers do have constant probabilities of choosing individual brands during certain periods of time. Such a hypothesis cannot be tested, however, unless a procedure independent of the test is available for identifying these consumers and the relevant time periods.

Summary

A model describing brand shifting behavior as a probabilistic process and incorporating the effects of past purchases and time elapsed between purchases has been outlined. A defense of this approach to the study of mechanisms underlying consumer brand choice has also been presented. What has not been discussed is the way in which such merchandising factors as price, advertising, product characteristics, retail availability, and promotions (price off, coupons, merchandise packs, etc.) influence the parameters of the model and the extensions of the model that might be required to incorporate such effects. Some earlier results of research on the influence of these variables have been incorporated into an aggregate "expected value" form of the model presented here (Kuehn, 1961). Much work, however, remains to be done.

References

Bush, Robert R., and Frederick Mosteller. *Stochastic Models for Learning.* New York: John Wiley, 1955.

Estes, William K. Individual Behavior in Uncertain Situations: An Interpretation in Terms of Statistical Association Theory. In Thrall, R. M., C. H. Coombs, and R. L. Davis (Eds.), *Decision Processes.* New York: John Wiley, 1954.

Frank, Ronald E. Brand Choice as a Probability Process. *Journal of Business,* Vol. 35, No. 1, January 1962, pp. 43-56.

Kuehn, Alfred A. An Analysis of the Dynamics of Consumer Behavior and Its Implications for Marketing Management. Unpublished doctoral dissertation, Graduate School of Industrial Administration, Carnegie Institute of Technology, 1958.

Kuehn, Alfred A. A Model for Budgeting Advertising. In Bass, Frank M., et al. (Eds.), *Mathematical Models and Methods in Marketing.* Homewood, Ill.: Richard D. Irwin, 1961.

9 Rational and Nonrational Thinking

(a) Projective Techniques in Marketing Research

MASON HAIRE* *(Psychologist)*

Two separate shopping lists were prepared, identical in all respects except that on one were the words "Maxwell House Coffee" and on the other "Nescafé." These lists were given to two different groups of housewives, but neither group knew of the existence of the other group or the other list. Each housewife wrote a description of the personality and character of the woman who for her group supposedly had the shopping list. Although no special attention was directed to the item of coffee, the responses indicated that each of the women with a supposed shopping list was regarded quite differently as to personality traits.

It is a well accepted maxim in merchandizing that, in many areas, we are selling the sizzle rather than the steak. Our market research techniques, however, in many of these same areas, are directed toward the steak. The sizzle is the subjective reaction of the consumer; the steak the objective characteristics of the product. The consumer's behavior will be based on the former rather than the latter set of characteristics. How can we come to know them better?

When we approach a consumer directly with questions about his reaction to a product we often get false and misleading answers to our questions. Very often this is because the question which we heard ourselves ask was not the one (or not the only one) that the respondent heard. For example: A brewery made two kinds of beer. To guide their merchandizing techniques they wanted to know

Source: Mason Haire, "Projective Techniques in Marketing Research," *Journal of Marketing,* Vol. 14 (April, 1950), pp. 649-656.

*Mason Haire is a professor of psychology at the Massachusetts Institute of Technology.

what kind of people drank each kind, and particularly, what differences there were between the two groups of consumers. A survey was conducted which led up to the questions "Do you drink ———— beer?" (If *yes*) "Do you drink the *Light* or *Regular*?" (These were the two trade names under which the company marketed.) After identifying the consumers of each product, it was possible to find out about the characteristics of each group so that appropriate appeals could be used, media chosen, etc.

An interesting anomaly appeared in the survey data, however. The interviewing showed (on a reliable sample) that consumers drank *Light* over *Regular* in the ratio of 3 to 1. The company had been producing and selling Regular over Light for some time in a ratio of 9 to 1. Clearly, the attempt to identify characteristics of the two kinds was a failure. What made them miss so far?

When we say "Do you drink *Light* or *Regular*?" we are at once asking which brand is used, but also, to some extent, saying "Do you drink the regular run-of-the-mill product or do you drink the one that is more refined and shows more discrimination and taste?" The preponderance of "Light" undoubtedly flows from this kind of distortion.

When we ask questions of this sort about the product we are very often asking also about the respondent. Not only do we say "What is ———— product like?" but, indirectly "What are *you* like?" Our responses are often made up of both elements inextricably interwoven. The answers to the second question will carry clichés and stereotypes, blocks, inhibitions, and distortions, whenever we approach an area that challenges the person's idea of himself.

There are many things that we need to know about a consumer's reaction to a product that he can not tell us because they are to some extent socially unacceptable. For instance, the snob appeal of a product vitally influences its sale, but it is a thing that the consumer will not like to discuss explicitly. In other cases the consumer is influenced by motives of which he is, perhaps, vaguely aware, but which he finds difficult to put into words. The interviewer-respondent relationship puts a good deal of pressure on him to reply and to make sense in his reply. Consequently, he gives us stereotypical responses that use clichés which are commonly acceptable but do not necessarily represent the true motives. Many of our motives do not, in fact, "make sense," and are not logical. The question-answer relation demands sense above all. If the response does not represent the true state of affairs, the interviewer will never know it. He will go away. If it does not make sense it may represent the truth, but the respondent will feel like a fool and the interviewer will not go away. Much better produce a cliché and be rid of him.

The Nature of Projective Tests

Still other kinds of motives exist of which the respondent may not be explicitly conscious himself. The product may be seen by him as related to things or people or values in his life, or as having a certain role in the scheme of things, and yet he may be quite unable, in response to a direct question, to describe these aspects of the object. Nevertheless, these characteristics may be of great importance as motives. How can we get at them?

Clinical psychologists have long been faced with a parallel set of problems. It is quite usual for a patient to be unable or unwilling to tell the therapist directly what kinds of things are stirring in his motivational pattern. Information about these drives are of vital importance to the process of cure, so a good deal of research has been directed towards the development of techniques to identify and define them. The development of projective techniques as diagnostic tools has provided one of the most useful means to uncover such motivations, and the market-researcher can well afford to borrow their essentials from the therapist.

Basically, a projective test involves presenting the subject with an ambiguous stimulus—one that does not quite make sense in itself—and asking him to make sense of it. The theory is that in order to make it make sense he will have to add to it—to fill out the picture—and in so doing he projects part of himself into it. Since we know what was in the original stimulus we can quite easily identify the parts that were added, and, in this way, painlessly obtain information about the person.

Examples of these tests come readily to hand. Nearly everyone is familiar with the Rorschach Test, in which a subject is shown a series of ink-blots and asked to tell what they look like. Here the stimulus is incomplete in itself, and the interpretation supplied by the patient provides useful information. This test yields fairly general answers about the personality, however, and often we would like to narrow down the earea in which the patient is supplying information.

The Thematic Apperception Test offers a good example of this function. Let us suppose that with a particular patient we have reason to suppose that his relation to figures of authority is crucial to his therapeutic problem. We can give him a series of pictures where people are shown, but where the relationship of authority or the characteristics of the authoritarian figure are not complete. He is asked to tell a story about each picture. If in each story the subordinate finally kills the figure of authority we have certain kinds of knowledge; if, on the other hand, he always builds the story so the subordinate figure achieves a secure and comfortable dependence, we have quite different information. It is often quite impossible to get the subject to tell us these things directly. Either he cannot or will not do so. Indirectly, however, he will tell us how he sees authority. Can we get him, similarly, to tell us how a product looks to him in his private view of the world?

Application of Projective Test in Market Research

Let us look at an example of this kind of thing in market research. For the purposes of experiment a conventional survey was made of attitudes toward Nescafé, an instant coffee. The questionnaire included the questions "Do you use instant coffee?" (If *No*) "What do you dislike about it?" The bulk of the unfavorable responses fell into the general area "I don't like the flavor." This is such an easy answer to a complex question that one may suspect it is a stereotype, which at once gives a sensible response to get rid of the interviewer and conceals other motives. How can we get behind this facade?

In this case an indirect approach was used. Two shopping lists were prepared. They were identical in all respects, except that one list specified Nescafé and one Maxwell House Coffee. They were administered to alternate subjects, with no subject knowing of the existence of the other list. The instructions were "Read the shopping list below. Try to project yourself into the situation as far as possible until you can more or less characterize the woman who bought the groceries. Then write a brief description of her personality and character. Wherever possible indicate what factors influenced your judgment."

Shopping List I
Pound and a half of hamburger
2 loaves Wonder bread
bunch of carrots
1 can Rumford's Baking Powder
Nescafé instant coffee
2 cans Del Monte peaches
5 lbs. potatoes

Shopping List II
Pound and a half of hamburger
2 loaves Wonder bread
bunch of carrots
1 can Rumford's Baking Powder
1 lb. Maxwell House Coffee (Drip Ground)
2 cans Del Monte peaches
5 lbs. potatoes

Fifty people responded to each of the two shopping lists given above. The responses to these shopping lists provided some very interesting material. The following main characteristics of their descriptions can be given:

1. 48 per cent of the people described the woman who bought Nescafé as lazy; 4 per cent described the woman who bought Maxwell House as lazy.

2. 48 per cent of the people described the woman who bought Nescafé as failing to plan household purchases and schedules well; 12 per cent described the woman who bought Maxwell House this way.

3. 4 per cent described the Nescafé woman as thrifty; 16 per cent described the Maxwell House woman as thrifty.

12 per cent described the Nescafé woman as spendthrift; 0 per cent described the Maxwell House woman this way.

4. 16 per cent described the Nescafé woman as not a good wife; 0 per cent described the Maxwell House woman this way.

4 per cent described the Nescafé woman as a good wife; 16 per cent described the Maxwell House woman as a good wife.

A clear picture begins to form here. Instant coffee represents a departure from "home-made" coffee, and the traditions with respect to caring for one's family. Coffee-making is taken seriously, with vigorous proponents for laborious drip and filter-paper methods, firm believers in coffee boiled in a battered sauce pan, and the like. Coffee drinking is a form of intimacy and relaxation that gives it a special character.

On the one hand, coffee making is an art. It is quite common to hear a woman say, "I can't seem to make good coffee," in the same way that one might say, "I can't learn to play the violin." It is acceptable to confess this inadequacy, for making coffee well is a mysterious touch that belongs, in a shadowy tradition, to the plump, aproned figure who is a little lost outside her kitchen but who has a sure sense in it and among its tools.

On the other hand, coffee has a peculiar role in relation to the household and the home-and-family character. We may well have a picture, in the shadowy past, of a big black range that is always hot with baking and cooking, and has a big enamelled pot of coffee warming at the back. When a neighbor drops in during the morning, a cup of coffee is a medium of hospitality that does somewhat the same thing as cocktails in the late afternoon, but does it in a broader sphere.

These are real and important aspects of coffee. They are not physical character-istics of the product, but they are real values in the consumer's life, and they influ-ence his purchasing. We need to know and assess them. The "labor-saving" aspect of instant coffee, far from being an asset, may be a liability in that it violates these traditions. How often have we heard a wife respond to "This cake is delicious!" with a pretty blush and "Thank you—I made it with such and such a prepared cake mix." This response is so invariable as to seem almost compulsive. It is almost unthinkable to anticipate a reply "Thank you, I made it with Pillsbury's flour, Fleischman's yeast, and Borden's milk." Here the specifications are unnecessary. All that is relevant is the implied "I made it"—the art and the credit are carried directly by the verb that covers the process of mixing and processing the ingredi-ents. In ready-mixed foods there seems to be a compulsive drive to refuse credit for the product, because the accomplishment is not the housewife's but the com-pany's.

In this experiment, as a penalty for using "synthetics" the woman who buys Nescafé pays the price of being seen as lazy, spendthrift, a poor wife, and as failing to plan well for her family. The people who rejected instant coffee in the original direct question blamed its flavor. We may well wonder if their dislike of instant coffee was not to a large extent occasioned by a fear of being seen by one's self and others in the role they projected onto the Nescafé woman in the description.

When asked directly, however, it is difficult to respond with this. One cannot say, "I don't use Nescafé because people will think I am lazy and not a good wife." Yet we know from these data that the feeling regarding laziness and shiftlessness was there. Later studies (reported below) showed that it determined buying habits, and that something could be done about it.

ANALYSIS OF RESPONSES

Some examples of the type of response received will show the kind of material obtained and how it may be analyzed. Three examples of each group are given below.

Descriptions of a Woman Who Bought,
Among Other Things, Maxwell
House Coffee

"I'd say she was a practical, frugal woman. She bought too many potatoes. She must like to cook and bake as she included baking powder. She must not care much about her figure as she does not discriminate about the food she buys."

"The woman is quite influenced by advertising as signified by the specific name brands on her shopping list. She probably is quite set in her ways and accepts no substitutes."

"I have been able to observe several hundred women shoppers who have made very similar purchases to that listed above, and the only clue that I can detect that may have some bearing on her personality is the Del Monte peaches. This item when purchased singly along with the other more staple foods indicates that she may be anxious to please either herself or members of her family with a 'treat'. She is probably a thrifty, sensible housewife."

Descriptions of a Woman Who Bought,
Among Other Things, Nescafé
Instant Coffee

"This woman appears to be either single or living alone. I would guess that she had an office job. Apparently, she likes to sleep late in the morning, basing my assumption on what she bought such as Instant Coffee which can be made in a hurry. She probably also has can [sic] peaches for breakfast, cans being easy to open. Assuming that she is just average, as opposed to those dazzling natural beauties who do not need much time to make up, she must appear rather sloppy, taking little time to make up in the morning. She is also used to eating supper out, too. Perhaps alone rather than with an escort. An old maid probably."

"She seems to be lazy, because of her purchases of canned peaches and instant coffee. She doesn't seem to think, because she bought two loaves of bread, and then baking powder, unless she's thinking of making cake. She probably just got married."

"I think the woman is the type who never thinks ahead very far—the type who always sends Junior to the store to buy one item at a time. Also she is fundamentally lazy. All the items, with possible exception of the Rumford's, are easily prepared items. The girl may be an office girl who is just living from one day to the next in a sort of haphazard sort of life."

As we read these complete responses we begin to get a feeling for the picture that is created by Nescafé. It is particularly interesting to notice that the Nescafé woman is protected, to some extent, from the opprobrium of being lazy and haphazard by being seen as a single "office girl"—a role that relieves one from guilt for not being interested in the home and food preparation.

The references to peaches are significant. In one case (Maxwell House) they are singled out as a sign that the woman is thoughtfully preparing a "treat" for her family. On the other hand, when the Nescafé woman buys them it is evidence that she is lazy; since their "canned" character is seen as central.

In terms of the sort of results presented above, it may be useful to demonstrate the way these stories are coded. The following items are extracted from the six stores quoted:

Maxwell House

1. practical
   frugal
   likes to cook

2. influenced by advertising
   set in her ways

3. interested in family
   thrifty
   sensible

Nescafé

1. single
   office girl
   sloppy
   old maid

2. lazy
   does not plan
   newlywed

3. lazy
   does not plan
   office girl

Items such as these are culled from each of the stories. Little by little, categories are shaped by the content of the stories themselves. In this way the respondent furnishes the dimensions of analysis as well as the scale values on these dimensions.

SECOND TEST

It is possible to wonder whether it is true that the opprobrium that is heaped on the Nescafé woman comes from her use of a device that represents a shortcut and labor-saver in an area where she is expected to embrace painstaking time-consuming work in a ritualistic way. To test this, a variation was introduced into the shopping lists. In a second experiment one hundred and fifty housewives were tested with the form given above, but a sample was added to this group which responded to a slightly different form. If we assume that the rejection in the first experiment came from the presence of a feeling about synthetic shortcuts, we might assume also that the addition of one more shortcut to both lists would bring the Maxwell House woman more into line with the Nescafé woman, since the former would now have the same guilt that the Nescafé woman originally had, while the

TABLE 1   PERSONALITY CHARACTERISTICS ASCRIBED TO USERS OF PREPARED FOODS

If They Use	No Prepared Food (Maxwell House alone)		Nescafé (alone)		Maxwell House (plus Pie Mix)		Nescafé (plus Pie Mix)	
They are seen as:	Number	Per Cent	Number	Per Cent	Number	Per Cent	Number	Per Cent
Not Economical	12	17	24	32	6	30	7	35
Lazy	8	11	46	62	5	25	8	40
Poor Personality and Appearance	28	39	39	53	7	35	8	40
N =	72		74		20		20	

Nescafé woman, already convicted of evading her duties, would be little further injured.

In order to accomplish this a second prepared food was added to both lists. Immediately after the coffee in both lists the fictitious item, "Blueberry Fill Pie Mix" was added. The results are shown in Table 1.

It will be seen immediately, in the first two columns, that the group to whom the original form of the list was given showed the same kind of difference as reported above in their estimates of the two women. The group with an additional prepared food, however, brought the Maxwell House Coffee woman down until she was virtually indistinguishable from the Nescafé. There seems to be little doubt but that the prepared-food-character, and the stigma of avoiding housewifely duties is responsible for the projected personality characteristics.

RELATION TO PURCHASING

It is still relevant to ask whether the existence of these feelings in a potential consumer is related to purchasing. It is hypothesized that these personality descriptions provide an opportunity for the consumer to project hopes and fears and anxieties that are relevant to the way the product is seen, and that they represent important parts of her motivation in buying or not buying. To test this hypothesis, a small sample of fifty housewives, comparable in every way to the group just referred to, was given the original form of the shopping list (Nescafé only). In addition to obtaining the personality description, the interviewer, on a pretext, obtained permission to look at her pantry shelves and determine personally whether or not she had instant coffee of any brand. The results of this investigation are shown in the Table 2.

The trend of these data shows conclusively that if a respondent sees the woman who buys Nescafé as having undesirable traits, she is not likely to buy instant coffee herself. The projected unacceptable characteristics go with failure to buy, and it does not seem unwarranted to assume that the association is causal.

Furthermore, these projected traits are, to some extent, additive. For instance, if a respondent describes the woman as having one bad trait only, she is about twice as likely not to have instant coffee. However, if she sees her as having two bad traits, and no good ones (e.g., lazy, can not cook), she is about three times as likely not to have instant coffee as she is to have it. On the other hand, if she sees her as having two good traits (e.g., economical, cares for family), she is about six times as likely to have it as not.

It was pointed out earlier that some women felt it necessary to "excuse" the woman who bought Nescafé by suggesting that she lived alone and hence could not be expected to be interested in cooking, or that she had a job and did not have time to shop better. Women who had instant coffee in the house found excuses almost twice as often as those who did not use instant coffee (12 out of 32, or 42 per cent, against 4 out of 18, or 22 per cent). These "excuses" are vitally important for merchandizing. The need for an excuse shows there is a barrier to buy-

TABLE 2   NESCAFÉ BUYER CHARACTERISTICS AS VIEWED BY OTHERS

The Woman Who Buys Nescafé is Seen As:	By Women Who Had Instant Coffee in the House (N = 32)		By Women Who Did Not Have Instant Coffee in the House (N = 18)	
	Number	Per Cent	Number	Per Cent
Economical[a]	22	70	5	28
Not economical	0	0	2	11
Can not cook or does not like to[a]	5	16	10	55
Plans balanced meals[b]	9	29	2	11
Good housewife, plans well, cares about family[a]	9	29	0	0
Poor housewife, does not plan well, does not care about family[b]	5	16	7	39
Lazy[b]	6	19	7	39

[a]The chances are 1 in 100. We are justified in rejecting the hypothesis that there is no difference between the groups.
[b]Differences this great would be observed only 5 times out of 100 in repeated samplings of a population whose true difference is zero.

ing in the consumer's mind. The presence of excuses shows that there is a way around the barrier. The content of the excuses themselves provides valuable clues for directing appeals toward reducing buying resistance.

Conclusions

There seems to be no question that in the experimental situation described here:

(1) Motives exist which are below the level of verbalization because they are socially unacceptable, difficult to verbalize cogently, or unrecognized.

(2) These motives are intimately related to the decision to purchase or not to purchase, and

(3) It is possible to identify and assess such motives by approaching them indirectly.

Two important general points come out of the work reported. The first is in the statement of the problem. It is necessary for us to see a product in terms of a set of characteristics and attributes which are part of the consumer's "private world," and as such may have no simple relationship to characteristics of the object in the "real" world. Each of us lives in a world which is composed of more than physical things and people. It is made up of goals, paths to goals, barriers, threats, and the like, and an individual's behavior is oriented with respect to these characteristics as much as to the "objective" ones. In the area of merchandizing, a product's character of being seen as a path to a goal is usually very much more important as a determinant of purchasing than its physical dimensions. We have taken advantage of these qualities in advertising and merchandizing for a long time by an intuitive sort of "playing-by-ear" on the subjective aspects of products. It is time for a systematic attack on the problem of the phenomenological description of objects. What kinds of dimensions are relevant to this world of goals and paths and barriers? What kind of terms will fit the phenomenological characteristics of an object in the same sense that the centimeter-gram-second system fits its physical dimensions? We need to know the answers to such questions, and the psychological definitions of valued objects.

The second general point is the methodological one that it is possible by using appropriate techniques, to find out from the respondent what the phenomenological characteristics of various objects may be. By and large, a direct approach to this problem in terms of straightforward questions will not yield satisfactory answers. It is possible, however, by the use of indirect techniques to get the consumer to provide, quite unselfconsciously, a description of the value-character of objects in his environment.

9 Rational and Nonrational Thinking

(b) Haire's Classic Instant Coffee Study— 18 Years Later

CONRAD R. HILL* (Marketing Educator)

Current marketing texts refer to Mason Haire's 1950 study as a classic, despite changing attitudes toward the possibility of quick and easy insights into consumer images. The author of this article takes a careful look at both Haire's study and motivational research.

Just as the post-Civil War American economy was sparked in part by the Protestant Ethic, a new powerful Consumer Ethic propels our affluence today. It energizes product innovations; it ferrets out new domestic and foreign markets; trade journals preach it; colleges legitimize it; and business groups ritualize it.

Although Consumerism provides opportunities it also presents problems due to consumers' fickleness—alternations from volatile whimsey to glaciered habituality. Necessarily, multi-million dollar advertising plans tend to be hunches about the state of consumer fickleness. Small wonder that marketers respond eagerly when behavioral scientists promise new ways to psyche the elusive consumer.

One of the most durable of these "new ways" has been the Mason Haire instant coffee study.[1] Although first published in 1950, the study continues to receive

Source: Conrad R. Hill, "Haire's Classic Instant Coffee Study—18 Years Later," © Journalism Quarterly, Vol. 45 (August, 1968), pp. 466-472.

*The author is a professor in the College of Business Administration at The University of Rhode Island.

[1] Mason Haire, "Projective Techniques in Marketing Research," Journal of Marketing, April 1950, pp. 125-39.

kudos from marketing and advertising research writers. The Boyd and Westfall[2] market research text unabashedly terms it "a classic (because it) illustrated the big advantages of projective techniques to uncover subconscious or socially unacceptable attitudes."

Other writers also endorse the study. Perry Bliss[3] refers to "the famous Mason Haire study" which was able to tap images that 'direct questioning' couldn't." The highly authoritative Marketing Science Institute[4] vouches for projective techniques also because motivations below the level of verbalizations are intimately related to purchase decisions. Although they cannot be identified and assessed by direct interview techniques, they can be inferred from the results of indirect projective techniques.

The Institute then commends Haire's study as a representative of useful research methods.

Although John Howard[5] states that "competent fundamental studies in which clinical theory is applied to buying behavior are badly needed but almost nonexistent in the literature," he singles out Haire's study as an example of good clinical research. Both Crane[6] and James MacNeal[7] endorse the efficiency of projective methods and also Haire's study.

(Not necessarily true! Haire's direct vs. indirect questions seem invidious. 1) he rejected instant coffee users; 2) he assumed implicitly that non-users disliked instant—"why do you dislike instant coffee?", 3) he then hailed his subsequent indirect data as truer than his direct question's data despite the negative pre-conditioning.)

A new research text by Green and Tull[8] echoes this general acceptance of Haire's study: "an early example of an MR Study that has come to be regarded as a classic . . ." For two pages, Green and Tull elaborate upon Haire's methods, findings and inferences.

Despite those accolades, evidence suggests these writers may be afflicted by a cultural lag about projective research. At a time when projectivists are becoming skeptical about projective research methods, academicians in marketing and advertising acclaim it;[9] at a time when practical marketers are becoming disenchanted

[2]Harper W. Boyd Jr. and Ralph Westfall, *Marketing Research*, rev. edition (Homewood, Ill.: Richard D. Irwin, Inc., 1964), pp. 162-63.

[3]Perry Bliss, ed., *Marketing and the Behavioral Sciences* (Boston: Allyn and Bacon, Inc., 1964), p. 80.

[4]Michael Halbert, *The Meaning and Sources of Marketing Theory* (New York: McGraw-Hill Book Co., 1965), p. 182.

[5]John Howard, *Marketing Theory* (Boston: Allyn and Bacon, Inc., 1965), pp. 95, 133 Fn.

[6]Edgar Crane, *Marketing Communications* (New York: John Wiley and Sons, 1965), pp. 192, 293.

[7]James U. McNeal, ed., *Dimensions of Consumer Behavior* (New York: Appleton-Century-Crofts, 1965), p. 240.

[8]Paul E. Green and Donald S. Tull, *Research for Marketing Decisions* (Englewood Cliffs, N.J.: Prentice-Hall, Inc., 1966), pp. 165-66.

[9]Bernard I. Murstein, *Theory and Research in Projective Technique* (New York: John Wiley and Sons, 1962). Murstein offers an extensive analysis of these criticisms as well as a thorough bibliography of studies in this field.

with MR's promise of quick and easy insights into consumers, marketing theorists continue to advocate it. For instance, Dr. Ernest Dichter[10] whose fertile Freudian imagination perhaps did most to promote motivational research, now acknowledges that "the field has lost much of its electricity." Dichter regards himself now as "a consultant in international marketing and not as a motivational researcher."[11]

Consequently, there's a suspicion that MR's easy insights into consumers tend to be contaminated insights.

First, should sample surveys borrow tools designed for clinical diagnoses of disturbed personalities?

Second, are MR's theoretical constructs—so basically Freudian—proper for a market place?

Third, can analysts—guided often by conflicting theoretical loyalties—produce reliable interpretations of data? It is no secret that identical data have produced as many conclusions as there were analysts.

Fourth, in previous studies, analysts have tended to use subjects' statements, not Ss per se, as analytical units. Obviously, data are overrepresented by garrulous Ss when that is done. Parenthetically, that is a criticism of Haire's study.

Although advocates of projective methods assure us their tools tap Ss' inner, private worlds; and that test data relate to overt behavior; and that any and all responses are meaningful for research, Murstein, [12] in a systematic review of these methods and theories, warns that a thorough clarification is overdue. This is necessary, he says, because projective methods are fraught with unknown amounts of confounding from these sources: 1) test stimuli factors, 2) background factors and 3) personality or organismic factors.

Those three sources as confounders may be assessed via their components. For instance, background factors include: the personalities, roles, statuses of the researcher; test locale; whether the test is individually or group administered; test instructions; and length of Ss' exposure to stimuli, among others.

The following personality factors are more or less crucial; Ss' ages, educations, sex, social classes, occupations, on-going responses, moods, response habits and verbal fluency.

Finally, test stimuli, the major source of confounding, should be assessed as to content and form. For instance, stimuli may be more or less relevant to the behavior under investigation. Furthermore, ambiguity, although a theoretical necessity in projective tests, may produce invalid data because Ss can and do censor responses to all test stimuli—including projective tests' stimuli.

Form relates to the number and sequence of stimuli and whether they are presented verbally, orally, pictorially, or in combinations thereof. Obviously, various

[10] Peter Bart, "Advertising: MR's Use is Dwindling," New York *Times* (Western edition), Dec. 18, 1962, p. 11.
[11] *Ibid.*
[12] Murstein, *op cit.*

combinations of form may elicit various levels of confounded responses depending on an Ss' personality factors. And so on! A suspicion emerges, therefore, that MR is too susceptible to cultural and technique biases to serve usefully as a device for advertising research.

Some Background to This Experiment

According to Murstein,[13] test stimuli are major sources of confounding in all research. Intuitively, Lewin's[14] concepts of positive and negative valences may be relevant here. For instance, Lewin's idea is that all behavior including acting, wishing, valuing, and thinking involve tensions and conflict due to the presence of positive (approach) stimuli and negative (avoidance) stimuli. Ss, then, are pushed and pulled by these approaches and avoidances if they cannot escape (Lewin's locomote)—either physically or psychologically—from the region of conflict.

Test stimuli, therefore, may possess varying directions and intensities of culturally loaded positive and negative valences. When Ss structure test stimuli, they inevitably encounter conflict because interview situations generate it. In geiger counter fashion, therefore, Ss register and assimilate and compare and compute plus and minus emissions from stimuli to provide an answer for an interviewer.

If that theoretical view is sound, then Mason Haire's[15] study suggests a method to explore positive and negative valences of stimuli. Haire first obtained, via direct questions, reasons why Ss disliked instant coffee. Next, he submitted grocery lists to each of two groups of these instant coffee dislikers; then they were asked to describe a hypothetical shopper who would use a "list of this kind." The lists varied on one item only—instant coffee and drip grind coffee were alternated.

one and one half pound of hamburger
two loaves of Wonder bread
bunch of carrots
one can of Rumford's baking powder
Nescafé instant coffee (Maxwell House Drip Grind coffee appeared on the other list)
two cans of Del Monte peaches
five pounds of potatoes

Ss' description of the shopper led Haire to infer that instant coffee suffered a negative image; drip grind coffee enjoyed a positive image. Haire concluded, therefore, that "dislike-for-instant's-taste" answers to his direct questions were masks for true attitudes. Disguised tests, on the other hand, were able to tap the true reasons behind these ego-protectors.

[13] Murstein, *op. cit.*
[14]George Levinger, "Kurt Lewin's Approach to Conflict and its Resolution: A Review with Some Extensions," *The Journal of Conflict Resolution,* December 1957, pp. 329-39.
[15]Haire, *op. cit.*

Haire inferred also that market resistance to instant coffee stemmed from "un-speak-able" cultural negativism, not from inherent product debilities—an important insight for marketers.

Product imagery, a commonplace marketing concept, says that all product and brands have a distinct image among consumers—including Haire's items. Those images, consequently, may be expected to exert congeries of positive pulls or nega-tive pushes upon Ss so that a final description of a shopper represents a reconcilia-tion of conflict.

In a context of Lewin's valences, did Haire's baking powder (intuitively a posi-tive valance) unduly contaminate his derived data? Would a "neutral" salt, if sub-stituted for baking powder, evoke different descriptions? Would a *neutral-negative* combination of *salt* and *instant coffee* elicit similar descriptions as a *positive-nega-tive* combination of *baking powder* and *instant coffee?*

In other words, Haire's method may be useful for the marketer, provided valence effects can be controlled.

NULL HYPOTHESIS

Ss' descriptions of a shopper with a grocery list containing baking powder and instant coffee will not differ from descriptions of a list containing salt and instant coffee.

Method

Haire's original method was duplicated as closely as his report permitted. Two grocery lists were used: one combined baking powder and instant coffee; the other replaced baking powder with salt. The other list items were identical to Haire's original list.

A total of 100 female shoppers was selected so that apparent age, income, edu-cation, and shopper locations were consistent with local demographics. The lists were mechanically randomized to avoid selection bias as to which S received which list treatment. This procedure yielded two sub-samples of 50 respondents each.

As per Haire, Ss were first qualified so that only non-users of instant coffee were admitted for further testing. Next, reasons for non-users were obtained (following Haire) by asking Ss what they disliked about instant coffee. Finally, Ss were asked to describe a hypothetical shopper who would use the preferred list.

Coding

Ss and not their statements alone were used as analytical units to provide positive, neutral and negative classifications of Ss' attitudes toward the shopper. Descriptive polarities were:

Positive	Negative
Large family	Small family
Good cook	Poor cook
Good planner	Poor planner
Smart	Stupid
Thin	Fat
Hard worker	Lazy
Neat	Sloppy
Good wife/mother	Poor wife/mother
High income	Low income

Neutral

A mixture of positive and negative descriptions, or an absence of clearly defined descriptions placed an S into this neutral category.

In addition, several Ss gratituitously commented about their lists' efficacy as a grocery list. These comments were also coded and tabulated for analysis.

Results

Of the 100 original Ss, editing revealed 14 incomplete protocols. The final sample included 41 with the salt, and 45 Ss with the baking powder list.

Table 1's reasons for disliking instant coffee are consistent with Haire's findings despite the intervening years.

TABLE 1   "WHAT DON'T YOU LIKE ABOUT INSTANT COFFEE?"*

	Baking Powder Respondents	Salt Respondents	N
Reasons per:			
Product Attributes:			
Poor taste	35	30	65
Scum on top	5	1	6
Poor aroma	4	4	8
	44	35	79
Other influences:			
Family dislikes	4	6	10
N	48**	41	89

*Actually, Haire's question was misleading. It mistakenly assumed that the Ss disliked instant coffee. Perhaps this is a reason for the consistent replies despite the ten-year span between the studies. See also: Conrad R. Hill, "Another Look at Two Important Coffee Studies." *Journal of Advertising Research,* December 1960, pp. 18-21.
**Column marginals do not add up to 45 because some Ss are included in more than one category.

Tables 2 and 3 test the null hypothesis that each list would elicit similar descriptions of the shopper.

TABLE 2   Ss CLASSIFIED BY LIST ACCORDING TO THEIR NEUTRAL AND AFFECT DESCRIPTIONS (POSITIVE/NEGATIVE) OF THE SHOPPER

	Salt List	Baking Powder List	N
Descriptions:			
Affect	22 (54%)	35 (78%)	57 (66%)
Neutral	19 (46)	10 (22)	29 (34)
N	41 (100)	45 (100)	86 (100)

Chi Square = 5.68, p. > .02, df = 1.

TABLE 3   AFFECT DESCRIPTIONS CLASSIFIED INTO POSITIVE AND NEGATIVE ATTITUDES TOWARD THE SHOPPER BY TYPE OF LIST

	Salt	Baking Powder List	N
Positive	4 (18%)	17 (49%)	21 (38%)
Negative	18 (82)	18 (51)	36 (62)
N	22 (100)	35 (100)	57 (100)

Chi Square = 5.35, p. > .05, df = 1.

Table 3 gives additional breakdowns of Table 2's affect descriptions into positive and negative attitudes. Unlike Haire's findings, these reveal that baking powder in concert with instant coffee tends to dilute the negativism evident in the neutral salt list.

Data in Tables 2 and 3 show that the descriptions produced by the lists do differ and that these differences are statistically significant at .05 level. The null hypothesis, therefore, is rejected and the alternate accepted that the two sets of stimuli did elicit differential descriptions of the shopper.

Discussion

Table 2 shows that the salt list's combination of neutral-negative stimuli split affect and neutral responses evenly while baking powder's positive-negative stimuli elicited significantly more affect than neutral responses.

Table 3 distributed Table 2's affect into positives and negatives. Now, the salt (neutral-negative) list's negative responses are significantly different from baking powder list's equal distribution of negative and positive descriptions.

In summary, it seems evident that Ss will follow dominent cue(s)—affect valences —when structuring or resolving a stimulus conflict presented them in an interview.

This suggests yeasaying and naysaying response styles reported elsewhere.[16] But in order to explain "valence effects" of a test stimuli, the context and background factors must be weighed. For instance, if a research topic is non-salient and if the interview is non-ego threatening, Ss are more apt to follow the dominant stimuli —the valence effect.

On the other hand, in ego threatening situations, or when a research topic is crucially salient, Ss will tend to censor their responses—the censoring effect. Both effects may occur in all interview forms—direct as well as indirect—so that disguise is no panacea. Haire's study, for instance, involved non-salience and non-ego threats so that valence effects are to be expected.

Consequently, these conclusions emerge: 1) As topic salience and ego threats in an interview situation increase, response censoring will increase also; 2) conversely, as salience and ego threats diminish, then valence effects will diminish. Both conditions distort the data to some degree.

Intuitively, Ss may be expected to be annoyed by tests that are difficult to structure or by those that are overly ambiguous. Consequently, Ss' annoyances may be verbalized as gratuitous asides. In turn, these asides may be indicators of salience or of non-salience of the test. Table 4, however, shows no difference in the number of gratuitous asides for the two lists.

TABLE 4   SALT AND BAKING POWDER LISTS' Ss WHO MADE GRATUITOUS COMMENTS ABOUT THEIR LIST'S EFFICACY

	Salt	Baking Powder	N
Made statements	12	15	27
No statements	29	30	59
N	41	45	86

Table 5 classified those gratuitous commentators into positives and negatives. Again, no differences are evident. Apparently, Ss found each list equally as structure-able—either equally easy or equally difficult.

TABLE 5   SALT AND BAKING POWDER Ss CLASSIFIED ACCORDING TO POSITIVE AND NEGATIVE COMMENTS ABOUT THEIR LISTS

	Salt	Baking Powder	N
Positive comments	6	9	15
Negative comments	6	6	12
N	12	15	27

[16]Arthur Couch, and Kenneth Kenniston, "Yeasaying and Naysaying Agreeing Response Set as a Personality Variable," "Journal of Abnormal and Social Psychology," LX, 1960, pp. 151-74.

Conclusions

These findings support Murstein's view that test stimuli color Ss' responses. Furthermore, this study suggests that projective tests' responses are partly a function of the valence effects of stimuli. A key first task in test design, therefore, is to assess the valence of proposed stimuli in order to avoid potentially biasing interpretations of data. Valence effect may be analogous to slanting—a type of leading question.

Returning to Haire's data, it is evident that the responses he obtained to disguised stimuli are not necessarily true attitudes toward instant coffee. Obviously, a careful assessment of the valence effects of ALL stimuli is necessary before such cavalier conclusions may be drawn.

In other words, research should not assume arbitrarily that any one stimulus in a battery is *the dominant* stimulus. It is doubtful, therefore, that quick and easy insights into consumer images are possible at current levels of research sophistication. At the same time, these present findings suggest that Haire-type designs seem valid provided valence effects of *all stimuli* are properly delineated.

Although some marketing writers see signs of an imminent union of marketing and the behavioral sciences, soberer evaluation of the many unresolved conceptual, theoretical and methodological problems suggests that a fruitful alliance is unlikely for years.

Limitations of the Study

The sample of respondents was judgmentally derived so that various confounding effects on responses may not have been randomized as hoped. Nevertheless, research that attempts to show the existence of certain associations but does not purport to make inferential leaps serves a purpose—if such associations are in fact demonstrated. To that end, this study seems worthy.

The assumption that hamburger, carrots, Wonder bread, Del Monte peaches and potatoes have neutral valences seems unrealistic—particularly, the branded items. Therefore, a thorough study would have to control for their effects as well.

As for reliability, this study was first performed in Lincoln, Nebraska, and duplicated three years later at Kalamazoo, Michigan. Similar data were obtained in each.

10 Personality and Personality Differences

Personality and Product Use

W. T. TUCKER *(Marketing Educator)* AND JOHN J. PAINTER* *(Marketing Educator)*

A key area of interest is the relationship between a consumer's personality and the uses he makes of products. This study, written in concise terms, hypothesizes and tests how certain market behavior is related to personality traits, and also demonstrates that through research additional light can be shed on the meaning (not merely the identification) of personality characteristics.

Perhaps no subject in marketing has received greater attention in the past few years than the relationship between personality and purchasing behavior. All of the furor over motivation research is clearly predicated on the premise that such a relationship exists, although some reporters seem to assume that all persons are, at base, alike. Yet even here, the factors referred to as common to all persons are most often those which personality studies have shown to be variables rather than constants. For instance, the importance of fear of the father image, which is reputed to militate against the use of banking services, must be conceived of as varying with some personality characteristic such as ego strength or emotional maturity if it is not to influence all persons in a highly similar way.

Talk about the importance of personality as a marketing variable has become common at advertising clubs and at marketing association meetings. The recent book by Pierre Martineau (1957) contains a chapter entitled "An Automobile for Every Personality." Charles Cannell (Ferber & Wales, 1958) says: "It may be that the determination of airplane travel has something to do with basic personal-

Source: W. T. Tucker and John J. Painter, "Personality And Product Use," *Journal of Applied Psychology,* Vol. 45 (October, 1961), pp. 325-329.

*W. T. Tucker is a professor of marketing at the University of Texas. John J. Painter is a professor of marketing at the University of Utah.

ity characteristics such as personal feelings of security or insecurity" (p. 10). And Ernest Dichter (Ferber & Wales) says confidently: "What we are searching for are psychological and personality elements which may have a dynamic effect on consumers' attitudes toward a product" (p. 26). Newman (1957) views personality as one of the major factors determining marketing behavior.

In the light of such points of view it may seem surprising that few efforts have been made to demonstrate that personality characteristics actually do influence product use. But the dearth of evidence on this point can be explained in part by supposition. First, the concept of personality itself has not been very clearly formulated. Second, the instruments available for the ready classification of personality types are few and generally suspect. Third, most self-respecting psychologists are apparently convinced that marketing behavior, pervasive as it may be, is of interest for commerical purposes only. Fourth, marketers probably have little understanding of the need for experimental evidence of their assumptions.

Yet it would seem that there is much to be learned about both personality and a large segment of human behavior by such studies. Scott's (1957) study of motion picture preferences is perhaps of less interest to the movie producer than it is to the individual who wants a clearer understanding of the personality factors isolated by the Minnesota Multiphasic Index. That these factors are less than completely clear is indicated by Scott's inability to provide a rationale for all of the significant correlations. And Eysenck's (Eysenck, Tarrant, Woolf, & England, 1960) recent findings that rigidity and extraversion relate to the number of cigarets smoked by an individual may be as important to the understanding of those characteristics as they are as a possible explanation of lung cancer in heavy smokers.

The present study was undertaken to test the hypothesis that marketing behavior is related to personality traits. At the same time, it was expected that the location of significant relationships would throw additional light on the meaning of personality characteristics studied.

Method

The Gordon Personal Profile was administered to 133 students of marketing along with a so-called Sales and Marketing Personality Index which included questions on the use of headache remedies, cigarets, chewing gum, deodorants, mouthwash, and other items commonly purchased by college students. Blind questions were interspersed to give the index the appearance of a personality or interest test. Results were then compared to determine the difference in personality trait scores for groups that professed to different rates of product use or interest. That the subjects accepted the index was indicated by the large number of students who asked after completing the forms if they could find out whether they would make good salesmen, advertisers, etc.

SUBJECTS

The subjects were all students of the first course in marketing at the University of Texas. The great majority were juniors; a few were in the last semester of their sophomore year, and others were in the beginning of their senior year. Since the Gordon Personal Profile has different norms for male and female students, and, since the frequency of use of a number of products was clearly related to sex, the 31 responses by females are not included in this report. Also, one subject was eliminated because he failed to fill out the Gordon Personal Profile completely. While this group of subjects can hardly be characterized as representative of even such a limited universe as college juniors, for purposes of this study their only necessary characteristic was that of providing a diverse group of scores on the Gordon Personal Profile and reasonable diversity in response to questions about products.

TEST MATERIALS

The Gordon Personal Profile was selected as the personality test to use since it measures four characteristics which seem intuitively meaningful as components of the "normal" personality and since it is based on college student norms. The profile rates persons on the variables of ascendency, responsibility, emotional stability, and sociability.

The form used to determine use of products or other marketing characteristics included nine questions relevant to the experiments and seven blind questions. Most of the experimental questions referred to frequency of use of a particular product, as in the following:

How frequently do you experience a headache that requires a headache remedy (aspirin, Bufferin, Anacin, etc.)
a. Never
b. Once or twice a year
c. About once a month
d. More often than once a month, but less than once a week
e. Once a week or more

Questions of this sort were asked about the use of headache remedies, vitamins, chewing gum, tobacco, mouthwash, alcoholic beverages, and deodorants. Two other questions related to the readiness with which the individual accepted new styles or fashions and preference in automobiles.

Blind questions were rather similar to those asked on interest tests:

Which of the following positions in an organization would you prefer to hold?
a. Secretary-Treasurer
b. Program chairman
c. President
d. Membership chairman
e. Ordinary member, no office

The list of 16 questions was pretested in order to insure their clearness and to make sure that multiple choice answers would elicit a reasonable spread of response. As a result of this pretesting, multiple choice answers were altered to fit the normal variations in frequency of use of various products. For instance, the most frequent use of headache remedies indicated by answers was "once a week or more," while the most frequent use of deodorants was described as "more than once a day," since the pretest demonstrated these to be common frequencies for heavy users.

PROCEDURE

Subjects filled out both forms at a single sitting of about 20 minutes, answering the Gordon Personal Profile first and the Sales and Marketing Personality Index second. While subjects were asked to fill in their sex, age, marital status, and year in school on the Gordon Personal Profile, names were not taken in order to encourage the greatest frankness in response. Each pair of tests handed out was numbered in advance.

INSTRUCTIONS TO SUBJECTS

Students in each class tested were given the following instructions:

As you all know, one of the difficult problems in business is the determination of an individual's interests, or what kind of job he can do best. Attempts to solve such problems have led to the development of a number of written tests—some of which take an hour or more to complete. You have in front of you two rather new tests that help to accomplish this for certain marketing jobs in just a few minutes. We know that one of these is moderately successful. We are interested in whether scores on the other are different or much the same. Do these tests really measure the same things?

To determine this, we need your help. We are not interested in your score as an individual but in the relationship of your score on one test with your score on the other.

For that reason, we do not want your name on the paper; we merely want you to answer the questions honestly and conscientiously. Instructions for each test appear at the top of the test.

First, make sure the red number on each of your tests is the same. Then fill in your age, sex, marital status, and year in school on Test #1, the Gordon Personal Profile. Then read the instructions on the test and answer the questions. When you are finished, go directly to the second test, read the instructions, then answer the questions.

You will find that on both tests there are some questions where none of the answers seem just right for you. Just pick the one that seems closest and do not worry about exact wording. Remember to read the test instructions carefully, since you have to answer each test in a somewhat different way.

ANALYTIC METHOD

Results were analyzed by comparing the difference in mean scores on one personality characteristic for groups with different product use patterns.

Table 1 shows the mean scores on responsibility for groups which answered the mouthwash question in each of the possible ways.

TABLE 1   MEAN RESPONSIBILITY SCORES FOR GROUPS WITH DIFFER-
ENT PATTERNS OF USE OF MOUTHWASH

Response	Mean Score	Number of Cases
Never use mouthwash	7.26	31
Quite infrequently	5.00	40
Once or twice a week	4.50	16
Once a day	3.90	10
More than once a day	6.50	4

While responsibility seems to be inversely related to frequency of use of mouthwash, despite relatively high scores for the four persons who use mouthwash more than once a day, the number of cases in some of the cells is too small for analysis of variance to show a significant relationship. For this reason, the last four groups were combined and compared using the t test with those who reported never using mouthwash. The resulting t of 2.12 is significant at the .05 level. The F test for homogeneity of variance was not significant.

This same method of analysis was used for each of the products on each of the personality characteristics, with the point for division into two groups being determined on the basis of scores and the number of subjects remaining in each of the groups.

It is entirely proper to question whether five-point scales of the sort used here should be dichotomized *after* observing the means of each of the categories. Such dichotomization obviously makes it possible to maximize the number of "significant" relationships. Where possible, it should therefore be avoided and some independent method should be used for dichotomization.

Since there is no apparent rationale for predicting relationships between personality characteristics and product use, it seems foolhardy to develop a purely arbitrary dichotomization method in the present case. Such a method could easily minimize relationships if it were only extremes of product use that related to personality measures and the cutting point closest to the median were arbitrarily used, for instance. It happens that dichotomizing the data shown in Table 1 by combining the top two categories and the bottom three does not lead to a significant t. The resulting quandary is more philosophical than statistical. It seems to the authors that refusing to locate the cutting point that leads to statistically significant differences is the more serious error when dealing with the kind of problem discussed here.

Results and Discussion

A total of 36 comparisons (9 product categories × 4 personality characteristics) included 13 significant relationships. As might be expected, some products were associated with no personality trait; others were associated with one or more; and one product, vitamins, was associated with all four of the personality traits.

Table 2 shows those relationships indicating the significance level. In addition, it shows correlation ratios in parentheses to indicate the approximate strength of the relationships.

The results clearly indicate that there is a relationship between product use and personality traits. This relationship apparently may include both frequency of use of a particular product and preference among different brands of a single product, since preference in automobiles is significantly related to scores on responsibility. At the same time, some products are used frequently or infrequently without relationship to any of the personality traits tested. Each personality trait seems to bear a relationship to the use of some products, each of the four traits scored by the Gordon Personal Profile relating to the use of at least two of the products considered in the present experiment.

It should be pointed out, however, that the relationships located between product use and personality are not particularly strong, certainly less strong than popular marketing concepts of the day suggest.

An obvious corollary to the conclusion that personality traits and product use are related is that the Gordon Personal Profile does isolate personality traits related to behavioral differences. Further, an examination of the pattern of significant relationships shown in Table 2 is persuasive that the four traits, ascendency, responsibility, emotional stability, and sociability, have considerable independence. The manual for the test indicates that the intercorrelations are generally low except for those between ascendency and sociability (.43) and between emotional stability and responsibility (.46). Those correlations were considerably higher in the present experiment, as shown in Table 3. The remaining correlations are quite low. It must be concluded that the Gordon Personal Profile does not measure four independent characteristics but two independent sets of related characteristics. However, it seems that one of a set of related characteristics can still prove to have enough relative independence to be conceptually valuable.

Most of the significant relationships between product use and character traits located are intuitively acceptable. One would expect that high ascendency and high sociability would be related to the rapid acceptance of new fashions, especially since ascendency is described largely as social leadership. On the other hand, there seems to be no particular reason for expecting all personality characteristics to be associated with the frequency of use of vitamins, unless one conceives that personality traits are most likely to affect behavior that society neither rewards nor punishes.

TABLE 2   SIGNIFICANT PERSONALITY TRAITS IN THE USE OR PREFERENCE FOR SOME CONSUMER PRODUCTS

	Ascendency	Responsibility	Emotional Stability	Sociability
Headache remedies	-.05 (.464)^c	—	-.05 (.320)^c	—
Acceptance of new fashions	.01 (.331)^c	—	—	.01 (.566)^c
Vitamins	-.05 (.332)^c	-.01 (.297)^c	-.01 (.091)^c	-.05 (.272)^c
Cigarettes	—	—	—	—
Mouthwash	—	-.05 (.224)^c	—	—
Alcoholic drinks	—	-.01 (.362)^c	—	—
Deodorants	—	.01 (.281)^c	—	—
Automobiles[a]	—	.05 (.295)^c	—	—
Chewing gum[b]	—	—	.01 (.331)^c	—

Note. In all cases except for the last two products, the sign indicates the nature of the relationship. High ascendancy is related to infrequent use of headache remedies, for instance, but with rapid acceptance of new fashions.
[a]Subjects who preferred the more popular makes of car such as Buick, Dodge, Mercury, Ford, Chevrolet, and Plymouth rated higher on the responsibility scale than those who stated a preference for such sports cars as the Corvette or Thunderbird.
[b]While there is no significant difference in personality trait scores and the amount of gum chewed, those who chew gum *only when offered it by someone else*, are significantly lower than others in responsibility and emotional stability.
[c]Correlation ratios.

113

TABLE 3   INTERCORRELATIONS AMONG PERSONALITY TRAITS

Traits	Ascend-ency	Respon-sibility	Emotional Stability
Responsibility	.058		
Emotional Stability	.035	.695	
Sociability	.708	.035	.086

The results cast some possible light on the nature of responsibility as a character trait. It is related to avoidance of vitamins and mouthwash, preference for popular cars and moderate drinking or abstinence. Since these are all modal characteristics of the group being tested, a reasonably strong case might be made for the fact that responsibility is closely related to the acceptance of group norms.

A comparison of the present results with those of Eysenck (1960) suggests that sociability on the Gordon Personal Profile is considerably different from extroversion, with which it might seem related. Eysenck's results showed a strong, significant correlation between extroversion and heavy cigarette smoking, while the present experiment did not even hint at such a relationship between sociability and heavy smoking. It is possible that the difference in age (Eysenck's subjects were considerably older) or difference in nationality (Eysenck's subjects were British) might explain this apparent contradiction.

Summary

The answers to the Gordon Personal Profile and a disguised product use questionnaire by 101 college of business students demonstrate that personality traits are often related to product use. Thirteen of a possible 36 such relations were significant at the .05 level or above.

A corollary conclusion is that the Gordon Personal Profile distinguishes personality traits related to behavioral differences, although the four traits are not "independent."

References

Eysenck, H. J., Tarrant, Mollie, Woolf, Myra, & England, L. Smoking and personality. *Brit. med. J.,* 1960, 5184, 1456-1460.

Ferber, R., & Wales, H. *Motivation and marketing behavior.* Homewood, Ill.: Irwin, 1958.

Martineau, P. *Motivation in advertising.* New York: McGraw-Hill, 1957.

Newman, J. W. *Motivation research and marketing management.* Boston: Harvard Univer. Press, 1957.

Scott, E. M. Personality and movie preference. *Psychol. Rep.,* 1957, 3, 17-18.

11 The Self

Perception of Self, Generalized Stereotypes, and Brand Selection

EDWARD L. GRUBB *(Marketing Educator)* AND GREGG HUPP* *(Marketing Executive)*

This study was designed to test a methodology for measurement of self-concept and consumer behavior in comparable terms and, therefore, to further substantiate the relationship of self-theory to consumer behavior. The results of the study were positive, indicating that owners of a specific make of automobiles perceive themselves as having self-concepts similar to those of others who own that make of automobile, and significantly different from owners of a competing brand.

Various theorists of consumer behavior have used self-theory to explain people's behavior in the market place. As Steuart H. Britt says:

A consumer may buy a product because, among other factors, he feels that the product enhances his own self-image. Similarly, a consumer may decide not to buy a product or not to shop at a particular store if he feels that these actions are not consistent with his own perceptions of himself [2, p. 186].

Though these general assumptions appear to be logical and are promising as a guide for marketing decision making, certain practical limitations still exist. These assumptions have not been thoroughly tested, and only a limited amount of empirical evidence, therefore, support them. The Advertising Research Foundation in its monograph, "Are There Consumer Types?" [1] summarizes various research

Source: Edward L. Grubb and Gregg Hupp, "Perception of Self, Generalized Stereotypes, and Brand Selection," *Journal of Marketing Research,* Vol. 5 (February, 1968), pp. 58-63.

*Edward L. Grubb is associate professor of marketing, School of Business Administration, Portland State College, Portland, Ore. Gregg Hupp is account executive, Marketing and Research Counselors, Inc., Dallas. The authors acknowledge the financial support of the Eastman Kodak Research Fund, College of Business Administration, University of Nebraska.

projects designed to determine the relationship between factors about consumers (including self) and their consumer behavior. The summary* indicates some positive results but also indicates doubts and problems.

General reasons are responsible for the limited quantity and quality of the empirical data. No complete theoretical foundation relating the self-concept and consumer behavior has been carefully outlined. Development of a total self-concept theory of consumer behavior would give researchers more complete theoretical knowledge to explain certain consumer phenomena. Further, such a theory would generate needed, meaningful hypotheses to serve as guides for research.

In addition, the presently accepted theory and empirical results do not indicate which aspects of a person's self-concept are causally related to his behavior in the market place. Application of current techniques may lead to measurement of elements of the self-concept not related to market behavior while other relevant aspects are ignored. The non-comparability between measurement of the self-concept and measurement of relevant aspects of consumer behavior is a major problem. It is difficult to find measurement scales equally applicable to the self-concept and brand or store image. For example, in semantic differential, such polar items as optimistic–pessimistic, introverted–extroverted, or sociable–shy, have meaning about a person's self-concept but are not relevant to the measurement of a brand profile. Solution of this problem is particularly important. If consumers select those brands or stores they consider self-enhancing, researchers must be able to measure, comparably, self-perception and the consumers' perception of the brand or store.

Purpose of the Study

The study was designed to develop a methodology that would better test the relationship between consumers' self-concepts and relevant aspects of their consumer behavior in terms meaningful to marketing theoreticians and practitioners. It was hoped that testing the methodology would provide further substantiation of the relationship between the self-concept and consumer behavior.

Theoretical Foundations

The study was based on previously developed theory relating the consumer's self-concept to his consuming behavior [8]. From infancy, a person develops perceptions, attitudes, feelings, and evaluations of himself as an object he classifies as his self. As the self takes form, it accumulates values and soon becomes a principal value around which life revolves—something to be safeguarded, cherished and, if possible, made still more valuable [9, p. 319].

Since the self-concept grows from reactions of parents, peers, teachers, and significant others; self-maintenance and self-enhancement depends on the reactions of these people. The person will strive for positive reactions from his significant references. The interaction process between two or more persons does not occur in a vacuum but is affected by the environmental setting and the personal attire of each person involved. As Goffman [6] stresses, these items become symbolic tools for goal accomplishments—and therefore self-enhancement—for people in the interaction process. That is, by using symbolic products a person is attempting to communicate to his significant references certain things about himself. If this communications process is successful, the significant references will react to him in the desired manner, and self-enhancement results.

For an individual consumer and his significant references, total understanding of the product's symbolic meaning includes perceptions of the kinds of people whom they believe use that product. When a person endorses a specific product in the interaction process, he is communicating that he wishes to see himself as associated with the kind of people he perceives consume the product.

Main Hypothesis

Based on this theory, the hypothesis was advanced: consumers of a specific brand of a product would hold self-concepts similar to the self-concepts they attribute to other consumers of the same brand. Further, consumers of a specific brand would hold self-concepts significantly different from self-concepts they attributed to consumers of a competing brand. If the person's references would accept this association, confirmation and enhancement of the person's self-concept would result.

Methodology

Research [5, 11, 12] indicates the symbolic meaning of the automobile to American consumers, so automobiles were the product category. A spring, 1966, survey of student automobile registrations at the University of Nebraska revealed that, except for Chevrolet and Ford, the two most popular make/model combinations for 1964 and 1965 automobiles were the standard Volkswagen 1200-1300 series and the Pontiac GTO series.[1] Seventy-five students registered Pontiacs and 83 students registered Volkswagens. Based on this popularity and the small likelihood that the two brands would have the same symbolic meaning, it was decided to use these for the brand category and to use the registered student owners for the study's universe.

A major undertaking was development of a measuring instrument to test the proposed hypotheses. After review of various methods, a modification of the semantic differential technique was selected. Instead of using opposite-meaning

---

[1] In 1964 the standard Volkswagen was identified as the 1200, and in 1965 as the 1300.

adjectives such as strong—weak, only one word was used for each trait. The respondent was to indicate the degree of applicability of each trait to the concept considered by selecting one of the following categories of applicability: not, slightly, moderately, quite, and very. For analytical purposes, each category was assigned a numerical value ranging from zero for the "does not apply" to four for the "applies very much."

Determination of the final trait words for the questionnaire meant preparing an extensive list of descriptive words that could be used to describe the self-concepts of Volkswagen and Pontiac GTO owners. A list of 98 descriptive words was compiled from the adjective check lists of Gough [7] and Cattell [3] from current advertising for each brand, and from published research sources. The final trait words were selected after giving the list to 112 University of Nebraska students. They were asked to indicate those words they felt best described the Pontiac GTO owners, those best describing the Volkswagen owners, and those describing owners of both makes. No word could be used in more than one category. It was decided to use only those terms that best described the owners of each make and therefore best differentiated between the self-concepts of the owner groups. From all responses, only those were selected which at least 70 percent of the respondents believed best described the owners of each make.

This process led to the selection of the following 16 words, 8 for each product.

Volkswagen 1200-1300 owners	Pontiac GTO owners
Thrifty	Status-conscious
Sensible	Flashy
Creative	Fashionable
Individualistic	Adventurous
Practical	Interested in the opposite sex
Conservative	Sporty
Economical	Style-conscious
Quality-conscious	Pleasure-seeking

For analysis, each of these eight trait words was used in the two larger multidimensional scales to measure self-concept traits of each respondent. The eight best descriptive trait words for the Volkswagen formed the multidimensional Volkswagen scale and the eight best descriptive words for the Pontiac formed the multidimensional Pontiac scale.

The completed questionnaire had these two basic scales (16 traits) that were given to each respondent to measure his self-concept, his perception of the self-concepts of the Volkswagen owners, and his perception of the self-concepts of Pontiac GTO owners. No respondent had any idea of the automotive relevance of each word. Each was asked to cooperate as a student representative, and was not told that he was asked to respond because of his auto registration.

Usable responses were obtained from 36 GTO owners and 45 Volkswagen own-ers. Since the study's results were not to be used for any generalizations about a broader universe of Pontiac and Volkswagen owners, this sample was considered satisfactory. The Pearsonian Measure of Skewness [4] was used to determine if skewness existed because of the restricted sample. The test results indicated that the data were markedly skewed only for the Volkswagen owner perceptions of other Volkswagen owners for the traits in the Pontiac scale. It was concluded that skewness of data was not a problem.

The analysis of the data was divided into four sections. Within the four sections, seven hypotheses were proposed and statistically tested by the analysis of variance.

Results

In summary, the results were positive and supported the hypotheses. Consumers of the two different brands of autos perceived themselves significantly different and held definite stereotype perceptions of the owners of each make. Further, they perceived themselves to be like others who owned the same make car and quite different from owners of competing brands.

DIFFERENCES IN SELF-CONCEPTS OF THOSE WHO CONSUME COMPETING BRANDS

Each respondent was asked to determine the degree of applicability of each of the 16 traits to himself. This procedure allowed for the measurement of the self-concepts of Pontiac GTO and Volkswagen 1200-1300 series owners and was im-portant to test the first hypothesis:

1. The self-concepts of Pontiac GTO owners will be significantly different from the self-concepts of Volkswagen 1200-1300 series owners.

Application of analysis of variance resulted in F values of 67.93 for the Pontiac scale and 15.75 for the Volkswagen scale, both statistically significant beyond the .01 level. Therefore, it can be concluded that for these groups, each not only con-sumes a different brand of the same product but also perceives itself differently.

Analysis of mean scores for the individual scale traits (Table 1) provides clarifica-tion of the difference in the two group's perceptions. Volkswagen owners rate themselves appreciably lower than Pontiac owners on such traits as status-conscious, fashionable, adventurous, interested in the opposite sex, sporty, style-conscious, and pleasure-seeking—all components of the Pontiac scale. In contrast, Pontiac owners rate themselves favorably on most component items of the Volkswagen scale, although not generally as high as do the Volkswagen owners. GTO owners see themselves as reasonably sensible, creative, individualistic, practical, conserva-tive, and quality-conscious. Volkswagen owners, however, see themselves as much more thrifty and economical.

TABLE 1   MEAN SCORES BY ITEM ON PONTIAC AND VOLKSWAGEN SCALES FOR BOTH OWNER GROUPS*

Item	Pontiac Owners			Volkswagen Owners		
	Self-Concept (1)	Pontiac Stereotype (2)	Volkswagen Stereotype (3)	Self-Concept (4)	Pontiac Stereotype (5)	Volkswagen Stereotype (6)
Pontiac Scale Items						
Adventurous	2.83	3.03	1.61	2.35	2.23	2.16
Fashionable	2.31	3.11	1.08	1.63	2.63	1.58
Flashy	1.31	2.75	.47	1.14	2.74	.86
Interested in the opposite sex	3.14	3.03	1.39	2.60	2.93	2.09
Pleasure-seeking	2.61	3.00	1.28	2.02	3.14	1.74
Sporty	2.42	3.39	.89	1.63	2.63	1.56
Status-conscious	2.42	2.97	.89	1.40	2.70	.98
Style-conscious	2.61	3.36	.72	1.74	3.07	1.02
Full scale	2.46	3.08	1.04	1.81	2.76	1.50
Volkswagen Scale Items						
Conservative	2.42	1.00	2.33	2.19	.74	2.23
Creative	2.25	2.19	1.28	2.19	1.47	2.14
Economical	1.83	1.31	3.33	2.77	.86	3.42
Individualistic	2.39	2.31	1.83	2.60	1.26	2.44
Practical	2.39	1.64	2.64	2.74	.91	3.33
Quality-conscious	3.03	2.94	1.83	3.02	1.81	2.88
Sensible	2.75	2.31	2.17	2.79	1.35	3.97
Thrifty	1.86	1.28	3.36	2.56	.58	3.28
Full scale	2.37	1.87	2.35	2.61	1.12	2.85

*To better substantiate the comparison of mean scores and to determine the effect of in-group variance or experimental error, z tests were conducted for each mean score comparison. Of the 88 comparisons where statistically significant differences were expected, 66 were significant at the .01 level. Of the 32 comparisons where no significant differences were expected, only 12 were found to be statistically significant at the .01 level.

DIFFERENCES IN SELF-CONCEPTS FOR COMPETING BRANDS

Each respondent was asked to give his estimation of the applicability of each trait of the two scales to owners of the GTO and Volkswagen sedan. This procedure allowed for measurement of the stereotype self-concept that the respondent attributed to the owners of each make. The results of the statistical analysis of these responses (Table 2) tested hypotheses 2 and 3.

2. Volkswagen owners will attribute to other Volkswagen owners a self-concept significantly different from that attributed to Pontiac GTO owners.

3. Pontiac GTO owners will attribute to other Pontiac GTO owners a self-concept significantly different from that attributed to Volkswagen owners.

TABLE 2   COMPARISON OF COMPETING BRAND OWNER STEREOTYPES

Category	Pontiac Scale		Volkswagen Scale	
	Mean	F	Mean	F
Volkswagen owners				
Pontiac stereotype	2.76	11.75*	1.12	54.25*
Volkswagen stereotype	1.50		2.85	
Pontiac owners				
Pontiac stereotype	3.08	174.70*	1.87	1.83
Volkswagen stereotype	1.04		2.35	

*Significant at .01 level.

Three of the four tests supported the hypotheses. Volkswagen owners had very definite views on the stereotypes of owners of the competing brands, and the stereotypes were very different as shown by statistically significant F values, 11.75 and 54.25. Pontiac GTO owners, however, perceived a meaningful difference between these two stereotypes only for the traits on the Pontiac scale, indicated by a statistically significant F value of 174.70.

Review of the mean scores for the individual traits adds greater meaning to these findings. Volkswagen owners felt that the traits of the Pontiac scale were quite applicable to Pontiac GTO owners (means of 2.23 to 3.14) but not very applicable to Volkswagen owners (means of .86 to 2.16). The reverse was true for the Volkswagen scale; Volkswagen owners felt that these traits were applicable to other Volkswagen owners (means of 2.14 to 3.28) but only slightly applicable to Pontiac GTO owners (means of .58 to 1.81).

Pontiac owners perceive other GTO owners as more status-conscious, flashy, fashionable, adventurous, interested in the opposite sex, sporty, style-conscious, and pleasure-seeking than Volkswagen owners. However, the Volkswagen scale perception portrait is mixed with GTO owners perceived as less thrifty, practical, conservative, and economical than Volkswagen owners but more creative, individualistic, and quality-conscious than Volkswagen owners.

SIMILARITY OF SELF-CONCEPT TO SAME-BRAND OWNER STEREOTYPE

If there are differences in the self-concepts of consumers of competing brands and if there are significant differences in the self-concepts they attribute to owners of each brand, it becomes important to determine whether the self-concepts of the owners of each brand are similar to or different from the stereotype they attribute to other owners of that brand. To test for this relationship, two hypotheses were generated.

4. The self-concept of Volkswagen owners will not differ significantly from the self-concepts they attribute to other Volkswagen owners.

5. The self-concept of Pontiac GTO owners will not differ significantly from the self-concept which they attribute to other Pontiac GTO owners.

In comparing the responses of Volkswagen owners for both scales (Table 3), the F values are not significant and the null hypothesis is accepted. It can be assumed for this sample that Volkswagen owners hold a self-concept confirming to their stereotype of the Volkswagen owner.

TABLE 3   COMPARISON OF SELF-CONCEPTS AND SAME BRAND OWNER STEREOTYPES

Category	Pontiac Scale		Volkswagen Scale	
	Mean	F	Mean	F
Volkswagen owners				
Self-concept	1.81	1.61	2.61	1.33
Stereotype	1.50		2.85	
Pontiac owners				
Self-concept	2.46	9.09*	2.37	2.59
Stereotype	3.08		1.87	

*Significant at .01 level.

For the GTO owner the results are less positive. For the Volkswagen scale the F value, 2.59, is not significant so the null hypothesis of "no significant differences in perception of self and stereotype" is retained. However, for the Pontiac scale the F value of 9.09 shows a significant difference in perception of self and others. Analysis of the component Pontiac scale items clarifies this contradictory significant difference. One trait, flashy, showed a highly atypical response distribution; Pontiac GTO owners had a self-concept mean score of 1.31, and GTO owners' stereotype had a mean score of 2.75. A second analysis of the scale after removal of "flashy" revealed an F value of .66, not statistically significant.

DIFFERENCES OF SELF-CONCEPTS FROM COMPETING BRAND OWNER STEREOTYPES

Validation of the theory requires not only determination that the self-concepts of consumers of a particular brand resemble the stereotype they attribute to others who consume the same brand, but also requires proof that their self-concepts are significantly different from the stereotype they attribute to those who consume competing brands. Testing of hypotheses 6 and 7 provided this information:

6. The self-concept of Volkswagen owners will be significantly different from the self-concept they attribute to GTO owners.

7. The self-concept of GTO owners will be significantly different from the self-concept they attribute to Volkswagen owners.

Confirmation of the hypotheses is again found (Table 4) in the responses of Volkswagen owners, but only partially in those of GTO owners. Analysis of the mean scores for individual scale items reveals that Volkswagen owners felt that the Volkswagen scale had significantly less applicability to GTO owners than to themselves. For the Pontiac scale the opposite is true, with these traits significantly more applicable to Pontiac owners than to themselves.

TABLE 4   COMPARISON OF SELF-CONCEPTS AND COMPETING BRAND OWNER STEREOTYPES

Category	Pontiac Scale		Volkswagen Scale	
	Mean	F	Mean	F
Volkswagen owners				
Self-concept	1.81	6.72*	2.61	69.79*
Pontiac stereotype	2.76		1.12	
Pontiac owners				
Self-concept	2.46	37.51*	2.37	.01
Volkswagen stereotype	1.04		2.35	

*Significant at .01 level

In comparing responses by Pontiac owners, the F value of 37.5 for the Pontiac scale is significant at the .01 level, supporting the hypothesis of significant differences between the self-perceptions of GTO owners and their perceptions of Volkswagen owners. Examination of individual scale traits further indicates extensive differences in mean scores. Pontiac owners generally felt that these traits, which they had previously indicated as highly characteristic of Pontiac owners, were only slightly applicable to Volkswagen owners.

Analysis of individual items for the Volkswagen scale reveals that GTO owners perceived the Volkswagen owner as more thrifty, practical, and economical than themselves but considered less sensible, creative, individualistic, and quality-conscious. These results parallel those obtained in testing hypothesis 3. The distribution of means resulting from this mixed portrait cancelled out differences within the scale creating similar overall means, and masked important differences in actual perceptions. The apparent similarity is, to a great degree, a statistical artifact [10].

Conclusions

Considering the limitations of the project, the results provide further empirical data supporting the relationship of self-concept to consumer behavior. These results also have application for the methodology of consumer research, providing empirical support for the proposed measurement of self-concept and consumer behavior in equal terms. Finally, if similar positive empirical data were obtained by more extensive research, marketing management would have an important behavioral tool for decision making.

LIMITATIONS OF THE STUDY

Several basic limitations existed. The universe selected contained University of Nebraska students, and a subsample of that. The use of students may have introduced a bias of greater homogeneity of perceptions of self than might exist for a broader based population. The two branded products selected for the test limited the general applicability of the results. Because of the price and use differences in the two automobiles, the degree of effective substitutability between them is quite small. This factor increases the possibility of substantial differences in the two brand's symbolic meanings and therefore increases the probability of positive results. Further, research might indicate that the greater the similarity of products under consideration, the greater the probability of fewer discriminating differences in self-concepts.

Another limitation was the two scales used for measurement of the respondents' self-concepts. Although these scales provided discriminating results, more refinement is needed to determine the interrelationships of each trait and to better clarify the meanings of each. If further use is to be made of the two scales, greater effort is needed to establish the scales' validity, particularly related to the owners of each make.

IMPLICATIONS FOR THEORY OF SELF-CONCEPT

The empirical data strongly supported the theory that consumers of different brands of a product class would perceive themselves to have significantly different self-concepts. The results also indicated that consumers of specific brands have definite perceptions about the self-concept characteristic of others who consume their brand as well as the self-concept characteristic of those who consume competing brands. The aspect to be tested is the relationship of consumers' self-concepts and their consumer behavior to the actions and perceptions of the consumers' parents, peers, and significant references.

If these results were to be further substantiated, the importance of proper promotion would be stressed. Promotion of a particular brand requires development of a strong consumer perception of the kind of people who own and use the product. If present and potential consumers of a product are to identify with a particular group for a specific self-concept, the promotional efforts must be directed to associate the product with the self-concept desired by the customers. These results also have meaning about the distribution of the product. Management must carefully control the distribution of the product so that those who first consume the product are the people appropriate for the desired image of the product. Having the "appropriate" people consume the product is a means of communicating the product's symbolic meaning to others.

These ideas for marketing management are not new but further support the importance of directing total effort to the development of the product's symbolic meaning. More important, management must point out the symbolic meaning of the product, to present and potential customers and their significant references, thus creating a common and accurate understanding.

References

1. "Are There Consumer Types?" New York: Advertising Research Foundation, 1964.

2. Steuart Henderson Britt, *Consumer Behavior and the Behavioral Sciences: Theories and Applications,* New York: John Wiley & Sons, Inc., 1966.

3. Raymond B. Cattell, *Description and Measurement of Personality,* New York: World Book Co., 1946.

4. Robert Ferber, *Statistical Techniques in Market Research,* New York: McGraw-Hill Book Co., Inc., 1949.

5. ———— and Hugh G. Wales, *Motivation and Market Behavior,* Homewood, Ill.: Richard D. Irwin, Inc., 1958.

6. Erving Goffman, *The Presentation of Self in Everyday Life,* Garden City, N. Y.: Doubleday and Co., Inc., 1959.

7. Harrison G. Gough, *Reference Handbook for the Gough Adjective Checklist,* Berkeley: University of California Press, 1955.

8. Edward L. Grubb and Harrison L. Grothwohl, "Consumer Self-Concept, Symbolism, and Market Behavior: A Theoretical Approach," *Journal of Marketing,* 31 (October 1967), pp. 22-7.

9. Theodore M. Newcomb, *Social Psychology,* New York: The Dryden Press, 1950.

10. Claire Selltiz, *et al., Research Methods in Social Relations,* New York: Holt, Rinehart, and Winston, 1964.

11. Thomas A. Staudt and Donald A. Taylor, *A Managerial Introduction to Marketing,* Englewood Cliffs, N. J.: Prentice-Hall, Inc., 1965.

12. Ralph Westfall, "Psychological Factors in Predicting Product Choice," *Journal of Marketing,* 26 (April 1962), 34.

12 Individual Differences

Differences Between Retailers' and Consumers' Perceptions

PETER J. McCLURE *(Marketing Educator)* AND
JOHN K. RYANS, JR.* *(Marketing Educator)*

Because of their close association with the public, retailers historically have been described as an excellent source of information about consumers. However, interviews reported here with consumers and appliance retailers reveal several interesting retailer misconceptions of consumers that may lead to ill-considered marketing strategies.

By definition a purchase transaction involves a buyer and a seller. Yet, consumer market researchers have tended to focus on the buyer by exploring such phenomena as attitude formation and behavior within and among decision-making units as well as developing a variety of demographic, socioeconomic, and psychological variables for use in segmenting markets. In these studies the seller, though playing an important role, is seldom considered in the analysis of purchase decision making in more than a peripheral manner.

Despite the lack of research, manufacturers have tended to consider retailers as an important source of information about consumers and have sought their help to gain a greater understanding of the marketplace. In such instances manufacturers often feel that if they could only be as close to consumers as retailers, many of the roadblocks to more successful marketing would be substantially reduced. They assume that because of the retailer's familiarity and frequency of contact with consumers, his observations of their behavior are more accurate than people more removed from retailing.

Source: Peter J. McClure and John K. Ryans, Jr., "Differences Between Retailers' and Consumers' Perceptions," *Journal of Marketing Research*, Vol. 5 (February, 1968), pp. 35-40.

*Peter J. McClure is assistant professor of marketing, Boston University. John K. Ryans, Jr. is associate professor of marketing, University of Maryland.

Yet investigation suggests retailers' perception, frequently differ from those of consumers, particularly about the relative importance of certain product attributes in the purchase decision. Furthermore, the retailers' ratings of competitors' brands differ significantly from consumers' on various products produced by these manufacturers.

In this article some differences between consumers' and retailers' views are developed in terms of:

1. importance to consumers of selected product attributes, such as price in the purchase decision for refrigerators, ranges, and automatic clothes washers,

2. retailers' opinions about competitors' brands (Frigidaire, General Electric, and Sears) and the consumers' images of various appliances of these three firms.

Research Design

The data for this discussion were generated in two studies, conducted simultaneously in Indianapolis in the Spring, 1964 (See [2 and 3]). One study dealt with consumers' images of selected appliance attributes and other aspects of consumer behavior. The other focused on appliance retailers' perceptions of how customers rate product attributes and their perceptions of other aspects of consumer behavior, brand attributes, and retailer-manufacturer relations.

SELECTION OF RESPONDENTS

The respondent in the consumer study was the female household head. A random sample was drawn from those 1960 census tracts of Indianapolis (updated for new dwellings) in which more than half of the dwelling units had $5,000 or greater annual income. This process yielded 282 interviews. The definition of the population reduced, but did not eliminate, the number of low income respondents in the study, the desired effect. One quarter of the respondents represented households with annual incomes of $10,000 and over, 63 percent with incomes between $5,000 and $10,000, and 12 percent with incomes under $5,000.

The respondent in the retailer study was the person in charge of merchandising major appliances in the firm. He was typically the owner or manager (of store or department), depending on the kind of firm. The retailer study involved a virtual census of appliance retailers in Indianapolis. From an initial listing of 123 retail outlets representing 99 separate firms with 24 branch locations, 89 successfully completed interviews represented 113 outlets. Of these, 29 percent were appliance stores, 36 percent furniture stores, 12 percent department stores, and 23 percent tire and miscellaneous stores. All major retailers participated in the study.

DATA COLLECTION

The interviews for the consumer study lasted about one hour and were done in the home. The retailer interviews were conducted at the respondent's place of work and varied from one and a half to three hours. Although the consumer and retailer interviews had different settings and contained several questions not common to both, care was taken to coordinate the particular questions and scaling devices generating the data discussed here.

Product Attributes. To measure the relative importance of price, style, service and warranty, extra gadgets, and ease of use in the purchase decision for refrigerators, ranges, and automatic clothes washers, consumers were asked "In purchasing a ————, the following characteristics are: . . . ." Each response was then given by the housewife on a seven interval scale ranging from zero (no importance) to six (very important). On the same scale, appliance retailers were asked to rate how important they thought the same features were to customers for the respective appliances.

Brand Attributes. A ten interval scale ranging from one to five (agree) and minus one to minus five (disagree) was used to measure consumers' images of attributes of particular brands of appliances (adapted from [1]). For example, consumers were asked, "Do you think that Frigidaire refrigerators are high priced?" The procedure was repeated using the phrases: "have good looking styles," "are trouble-free," and "have extra gadgets" for Frigidaire refrigerators, General Electric, and Sears refrigerators, ranges, and automatic clothes washers. Housewives were permitted to rate the products even if they used these particular brands since the objective was to obtain an indication of consumers' images regardless of their viewpoint.

Retailers given comparable scales and phrases were asked to rate the three brands used in the consumer study but not specific appliances. They were asked not to rate the major brand they carried if it was one of these. It was felt that less response bias would be introduced this way. Unfavorable responses about their own supplier would be an indirect criticism of themselves, whereas a favorable rating of the other brands would not necessarily imply an unfavorable image of their own suppliers.

ANALYSIS OF DATA

A two-tailed Mann-Whitney U Test, corrected for ties, was used to test the null hypothesis of no difference between the distribution of consumers' and retailers' responses [4]. For each pair of consumer and retailer distributions tested, the more positive distribution was determined by noting the sign associated with the difference $U-u_v$ [4, p. 121]. If the sign was positive, the distribution of consumers' responses would be more positive than the retailers'. If the sign was negative, the distribution of retailers' responses would be more positive than the consumers'.

An analysis of the data showed that there might be a difference between the consumers' and retailers' ratings because of the way each group reacted to the scales. The research revealed, however, that the relative rating levels for consumers and retailers differed from one scale to another in direction as well as magnitude. These relative differences provide the basis for the following discussion.

Relative Importance of Product Attributes

Though the retailers' ratings of the relative importance consumers put on various product attributes in the appliance-purchase decision were generally consistent—in rank order—with the ratings given by the consumers, they tended to understate the degree of importance consumers attach to such attributes. The retailers underestimated the importance consumers attributed to the various product attributes in all cases except price of automatic clothes washers and extra gadgets on ranges and automatic clothes washers (Table 1).

Differences between the respective distributions of retailers' and consumers' responses were most pronounced for two attributes—service and warranty and ease of use—that resulted in the high levels of significance in Table 1. The retailers tended to consider the two attributes relatively less important than they were to consumers. Though 81 to 82 percent of the consumers in rating the three appliances on the importance of service and warranty felt strongly enough to use the extreme interval (plus six), only 54 to 68 percent of the retailers did. Similarly, 67 to 68 percent of the consumers used the same extreme interval in rating the appliances on ease of use compared with only 30 to 51 percent of the retailers. These observations indicate a possible misunderstanding of consumers by retailers that may make retailers emphasize service and ease of use too little in their marketing strategy.

Among the three major appliances investigated, the appliance retailers and consumers were least similar in their responses on ranges. These differences were exhibited especially for service and warranty and extra gadgets. Considering the saturation of this product relative to automatic clothes washers, for example, such a finding is unexpected and is apparently inconsistent with the commonplace assumption that retailers are knowledgeable about consumers.

Retailers were best able to perceive the importance consumers placed on various product attributes for automatic clothes washers. This may reflect the greater usefulness of automatic clothes washers when compared with refrigerators and ranges, and consequently, the more intense response of retailers to the consumers' concern for service and ease of use.

The least difference was shown between the importance retailers and consumers attributed to the price of refrigerators, extra gadgets on automatic clothes washers, and style of ranges.

PRICE: THE RETAILERS' DEMON

Retailers generally reacted strongly on all questions about price, whether they related to the importance of price to consumers, the use of price as a strategy element, or the need for resale price maintenance. The reaction was noticeable regardless of whether open-end questions or rating scales were used. In response to structured questions, more than 88 percent of the retailers felt that price was an important consideration in the purchase of major appliances and that consumers were price conscious. In some other instances, the retailers conceded the import-

TABLE 1 RETAILERS' AND CONSUMERS' RATINGS' IMPORTANCE OF GIVEN ATTRIBUTES IN THREE MAJOR APPLIANCES

Attribute	Appliance	Respondent*	Ratings (Percent)					Ratings More Positive		Significance Level for Mann-Whitney U
			Of No Importance			Very Important		Retailers	Consumers	
			0-2	3	4	5	6			
Price	Refrigerators	Retailers	6	16	12	23	43		x	.85
		Consumers	16	10	14	7	53			
	Ranges	Retailers	3	16	18	24	39		x	.36
		Consumers	18	7	13	5	57			
	Automatic clothes washers	Retailers	5	13	12	20	50	x		.30
		Consumers	18	8	16	6	52			
Style	Refrigerators	Retailers	5	27	24	21	23		x	.11
		Consumers	18	10	16	15	41			
	Ranges	Retailers	6	13	28	22	31		x	.64
		Consumers	17	9	17	13	44			
	Automatic clothes washers	Retailers	25	29	21	5	20		x	.34
		Consumers	29	16	15	9	31			

Category	Product	Respondent								p
Service and warranty	Refrigerators	Retailers	3	7	12	15	63		x	.001
		Consumers	1	2	7	8	82			
	Ranges	Retailers	7	10	11	18	54		x	.001
		Consumers	2	1	7	8	82			
	Automatic clothes washers	Retailers	0	6	8	18	68		x	.02
		Consumers	2	2	6	9	81			
Extra gadgets	Refrigerators	Retailers	52	27	12	3	6		x	.30
		Consumers	44	16	14	8	18			
	Ranges	Retailers	25	33	23	9	10	x		.01
		Consumers	49	15	14	5	17			
	Automatic clothes washers	Retailers	34	42	11	5	8	x		.66
		Consumers	48	13	16	8	15			
Ease of use	Refrigerators	Retailers	8	11	23	28	30		x	.001
		Consumers	5	4	10	14	67			
	Ranges	Retailers	1	10	19	30	40		x	.001
		Consumers	7	3	10	13	67			
	Automatic clothes washers	Retailers	0	7	15	27	51		x	.02
		Consumers	4	4	10	14	68			

*n equals 82 for the retailer ratings and 280 for the consumer ratings.

131

ance of other factors in consumer decisions about particular products, as reported in Table 1.

During the interviews, the topic mentioned most frequently by retailers was price. For example, often when an apparently unsuccessful appliance retailer tried to explain his predicament, he would blame the pricing practices of competitors or the "bait advertising" of the "big store downtown." Other retailers complained that customers visited their store only to compare prices and then bought elsewhere, or that the discount store prices were forcing them out of business. However, despite such findings, price was not the only appliance attribute considered important by the consumer (see Table 1).

Store Owners. Although nearly all appliance retailers thought price was an important consideration, many felt that factors such as brand preference or product quality offset price considerations. However, store owners, particularly the small store owners rather than store or department managers, tended to feel that price considerations override all other customer considerations. Furthermore, it was the store owner group that generally rated price as especially significant to consumers purchasing refrigerators, ranges, and automatic clothes washers. For example, more than 81 percent of the owners, as compared with 47 percent of the managers, rated price as extremely important (five or six) to the consumer in the purchase of refrigerators. The owners also consistently ranked price high as a strategy element and considered haggling over price basic to the retail transaction. Certainly, smaller retailers would be expected to find it difficult to compete with larger, more aggressive stores on price; it is not surprising that this attribute would be used to explain their current plight. Yet the consumers' replies did not support the retailers' assumption that price is all important.

Competition Misconceptions

The retailers frequently perceived competitive brands (carried by competitive retailers) much differently than consumers did. For example, a retailer may view a competitor's brand as substantially lower in price and also much less trouble-free than consumers do. As a result, he may stress the trouble-free performance of his brand and quietly worry about price. Unfortunately for this retailer and this brand's manufacturer, consumers may not share his views and instead may feel there is not as much price differential as the retailer believes and the products of the competitive brand have much better quality than he judges. The following data reveal some of these misconceptions.

RETAILERS' IMAGES AND CONSUMERS' IMAGES

Considerable variation was found between the retailers' images of competitive brands and the consumers' images of selected appliances of those brands. For example, for the competitive Frigidaire and General Electric brands, retailers rated their prices relatively higher than did consumers—specifically Frigidaire refrigerators and General Electric refrigerators, ranges, and automatic washers (Table 2). The difference was greatest for Frigidaire.

The reverse relationship was found for Sears. Although consumers viewed Sears' appliances as relatively lower priced than the Frigidaire and General Electric ones, retailers perceived an even greater price differential for these competitive brands. They rated product prices for Sears much lower than they did the price levels for Frigidaire and General Electric. Where only 31 percent of the retailers used the positive (agree) intervals in rating Sears on high prices, 89 and 81 percent used the same intervals when rating Frigidaire and General Electric, respectively. Consequently, the responses of retailers on price were more positive than consumers for Frigidaire and General Electric and less positive for Sears, especially for consumers' images of Sears' ranges.

These data suggest that the retailers exaggerated price differences the consumers perceive among the three brands. Perhaps this observation could be explained as a random event if it were not for the consistency in the distributions of the remaining three attributes (Table 2). In only one other instance—extra gadgets involving retailers' images of Sears and consumers' images of Sears' refrigerators—were the retailers' responses more positive.

Trouble-Free Attribute. The widest variation between retailers and consumers was associated with the trouble-free attribute of Sears' appliances. Although retailers were generally more critical of this characteristic than were consumers (consumers' ratings were more positive), retailers' responses were noticeably more negative on Sears. Consumers rated Sears' refrigerators and ranges only slightly below General Electric and actually rated automatic clothes washers slightly above. However, retailers rated Sears substantially below General Electric, which resulted in the extremely high levels of significance in Table 2.

It may be that the retailers' historic images of particular brands have not been updated to reflect the effect of their competitors' merchandising efforts on consumer attitudes. Although consumer attitudes toward brands of appliances are not likely to change swiftly, the efforts of a manufacturer over several years can leave their impact. In this context it is not unreasonable to assume that historic images may have pictured Frigidaire refrigerators as the higher-priced, higher-quality brand and Sears as the lower. Further, the same historic relationship among the three appliances of General Electric and Sears has often been expressed. With the exception of the trouble-free attribute of automatic clothes washers, the present data substantiate this rank ordering of brand images among consumers. However, the exaggerated stereotype expressed by the retailers differs markedly from the consumers' views for both price and quality.

TABLE 2   RETAILERS' AND CONSUMERS' RATINGS OF BRAND ATTRIBUTES OF THREE MAJOR APPLIANCES

Attribute and Brand	Respondents	Appliance	Ratings (Percent)					Ratings More Positive		Significance Level for Mann-Whitney U
			Disagree		Agree		Base	Retailers	Consumers	
			−5 to −4	−3 to −1	+1 to +3	+4 to +5				
High priced										
Frigidaire	Retailers	Refrigerators	3	8	62	27	75	x		.001
	Consumers		7	27	51	15	257			
General Electric	Retailers		3	16	65	16	68			
	Consumers	Refrigerators	6	28	50	16	257	x		.08
		Ranges	5	27	51	17	248	x		.19
		Automatic clothes washers	4	30	52	14	247	x		.08
Sears	Retailers		28	41	26	5	78			
	Consumers	Refrigerators	17	51	30	2	256		x	.06
		Ranges	11	45	38	6	244		x	.001
		Automatic clothes washers	17	49	28	6	261		x	.05
Good looking style										
Frigidaire	Retailers	Refrigerators	1	5	52	42	76			
	Consumers		1	2	42	55	257		x	.02

General Electric							
Retailers	1	7	52	40	68		
Consumers							
Refrigerators	1	3	46	50	258	x	.04
Ranges	0	2	50	48	251	x	.11
Automatic clothes washers	0	4	52	44	250	x	.41
Sears							
Retailers	2	23	50	25	80		
Consumers							
Refrigerators	0	7	55	38	256	x	.001
Ranges	0	6	60	34	244	x	.01
Automatic clothes washers	1	7	53	39	261	x	.001
Trouble-free							
Frigidaire							
Retailers	4	20	56	20	66		
Consumers							
Refrigerators	2	13	45	40	257	x	.01
General Electric							
Retailers	10	25	42	23	60		
Consumers							
Refrigerators	5	16	47	32	258	x	.01
Ranges	1	17	52	30	250	x	.01
Automatic clothes washers	5	23	45	27	250	x	.19
Sears							
Retailers	22	29	41	8	69		
Consumers							
Refrigerators	4	23	45	28	255	x	.001
Ranges	1	19	53	27	243	x	.001
Automatic clothes washers	4	23	41	32	260	x	.001

TABLE 2   RETAILERS' AND CONSUMERS' RATINGS OF BRAND ATTRIBUTES OF THREE MAJOR APPLIANCES
(continued)

Attribute and Brand	Respondents	Appliance	Ratings (Percent)					Ratings More Positive		Significance Level for Mann-Whitney U
			Disagree		Agree		Base	Retailers	Consumers	
			−5 to −4	−3 to −1	+1 to +3	+4 to +5				
Extra gadgets										
Frigidaire	Retailers	Refrigerators	1	14	66	19	73			
	Consumers	Refrigerators	0	13	55	32	255		x	.31
General Electric	Retailers	Refrigerators	3	11	63	23	64			
	Consumers	Refrigerators	1	11	57	31	257		x	.22
		Ranges	0	11	50	39	250		x	.11
		Automatic clothes washers	2	10	59	29	250		x	.73
Sears	Retailers	Refrigerators	1	25	54	20	75			
	Consumers	Refrigerators	2	20	61	17	255	x		.63
		Ranges	0	14	57	29	245		x	.02
		Automatic clothes washers	1	19	53	27	258		x	.26

Conclusion

Though there are undoubtedly exceptions to these findings, especially among other products and kinds of retailers, these observations are indicative of appliance retailers and consumers in a major market area.

If so, why are retailers not better informed of their customers and their customers' views; how they can be made more aware? Their familiarity and frequency of contact with customers make them the envy of many manufacturers operating from remote corporate offices. Yet, this familiarity and frequency of contact do not seem to give retailers a highly accurate understanding of consumers. Thus:

1. Retailers consistently underestimate the strengths with which consumers view the importance of service and warranty, ease of use, and style in the appliance purchase decision. (Retailers are most accurate in their portrayal of consumers' views on automatic clothes washers and least accurate on ranges.)

2. Price is the special concern of appliance retailers who own their stores as contrasted with buyers or managers of larger stores.

3. Retailers tend to view attributes of competitive brands differently from consumers. These images are either over-sensitive or under-sensitive to specific attributes and seem to reflect historic stereotypes rather than current consumer brand images.

This study dealt with retailers in the aggregate. If each retailer is considered individually, the identification of that retailer's market in terms of current and prospective customers becomes vague for all but retail giants. Even so, the interested retailer can investigate his misconceptions of his market. Manufacturers faced with the problems of centralizing more of their production operations, yet are dependent on thousands of small and middle-sized retailers for distribution, are especially vulnerable. The national manufacturer must develop marketing programs suitable for hundred of retailers; consequently, his research should be aimed at developing propositions suitable for generalization over large categories of retailers.

References

1. Irving Crespi, "Use of a Scaling Technique in Surveys," *Journal of Marketing,* 25 (July 1961), 69-72.

2. Peter J. McClure, "An Analysis of Consumers' Images of Major Appliances and Brands of Appliances in Terms of Four Forms of Segmentation," Unpublished D.B.A. dissertation, Graduate School of Business, Indiana University, 1966.

3. John K. Ryans, Jr., "An Analysis of Appliance Retailer Perceptions of Retail Strategy and Decision Processes," Unpublished D.B.A. dissertation, Graduate School of Business, Indiana University, 1965.

4. Sidney Siegel, *Nonparametric Statistics for the Behavioral Sciences,* New York: McGraw-Hill Book Company, Inc., 1956, 116-27.

GROUP INFLUENCES

13. Imitation and Suggestion

"The Influencing Role of the Child in Family Decision Making," Lewis A. Berey (Marketing Educator) and Richard W. Pollay (Marketing Educator), *Journal of Marketing Research,* Vol. 5 (February, 1968), pp. 70-72.

14. The Family

"Husband-Wife Interaction in Decision Making and Decision Choices," William F. Kenkel (Sociologist), *The Journal of Social Psychology,* Vol. 54 (August, 1961), pp. 255-262.

15. Social Influences

"Effects of Group Influences on Consumer Brand Preferences," James E. Stafford (Marketing Educator), *Journal of Marketing Research,* Vol. 3 (February, 1966), pp. 68-75.

16. Influences of Social Class

"Social Class and Life Cycle as Predictors of Shopping Behavior," Stuart U. Rich (Marketing Educator) and Subhash C. Jain (Marketing Educator), *Journal of Marketing Research,* Vol. 5 (February, 1968), pp. 41-49.

17. Influences of Role

"Homemaker Living Patterns and Marketplace Behavior—A Psychometric Approach," Clark L. Wilson (Psychologist), in John S. Wright and Jac L. Goldstucker, Editors, *New Ideas for Successful Marketing,* (Chicago: American Marketing Association, 1966), pp. 305-336

18. Influences of Innovators and Leaders

"The Effect of the Informal Group Upon Member Innovative Behavior," Thomas S. Robertson (Marketing Educator), in Robert L. King, Editor, *Marketing and the New Science of Planning* (Chicago: American Marketing Association, 1968), pp. 334-340.

Every consumer is influenced by a number of different groups. His earliest and closest affiliation is with his family. But the consumer also is influenced by ethnic and religious factors, by social classes, by role, and by various innovators and leaders. The six selections in Part IV deal with *sociological* influences on the consumer.

13 Imitation and Suggestion

The Influencing Role of the Child
in Family Decision Making

LEWIS A. BEREY *(Marketing Educator)* AND
RICHARD W. POLLAY* *(Marketing Educator)*

The role of children as influencers of consumer decisions was investigated by studying interactions between mothers and children. Purchase behavior by the mother of a child's preferred packaged cereals was related to the child's assertiveness and the mother's child-centeredness.

There are at least three main reasons why attention to the role of the child in the market is warranted: (1) the size of the child market is rapidly growing,[1] (2) obviously children influence the family's decision making, and (3) adult consumer behavior is the direct antecedent of child consumer behavior. McNeal [3] discusses the behavior of children as direct consumers of certain low priced, low importance (to the family) products, when the child spends money on what he wants. Wells [6] discusses children's responses to different kinds of television programming and advertising appeals; both Wells and LoSciuto [5] and Garnatz [2] have studied the patterns of child behavior and influence within the store setting. These last two studies begin to approach the broader, more interesting, and more important question of how the child influences family purchasing decision, but they look at the parent-child interaction within the store—only a small sampling of

Source: Lewis A. Berey and Richard W. Pollay, "The Influencing Role of the Child in Family Decision Making," *Journal of Marketing Research,* Vol. 5 (February, 1968), pp. 70-71.

*Lewis A. Berey is marketing research assistant, General Mills, Inc. Richard W. Pollay is assistant professor of business administration, University of Kansas. The research was done when Berey was a student at the University of Kansas. The authors are indebted to Glenn Johnson and R. Fred Frevert for their critique of the results and especially to Merlin Spencer for his suggestions during most phases of the project.
[1] See McNeal [3] for estimates of this trend's strength.

141

the total influencing process. It seem advantageous to also measure some more pervasive behavioral characteristics of the parent, the child, and their interaction.

Most products are not directly available to the young child and must be obtained through an intermediary purchasing agent, the parent. The extent of the influence a child may have on the parent's purchase decision seems dependent on at least two primary factors, the child's assertiveness and the parent's child-centeredness. Examination of the flow of influence from the child to the parent shows that the child's assertiveness is clearly related to the amount of input initiated at the child's end of this communication channel. The receiving end of the communications channel is the parent and the extent of influence a child may have obviously depends on how well the parent is "tuned in" to the child.

This study focused on a product class, ready-to-eat breakfast cereals in which the mother-child relationship seemed predominant, thus reducing the potential complexity of the influence and purchase process down to a simple dyad that could be effectively studied. Assuming that a successful influence attempt would increase the purchase probability of a child's favorite brand, the hypotheses are:

1. The more assertive the child, the more likely the mother will purchase the child's favorite brands of breakfast cereal.

2. The more child-centered the mother, the more likely she will purchase the child's favorite brands of breakfast cereal.

Research Methodology[2]

FIELD OPERATIONS

The sample consisted of 48 students from an urban, private school system, their mothers, and their teachers. The students were from middle to upper-middle income families and were eight to eleven years old.[3]   A questionnaire was given to three classes of children at their school; the children recorded their responses on a standard answer sheet. To control for possible inter-child influence in the group situation, the children were asked to spell words as best they could and to raise their hands if they did not understand a question.[4] Information was obtained on each child's age, three favorite cereals, and his other preferred cereals, to a maximum of ten.

Three teachers of the children rated, on a three-point scale, the verbalness, leadership, persistence, and initiative of each child relative to his classmates. Children were rated separately to minimize inter-attribute bias or halo effect. The third

[2]Details on methodology and results are in [1].

[3]McNeal's [3] reported patterns of child consumer behavior suggest that at age nine the child's tastes for goods begin to go beyond his independent economic means. At this age, then, we would expect to see initiation of a continuing influence on the family's decision making.

[4]For a discussion of recommended interviewing procedures for use with children, see [6].

phase of the field research consisted of a personal interview with each child's mother in her home within three days after the child's interview.[5] When the child was at home during the interview, the mother was instructed to respond without consulting the child. Each mother was first asked to name her child's preferred cereal brands. Her inventory of cereals was checked, and she was asked whether she was out of any particular cereals bought within the past two weeks. Information was obtained on the mother's involvement in the child's activities, the number of children living at home, and the number of trips monthly that her child made to the supermarket alone and with her, and the mother's employment, if any.

INDEX CONSTRUCTION

Indexes for these variables were constructed: (a) the child's assertiveness, (b) the mother's child-centeredness, (c) her brand name recall, and (d) her purchases of the child's favorite cereals. The child's assertiveness index was the total of the teacher's ratings. Possible index scores ranged from 4 through 12; the maximum score resulted from rating a child as often verbal, often a leader, often demonstrating initiative, and very persistent.

The child-centeredness index was constructed for each mother based on her time involvement in the child's activities. For every club, group, or activity of the child, the mother was given 0, 1, or 2 points depending on whether she reported the frequency of her participation as rarely, sometimes, or often. An additional point was given if the mother reported that she often drove the child to the activity. The total points were divided by the number of the child's activities to get a measure of average involvement.[6] For the *brand name recall index* the mother was given five points for each brand she recalled that the child had previously preferred.

The purchase index was constructed giving five, four, three, or two points if the pantry inventory showed, respectively, the first, second, or third choices or other preferred brands. Assuming the greater a child's influence, the smaller the probability of the cereal not being in stock, the mother was given one less point than listed above if she reported recent purchase of a preferred cereal but was currently out of stock.

---

[5] Several interviewers were used, although, ideally, one researcher should have done all interviewing. As a measure of possible error, a chi-square analysis was performed on several of the mothers' responses that could have been affected by different intensities of interviewer probing. No significant differences were found for the mothers' responses obtained by each of the interviewers.

[6] This is obviously a crude measure of child-centeredness, but it has the advantage of needing only data easily obtained. Ideally a psychometric instrument might be used, but would require further invasion of privacy, already violated by the pantry check and the researcher's interviewing of the child outside the mother's presence.

Results and Discussion

The mother's purchase behavior was independent of these control variables: (a) the child's age, (b) the number of other children in the home, (c) the mother's outside employment, (d) the number of trips to the store the child made alone, and (e) the number of trips to the store the child accompanied his mother.[7]

Although the association between child-centeredness and purchase is significant at the .05 level, the direction of the Spearman rank correlation ($r_s = -.27$) is opposite to that previously hypothesized. Instead of highly child-centered mothers showing a greater tendency to purchase their children's favorite cereals, they have a tendency to purchase these cereals less frequently. An explanation could be that the mother who is more child-centered has a greater tendency to purchase cereals following her view of what is right and healthful. Since the child usually prefers presweetened cereals, the child's preference differs from the mother's selection and, given her overriding concern for the child's well-being, she tends to ignore the child and to purchase what she thinks will do the child the most good.[8] In addition, the mother low in child-centeredness may be more likely to purchase the brands the child prefers to placate the child.

When the child's assertiveness is compared with the mother's purchase behavior, the rank correlation coefficient ($r_s = .04$) is not significant, so Hypothesis I is rejected, and it is concluded that the child's degree of assertiveness has little effect on whether the mother purchases her child's favorite cereals. This conclusion, however, must be made with reservations. The correlation between the child's assertiveness and the mother's child-centeredness was significant at the .10 level ($r_s = .19$), reflecting the interdependence of the interaction variables in the continuing mother-child relationship. Thus, it might be expected that the child's assertiveness would be negatively related to purchase behavior, as was the mother's child-centeredness. Because there is no negative relationship suggests that assertiveness of a child might increase the likelihood of the child's having his favorite cereals purchased.[9]

The relationship between the mother's brand recall of her child's favorite cereals and her purchase of these cereals was significant beyond the .01 level ($r_s = .49$), but neither the child's assertiveness ($r_s = .03$) nor the mother's child-centeredness

[7]A 2x2 chi-square analysis, corrected for continuity, yielded the following values of chi square and levels of significance respectively: .904(.25), .094(.40), .816(.25), .071(.40), and .168(.35).

[8]The dispersion between the proportion of presweetened cereals mentioned by the children (.52) and the proportion of presweetened cereals in the marketplace.(.42), based on [4], was such that the null hypothesis was rejected at the 99 percent level and the alternative hypothesis accepted of a significant difference between the child's preferences and the market offering. The market offering probably overstates the acceptability of presweetened cereals to the mothers and, if so, the difference between the mother's and child's independent product selections would be even greater than the difference between these statistics.

[9]The size of the sample prohibited effective statistical analysis between assertiveness and purchase while controlling the effect of child-centeredness.

$(r_s = -.12)$ was significantly related to the mother's brand name recall. The fact that the correlation with child's assertiveness is more positive again seems to suggest that assertiveness leads to some increase in brand recall. The negative correlation apparently results from the child-centered mother who does not tend to buy the child's preferred cereals. Her recall is prohibited by lack of experience with the product and also, perhaps, by dissonance reduction, so she will not recall that her child's favorite cereals are not the purchased ones.

Since this study is cross-sectional, not longitudinal, it reports differences between children and between mothers. Nothing here implies that a given child cannot increase the likelihood of getting his favorite cereal purchased by becoming more demanding and assertive or that a mother can become more child-oriented and decrease her purchasing of the cereals her child prefers, though such generalizations seem intuitively acceptable.

Implications

Though child-centeredness of the mother may increase her receptivity to influence by the child, for cereals there is apparently the stronger effect of the mother being in strong disagreement with the child over what brands to purchase. Awareness of the strength of this "gatekeeper" effect has some strong implications for firms marketing any product with which the child is eventually involved. Given that the mother is not only a purchasing agent for the child but also an agent who superimposes her preferences over those of the child, it is clear that a lot of advertising would be well directed at the mother,[10] even if the mother is not a "consumer" of the product. Without such advertising, the child's influence attempts may be largely ignored if the mother thinks the brand desired is an inferior good.

The rejection of a child's attempted influence may also stem from the mother's perceptions of the quality of information the child possesses, with the perceived legitimacy of the child's influence attempts, and with the mother's opinion of the promotional stimulus that initiated the child's interest. A commerical the mother perceives as silly and unconvincing may cause her to discredit the product.

References

1. Lewis A. Berey, "A Study of Children's Influence on Parental Buying Behavior," Master's thesis, University of Kansas, 1967.
2. George Garnatz, "Children Have Market Influence," Unpublished paper, Kroger Food Foundation, Cincinnati, 1954.

[10] Recently some children's cereals have been promoted on television in the early afternoon and later evening hours. The appeals are directed toward the mother, but to our knowledge the consequence of such a strategy has yet to be determined.

3. James U. McNeal, *Children as Consumers,* Austin, Texas: Bureau of Business Research, University of Texas, 1964.

4. A. C. Nielsen, *Competitive Tabulation of Ready-to-Eat Cereals–Kansas City District,* Unpublished manuscript, A. C. Nielsen Company, Chicago, October 1965.

5. William D. Wells and Leonard A. LoSciuto, "Direct Observation of Purchasing Behavior," *Journal of Marketing Research,* 3 (August 1966), 227-33.

6. William D. Wells, "Children as Consumers," in Joseph W. Newman, ed., *On Knowing the Consumer,* New York: John Wiley & Sons, Inc., 1966, 138-45.

14 The Family

Husband-Wife Interaction in Decision Making and Decision Choices

WILLIAM F. KENKEL* (Sociologist)

The discussions of married couples, as they decided what to do with a supposed $300 gift, were tape-recorded and analyzed by a special system of interaction process analysis. The relative amounts of time talking by husband and wife apparently was a significant factor as to the types of items they decided on buying.

A. The Behavior of Spouses

A number of studies have discovered that married couples differ with regard to the roles they play when engaging in joint decision making (4, 6). Frequently the husband does more of the talking and contributes more ideas toward a solution of the problem, but wives have been found to outperform their husbands in these respects. The wife has been observed to do more to keep the decision making session running smoothly, but sometimes husbands play this part or both husband and wife share the part equally. Couples vary, too, with regard to which spouse has more influence (3).

When in the course of observing a substantial number of married couples such variation in their behavior is noted, one is led to hypothesize certain effects or results of different interaction patterns. Do couples where the husband is the "idea man" make as rational decisions as other couples? Are they as happy as other couples? Is there any evidence that essentially equal performance by husband and

Source: William F. Kenkel, "Husband-Wife Interaction in Decision Making and Decision Choices," The Journal of Social Psychology, Vol. 54 (August, 1961), pp. 255-262.

[1] Acknowledgment is due the Research Foundation and the Industrial Science Research Institute, Iowa State University, for their support in our studies of family decision making.
*William Kenkel is professor of sociology at Iowa State University.   **147**

wife of the different tasks called for in decision making results in a more efficient, more rational, or otherwise different decision outcome? The questions, with their implied propositions, could be continued. Probably most sociologists would expect that the different modes of spousal interaction would have some effect either on the relationship of the couple, their performance of task at hand, or both. Lewin's (5) early study of autocratic and democratic groups is related to the present issue, for it indicates that the role behavior of members of small groups affects the productivity of the group as well as the human relationships. Again, Torrence (7) found that the way in which power is distributed in small groups has consequences for the group's decisions. Strodtbeck (6) reports a relationship between spousal roles in decision making and "winning" a decision. The above and other studies should serve to make us sensitive to the role relationships of husbands and wives in decision making interaction.

This paper is restricted to an investigation of the relationship between the behavior of spouses in a decision making session and the decision outcome. Since the decision problem presented to the couples involved their spending a hypothetical gift of money, the outcome is in terms of the kinds of items they chose to buy. By virtue of the part played in the decision making session, the spouses had varying opportunity to control the way in which the gift money was to be spent. There emerged, in addition, something approaching a typical masculine and feminine role in decision making. We need now to investigate whether either the differential ability to control the couple's resources or departure from the typical spousal role were reflected in the kinds of items the couple chose to purchase. While it is reasonable to assume that need, family goals, and other factors would help determine what kinds of goods are purchased, it is an intriguing hypothesis that the decision making role pattern of the couple has a demonstrable effect on the way in which they spend, or intend to spend, their money.

B. Study Design

Fifty married couples in which the husband was a college student formed the controlled sample for this study. A pretested decision making problem, discussed in more detail in an earlier paper (4), was utilized. Each couple was asked to assume that they had received a gift of $300 with the stipulation that it could not be saved nor could it be used for anything that they had previously decided to buy. They were asked to discuss together how they should spend the money and to reach an agreement, within about a half an hour, on a list of items they would like to purchase. The ensuing decision making session was tape recorded.

Bales' system of Interaction Process Analysis was used to analyze the behavior of the spouses during the problem solving session (1). This system involves a set of 12 categories which can be used to describe all behavior to which an observer can assign meaning. It enables us, therefore, to produce an objective account of the qualitative and quantitative contributions of husbands and wives during the session.

The present analysis is restricted to: (1) the relative amount of talking done by each spouse (total actions in all twelve of Bales' categories), (2) their relative performance that had to do with keeping the discussion running smoothly (Bales' Categories 1 and 2), and (3) their relative performance of actions consisting of giving ideas, suggestions, opinions, analysis, and the like (Bales' Categories 4, 5, and 6). An operational definition was developed and the couples were classified as "about the same," "husband high," or "wife high" with regard to their total talking, performance of social emotional actions, and performance of task actions.

From the tape record of each couple's discussion there was abstracted a list of all items the couple chose to purchase with their gift money, the cost of the item, and whether husband or wife first suggested the item. Some method of classifying the items was patently necessary. The following system was devised (Table 1).

TABLE 1

Category	Typical Items
1. Wife-personal:	clothing of all sorts, jewelry, golf lessons.
2. Wife-household:	washing machine, dryer, new stove, cooking utensils.
3. Husband:	books, shotgun, clothing, fishing equipment, watch.
4. Joint family:	furniture, vacation trip, television, car down payment.
5. Children:	play equipment, clothing, toys, new furniture.

It should be noted that the classificatory system here employed emphasizes the *user* of the item rather than the *nature* of the item. Thus a dress for the wife is classified as "wife-personal" rather than as "clothing." It is thought that classification by user should reflect more readily the effect of spousal roles on the decision choices. In other words, if the interaction pattern of the couple affected the sorts of items they chose to purchase, it should be more apparent with the classification system here employed than if the items were categorized in some other way. Very little difficulty was experienced in classifying the items to our system. About 80 percent of all of the items mentioned by the 50 couples were able to be placed in one of the five categories.

For each couple we next computed the per cent of all items on their final list that fell into each of the categories and the per cent of the hypothetical gift money utilized for each category. The correlation between the per cent of items and the per cent of money was found to be +.85. This indicates that, in general, the more items a couple chose in a given category, the more money they spent in that category. The lowest correlations, .68 and .75, were found with respect to wife-household and children's categories, respectively. In the former case, fewer items tended to account for more of the money; children's items, on the other hand, tended to use up a disproportionately small proportion of the money. In the present analysis we will deal only with the proportion of the total list of items the 50 couples devoted to each item category.

C. Findings

1. TOTAL TALKING

A number of studies have discovered that the total amount of talking a person does in a small problem-solving group has a bearing on his influence and thus on the solution produced by the group. Strodtbeck (6) reports, for example, that among 34 couples the spouse who talked most won most of the decisions in 24 of the cases. Bass (2) found a correlation of .93 between the total time spent talking and the votes for having demonstrated leadership that men in an eight-man discussion group received. In short, the relative amount of talking done by participants in a decision making group would seem to be a variable crucial for investigation.

In 40 per cent of the cases of the present study, the husband and wife did about the same amount of talking during the experimental session. As is apparent in Table 2, these couples differed from the remaining couples with regard to how they spent their gift money. The difference is obvious in four of the five possibilities. When the spouses talked about equally, they were more likely than any others to choose wife-household items and were less likely than others to choose items for the husband and children. They were also less likely than the cases where the wife out-talked her husband to choose goods for the personal use of the wife.

TABLE 2   DISTRIBUTION OF TOTAL AMOUNT OF TALKING AND PROPORTIONS OF THE ITEMS SELECTED IN FIVE USER CATEGORIES

| Action Distribution | Per cent items in category | | | | |
	Wife-Personal	Wife-Household	Husband	Joint Family	Children
About the same	7.6	14.8	15.1	30.7	13.2
Husband higher	8.6	8.2	18.5	34.7	16.4
Wife higher	10.8	8.4	23.8	29.8	23.0

In the bulk of the remaining cases, 42 per cent of the total group, the husband talked more than his wife. In these families the items selected were more frequently for the use of the entire family than in the other two types of families. When the husband did more of the total talking than his wife, the couple chose more items for the children and husband, but fewer household items, than when the couple talked about the same amount. When the cases in which the husband out-talked his wife are compared with the couples who talked about equally, there is about a 3 per cent or greater difference in the proportion of items selected in four of the five categories.

Due to their small numbers, little comment can be made on those cases in which the wife out-talked her husband. The strong tendency for more of the items to be for the use of children can be noted. It is also suggestive that when the wife talks more than her husband the couple chooses more goods for the personal use of the wife. At the same time, husbands seem to fare best, in terms of the proportion of the list of items that are for their use, when the woman does more of the talking.

2. THE "IDEA-MAN" ROLE

The fact that the relative amount of talking done by persons taking part in decision making with their spouses seemed to be related to their choices is intriguing. In an effort to explain the relationship, analyses were made of the distribution of the spouses' actions according to the nature of the actions. Particularly important was thought to be the task-related behavior. This consisted of giving actual suggestions on the way to spend the money, evaluating the choices of self or other, giving information about the items, expressing desires or feelings, and similar "giving" behavior related to the task at hand. Such behavior, of course, is requisite to the development of a suggested list of items to be purchased, and it could well be imagined that the way in which the couple divided up this task-oriented role would have a bearing on the decision outcome.

In 60 per cent of the cases the husband contributed more of the ideas and suggestions than did his wife. Among such couples, in two of the five categories, wife-household and joint family, the proportion of items was substantially higher than in the cases in which husband and wife contributed ideas about equally. Table 3 also shows that when the husband was the "idea man" fewer of the items were for the children but more were for the family as a whole than when the wife led in ideas. The remaining differences do not appear to be substantial.

TABLE 3   DISTRIBUTION OF IDEAS AND PROPORTION OF ITEMS SELECTED IN FIVE USER CATEGORIES

Action Distribution	Wife-Personal	Wife-Household	Husband	Joint Family	Children
About the same	8.1	19.9	15.5	41.8	14.0
Husband higher	8.7	10.3	17.8	34.7	16.9
Wife higher	7.4	9.6	19.5	23.6	21.2

Husbands and wives contributed about the same number of ideas in 26 per cent of the cases studied. These couples were decidedly more likely than any others to choose items to be used by the entire family. They were also much more likely to select household items used primarily by the wife. In addition, they were considerably less likely than couples in which the wife led in ideas to allocate their resources for goods for the children. When the wife contributed more of the ideas, as she did in 18 per cent of the cases, more of the items were for the children, and fewer were for the use of the entire family.

3. SOCIAL-EMOTIONAL ACTIONS

The behavior of the spouses that was classified as "Social-emotional, positive" included such actions as raising the other person's status, expressing affection, showing consideration or satisfaction, joking, and laughing. In 72 per cent of the cases wives performed more of the social-emotional or expressive actions than did husbands. About equal performance was discovered in 8 per cent of the cases, while 20 per cent of the husbands outperformed their wives in this area.

It is interesting that for every category of decision choice there is a noticeable difference between couples in which the wife was the social-emotional leader and other couples. When the wife specialized in the expressive role, as indicated in Table 4, the items chosen were less frequently for her personal use and were more

TABLE 4   DISTRIBUTION OF SOCIAL-EMOTIONAL ACTIONS AND PRO-
PORTION OF ITEMS SELECTED IN FIVE USER CATEGORIES

Action Distribution	Categories				
	Wife-Personal	Wife-Household	Husband	Family	Children
About the same	3.1	12.5	30.7	38.2	12.5
Husband higher	11.9	6.3	21.1	22.1	11.1
Wife higher	7.1	14.3	16.7	35.5	21.1

frequently for the children, for the family as a whole, and for the household, than when the husband was the social-emotional leader. It should be noted that when the wife was the social-emotional leader about twice as many items were selected for her husband's as for her own use. All of this seems to add up to a picture of outgoing, sympathetic women ministering to the needs of the children and husband and thinking more of what is needed for them, the family as a whole, and the home than of their personal needs.

When the husband contributed most of the social-emotional actions the proportion of personal items for the wife goes up and household items decrease. This may indicate that the personality type capable of playing this role, a minority among the males in the sample, has greater sensitivity to the needs of his wife and thinks first of her personal wishes and then of household items. Not fitting this picture of the empathic, sensitive, altruistic male, however, are the findings that the husband himself gets a liberal share of the gift money, more so than when the wife is the social-emotional leader, and that joint family and childrens' items also are reduced. There exist too few cases of husband and wife sharing equally the expressive role to allow detailed analysis. It can be noted, however, that in almost every instance such couples differed noticeably from both of the other types of couples.

D. Discussion

Our intent in this research was to explore the relationship between certain variables in an experimental setting, rather than to describe the situation in any universe. The variables with which we were concerned were the interaction patterns of husbands and wives in decision making and the nature of their choices. The smallness of the sample and its controlled, rather than random, nature make it inadvisable to employ the usual statistical tests of the significance of the discovered relationships. Nevertheless, some summary indication of the extent to which a relationship was found would seem to be in order.

Taking the findings reported in the three tables together, there were 45 possibilities for differences to occur in the proportion of consumer items selected by the couples with the different interaction patterns. Of these 45 possibilities, 32 showed a difference of 3 per cent or more, 19 a difference of 5 per cent or more, and 7 a difference of about 10 per cent or more. This would seem to indicate that the way in which spouses divide up the task, social-emotional, and total actions in decision making has some bearing on the kind of items they actually choose. The relationship does not seem to be strong.

It is interesting that the way in which the spouses behaved with respect to the production of ideas and suggestions failed to show through with a strong bearing on the particular gift items they selected. Distribution of ideas was found to be less important than the distribution of social-emotional actions or the total amount of talking. The importance of expressive behavior seems to indicate that the subtleties of spousal interaction in decision making require more attention.

If one is accustomed to think of consumer choices being influenced chiefly by object needs, wants produced by advertising, family goals and values, and the like, than it is indeed impressive that even some relationship was discovered between how couples decide to spend a sum of money and the roles they play in reaching the decision. The findings of the present research serve to remind us of the importance of spousal interaction in problem solving situations. The present research perhaps suggests a line of inquiry which, if a larger sample was employed, may lead to more definitive findings.

References

1. Bales, R. F. Interaction Process Analysis. Cambridge, Mass.: Addison-Wesley Press, 1951.
2. Bass, B. M. An analysis of leaderless group discussion. *J. Appl. Psych.*, 1949, 33, 527-533.
3. Kenkel, W. F. Influence differentiation in family decision making. *Social Soc. Res.*, 1957, 42, 18-25.
4. Kenkel, W. F., & Hoffman, D. K. Real and conceived roles in family decision making. *Marr. & Fam. Liv.*, 1956, 18, 311-316.
5. Lewin, K., & Lippitt, R. An experimental approach to the study of autocracy and democracy. *Sociometry*, 1938, 1, 292-300.

6. Strodtbeck, F. L. Husband-wife interaction over revealed differences. *Amer. Sociol. Rev.,* 1951, 16, 468-473.

7. Torrance, E. P. Some consequences of power differences on decision making in permanent and temporary three-man groups. *In:* Hare, P. and others, *Small Groups.* New York: Knopf, 1955.

15 Social Influences

Effects of Group Influences on Consumer Brand Preferences

JAMES E. STAFFORD* *(Sociologist)*

The exploratory study reported here attempts to identify if and how informal social groups influence the brand preferences of their members. The results suggest, first, that consumers are influenced by such groups; and second, that the extent and degree of brand loyalty behavior within a group is more closely related to the behavior of the informal leader than to the cohesiveness of the group.

Most earlier marketing researchers described consumer brand preference behavior without attempting to uncover and analyze experimentally determinants of such brand preferences [2, 3]. With the advent of sophisticated mathematical models, however, renewed interest was shown in conducting experimental studies leading to an explanation of the process of brand preference behavior [4, 5, 8]. To date, the most important contributions of these studies have been their reliance on realism and their emphasis on brand loyalty as a probability process. For the most part, factors other than economic ones were not considered important, or at least they were de-emphasized. In recent years, however, marketing men generally have conceded that such social factors as acculturation, social class, ethnic groups and identification all play some role in consumer decision making. The question today is exactly how, in what way, and to what extent social factors influence consumer behavior.

Source: James E. Stafford, "Effects of Group Influences on Consumer Brand Preferences," *Journal of Marketing Research,* Vol. 3 (February, 1966), pp. 68-75.

*J. E. Stafford is an assistant professor of marketing and advertising, University of Houston. Grateful acknowledgment is made to W. T. Tucker, University of Texas, for his valuable suggestions and constructive criticism, and to the Ford Foundation who partially supported this project.

A second thought which suggested this study revolves around the concept of group or interpersonal influence. From both a theoretical and empirical point of view, the literature of the behavioral sciences fully supports the idea that certain groups, and particularly certain individuals within the group, influence member behavior. While a great deal of marketing research has been conducted on various aspects of consumer behavior, there have been only a few analytical attempts [7, 9] to determine if such interpersonal interactions do, in fact, influence consumer behavior.

The lack of empirical research on determining whether small, informal, social groups influence the purchasing behavior of their members led to this design of an experiment which would, first, indicate whether this influence exists and, second, describe and explain the process of group influence on one particular type of consumer behavior—brand preferences. The main objective was to explore in as much detail as possible if and how a consumer's brand preferences might be conditioned by intergroup communications and the perception of brand preferences of fellow group members.

The overall design of the experiment consisted of sociometrically selecting ten groups of women who were close friends, neighbors, or relatives; who might go shopping together; and who were given a common experimental task to perform. The assumption was that the resulting groups were "real" in some sense other than that of being arbitrarily brought together for the study. This did not mean that the groups had to have traditions of long standing, but they had to have real interaction among the individuals making up the group.

By analyzing first the relationship between the groups and their subsequent observed brand preference behavior, it was hoped that the influence of groups on the brand preferences of their members could be shown statistically. Second, by analyzing the interaction processes of each group, it was also hoped to illustrate that the degree of influence exerted varies according to the internal cohesiveness[1] of the group, and according to the type and strength of informal leadership exhibited.

Review of Group Theory

During the past two decades there has been a resurgence of interest in individual-group relationships. This resurgence continued to build momentum until, today, the study of small groups has become a central area of theorization and experimentation for social psychologists. The major character of this trend, as contrasted with the individualistic emphasis, is the realization that group situations generate differential effects of significant consequence. Group interaction is seen as a major determinant in attitude formation and attitude change, as well as for other phenomena (satisfaction of social needs) of importance to the individual.

---

[1]Cohesiveness refers to the attraction a group has for its members. The greater the attractiveness of the group, the more cohesive the group.

As is typical in the behavioral sciences, there is no one accepted definition of "groups." The most common definition revolves around the term "reference groups" which can include groups to which a person actually belongs, to which he aspires to belong, or dissociative groups to which he aspires *not* to belong. Thus, for one member a group may be a membership group while for another it is a reference group. Most social psychologists consider reference groups as a person's major source of values, norms, and perspectives.

Reference groups influence behavior in two major ways. First, they influence *aspiration levels* and thus play a part in producing satisfaction or frustration. If the other members of a particular reference group (for example, neighbors) are wealthier, more famous, better gardeners, *etc.,* one may be dissatisfied with his own achievements and may strive to do as well as the others.

Second, reference groups influence *kinds* of behavior. They establish approved patterns of using one's wealth, of wearing one's prestige, of designing one's garden. They thus produce conformity as well as contentment (or discontentment). These two kinds of influence have, in general, a great deal in common. Both imply certain perceptions on the part of the individual, who attributes characteristics to the reference group which it may or may not actually have. Both involve psychological reward and punishment.

Reference behavior itself is a cognitive process in which individuals evaluate their statuses, behavior, norms, and values by means of referents.[2] The four objects of evaluation—norms, values, statuses, and behavior—may be grouped into objective (statuses and behavior) and subjective (norms and values) categories. It is recognized that the contents of each category have important linkages with those of the other, but for purposes of analysis the distinction may be made.

Reference behavior is characterized by three general dimensions—knowledge, affectivity, and sanctions. These dimensions appear as interrelated variables which come into play in all forms of reference behavior.

For a phenomenon to be used, the individual must be aware (have knowledge) of its existence, and the degree and kind of knowledge serve as guides to his use of the referent. Through direct and indirect communication, members learn the norms and values of their informal groups and see how the normative structure is expressed in the status arrangements and corresponding behavior patterns.

The sanctions perceived by individuals constitute another dimension of reference behavior. The concept of referents indicates the existence of myriads of potential referents and, yet, the actual number of referents utilized by any one person is necessarily limited. When an individual perceives a potential referent, such as an informal social group, to be the source of positive sanctions (rewards) or negative sanctions (punishment or the withholding of anticipated rewards) which relate to himself, at that moment the informal group becomes an actual referent and is used in the evaluation of norms, values, statuses, and behavior.

[2] Referents are whatever individuals employ in evaluating their own statuses, behavior, norms, and values. In this paper the small, informal social group is the main referent being considered, although there are many other phenomena that one could use as referents.

The third dimension of reference behavior—affectivity—relates to the degree of identification a person has for a particular group. Recognition of the importance of a person's degree of identification to a reference group is very valuable to an understanding of how groups influence the behavior of their members.

Because of the segmentation of life in an industrialized, mass society, important decisions faced by an individual can involve the perspectives of many referents without any perceived conflicts between them. In general, the more restricted the application of results of a process of evaluation, the more limited will be the number of referents mobilized in the process. If, for example, an individual was planning a small purchase (a gallon of milk), he would probably utilize very few referents to make a decision. On the other hand, if he were planning to purchase a new car, then he would probably evaluate his decision alternatives by considering a much larger number of referents. While determination of any rank order of influence potential is very difficult to accomplish, some mention can be made of two other concepts which have evolved out of group theory, and which are quantitatively measurable—group cohesion and group leadership.

Informal structuring tends to occur in all groups after a period of time during which the members have interacted with one another. Homans contended that "the usual outcome of interaction is the formation of interpersonal bonds of affect and respect [6]." The recipient of affect and respect was said to have social rank within the group. Differential social ranks provided the basis for informal structuring.

Were all members of a group to like and respect each other highly, no substructures would be said to exist. This condition would define complete, 100 percent positive cohesion. All social ranks would be equal. If, on the other hand, every member ignored every other one, each member would be considered a separate substructure, a one-man clique. This would define the state of zero cohesion. Internal social influence would be equal to zero. Much evidence exists to support the proposition that inter-group pressure to conform on matters of importance varies directly with cohesion. In a very cohesive group, a member will experience a great deal of pressure to conform. In a less cohesive group, pressure to conform is expected to vary directly with the amount of deviation from the group norms, at least up to a point.

The concept of "group leaders" developed from the evolution of role differentiation within the group. Except in very unusual circumstances, informal role differentiations are expected to occur in every group. As a result of this role differentiation process, each person in the group has a certain social rank or status. The more status an individual has, the greater his prestige; the greater one's prestige, the higher he is in the informal hierarchy and the more "social power" he possesses. Social power has been defined as the total amount of opinion change one person could induce another to make. The concept could, of course, be broadened to include the overt as well as the convert changes a member can effect in another member of the group. When a group member has social power over other members, he also usually has high status and is normally considered the group leader.

Methodology

OBJECTIVES AND HYPOTHESES

Considering the fertile field for research in consumer behavior offered by reference group theory, it seemed very pertinent to relate reference theory and consumer behavior in an empirical study. The first and foremost objective of the study, therefore, was to show statistically that small, informal groups do influence certain aspects of consumer behavior. In hypothesis form, the first objective was:

1. Small, informal social groups exert influence toward conformity on member brand preferences.

The second and third objectives were closely related to the first. In fact, they could be considered secondary objectives. Assuming support for the first goal, this part of the study attempted to determine how and to what degree informal groups influence member behavior. From a theoretical standpoint, group cohesion and group leadership played important roles in forming group opinions and behavior patterns. Specifically, then, Hypotheses 2 and 3 were:

2. The degree of influence exerted on a member by the group is directly related to the "cohesiveness" of that group.
3. Within a group, the "leader" is the most influential member with respect to member behavior patterns in purchase situations (brand preferences in this study).

RESEARCH DESIGN

The research design attempted to analyze the relationship among several variables (group influences and brand preferences) under controlled but "real-life" conditions. The broad steps of the research were as follows:

1. Specification and delineation of the first major variable of interest—small, informal groups. A two-stage, systematic random sample of ten housewives from one Census tract in Austin, Texas, was used as a representative basis to obtain ten informal groups. Each member of the original sample was asked to take a sociometric test, which was used to determine the interpersonal relationships of interest and to disclose the feelings which individuals have toward each other in respect to a group situation they are considering at that moment. Since consumer behavior was the broad topic of study, each woman was asked to nominate four friends, relatives or neighbors with whom "she likes to or would be willing to go shopping." The use of an activity criterion, rather than a request for a general statement of friendship, was intended to reveal the specific basis on which a selection was made, as well as to uncover group interactions closely associated to some common activity like buying behavior. The end result of the sociometric test was ten groups of women who were friendly toward each other, who interacted, and who all were oriented toward one criterion—shopping behavior. The rest of the experiment

dealt with how the influence of interpersonal relationships on a person's brand preferences could be observed.

2. A particular product, bread, was selected as a vehicle for the brand preference study because of ease of handling, frequent use, and financial considerations. Thin sliced white bread from a local bakery was packaged in identical clear unmarked cellophane bags. Large labels (2" × 2") with the letters, "H," "L," "M," "P," were designated as "brands" to be placed on the bread. These four middle-alphabet consonants were chosen because, first, they were easy to remember and, second, they have about the same frequency of use in English. It was not assumed that these symbols (brands) were completely neutral because it is probable that no set of symbols could be neutral, equally pleasing, or have common meanings for all individuals.

3. The experiment itself was relatively simple. Called on at home twice a week (Tuesday and Friday) for eight weeks, each of the forty-two women in the study was given her choice of the four previously unknown brands of bread. The four brands were placed on a tray so the participant could easily see and choose the one she wanted. In order to control for position bias, the position of the brands on the tray was varied each day in Latin square design. The women were not aware that all of the brands were from the same bakery, or that the study was concerned with analyzing inter-group influences. Rather, they were told the purpose of the study was to discover how women go about choosing a brand of bread from several about which they knew nothing.

4. At the end of the test period, each woman was given a short questionnaire covering brand preferences and general opinions regarding the bread. The questionnaire also provided specific information for determining group cohesion, group leadership, and intergroup communication patterns.

5. Analysis of the data included determination of (a) group influences on brand choices and preferences; (b) influence of the degree of group cohesion on brand preferences; (c) influence of group leaders on brand choices of other group members, and (d) comparisons of actual brand choices with brand preferences.

Results

By analyzing the similarities and differences of brand choice patterns within the entire sample and among the members of each group, it was expected to determine whether the group was in fact a source of influence on member brand preferences. On the assumption that the data were neither correlated nor binomial, two-way analysis of variance (F-test) was a valid tool to use to test the first hypothesis. If the study was properly designed to show that groups influence member brand preferences, then the statisitcal result should be a significant difference between the groups in the brands preferred. In other words, while within-group brand preferences should be similar, the groups themselves should vary among one another with respect to brand preferences. The results are presented in Table 1.

TABLE 1   ANALYSIS OF VARIANCE SUMMARY FOR THE INFLUENCE OF INFORMAL GROUPS ON BRAND PREFERENCES

Source of Variation	Sum of Squares	Degrees of Freedom	Variance Estimates by Pooling	F
Brands	22.90	3	7.60	.74
Groups	181.30	9	20.10	1.97*
Interaction	1,580.40	155	10.20	

*p = .05

Statistically, the results of the analysis of variance test supported the first hypothesis. A significant difference was found between the groups with respect to preferred brands, while there was no significant difference between the brands themselves. Also, there was no significant interaction effect between brands and groups, thus disposing of one major source of statistical ambiguity. The first result, while explaining nothing of the determinants of group influence, did provide sufficient stimulus to carry on a more detailed analysis of the process of group influence.

While analysis of variance was a valuable and powerful tool in determining whether the groups did, in fact, influence member brand preferences, it provided no clues as to *how* this influence was initiated and whether this influence was exerted toward member conformity. Theoretically speaking, two factors—cohesiveness and informal leadership—have an important bearing on the effectiveness of internal group influences.

Essentially, group cohesiveness was measured by having each member of the group rate every other member of that group on a seven point bipolar scale which ranged from Best Friend (+3) to Hated (−3), with Don't Know (0) as the center point. The algebraic sum of points given by all the group members was termed "Lib units [1]." The higher the mean Lib score for a group, the more cohesive (positive or negative) was the group.

Group leadership was defined operationally as the sum of three different sources of influence: attractiveness, expertness, and communications centrality. First, the attractiveness of each group member to every other group member was measured by taking the mean Lib score that person received on the group cohesion measurement. The individual who was most attractive or best liked by her group was considered to be a potential informal leader of the group. Second, expertness as a form of leadership was described rather arbitrarily as the woman in each group who had been a member of the first bread panel study conducted by Tucker [10]. Because of her previous experience on a similar study, it was believed that this individual might be considered an expert in this study, with her opinions being therefore more influential. Finally, the leader was defined as the individual in the central position of that group's communication network. Each woman was asked to tell how often (times per week) she called, was called by, or saw in person each of the other group members. By classifying this data, it was possible to describe rather accurately the communication patterns of each group. The women in the group with the highest frequency of communications (central position) was defined as the leader.

EFFECT OF COHESIVENESS ON BRAND PREFERENCES

The main function of this section of the study was to determine whether cohesiveness influenced the degree to which members would conform to each other's brand preferences. In other words, would members of more cohesive groups be more likely to prefer the same brand than members of less cohesive groups? A second consideration from a slightly different point of view from the above was: would members of more cohesive groups tend to be more or less brand loyal than members of less cohesive groups? Does increased cohesion lead to similarities in general behavior (brand loyalty) even though the loyalty may be expressed on different brands?

As shown in Table 2, there appeared at first to be no relationship between cohesiveness and similarity among member brand preferences.

TABLE 2   THE RELATIONSHIP BETWEEN COHESIVENESS AND THE BEST LIKED BRAND OF EACH GROUP

Rank Order of Groups from Highest to Lowest in Cohesiveness	Cohesiveness in Mean Lib Scores	Percent Best Liked Brand Chosen by the Group
1	3.00	66.6
2	2.50	65.6
3	2.00	30.9
4	1.90	50.0
5	1.40	25.3
6.5	1.10	28.2
6.5	1.10	29.7
8	1.00	43.7
9	0.90	50.0
10	0.65	34.2

The two groups highest in cohesiveness also had the highest percentage of mutually preferred brands. Group 8 and 9, however, also exhibited high degrees of internal similarity for the best liked brand. As a result, no concrete conclusions could be drawn from these data regarding the importance of cohesiveness in the effectiveness of group influence.

In an attempt to approach the determination of the influence of cohesiveness from a different direction, the collected data were reanalyzed and rearranged as shown in Table 3.

Since it was known that group cohesion and leadership were closely related, Table 3 was revised to include not only the group's best liked brand but also that of the

TABLE 3   COMPARISONS OF BEST LIKED BRANDS OF LEADERS AND GROUPS TO GROUP COHESION

Rank Order of Groups from Highest to Lowest in Cohesiveness	Cohesiveness in Mean Lib Scores	Leader's Best Brand Liked	Percent Best Liked Brand Chosen by Leader	Entire Group's Best Liked Brand	Percent Best Liked Brand Chosen by Group (Leader Excluded)
1	3.0	H	68%	H	56%
2	2.5	M	100	M	48
3	2.0	H	43	H	31
4	1.9	P	83	P	50
5	1.4	H	43	H	25
6.5	1.1	M	37	P	28
6.5	1.1	L	40	H	29
8	1.0	P	43	H	28
9	0.9	M	100	M	50
10	0.6	P	43	M	34

leader's. Notice that in the five most cohesive groups, the preferred brand of the group and the leader were the same. In the five less cohesive groups there was only one occurrence of preference similarity (Group 9).

No relationship was discovered between the degree of cohesiveness and the extent and strength of brand loyalty[3] in the group. In Table 4, for example, two groups ranked low in cohesiveness (8th and 9th) both had as many members brand loyal as the two top ranked groups. Also shown in the table was the fact that the average length of a brand loyalty run varied indiscriminately regardless of cohesiveness.

TABLE 4   THE INFLUENCE OF GROUP COHESIVENESS ON THE EXTENT
OF STRENGTH OF BRAND LOYALTY

Rank Order of Groups from Highest to Lowest in Cohesiveness	Percent of Each Group Brand Loyal	Mean Length of Group's Brand Loyalty Runs
1	100%	8.0
2	100	10.5
3	50	4.0
4	80	7.0
5	60	2.6
6.5	100	5.2
6.5	40	2.6
8	200	9.7
9	100	6.0
10	60	3.6

In this study, cohesiveness appeared to have its most important function in providing an agreeable environment in which informal leaders could effectively operate.

EFFECT OF GROUP LEADERSHIP ON BRAND PREFERENCES

Group leadership, as previously mentioned, was measured in three ways: by attraction, expertness, and position centrality in the communications network. Since each was an independent measurement, it was possible that any or all of them would delineate a different group leader. Table 5 was the result of a cross tabulation of the measurements.

In six of the ten groups, the leader was the same individual regardless of the leadership measurement. In three of the other four groups it was impossible to obtain a meaningful measurement of individual attraction because (1) all of the members were related, or (2) all individuals in the group were liked by each other to about the same degree. The individual from each group ultimately selected as

[3]Brand loyalty has been operationally defined as "three consecutive choices of the same brand."

TABLE 5   COMPARISONS OF THE RESULTS OF THE THREE GROUP
LEADERSHIP MEASUREMENTS*

Group	Individual	A	E	C	Group	Individual	A	E	C
1	1	None	X	X	6	27	X	X	X
	2					33			
	3					40			
	4					28			
	5								
2	6		X	X		26	X	X	X
	7	X				34			
	8					25			
	9					28			
	44					17			
3	11	X	X	X	8	29	X	X	X
	12					35			
	13					30			
	14								
	15								
4	16	None	X		9	42	X	X	X
	10					41			
	36			X		21			
						31			
						32			
5	22	X	X	X	10	19			
	23					20	None	X	X
	24								
	43								
	18								

*Leadership measurements

A = attraction

E = expertness

C = communications centrality.

the leader for purposes of analysis was the member who had the highest average on the three measurements.

In order to substantiate the importance of informal leadership to effective group influence, one must refer back to Table 3. An important aspect of this table was that it indicated a definite relationship between how well the leader preferred his best liked brand and what brand was preferred (including the strength of this preference) by the other members of the group. In other words, regardless of the degree of cohesiveness, the more frequently the leader chose his best liked brand, the higher the likelihood that the rest of the group would prefer that brand more often than expected by chance. For example, in the group ranked ninth in cohesiveness, the leader selected one brand sixteen consecutive times; her fellow group members preferred the same brand 50 percent of the time when it was expected by chance only 25 percent of the time.

Table 6 indicates this relationship even more clearly. Working down the figures in the table, it is seen that the more frequently a leader chose one brand, the higher

TABLE 6   COMPARISONS OF FREQUENCY OF CHOICE OF BEST LIKED BRANDS OF THE LEADER AND MEMBERS OF EACH GROUP

Group Leader's Best Liked Brand	Percent Best Liked Brand Chosen by Leader (Ranked from Highest to Lowest in Percent of Time Chosen	Entire Group's Best Liked Brand	Percent Best Liked Brand Chosen by Group (Leader Excluded)
M	100%	M	50%
M	100	M	48
P	83	P	50
H	68	H	56
P	43	M	34
H	43	H	31
M	43	P	28
H	43	H	25
L	40	H	29
M	37	P	28

the probability that the rest of her group would like and take the same brand. Once the leader's preference for a certain brand dropped below 68 percent, the group's frequency and similarity of brand preference to that of the leader declined rapidly. In the four highest ranked groups, the leaders and members not only preferred the same best liked brand, but preferred them an exceptionally high percentage of the time compared to the rest of the groups. In only two of the six remaining groups did the leaders and other members prefer the same brand, and then only at percentage levels expected by chance.

To further substantiate the hypothesis that group leaders are a key element in understanding how groups influence the behavior of members, the data were analyzed in order to compare the leader's degree of brand loyalty[4] and the percentage of brand loyalty among the other members of the group. Table 7 summarizes the results of this analysis.

[4]While brand loyalty has been operationally defined as three consecutive choices of the same brand, it is logically assumed in this discussion that a person who selected the same brand 16 times in a row has a much higher degree of brand loyalty than an individual who selects the same brand three consecutive times.

TABLE 7   COMPARISON OF THE DEGREE OF BRAND LOYALTY OF THE
GROUP LEADER WITH THE PERCENTAGE OF BRAND LOYALTY
IN THE GROUP

Group Leader's Degree of Brand Loyalty (Length of Longest Consecutive Run of One Brand)	Percent of Group (Excluding Leader) Becoming Brand Loyal (3 Consecutive Choices of One Brand)	Number in Group (n)
16	100%	2
15	100	5
12	75	5
9	100	3
6	100	3
5	100	5
3	50	5
3	25	5
2	45	5
2	55	4
		42

Once the leader's brand loyalty reached a certain degree of strength (5 consecutive times), then the probability was much greater that most of his group would also become brand loyal. Further increases, however, in the leader's degree of brand loyalty had no measurable effect, since 100 percent brand loyalty was the highest that could be obtained.

Summary and Conclusions

The study led to the following tentative conclusions:

First, an analysis of variance test indicated that the informal groups had a definite influence on their members toward conformity behavior with respect to brands of bread preferred. At the same time, there was no significant preference shown for any one of the four brands used in the study. Interaction between the groups and brands was found not to be significant.

Second, it was hypothesized that the cohesiveness of a group would be an important determinant of the degree of brand loyalty exhibited by members. No statistical significance, however, was found between the level of cohesiveness and the degree of member brand loyalty. Only when cohesiveness and leadership were combined was any relationship with member brand loyalty uncovered. In more cohesive groups, the probability was much higher that the members would prefer the same brand as the group leader. Thus, cohesiveness appeared to have its most important function in providing an agreeable environment in which informal leaders could effectively operate.

Finally, leaders were found to influence fellow group members in two ways. First, the higher the degree of brand loyalty exhibited by a group leader, the more likely were the other members to prefer the same brand. Second, the greater the degree of leader brand loyalty, the higher was the percentage of his group also becoming brand loyal. In other words, the extent and degree of brand loyalty within a group was closely related to the behavior of the informal leader.

Like most exploratory studies of this nature, this experiment had certain inherent limitations—the groups obtained may not have been the ones most relevant to the purchase of bread, the number of groups studied was small, and only one product was used. Similarly, the product itself (bread) was a limiting factor. Susceptibility to group influence probably varies across products with the more conspicuous or socially important products being more susceptible. Also, the influence of the leaders on member brand preferences might be much less in the "real world" where differences do exist among products. If these statements are true, then the product used in this study may have been one which maximized the difficulty of locating and measuring the interpersonal influences of group members. Since in this experiment, the influence of groups (and leaders) was substantiated on such a common and minor purchase as bread, then there is good reason for presuming similar influence on a broad spectrum of consumer behavior. One of its primary values of this type of interdisciplinary study lies in the fact that the results usually lead to interesting and provocative implications, as well as providing new avenues and directions for research. By altering the selection process of the informal groups, and by testing products other than bread, a more thorough understanding of social influence on consumer behavior should be possible.

References

1. W. C. Bonney and C. E. George, *Measurement of Affective Adaptation Residuals,* Technical Report 5 (Office of Naval Research, Agricultural and Mechanical College of Texas), 1961.

2. George Brown, "Brand Loyalty—Fact or Fiction?" *Advertising Age,* 23 (June 9, 1952), 53-5.

3. Ross Cunningham, "Brand Loyalty—What, Where, How Much?" *Harvard Business Review,* 34 (January-February 1956), 116-28.

4. Ronald E. Frank, "Brand Choice as a Probability Process," *Journal of Business,* 35 (January 1962), 43-56.

5. Frank Harvey and Benjamin Lipstein, "The Dynamics of Brand Loyalty: A Markovian Process," *Operations Research,* 10 (January-February 1962), 19-40.

6. George Homans, *Social Behavior: Its Elementary Forms,* New York: Harcourt, Brace and World, Inc., 1961, 118-9.

7. Elihu Katz and P. F. Lazarsfeld, *Personal Influence,* Glencoe, Ill.: The Free Press of Glencoe, 1955.

8. A. A. Kuehn, "Consumer Brand Choice—A Learning Process?" in *Quantitative Techniques in Marketing Analysis,* R. E. Frank, A. A. Kuehn, and W. F. Massy, eds., Homewood, Ill.: Richard D. Irwin, Inc., 1962, 390-403.

9. S. J. Shaw, "Behaviorial Science Offers Fresh Insights on New Product Acceptance," *Journal of Marketing,* 29 (January 1965), 9.

10. W. T. Tucker, "The Development of Brand Loyalty," *Journal of Marketing Research,* 1 (August 1964), 32-5.

16 Influences of Social Class

Social Class and Life Cycle as Predictors of Shopping Behavior

STUART U. RICH *(Marketing Educator)* AND
SUBHASH C. JAIN* *(Marketing Educator)*

Traditionally it has been held that consumer buying behavior can be classified by social class and stage in the family life cycle. But recently it has been suggested that these distinctions have been obscured by the leveling effects of social and economic changes.

From data of an extensive empirical study of women's shopping behavior, the authors suggest that in many instances the earlier market segmentation concept may be outmoded.

This article is concerned with application of concepts of social class and life cycle to consumer shopping behavior for the purposes of segmenting the market. That these concepts help in understanding the consumer is generally accepted. As Martineau said,

The friends we choose, the neighborhoods we live in, the way we spend and save our money, the educational plans we have for our children are determined in large degree along social class lines. A rich man is not just a poor man with more money. He probably has different ideals, different personality forces, different church membership, and many different notions of right and wrong, all largely stemming from social class differentials. With its disciplinary pressures of approval and disapproval, belonging versus ostracism, social class is a major factor shaping the individual's style of life [16].

Source: Steuart U. Rich and Subhash C. Jain, "Social Class and Life Cycle as Predictors of Shopping Behavior," *Journal of Marketing Research,* Vol. 5 (February, 1968), pp. 41-49.

*Stuart U. Rich is professor of marketing, School of Business Administration, University of Oregon. Subhash C. Jain is assistant professor of marketing, School of Business Administration, University of Dayton.

Thus for a marketing program to be effective, it must be designed to reach the social class that fits one's product or service. Similarly, life cycle has been used as an independent variable in analyzing housing needs and uses, income, finances, and the purchase of a standard package of items to be consumed at each stage in life [3].

However, recent changes in social and economic circumstances of consumers—such as increase in discretionary income, leisure time, opportunities for higher education, increasing social benefits, movements to suburbia—have raised some doubts about the effectiveness of social class and life cycle to explain consumer behavior. Several articles [6, 15, 19, 26, 27] in academic and professional journals indicate how people supposedly of different classes tend to resemble each other in the market place. This was also reflected in the *Wall Street Journal*.

It is no news that blue-collar pay is rising. It's not even particularly news that blue-collar workers have been raising their pay somewhat faster than white-collar workers. The extent to which these blue-collar increases have been creating what is in effect a new class blending traditional blue-collar and white-collar spending habits, social customs and ways of thinking, is perhaps not so well realized. But recently this has become the most striking of all blue-collar trends [14, p. 1].

A similar trend has been noted about life cycle. As a J. C. Penney's executive said,

The youth market is influenced by the population explosion, education which teaches reason rather than memorization, sweeping changes in social attitudes. Young people have a "no depression complex," a refreshing honesty and self-effacing humor. They also have a higher level of 'taste achievement. which they have acquired themselves. The youth market is witty, wordly, and has money to spend. This market has influence on all the other markets (parents, young adults, older people who respond to youth) [7].

In summary, the traditional distinctions between the various social classes and stages in the family life cycle seem to be quickly diminishing. The main objective of this article is to report the findings of a study done to test the usefulness of social class and life cycle in understanding consumer behavior during changing socioeconomic conditions.[1] In presenting our findings, other studies and certain statements and assertions will be referred to which our empirical findings support or refute.

Method

The data used in this study were originally collected by one of the authors for a comprehensive work in 1963 on shopping behavior of department store customers [22]. The data consisted of about 4,000 personal and telephone interviews in Cleveland and New York. For this article part of the data was reanalyzed, namely

[1]This study was done for a doctoral dissertation [10].

the results of 1,056 personal interviews with a probability sample representing all women 20 years of age and older residing in the Cleveland standard metropolitan statistical area. In collecting the original data, a random procedure divided this Cleveland area into 19 zones and selected a sample of places—one place in each zone. This random procedure was repeated and a second, independent sample was drawn, providing a replicated probability sample.[2]

The two major variables used here were social class and family life cycle. Social class was stratified by a multiple-item index, Warner's Index of Status Characteristics [28] widely used in social research.[3] In this index Warner had four variables, source of income, occupation, dwelling area, and house type. This index was modified and source of income and house type were replaced with the amount of income and education of family head. Warner originally used source of income only because of the difficulty in obtaining income amount. It has been found that house type, which is mainly a reflection of house value, is mainly dependent on occupation. If house type and occupation were used, occupation would have been weighed very heavily. Therefore, education—also an important determinant of social class—was substituted for house type.

To measure life cycle, the following breakdown was used: under 40 without children, under 40 with children, 40 and over without children, 40 and over with children, This gave a measure of the effects of age, married status, and children in the household—all important determinants of shopping behavior. Using 40 as the dividing point for age indicated whether there were preschool children in the household, another important factor influencing shopping habits [22].

Highlights of the differences in shopping behavior of women in various social classes and stages in the life cycle are described here. Chi-square tests were used to ascertain which of these differences were significant at the .05 level and to determine, for instance, whether social class affected women's interest in fashion and choice of shopping companions.

Factors Affecting Shopping

INTEREST IN FASHION

If traditional distinctions between the women in various social classes and stages of the life cycle are disappearing an indication would be expected in women's interest in fashion. Respondents' interest in fashion was measured from these five statements, each printed on a separate card and handed to the respondent. She was asked to state her preferences, which were noted by the interviewer.

1. I read the fashion news regularly and try to keep my wardrobe up to date with fashion trends.

[2]For a step-by-step description of the research procedure used, including sample design, see "Technical Appendix on Research Methodology" [22].
[3]For a full discussion of different methods of social stratification and how and why we used Warner's Index, see Chapter 2 [10].

2. I keep up to date on all fashion changes although I don't always attempt to dress according to these changes.

3. I check to see what is currently fashionable only when I need to buy some new clothes.

4. I don't pay much attention to fashion trends unless a major change takes place.

5. I am not at all interested in fashion trends.

In Table 1, the fashion interests of the women belonging to various social classes are compared. Fashion plays an important part in the lives of all women regardless of class. Except for the lower-lower class, in which a slightly higher percentage of women than in other classes showed no interest in fashion at all, very small percentages of women among all other classes found fashion uninteresting.

King made essentially the same point, emphasizing the broad appeal of fashion [13]. This finding supports Weiss's remark, "Fashion today is the prerogative of a substantial majority of our population—men, women and children" [29, p. 104]. However, these findings do not entirely agree with the traditional research of Barber and Lobel who found that social class differences determined the definition of women's fashion [1]. Although this was true for knowing fashion changes, it did not apply to keeping the wardrobe up to date, which concerned all women.

TABLE 1   INTEREST IN WOMEN'S FASHIONS BY CLEVELAND WOMEN SHOPPERS, BY SOCIAL CLASS

Statement on Degree of Interest	Social Class[a]					
	L-L	U-L	L-M	U-M	L-U	U-U
Read news regularly and keep wardrobe up to date	14%	8%	9%	10%	19%	9%
Keep abreast of changes but not always follow	19	29	42	50	47	64
Check what is fashionable only if buy new clothes	15	22	15	17	17	9
Only pay attention to major fashion changes	22	23	19	14	14	18
Not at all interested in fashion trends	24	16	12	9	3	—b
Don't know	6	2	3	—	—	—
Total	100%	100%	100%	100%	100%	100%
Number of cases	132	346	265	206	36	11

[a]In this and subsequent tables, L = lower, M = middle, and U = upper.
[b]In this and subsequent tables, a dash represents less than .5 percent.

The present survey also showed that women in different stages of the life cycle did not vary significantly in their fashion interests. For instance, 48 percent of women

40 or over with children either read the fashion news regularly or kept up to date on all fashion trends compared with 50 percent of women under 40 with children. Katz and Lazarsfeld, however, found that interest in fashion declined with the life cycle [12].

Table 2 summarizes the methods that women in various social classes used for following fashion trends. Except for watching television and listening to the radio, where the differences between social classes were not significant, the helpfulness

TABLE 2   METHODS HELPFUL TO CLEVELAND WOMEN ON FASHION TRENDS, BY SOCIAL CLASS

Method	Social Class					
	L-L	U-L	L-M	U-M	L-U	U-U
Going to fashion shows	5%	3%	7%	9%	22%	18%
Reading fashion magazines	14	13	11	23	36	27
Reading other magazines	17	18	26	31	28	46
Reading fashion articles in papers	22	34	46	45	56	64
Looking at newspaper ads	39	57	60	68	67	91
Going shopping	36	50	53	63	75	73
Discussing fashion with others	21	22	29	34	36	46
Observing what others wear	22	36	81	51	58	55
Watching television	32	28	25	26	25	46
Listening to the radio	2	5	5	2	8	—
Don't know	3	1	1	—	—	—
No interest in fashion	30	18	14	10	3	—
Total[a]	243%	285%	358%	362%	414%	466%
Number of cases	132	346	265	206	36	11

[a]Total exceeds 100 percent because of multiple responses.

of the various methods shown in keeping women up to date on fashion changes increased with social class level. The rate of increase varied, however, with different methods. For example, in the category "discussing fashion with others," there was relatively little difference between the lower and middle classes. In "looking at newspaper ads," there was a sharp rise in helpfulness from the lower-lower class to the upper-lower class, but the difference is not particularly significant until the upper-upper class. In summary, the traditional view of greater fashion interest for higher social classes generally holds true for particular methods used to keep informed of fashion, although the increase in interest is seldom in any direct proportion to the increase in social level.

Unlike social class, life cycle did not affect fashion interest. There were no significant differences in the methods used by women in various stages of the family life cycle for being informed of fashion changes.

SOURCES OF SHOPPER INFORMATION

Newspaper ads are an important source of shoppers' information. The degree of helpfulness which women attributed to newspaper advertising was analyzed. Women in various social classes seemed to find newspaper ads helpful to about the same degree, except a slightly greater percentage of women in the lower-lower class found them somewhat more helpful.

Another measure used to study the importance of newspaper ads was to analyze the regularity with which women in different social classes looked at newspaper ads. Here again, women of different status groups showed no significant differences in the regularity of their looking at newspaper ads. These results agreed with findings of a recent study reported in *Editor and Publisher:*

> The daily newspaper's coverage of the market place on the average day is nearly universal. Almost every household, 87%, gets a newspaper. . . . The mass exposure opportunity represented by this high percentage of page opening is remarkably consistent for men and women of all ages, incomes, educational attainments and geographical locations [25].

Carman has reported a similar finding about the importance of newspaper ads as a source of information for members of different social classes [2, p. 29].

Among women in the various stages of the family life cycle, those with children considered the newspaper ads more helpful. For instance, 88 percent of the women 40 and over with children founds ads helpful compared with 73 percent of those without children. Among the women under 40 with and without children, the percentages were 81 and 70, respectively. Further analysis showed that women with children looked at newspaper ads more often than those without children. Age itself had little effect on either the regularity of looking at ads in newspapers or the helpfulness attributed to these ads.

This finding about life cycle differs from what Miller pointed out in 1954,

> The younger housewives are easier to educate to an awareness of product and brand; it is easier to get across to the younger housewives the reasons why they should try it or buy it; and the younger housewives are less fixed in their buying habits and brand loyalty, and will be more inclined to change their buying patterns in response to advertising [17, p. 65].

Again we note that some of the traditional distinctions among the social classes and stages in the family life cycle may be disappearing.

INTERPERSONAL INFLUENCES IN SHOPPING

Interpersonal influences play an important part in shopping deicisions. For practical application to marketing , it is necessary to know who these influencers are for each segment of the market. The traditional view has been that upper classes interacted more with members of the immediate family and put great emphasis on lineage. The middle class, though, was generally considered self-directing, had initiative, and was dependent on themselves and their friends more than on relatives. Like the upper classes, the lower classes depended on relatives and family members more often [8, p. 286]. Our findings differed in some respects from this view.

Tables 3 and 4 present data on the impact of interpersonal influences on shopping decisions under two categories, helpfulness attributed to discussing shopping with

TABLE 3   DISCUSSION OF SHOPPING WITH OTHERS, CLEVELAND WOMEN, BY SOCIAL CLASS

Consider It Helpful With	Social Class[a]		
	Lower	Middle	Upper
Friends	34%	37%	50%
Husband	13	18	24
Mother	5	5	6
Other family members	20	14	18
No one	36	39	32
Total[b]	108%	113%	130%
Number of cases	478	471	47

[a]Significant differences were noted even when we divided the respondents into six social classes. However, to save space here in some instances only three classes are shown.
[b]Total exceeds 100 percent because of multiple responses.

others and persons with whom respondents usually shopped. In both categories, women in various social classes showed no significant difference in the influence of friends on shopping. The husband was slightly more important as a shopping influence for the middle and upper classes than for the lower classes, and children were more likely to be taken on shopping trips by the middle and upper classes. However, mother and other family members were not mentioned to any large extent by the lower classes as traditional research would indicate.

Note also in Table 3 that the proportion of women who attributed no help to discussing shopping with others was not significantly different for the three classes. This does not agree with what Rainwater, Coleman, and Handel said, "the working class largely depended on word-of-mouth recommendation before making major purchases" [21, p. 210].

SHOPPING ENJOYMENT

Most women enjoyed shopping regardless of their social class. However, women in different social classes had varying reasons for enjoying shopping. Some reasons —such as the recreational and social aspects of shopping, seeing new things and

TABLE 4   PERSONS WITH WHOM CLEVELAND WOMEN USUALLY SHOP, BY SOCIAL CLASS

Usually Shop With	Social Class					
	L-L	U-L	L-M	U-M	L-U	U-U
Friends	32%	31%	26%	34%	39%	46%
Husband	20	25	32	35	33	9
Mother	5	7	9	9	3	—
Children	10	15	22	23	28	—
Other family members	21	23	16	10	8	18
No one in particular	26	20	17	22	17	36
Never shops with others	—	2	1	2	—	—
Total[a]	114%	123%	123%	135%	128%	109%
Number of cases	132	346	265	206	36	11

[a] Total exceeds 100 percent because of multiple responses.

getting new ideas, and bargain hunting and comparing merchandise—were mentioned by all social classes without any significant difference. Another reason, namely acquiring new clothes or household things, was more enjoyable for the two lower classes. However, a pleasant store atmosphere, display, and excitement were specified as reasons for enjoying shopping by a greater proportion of the women in the upper-middle, lower-upper, and upper-upper classes. Stone and Form found that enjoyment in shopping was not a function of social status [24]. This was in accord with our general finding on shopping enjoyment although, as just noted, the reasons for enjoyment sometimes varied among social classes.

Life cycle did not have any effect on the enjoyment of shopping for clothing and household items. For instance, 38 percent of the women over 40 with children enjoyed shopping for such reasons as pleasant store atmosphere, displays, and excitement compared with 36 percent in this age group without children. For women under 40 without children, the percentages were 37 and 41, respectively.

Stone and Form claimed that younger women with children enjoyed shopping more than other women. In this study, neither age nor the presence of children in the family seemed to make any difference for women in their enjoyment of shopping.

SHOPPING FREQUENCY

The frequency with which women shopped during the year was significantly associated with social class. For example, 38 percent of the women in the upper class and 34 percent in the middle class shopped 52 or more times a year compared with 24 percent in the lower class. These findings do not match those of Stone and Form. According to them, women in either the upper or the middle class shopped less often than women in the lower or working class.

Younger women shopped more often than older women, but presence of children did not make any significant difference within the two age groups (Table 5). Stone and Form found the frequency of shopping trips mainly dependent on children in the family.

TABLE 5   FREQUENCY OF SHOPPING TRIPS OF CLEVELAND WOMEN, BY LIFE CYCLE

| Times Per Year | Stage in Life Cycle | | | |
| | Under 40 | | 40 and Over | |
	No Child	Child	No Child	Child
52 or more	30%	30%	25%	31%
24 to 51	33	25	17	20
12 to 23	23	28	18	21
6 to 11	2	4	6	7
1 to 5	12	12	27	21
Less than once	—	—	2	—
Never	—	—	1	—
Don't know	—	1	4	—
Total	100%	100%	100%	100%
Number of cases	66	474	240	276

IMPORTANCE OF SHOPPING QUICKLY

The higher the social status of a woman, the more she considered it important to shop quickly. Thus, 39 percent of upper class women regarded it important to always shop quickly, though only 30 percent in the lower class and 34 percent in the middle class did. Only 10 percent of upper class women felt it was not important to shop quickly compared with 19 percent and 29 percent in the middle and lower classes, respectively. According to Stone and Form, however, the upper and lower classes spent more time shopping than did the middle class. Huff found that women of high social status spent the most time on an average shopping trip [9].

For life cycle, Stone and Form found that women in their forties felt most hurried, and women in their twenties were divided evenly between those who felt they had adequate time and those who did not. In their study age was found to be the determining factor of the importance of shopping quickly. In this study, women under and over 40 with children put more stress on quick shopping than those without children. These findings thus show different behavior patterns about the importance of shopping quickly.

BROWSING

Tendency to browse without buying anything was more prominent among the upper-lower (41 percent), lower-middle (44 percent), and upper-middle (42 percent) classes. Yet women in the lower-lower, lower-upper, and upper-upper classes mentioned it less often (Table 6). Stone and Form discovered that lower class women did more browsing than middle and upper class women, a finding obviously different from this study's.

TABLE 6   BROWSING OF CLEVELAND WOMEN, BY SOCIAL CLASS

Regularity of Occurrence	Social Class					
	L-L	*U-L*	*L-M*	*U-M*	*L-U*	*U-U*
Regularly or fairly often	29%	41%	44%	42%	22%	18%
Once in awhile	30	37	35	36	31	27
Never	40	21	20	22	44	55
Don't know	1	1	1	—	3	—
Total	100%	100%	100%	100%	100%	100%
Number of cases	132	346	265	206	36	11

Further, women under 40 with or without children, browsed more (24 percent and 22 percent, respectively) than women 40 and over (12 percent for those with and without children); but Stone and Form did not find the life cycle to have any relationship here. Again, traditional distinctions among the various social classes and stages in the family life cycle may be changing.

DOWNTOWN SHOPPING

Several authors have reported how the continued expansion of the shopping centers has challenged the traditional role of the downtown area [5, 11, 23]. In this study, the lower the social status, the greater the proportion of downtown shopping (Table 7). Sixty-eight percent of lower-lower class women were desig-

TABLE 7   SHOPPING DONE DOWNTOWN BY CLEVELAND WOMEN, BY SOCIAL CLASS

Proportion of Downtown Shopping[a]	Social Class					
	L-L	*U-L*	*L-M*	*U-M*	*L-U*	*U-U*
High	68%	50%	42%	33%	22%	18%
Low	19	33	37	50	59	64
None	11	15	19	15	16	18
Don't know	2	2	2	2	3	—
Total	100%	100%	100%	100%	100%	100%
Number of cases	132	346	265	206	36	11

[a] High downtown shoppers shop downtown half or more of the time; Low downtown shoppers, one-quarter or less of the time;
None means women who do not shop downtown.

nated as high downtown shoppers, only 22 percent of the lower-upper class and 18 percent of the upper-upper class were considered to be so. This finding is different from that reported in *Workingman's Wife*, "A comparison between the shopping of middle class women and working class women shows the provinciality of the latter. Fewer working class than middle class women classify themselves as 'regular shoppers' in the central business districts" [21, p. 21]. Thus there is a change in downtown clientele. Once the upper class shopped downtown more often; now it may be the lower classes who patronize downtown more.

This also suggests that suburban shopping centers are becoming increasingly more important for the upper classes. This has been noted in *Women's Wear Daily*, "It is a mistake to promote just $25 dresses in a suburban store. . . . We have found, from experience, that higher price clothes do sell in depth in the suburbs" [20, p. 40].

Cross tabulations by life cycle showed a tendency for young people to patronize shopping centers more than older people, as suggested by other findings.

No significant differences on downtown shopping existed among the women in the various social classes living in the city. However, among the suburbanites, social class was inversely related to downtown shopping. For instance, among the city dwellers about 60 percent of the women in the two lower and two middle classes were ranked as high downtown shoppers. Yet, among the out-of-city residents 43 percent of lower-lower class women and 37 percent of upper-lower class were considered high in-town shoppers; only 32 percent in the lower-middle and 27 percent in the upper-middle class were high downtown shoppers. The percentages for the two upper classes further decreased to 22 percent and 18 percent, respectively.

In contrast, about 70 percent of the women in the two upper classes (living in the suburbs) were low downtown shoppers, though the same percentage was 29 percent for the lower-lower class and 40 percent for the upper-lower class. However, when the high and low categories were considered together and compared with the "none" group, downtown shopping by suburbanites increased in each higher social class.

In general, a greater proportion of higher class women shop downtown, but women in the lower classes appear to shop more intensively in the central business district.

TYPE OF STORE PREFERRED

As seen in Table 8, higher class women more often named the regular department store as their favorite. The department store maintained a broad image as a favorite store since 51 percent of the lower-lower class women and 60 percent of the upper-lower class designated it their favorite store. A greater percentage of lower-lower (14 percent) and upper-lower (11 percent) women favored the discount store than did women in either the middle or upper classes.

TABLE 8   KIND OF FAVORITE STORE OF CLEVELAND WOMEN, BY
SOCIAL CLASS

Kind of Store	Social Class					
	L-L	U-L	L-M	U-M	L-U	U-U
Regular department	51%	60%	77%	83%	88%	91%
Discount department	14	11	6	2	—	9
Variety and junior department	2	6	6	5	—	—
Mail order	9	14	5	2	3	—
Medium to low specialty	2	2	1	—	6	—
Neighborhood	11	2	1	1	3	—
Others	11	5	4	7	—	—
Total	100%	100%	100%	100%	100%	100%
Number of cases	132	346	265	206	36	11

Several writers have emphasized that women in various social classes differ in
the department stores they patronize and have different expectations about each
store [4, 16, 18]. Therefore, the authors looked at the particular stores which
women named as their favorites among the different regular department stores.
Three department stores in Cleveland were mentioned far more often than others,
and these were called a high fashion, a price appeal, or a broad appeal store.

As shown in Table 9, the high fashion store became more important for each

TABLE 9   KIND OF DEPARTMENT STORE FAVORED BY CLEVELAND
WOMEN

Kind of Department Store	Social Class					
	L-L	U-L	L-M	U-M	L-U	U-U
High fashion store	4%	7%	22%	34%	70%	67%
Price appeal store	74	63	36	24	19	18
Broad appeal store	22	30	42	42	11	15
Total	100%	100%	100%	100%	100%	100%
Number of cases	67	208	204	71	32	10

higher class. But, the price appeal store was inversely related to social class. The
broad appeal store was mentioned by the two middle classes more often. These
findings generally agreed with what Martineau discovered.

The blue collar individual, as his family income goes up, proceeds from cars to
appliances to home ownership to apparel. He and his family are candidates for
almost any store, and the most successful stores which would traditionally appeal
to them have held them by steadily trading up, both in merchandise, store facilities

and their image. . . . The point again is that this person has changed. He is not the same guy. He has long since satisfied his needs and wants and now he is interested in satisfying his wishes [15, p. 56].

The high preference of the lower class shoppers for the regular department stores is therefore not surprising.

The kind of department store women in the various social classes mentioned most often was also analyzed for the following kinds of merchandise: women's better dresses; house dresses and underwear; children's clothing; men's socks and shirts; furniture; large appliances; towels, sheets, blankets and spreads; and small electrical appliances and kitchen utensils. Here again the two upper classes specified the high fashion store as their favorite for the first five of these eight kinds of merchandise. Women in the two lower classes shopped at the price appeal store most of the time for all items.

Analysis of the favorite store of women in various stages of the life cycle showed that the regular department store ranked high among all women except that younger women with children showed somewhat less preference for it. Table 10 shows that 57 percent of the younger women with children and 65 percent of the

TABLE 10   KIND OF FAVORITE STORE OF CLEVELAND WOMEN, BY LIFE CYCLE

Kind of Favorite Store	Stage in Life Cycle			
	Under 40		40 and over	
	No Child	Child	No Child	Child
Department	65%	57%	83%	79%
Discount	9	13	2	2
Mail order	5	11	2	7
All others	21	19	13	12
Total	100%	100%	100%	100%
Number of cases	66	474	240	276

of the younger women without children mentioned the regular department store as their favorite. Discount stores were preferred by the younger women a little more than by the older ones. No significant differences were revealed between the types of stores favored by women in various stages of the family life cycle for the eight kinds of merchandise individually.

Conclusion

Socioeconomic changes in income, education, leisure time, and movement to suburbia cut across traditional class lines and various stages in the life cycle. Some authors like Rainwater, Coleman, and Handel have found social class a significant factor in determining consumer behavior [21]. However, recent writings seem to indicate that social class distinctions have been obscured by rising incomes and educational levels [14, 15].

Our empirical findings tend to support the second viewpoint. The random sampling procedure used assured every Cleveland woman 20 years of age or older an equal chance of being selected, and interviewer bias was closely controlled. Hence, we are able to generalize about shopping behavior in Cleveland. Admittedly, all findings cannot be applied to women in other cities. However, in the original study, which included Cleveland and New York-northeastern New Jersey metropolitan areas, many patterns of shopping behavior for women in particular income or life cycle categories were almost identical in the two areas despite the contrasting patterns of size, geographical location, demography, and kinds of stores found in these two cities [22].

Spot checks made of Cleveland and New York women in the present study again produced similar results. For instance, among women under 40 with children in Cleveland, 30 percent shopped 52 or more times per year compared with 34 percent for this group in New York. For women 40 and over with children, the percentages were 31 and 30 for the two cities. On the importance of being able to shop quickly, 30 percent of the lower social class women in Cleveland felt this was always important, as did 34 percent of the middle class women and 39 percent of the upper class women. In New York these percentages were 29, 36, and 39, respectively. In other words, there seems to be evidence that many of the shopping behavior patterns of Cleveland women exist in other cities.

The findings thus question the usefulness of life cycle and social class concepts in understanding consumer behavior in view of recent changes in income, education, leisure time, movement to suburbia, and other factors. Students of marketing and store executives may need to reconsider how far these sociological concepts should be used for segmentation purposes and what their probable impact will be on marketing policies and programs.

References

1. Bernard Barber and Lyle S. Lobel, "Fashion in Women's Clothes and the American Social System," *Social Forces,* 31 (December 1952), 124-31.

2. James M. Carman, *The Application of Social Class in Market Segmentation,* Berkeley, Calif.: University of California, 1965.

3. Lincoln Clark, ed., *The Life Cycle and Consumer Behavior,* Vol. 2, New York: New York University Press, 1955.

4. Richard P. Coleman, "The Significance of Social Stratification in Selling," in Martin L. Bell, ed., *Marketing: A Maturing Discipline,* Chicago: American Marketing Association, December 1960, 177.

5. Thomas Lea Davidson, *Some Effects of the Growth of Planned and Controlled Shopping Centers on Small Retailers,* Washington, D. C.: Small Business Administration, 1960.

6. Editors of *Fortune, Market for the Sixties,* New York: Harper and Row, 1960.

7. "Experts Set Youth Market Guidelines," *Women's Wear Daily,* 113 (October 18, 1966), 19.

8. August B. Hollingshead, "Class Differences in Family Stability," in Reinhard Bendix and Seymour Martin Lipset, eds., *Class, Status and Power,* New York: The Free Press, 1965.

9. David L. Huff, "Geographical Aspects of Consumer Behavior," *University of Washington Business Review,* 18 (June 1959), 27-35.

10. Subhash Jain, "A Critical Analysis of Life Cycle and Social Class Concepts in Understanding Consumer Shopping Behavior," Unpublished doctoral dissertation, University of Oregon, 1966.

11. C. T. Johanssen, *The Shopping Center Versus Downtown,* Columbus, Ohio: The Ohio State University, 1955.

12. Elihu Katz and Paul F. Lazarsfeld, *Personal Influence,* Glencoe, Ill.: The Free Press, 1955, 263-8.

13. Charles W. King, "Fashion Adoption: A Rebuttal to the Trickle Down Theory," *Proceedings,* Summer Conference, American Marketing Association, June 1964, 108-25.

14. Frederick C. Klein, "Rising Pay Lifts More Blue Collar Men into a New Affluent Class," *The Wall Street Journal,* 165 (April 5, 1965).

15. Pierre Martineau, "Customer Shopping Center Habits Change Retailing," *Editor & Publisher,* 96 (October 26, 1963), 16, 56.

16. *Motivation in Advertising,* New York: McGraw-Hill Book Company, 1957, 166-7.

17. Donald L. Miller, "The Life Cycle and the Importance of Advertising," in Lincoln Clark, ed., *The Life Cycle and Consumer Behavior,* Vol. 2, New York: New York University Press, 1955.

18. Vance Packard, *The Status Seekers,* New York: Pocket Books, Inc., 1961, 113.

19. Peter G. Peterson, "Conventional Wisdom and the Sixties," *Journal of Marketing, 26* (April 1962), 63-5.

20. Trudy Prokop, "Jack Weiss: No Gambler, But a Man of Decision," *Women's Wear Daily,* 113 (November 28, 1966), 40.

21. Lee Rainwater, Richard Coleman, and Gerald Handel, *Workingman's Wife,* New York: MacFadden-Bartell Corp., 1962.

22. Stuart U. Rich, *Shopping Behavior of Department Store Customers,* Boston, Mass.: Division of Research, Graduate School of Business Administration, Harvard University, 1963.

23. George Sternlieb, *The Future of the Downtown Department Store,* Cambridge, Mass.: Harvard University, 1962.

24. Gregory P. Stone and William H. Form, *The Local Community Clothing Market: A Study of the Social and Social Psychological Contexts of Shopping,* East Lansing, Mich.: Michigan State University, 1957, 20.

25. "Survey Proves High Exposure for Ads on Newspaper Pages," *Editor & Publisher,* 97 (October 3, 1964), 17-8.

26. Thayer C. Taylor, "Selling Where the Money Is," *Sales Management,* 91 (October 18, 1963), 37-41, 122, 124, 126.

27. ———, "The I AM ME Consumer," *Business Week,* (December 23, 1961), 38-39.

28. W. Lloyd Warner, M. Meeker, and K. Eells, *Social Class in America,* Chicago: Social Research, Inc., 1949.

29. Edward B. Weiss, "The Revolution in Fashion Distribution," *Advertising Age,* 34 (June 24, 1963), 104-5.

17 Influences of Role

Homemaker Living Patterns and Marketplace Behavior— A Psychometric Approach*

CLARK L. WILSON** *(Psychologist)*

This is a study of the patterns of daily behavior, interests, and opinions of housewives. The relationship of these patterns to their purchasing habits of various classes of products and media exposure was studied. The results indicate that certain nondemographic variables significantly increase our ability to account for variations in these activities.

Introduction

It is a demonstrable fact that no single product or service is sold to everyone. At least, no such product has been identified to date.

Even if a product can be cited that sells to almost everyone, it is still a good bet that it would not be used in even approximately equal amounts by all households or users. If we divide the using group into two equal halves—the heavier-using half and the lighter-using half—we will find that the average heavy-user consumes from three to ten times as much as the light.

Source: Clark L. Wilson, "Homemaker Living Patterns and Marketplace Behavior—a Psychometric Approach," in John S. Wright and Jac L. Goldstucker, Editors, *New Ideas for Successful Marketing* (Chicago: American Marketing Association, 1966), pp. 305-336.

*I am happy to acknowledge the support of Batten, Barton, Durstine & Osborn, Inc. (BBDO). This study was begun and all the data were collected while the writer was Vice President, Research, at that agency. The analysis and reporting were completed while the writer was Ford Foundation Visiting Professor at Harvard University, Graduate School of Business Administration and a consultant to BBDO. The support of the Ford Foundation and Harvard Business School are also gratefully acknowledged.

**Clark L. Wilson was Ford Foundation Visiting Professor, Harvard Business School at the time of doing this research.

Consequently, it is an axiom that the more one knows about his customers the more effectively he can market a product.

This study is aimed at that objective of developing better and more complete methods of consumer description. It goes beyond that basic objective and tries to demonstrate the potential practical value of such descriptions.

Succinctly, the basic hypotheses under investigation are two:

(1) People (in this study, housewives) live according to established behavior and attitude patterns which can be *identified* and *measured*.

(2) These Living Patterns, in turn, are related to other behaviors of more direct economic importance, such as product purchase and media exposure so that knowledge of such Living Patterns over and above knowledge of demographic characteristics, can be of economic value in marketing management.

The Study

A 13-page questionnaire was sent to 600 women in August 1963. These women were members of a regular commercial mail panel maintained by the Home Testing Institute, Manhassett, New York.

Four hundred eighty questionnaires were returned (80% of those mailed out) and of this number 466 were fully usable. That part of the questionnaire of concern here consisted of 157 questions on everyday behavior. The general type of question will become evident in the results which follow. To each question the housewife was asked to respond with a "Yes," "?," or "No."

Factor analysis was the method used to identify the dimensions (or scales) measured by these questions.

Results

To look at the results of the study, an examination of Table 1 will serve to illustrate some basic concepts and explain some additional terms.

Table 1 contains three columns of information: "Item" and "% Answering 'Yes'" are, respectively, verbatim reportings of the original items in the questionnaire and the percentage of respondents who checked the "Yes" response. The final column, "Scale Loading," presents the results of the factor analysis.

It will be remembered that through the process of factor analysis a series of items or questions are identified which tend to form a common pattern and along which people vary in a common way. Since, quite logically, not all questions are identical, it follows that they do not all measure the basic underlying dimension to the same degree. Factor analysis provides a "loading" which is a numerical quantity ranging from −1.00 to +1.00. The higher the positive *loading* the more the particular question indicates the underlying dimension. Negative loadings are interpreted in the reverse.

TABLE 1   SCALE 1 - COMMUNITY MINDEDNESS[a]

Item	% Answering "Yes"	Scale Loading
I like to work on community projects.	45%	.60
I am an active member of more than one service organization.	20	.58
I like to organize community projects.	18	.58
One of my favorite community activities is working with boys and girls in Scouting or other group activities.	30	.52
I do volunteer work for a hospital or service organization on a fairly regular basis.	18	.50
I go to the women's club, church ladies' group or some other women's group which meets regularly.	50	.46
I have helped to collect money for the Red Cross or United Fund or March of Dimes.	58	.43
One of the duties of American women is to take an active part in community activities.	72	.42
I have personally worked in a public campaign or for a candidate or an issue.	22	.39
I am active in the PTA.	29	.37

[a] Number of Items: 10
Average Score: 3.9
Estimated Reliability: .72

The maximum possible loading of +1.00 means, "This item unequivocally is the dimension." In practical work with factor analysis, loadings that high never appear. Generally, a loading of .40 or up is considered to be quite healthy and one over .50 to be strong. In this study the writer has generally adopted a loading of .30 as a minimum acceptable. In short, then, the higher the "loading" the more that particular question defines the basic dimension being measured.

As noted, this particular scale is called "Community Mindedness." The process of giving a label to a dimension through factor analysis is a highly subjective proposition. Essentially, the person conducting the research puts a label on the results that, to him, best typifies the common variance or sense that seems to underlie the various items in the scale.

Looking at the first five items which have loadings of .50 or higher, one sees a rather consistent community and service dimension running through them. These dimensions do not appear to be violated in the other items with lower loadings. Therefore, in general, it appears to be fairly reasonable to identify this particular scale as "Community Mindedness."

It will be noticed that at the bottom of the table appears "Estimated Reliability: .72" This is a reasonably precise statistical term which actually carries much of the same meaning given it in everyday language. It may be thought of it as stability or consistency. In short, it is the extent to which the scale would likely give consistent results as it is used from time to time. Another way of saying it is that *reliability* indicates the extent to which the measurements are free from chance errors or error variance. A *reliability of .72 indicates that 72% of the variance measured by the scale is true or consistent variance and 28% of it is just a matter of chance.*

The reason reliability is important is that if one tries to relate the measurements on a scale to any other kind of behavior—in this case marketplace behavior—he must have some sort of stability in the measurements he makes. If a scale of measurements were completely unreliable it would, by definition, be impossible to relate the scores obtained on that scale to any other kind of behavior. Thus, to make progress toward the basic goals of this study one needs at least some scales of adequate reliability.

Tables 2 through 13 show some of the better defined scales obtained in the study. In each case only a few of the leading items are presented. At the bottom of each table the number of items in the full scale are given.

TABLE 2   SCALE 2 - HAPPY HOUSEKEEPER[a]

Item	% Answering "Yes"	Scale Loading
I really enjoy cleaning my house.	70%	.65
I really like most forms of housework.	68	.65
My idea of housecleaning is "once over lightly."	10	−.50
My husband compliments me on the way I run the house.	57	.45
Keeping my home nice satisfies my creative needs.	70	.44

[a]Number of Items: 7
Average Score: 4.1
Estimated Reliability: .75

The items in Scale 2 appear to consistently describe someone who is positively disposed to keep her house in a neat and orderly manner and to enjoy it.

There is a negative loading for the item, "My idea of housecleaning is once over lightly," with a loading of −.50. It should be kept in mind that the "Yes" responses on these scales are being scored. The results here indicate that the "Yes" response to the third item is actually the *opposite* in meaning to the "Yes" responses on the other items. The basic thrust of this item is in the opposite direction from the other

TABLE 3   SCALE 3 - FASHION CONSCIOUS[a]

Item	% Answering "Yes"	Scale Loading
I dress for comfort, not for fashion.	67%	−.56
I usually have at least one outfit that is the very latest style.	49	.54
I enjoy trying the latest style in hair-do's.	12	.52
Dressing smartly is an important part of my life.	58	.50
Fashion in clothes is more important than comfort to me.	9	.50

[a]Number of Items: 10
Average Score: 3.6
Estimated Reliability: .75

TABLE 4   SCALE 4 - "SPECIAL" SHOPPER[a]

Item	% Answering "Yes"	Scale Loading
I shop for specials.	77%	.66
I study the food ads each week so I can make the best buy.	77	.66
I watch the advertisements for announcements of sales.	86	.64
When I find a coupon in the paper, I usually clip it and redeem it the next time I go shopping.	59	.48

[a]Number of Items: 4
Average Score: 2.4
Estimated Reliability: .41

190

TABLE 5   SCALE 5 - LOYAL VS. VENTURESOME SHOPPER[a]

Item	% Answering "Yes"	Scale Loading
I keep away from brands I never heard of.	49%	.60
As a rule I don't buy new products until I hear something about them from people who have tried them.	42	.57
Once I have made a choice on brands I am likely to use it regularly without trying any others.	49	.56
I enjoy trying new products before other people do.	67	−.34
To me, half the fun of shopping is in trying new things.	65	−.31

[a]Number of Items: 5
Average Score: 0.1
Estimated Reliability: .65

TABLE 6   SCALE 6 - CHILD ORIENTED[a]

Item	% Answering "Yes"	Scale Loading
I spend a lot of time with my children talking about their activities, friends and problems.	82%	.57
I take a lot of time and effort to teach my children good habits.	81	.54
I try to arrange my home for my children's convenience.	74	.46
When my children are ill in bed, I drop most everything else in order to see to their comfort.	81	.43

[a]Number of Items: 7
Average Score: 6.1
Estimated Reliability: .72

TABLE 7   SCALE 7 - SPORTS SPECTATOR[a]

Item	% Answering "Yes"	Scale Loading
I follow the baseball results in the paper.	24%	.67
I read the sports section of the paper.	26	.65
I like to watch or listen to baseball or football games.	40	.65

[a]Number of Items: 6
Average Score: 1.9
Estimated Reliability: .66

TABLE 8   SCALE 8 - ARTS ENTHUSIAST[a]

Item	% Answering "Yes"	Scale Loading
I enjoy going to concerts.	36%	.60
I enjoy going through an art gallery.	51	.58
I enjoy listening to classical records.	58	.56
I spend some leisure time in museums.	25	.47

[a]Number of Items: 6
Average Score: 2.3
Estimated Reliability: .65

TABLE 9   SCALE 9 - ACTIVE ATHLETE[a,b]

Item	% Answering "Yes"	Scale Loading
I used to bowl, play tennis or golf or other active sports quite often.	48%	.49
I was active in sports when I was in school.	48	.37
I go bowling often.	9	.33

[a]Number of Items: 5
Average Score: 1.9
Estimated Reliability: .41
[b]Note that this scale is separate from Scale 7, Sports Spectator. This one involves active participation while number 7 represents a more passive interest.

TABLE 10   SCALE 10 - WEIGHT WATCHER[a]

Item	% Answering "Yes"	Scale Loading
I have gone on a strict diet to control my weight one or more times.	44%	.69
I have bought Metrecal or other diet supplements for myself.	29	.68
I take advantage of low calorie foods to help me and/or my family keep our weight down.	46	.57
I definitely watch what I eat to keep my weight down.	44	.46

[a]Number of Items: 4
Average Score: 1.8
Estimated Reliability: .71

TABLE 11   SCALE 15 - BEAUTY CONSCIOUS [a]

Item	% Answering "Yes"	Scale Loading
I nearly always wear nail polish and have several different shades to go with my clothes.	16%	.76
I nearly always wear nail polish.	23	.68
I have several different shades of lipstick to go with different dresses.	44	.36
I use eye shadow three times a week or more.	10	.33

[a]Number of Items: 4
Average Score: 0.9
Estimated Reliability: .72

TABLE 12   SCALE 17 - ENERGETIC[a]

Item	% Answering "Yes"	Scale Loading
I have a lot of energy.	53%	.60
I am able to work for long periods of time without feeling tired.	48	.60
I often wonder where others get all the energy they seem to have.	64	−.53

[a]Number of Items: 4
Average Score: 0.2
Estimated Reliability: .61

TABLE 13   SCALE 19 - BUTTERFLY[a]

Item	% Answering "Yes"	Scale Loading
I have to entertain frequently in order to repay the invitations I get.	27%	.43
I go out to lunch with my friends quite often.	18	.39
I go to the beauty parlor nearly every week.	14	.32
I often buy products or brands just on impulse.	40	.31

[a]Number of Items: 4
Average Score: 1.0
Estimated Reliability: .34

items in the scale. So, a "No" response apparently measures the same dimension in the same direction as a "Yes" to the other items. This can be observed to be the possible reason that only 10 per cent of the sample of housewives answered "Yes" to this response. Negative loadings are encountered from time to time and are a help in interpreting the results.

It should be noted that each scale is numbered and there are missing numbers. Altogether there were 20 such scales. In the interest of time only some of the stronger scales (in terms of reliability and/or length) have been presented here. The others are fully described in the basic study monograph (Wilson, 1966). They are also referred to in the tables which follow.

One question that will be in the minds of marketing researchers is, "Do these kinds of scales really measure anything different from demographics?" Of course, the answer depends somewhat on what one includes in demographics. If such things as age, income, family size, place of residence and the like are included, Table 14 will answer the question.

TABLE 14   PERCENT OF VARIANCE IN LIVING PATTERN SCALES
ACCOUNTED FOR BY DEMOGRAPHIC CHARACTERISTICS

Scale Number	Name	% Total Variance Estimated True (Reliability)	% Total Variance Accounted for by Demographic Characteristics
(Col. 1)	(Col. 2)	(Col. 3)	(Col. 4)
1	Community Mindedness	72%	43%
2	Happy Housekeeper	75	8
3	Fashion Conscious	75	4
4	"Special" Shopper	41	3
5	Loyal vs. Venturesome Shopper	65	3
6	Child Oriented	72	3
7	Sports Spectator	66	5
8	Arts Enthusiast	65	10
9	Active Athlete	41	6
10	Weight Watcher	71	8
11	Phlegmatic	23	11
12	Church Goer	67	23
13	Routine Minded	69	2
14	Budget Minded	68	6
15	Beauty Conscious	72	8
16	Modern Family Manager	70	19
17	Energetic	61	3
18	"Dress for Husband" Oriented	58	1
19	Butterfly	34	5
20	Undefined	40	21

In this table, Column 3 shows the reliability coefficients which are equivalent to percentage estimates of the true variance being measured. Conceptually, this may also be considered as the maximum amount of variance any other independent variable or set of variables might account for if one considered each Living Pattern as the dependent variable. In Column 4 is the maximum multiple R^2 obtained from a regression on each Living Pattern variable using a set of 13 demographic characteristics as independent variables.

As will be seen, the overlap is relatively small in most instances. In the case of Scale 1, Community Mindedness, the demographic variable obtained by counting the number of clubs a woman said she belonged to, accounted for 42 out of the

43 per cent of the figure in Column 4. The same variable accounted for most of the relationship with Scale 12, Church Goer.

Of particular interest may be the very low 3 per cent overlap between Scale 6, Child Oriented, and demographics. Number of children in the family did not account for much of the variance in the Child Oriented Scale.

REPORTED PURCHASING BEHAVIOR

Now we will see if these scores are of a *practical* significance by looking at the amount of information they give us, over and above demographic measurements in relation to *homemakers' reported purchasing of products.*

The method of presenting the results is in terms of variance accounted for. In this case, it is a matter of the variance in purchasing levels that can be accounted for by demographic characteristics *alone* versus demographic characteristics *plus* Living Pattern scale scores.

In addition to the amount of variance in purchasing accounted for by each of the two sets of variables, the reader will find a list of the principal variables, both demographic and Living Pattern, that account for most of the variance. Table 15 shows the results on soft drinks. Tables 16 through 21 show the results for a few of the 23 product classes studied.

TABLE 15   SOFT DRINK CONSUMPTION (By Homemaker Personally)

Percentage of Variance Explained:

By Demographics <u>Only</u>	6%
By Demographics plus Living Patterns	12

Principal Variables Contributing:

<u>Demographic:</u>	#21 (+) Family Size
	31 (+) Husband's Education
	34 (+) Inner-Outer Market
<u>Living Patterns:</u> Scale	# 2 (+) Happy Housekeeper
	8 (−) Arts Enthusiast
	16 (−) Modern Family Manager

Table 15 refers to reported soft drink consumption by the homemaker herself. She is not asked about her family as a whole. Among this sample of women, 6 per cent of the variance in personal soft drink consumption can be explained by demographic characteristics alone. It should be remembered, again, that children are not included in these data. If they were one might expect that *age* of children would account for a great deal more than 6 per cent of the variance. However, in contrast to the 6 per cent for demographics the addition of Living Patterns increases the explained variance to 12 per cent. The first reaction of some people will be that even by including Living Patterns there is not much variance. However, lest

TABLE 16   LIPSTICK PURCHASE

Percentage of Variance Explained:

By Demographics Only	11%
By Demographics plus Living Patterns	29

Principal Variables Contributing:

Demographic:		#24 (+) Number of Teens (Age 10 to 19)
		25 (+) Income
		31 (+) Husband's Age
Living Patterns:	Scale	1 (−) Community Minded
		3 (+) Fashion Conscious
		6 (+) Children Oriented
		9 (+) Active Athlete
		15 (+) Beauty Conscious
		18 (−) "Dress for Husband" Oriented
		19 (+) Butterfly

TABLE 17   KITCHEN FLOOR WAX USAGE

Percentage of Variance Explained:

By Demographics Only	3%
By Demographics plus Living Patterns	10

Principal Variables Contributing:

Demographic:		#24 (+) Number of Teens (Age 10-19) in the Home
Living Patterns:	Scale	5 (−) Loyal vs. Venturesome Shopper[a]
		6 (+) Children Oriented
		7 (−) Sports Spectator
		9 (+) Active Athlete

[a]Venturesome shoppers buy more of product.

TABLE 18   STOMACH REMEDY USAGE

Percentage of Variance Explained:

    By Demographics Only   3%

    By Demographics plus Living Patterns   8

Principal Variables Contributing:

Demographic:	None	
Living Patterns:	Scale	11 (+) Phlegmatic
		14 (+) Budget Minded

TABLE 19   NUMBER OF WASH LOADS PER WEEK

Percentage of Variance Explained:

    By Demographics Only   27%

    By Demographics plus Living Patterns   33

Principal Variables Contributing:

Demographic:	#21 (+) Family Size	
	27 (+) Number of Cars	
	32 (+) Husband's Age	
Living Patterns:	Scale	6 (+) Child Oriented
		88 (−) Arts Interest
		9 (+) Active Athlete
		16 (−) Modern Family Manager

TABLE 20   KITCHEN AND BATHROOM CLEANSER USAGE

Percentage of Variance Explained:

    By Demographics Only   3%

    By Demographics plus Living Patterns   10

Principal Variables Contributing:

Demographic:	None	
Living Patterns:	Scale	2 (+) Happy Housekeeper
		5 (−) Loyal vs. Venturesome Shopper[a]
		9 (+) Active Athlete

[a]Venturesome shoppers buy more of the product.

198

TABLE 21   WINE PURCHASE

Percentage of Variance Explained:	
By Demographics <u>Only</u>	17%
By Demographics plus Living Patterns	22

Principal Variables Contributing:	
<u>Demographic</u>:	#25 (+) Income
	32 (+) Husband's Education
	33 (+) Market Size
<u>Living Patterns</u>:	None

he go too far, the reader should be reminded that demographics alone, on which researchers have relied so heavily in the past, account for less. It will be shown later that as one approaches 30 per cent of variance accounted for, the pay-off may become quite practical.

MEDIA

To the marketing manager a medium is, of course, a channel of communication to customers or prospects through which advertising messages can be transmitted.

In the past the principal manner of solving the problem of selecting the most efficient media has been to obtain a profile of the demographic characteristics of product users or prospects. With this profile in hand the media buyer searched the demographic profiles of media and made the best match he could. If consumer research had indicated that housewives with families of four or more persons were heavy users of the product in question, the media buyer would produce a list of magazines and broadcast opportunities all evaluated in terms of large family audiences.

This general method of matching media and product profiles was limited in accuracy to the extent that variation in product use and media exposure are both accounted for by common Demographic Characteristics. The following present the reported media exposure relationships in the same manner as reported purchasing behavior.

The method used to evaluate media in the following paragraphs might appropriately be considered for general use a technique for scanning potential media. It involves making estimates of average product consumption by the readers or viewers of each medium on the basis of our increased knowledge of customer profiles. By so doing the advertiser may compare one medium with another on the basis of estimated product use by the audience.

The approach is essentially one of matching the product user profile with the profiles of each medium under consideration. (In the case of selecting media for new products one might use the profile obtained in concept tests, blind product

TABLE 22   TOTAL TV WATCHING HOURS

Percentage of Variance Explained:

By Demographics Only	8%
By Demographics plus Living Patterns	20

Principal Variables Contributing:

Demographic:		#31 (−) Husband's Age
		33 (+) Market Size
Living Patterns:	Scale	5 (−) Loyal vs. Venturesome Shopper
		7 (+) Sports Spectator
		14 (+) Budget
		17 (−) Energetic
		18 (−) "Dress for Husband" Oriented
		19 (+) Butterfly
		20 (−) Undefined

TABLE 23   AMERICAN HOME

Percentage of Variance Explained:

By Demographics Only	6%
By Demographics plus Living Patterns	12

Principal Variables Contributing:

Demographic:		#23 (+) Number of Adults (Over Age 19)
Living Patterns:	Scale	12 (+) Church Goer

TABLE 24   BETTER HOMES AND GARDENS

Percentage of Variance Explained:

By Demographics Only	6%
By Demographics plus Living Patterns	11

Principal Variables Contributing:

Demographic:		#31 (+) Husband's Age
Living Patterns:	Scale	7 (+) Sports Spectator
		12 (+) Church Goer

TABLE 25   FAMILY CIRCLE

Percentage of Variance Explained:			
By Demographics Only			2%
By Demographics plus Living Patterns			13
Principal Variables Contributing:			
	Demographic:	None	
	Living Patterns:	Scale	4 (+) "Special" Shopper
			5 (−) Loyal vs. Venturesome Shopper
			12 (+) Church Goer
			14 (−) Budget
			15 (−) Beauty Conscious
			16 (+) Modern Family Manager
			17 (−) "Dress for Husband" Oriented

TABLE 26   GOOD HOUSEKEEPING

Percentage of Variance Explained:			
By Demographics Only			6%
By Demographics plus Living Patterns			14
Principal Variables Contributing:			
	Demographic:		#23 (+) Number of Adults (Over Age 19)
	Living Patterns:	Scale	16 (+) Modern Family Manager

TABLE 27   HOLIDAY

Percentage of Variance Explained:			
By Demographics Only			5%
By Demographics plus Living Patterns			9
Principal Variables Contributing:			
	Demographic:		#32 (+) Husband's Education
	Living Patterns:	Scale	8 (+) Arts Enthusiast
			14 (−) Budget Minded

201

TABLE 28   LADIES' HOME JOURNAL

Percentage of Variance Explained:

By Demographics Only	1%
By Demographics plus Living Patterns	10

Principal Variables Contributing:

Demographic:	None	
Living Patterns:	Scale	7 (+) Sports Spectator 8 (+) Arts Enthusiast 16 (+) Modern Family Manager

TABLE 29   LIFE

Percentage of Variance Explained:

By Demographics Only	4%
By Demographics plus Living Patterns	13

Principal Variables Contributing:

Demographic:		#23 (+) Number of Adults (Over Age 19) 25 (+) Income 26 (−) Own-Rent Home[a]
Living Patterns:	Scale	3 (+) Fashion Conscious 8 (+) Arts Enthusiast 19 (+) Butterfly

[a]Renting a home increases the likelihood of claiming to read Life.

TABLE 30   LOOK

Percentage of Variance Explained:

By Demographics Only	6%
By Demographics plus Living Patterns	13

Principal Variables Contributing:

Demographic:	None	
Living Patterns:	Scale	2 (−) Happy Housekeeper 3 (+) Fashion Conscious 20 (−) Undefined

TABLE 31   MADEMOISELLE

Percentage of Variance:		
By Demographics Only		6%
By Demographics plus Living Patterns		15

Principal Variables Contributing:

Demographic:		#29 (+) Education
Living Patterns:	Scale	5 (−) Loyal vs. Venturesome Shopper[a]
		13 (+) Routine
		15 (+) Beauty Conscious

[a]Venturesome shopper more likely to claim to read Mademoiselle.

TABLE 32   McCALL'S

Percentage of Variance:		
By Demographics Only		5%
By Demographics plus Living Patterns		12

Principal Variables Contributing:

Demographic:		#30 (+) Number of Clubs
Living Patterns:	None	

TABLE 33   RELATIVE CONTRIBUTION TO VARIANCE IN LIPSTICK PURCHASING BY LIVING PATTERN SCALES AND DEMOGRAPHIC CHARACTERISTICS

Variable Number	Name	Weight	
25	Income	(+)	.23
3	Fashion Conscious	(+)	.22
15	Beauty Conscious	(+)	.16
9	Active Athlete	(+)	.14
1	Community Minded	(−)	.11
18	"Dress for Husband" Oriented	(−)	.10
19	Butterfly	(+)	.09
24	Number of Teens (Age 10-19)	(+)	.08
6	Child Oriented	(+)	.07
31	Husband's Age	(+)	.06

placements or preliminary copy tests. In such cases it would be possible to identify the people who respond favorably and develop a preliminary product use profile.) The method of making these estimates is *multiple regression analysis.*

It will be remembered that in previous results we have discussed the relationship of one measure to another in terms of amounts of variance. For example, certain Living Patterns account for substantial amounts of variance in product and media usage as do certain Demographic Characteristics, and the like.

For instance, in studying lipstick purchasing (Table 16) we identified a total of 10 Living Pattern Scales and Demographic Characteristics that account for variance in lipstick purchase. In the table which follows, the same 10 variables are listed. However in this table the regression weights are shown.

In principle, the use of these weights is as follows: (a) for each person in the sample an index of product purchase is computed; (b) this is done by taking that person's score on each characteristic or Living Pattern Scale and multiplying it by the appropriate weight to obtain a weighted score for each variable; (c) then the sum of all the weighted scores equals an index projection of product purchase.

For example, in the case of lipstick purchase each housewife's coded income level was multiplied by (+) .23; her score on Scale 3, Fashion Conscious, was multiplied by (+) .22. Finally, a score was derived for each person which is tantamount to a projection of her level of lipstick purchase.

One or two additional facts should be noted. For example, Scale 1, Community Minded, and Scale 18, "Dress for Husband" Oriented, are weighted (−) .11 and (−) .10, respectively. This merely means that the weighted scores for each person on these two variables are *subtracted* from the total estimate.

The way we arrive at the projection for each medium is to first make a projection for each reader or viewer according to the system outlined above and then take an average for all people claiming exposure to each medium.

As one would expect, the product use projection would be higher for those media that have more scales and characteristics in their profiles in common with the product under consideration. This is especially true if the common scales are those with high weights.

Before looking at some actual figures to examine this system of media scanning more closely, at least one question that is probably in the practical reader's mind should be answered. To arrive at a projected level of product purchase for each medium it is not necessary to have the complete profile for *each* member of *each* audience. The projected average product use can be made if one has only the *average* value for the audience on each relevant profile variable.

Other extensions and modifications of this line of thought will be made in future papers.

For example, a marketing manager of lipstick could conduct a profile study on his own product. If present results are indicative he would find 10 variables important in his product profile. In the process he would obtain a weight for each of the 10 variables. Hopefully, he could find an average value for the audiences of considered media on each of his ten variables. If so, he could proceed.

TABLE 34   NUMBER OF WASH LOADS PER WEEK [a,b]

Top Ten Magazines

Magazine	Cross Tabulation Rank	Regression Estimate Rank
True Story	1	1
True Confessions	2	2
Glamour	33	7-8
True	4	10
Mademoiselle	5-6	6
Mechanix Illustrated	5-6	3
Good Housekeeping	7	16
Modern Romance	8	5
Modern Screen	9-10	4
Harper's	9-10	13-14
Average Rank	5.5	7.4

Bottom Ten Magazines

Magazine	Cross Tabulation Rank	Regression Estimate Rank
Saturday Review	31	33
Family Circle	32	28-29
Holiday	33	24-27
Popular Science	34-35	24-27
Reader's Digest	34-35	30
Atlantic Monthly	36	39
New Yorker	37	36-37
Newsweek	38	32-33
Time	39	36-37
U.S. News & World Report	40	40

[a]A comparison of rankings of magazine efficiencies in terms of average product purchases estimated by cross tabulations and by regression estimates.
[b]Purchase pattern variance explained by Demographic Characteristics plus Living Pattern scales 33%.

What can be expected from the system is best shown by the following four tables. In two of these, Number of Wash Loads per Week and Lipstick Purchases, the amount of purchase variance accounted for was high, 33% and 29% respectively. For Soft Drink Consumption, only 8% was accounted for, and for Stomach Remedies, 12%. As we will see, the media matching is much more effective when a relatively high level of purchase pattern variance can be explained.

The tables that follow show a comparison of the magazines evaluated as most efficient and least efficient by two methods. TV was not included in this analysis.

The first method is equivalent to the traditional one of conducting a survey among product users and find which magazines are read most. In this case we have,

TABLE 35   LIPSTICK PURCHASES[a,b]

Top Ten Magazines

Magazine	Cross Tabulation Rank	Regression Estimate Rank
House Beautiful	1	1
Saturday Review	2	7
Glamour	3	5
Harper's	4-5	6
Mademoiselle	4-5	4
Vogue	6	8.5
New Yorker	7	2
Business Week	8	11.5
Esquire	9-10	8.5
Saturday Evening Post	9-10	18.5
Average Rank	5.5	7.2

Bottom Ten Magazines

Magazine	Cross Tabulation Rank	Regression Estimate Rank
Better Homes and Gardens	30-31	18-19
Good Housekeeping	30-31	25-26
U.S. News & World Report	32	25-26
Field & Stream	33	37
Reader's Digest	34	30
Time	35	15
Modern Romance	36	40
Sports Afield	37	39
Outdoor Life	38	38
Atlantic Monthly	39-40	22-23
Mechanix Illustrated	39-40	36
Average Rank	35.5	28.0

[a]A comparison of rankings of magazine efficiencies in terms of average product purchases estimated by cross tabulations and by regression estimates.
[b]Purchase pattern variance explained by Demographic Characteristics plus Living Pattern scales 29%.

in effect, evaluated each magazine by the average amount of product used by the readers in its audience. So, the first method of evaluation is based on this more usual kind of survey cross-tabulation. Each magazine is given a rank. For the top 10 these ranks run from 1 to 10 with ties being designated as, for example, 5-6 for a tie between ranks 5 and 6, etc. The column headed, "Cross-Tabulation Rank" contains the information obtained in this manner.

The other method used is that discussed in the previous paragraphs. By that method, a rank for each magazine was also prepared. These appear in the column headed, "Regression Estimate Rank."

TABLE 36   SOFT DRINK CONSUMPTION[a,b]

Top Ten Magazines

Magazine	Cross Tabulation Rank	Regression Estimate Rank
True Confessions	1	1
True Story	2	3
Modern Romance	3	5
Modern Screen	4	2
Esquire	5	11-12
Mademoiselle	6	7
Glamour	7	9
Business Week	8	31-32
Harper's	9	9
Life	10	29
Average Rank	5.5	12.6

Bottom Ten Magazines

Magazine	Cross Tabulation Rank	Regression Estimate Rank
McCall's	31	26-27
Family Circle	32	33-36
Popular Science	33	22-23
Sports Afield	34	13-14
Ladies' Home Journal	35	33-36
Outdoor Life	36	24-25
Reader's Digest	37	38-39
Better Homes and Gardens	38	29
New Yorker	39	31-32
National Geographic	40	33-36
Average Rank	35.5	29.0

[a]Comparison of rankings of magazine efficiencies in terms of average product purchases estimated by cross tabulations and by regression estimates.
[b]Purchase pattern variance explained by Demographic Characteristics plus Living Pattern scales 12%.

The basic evaluation of the regression method will, then, be to see how closely the ranks obtained by that method agree with those obtained by the cross-tabulation of the survey among product user.

For demonstration, the ranks assigned to the top 10 and the bottom 10 magazines selected by the cross-tabulation methods are shown and the ranks of those same magazines by the regression method are compared.

To obtain an impression of the results the most effective way is to scan the two columns of each table labeled "Cross Tabulation Rank" and "Regression Estimate Rank." The extent to which they agree is indicative of the success of the latter.

TABLE 37   USE OF STOMACH REMEDIES [a,b]

Top Nine Magazines[c]

Magazine	Cross Tabulation Rank	Regression Estimate Rank
True Story	1	3-4
American Home	2	14-17
True Confessions	3	1
Popular Science	4	10
Modern Romance	5-6	2
Atlantic Monthly	5-6	30-31
Esquire	7	23-28
Popular Mechanics	8-9	8-9
Family Circle	8-9	23-28
	*	
Average Rank	5.5	15.4

Bottom Ten Magazines

New Yorker	31	38
Holiday	32	29
Good Housekeeping	33	23-28
Field & Stream	34-35	7
Better Homes and Gardens	34-35	30-31
Look	36-37	18-22
Newsweek	38	37-39
Saturday Review	38	37-39
Sports Afield	39	3-4
National Geographic	40	40
Average Rank	35.5	25.5

[a] A comparison of rankings of magazine efficiencies in terms of average product purchases estimated by cross tabulations and by regression estimates.
[b] Purchase pattern variance explained by Demographic Characteristics plus Living Pattern scales 8%.
[c] No tenth magazine is shown because of an excessive number of ties.

In the first two tables (Tables 34 and 35) out of the 10 top magazines picked for each product by the Cross Tabulation method, eight were also picked by the regression method using demographics and Living Patterns scores. In these two instances approximately 30 per cent of the product purchase variance had been accounted for. As the amount of purchase variance accounted for decreases, the results are less exciting.

Conclusion

The results presented here are intended to give an idea of what this writer feels is the promise for the future in this line of research. The vast amount of work done in mental testing can be tapped for service to marketing management.

This first effort has demonstrated that there are such things as patterns in daily living behavior. At least the respondents in this research reported them in a systematic way.

Furthermore, there are good indications that these patterns have some significance for marketing management. In fact, it would appear that if one can account for something around 30 per cent or more of the variance of the purchase of his product he can begin to obtain some practical pay-off.

Of course, no research project ever provides the final word on an avenue of exploration. This one, surely, is only the beginning. Much more work needs to be done. It is hoped that others will be tempted to explore this kind of thinking. I, myself, expect to.

The results here are all drawn from one sample, and thus, subject to some circularity. However, in the basic monograph I have attempted to minimize any tendency to overstate the results and remain quite conservative.

Reference

Wilson, Clark L. *Homemaker Living Patterns and Marketplace Behavior,* Harvard Business School, Division of Research, Boston 1966 (Univ. Press).

18 Influences of Innovators and Leaders

The Effect of the Informal Group Upon Member Innovative Behavior

THOMAS S. ROBERTSON* *(Marketing Educator)*

The impact of small, informal neighborhood groups on member innovative behavior is assessed. Group characteristics, in terms of interaction and sentiment, are related to aggregate group response to innovation.

The relationship of the member to the group is further related to his individual innovative response.

Innovative behavior is an *activity* engaged in by individuals. Within the confines of a social system, such as a neighborhood, individuals meet, see, and talk with one another—*interaction* occurs. If such interaction among a set of people is on a continuing basis, *sentiment* may exist within the group in terms of differential liking among group members and the formation of group ideology and norms governing expected activity patterns.

The research objective of this study can be formulated in terms of this conceptual scheme, developed by Homans,[1] so as to assess the effect of interaction and sentiment variables upon the activity of new product adoption, both on a group and individual basis.

Source: Thomas S. Robertson, "The Effect of the Informal Group Upon Member Innovative Behavior," in Robert L. King, Editor, *Marketing and the New Science of Planning* (Chicago: American Marketing Association, 1968, pp. 334-340.

*Thomas S. Robertson is Assistant Professor, Graduate School of Business Administration, Harvard University.
[1]George C. Homans, *The Human Group* (New York: Harcourt, Brace & World, Inc., 1950).
Research underlying this paper was carried out under the joint financial support of the Bureau of Business and Economic Research and the Division of Research, UCLA. Thanks are expressed to Mr. Jim Koch and Mr. Brian Horsfall for their roles in the completion of this project.

Relevant Concepts

INTERACTION AFFECTS ACTIVITY

Homans postulates that: "Persons who interact with one another frequently are more like one another in their activities than they are like other persons with whom they interact less frequently." Myers has found that the exercise of opinion leadership in the interaction process is reflected in likeness of innovative activity patterns among group members.[2]   Other research evidence is that the innovator is generally higher on opinion leadership than the average group member.

SENTIMENT AFFECTS ACTIVITY

It is basic to sociological theory that group norms affect member behavior. Rogers has used the ideal types of "modern" and "traditional" norms to account for high and low innovativeness in social systems. Festinger proposed that there will be high reliance upon social reality and normative influence when the physical reality is ambiguous or unstructured,[3] as perhaps in the case of new products.

Research by Festinger and Back has found that the greater the attractiveness of the group to its members, the greater the amount of influence successfully exerted upon the members, and the greater the behavioral conformity resulting. Coleman, Katz, and Menzel have documented the "interaction" or "snowball" effect in new product diffusion, that the socially more integrated members of a social system adopt sooner than the socially less integrated members.[4]   Literature exploring the perceived risk concept has found that if the individual is experiencing risk, he will seek to reduce it. Arndt has documented that avoiding new products is a risk-handling tactic used by high-risk perceivers.[5]

These concepts are drawn from a variety of contexts and research traditions. The basic question is whether the hypotheses will be confirmed for consumer innovative behavior across product categories. If such activity is not of sufficient relevance to the groups studied, lack of positive relationships may well occur.

[2] John G. Myers, "Patterns of Interpersonal Influence in the Adoption of New Products" In *Proceedings of the American Marketing Association*, ed. Raymond M. Haas, Chicago, 1966, pp. 750-757.

[3] Leon Festinger, "Informal Social Communication," *Psychological Review*, Vol. 57, September, 1950, pp. 271-281.

[4] James S. Coleman, Elihu Katz, and Herbert Menzel, *Medical Innovation: A Diffusion Study* (Indianapolis: The Bobbs-Merrill Company, 1966), chapter 7.

[5] Johan Arndt, "Perceived Risk and Word of Mouth Advertising," In *Perspectives in Consumer Behavior*, eds. Harold H. Kassarjian and Thomas S. Robertson (Glenview: Scott, Foresman and Company, 1968), pp. 330-337.

Hypotheses

GROUP ANALYSIS

Interaction (I).

I-1. Communication about innovation among group members will be positively related to: a) group similarity of, and b) extent of innovativeness.

I-2. Exercise of opinion leadership within the group will be positively related to: a) group similarity of, and b) extent of innovativeness.

Sentiment (S).

S-1. Favorability of the group norm on innovation will be positively related to extent of innovativeness.

S-2. Group cohesiveness will be positively related to similarity of innovativeness.

S-3. Perceived risk will be negatively related to extent of innovativeness.

INDIVIDUAL ANALYSIS

Interaction (I).

1-3. Communication about innovation with other group members will be positively related to the individual's innovativeness.

I-4. Exercise of opinion leadership within the group will be positively related to innovativeness.

Sentiment (S).

S-4. Favorability of the norm on innovation which the individual reflects will be positively related to innovativeness.

S-5. Social integration will be positively related to innovativeness.

S-6. Perceived risk will be negatively related to innovativeness.

Research Design

Research was conducted in the spring of 1967 in the Los Angeles suburb of Encino. The neighborhood selected was middle class in profile with almost all heads of households holding white collar or semi-professional positions. Most households were composed of families with children living at home.

The design of the research involved identification of small, informal neighborhood groups. These groups were preferred—for purposes of investigating buying behavior—to formal groups, such as PTA or church groups, which carry out explicit functions and possess a specified organizational structure. It was felt that the formal group is not the relevant reference group for most consumption-related activities. Consumer information may be transferred within the formal group, but it is more incidental to the ongoing group purpose. It is realized that the informal neighborhood group need not be the relevant reference point for buying activities either.

Another possible approach would have been to identify a defined social system in terms of some common attribute, such as residing in the same apartment complex, which would have again simplified the research design. A pilot venture along these lines in the Los Angeles area, however, revealed that too little inter-action occurred among residents to identify groups meaningfully. A married students' housing project, where interaction is considerable, could have again been used, as in other research by Arndt and Myers, but the range of consumption of concern to student wives is limited.

SAMPLING

Identification of informal neighborhood groups proceeded as follows:

1. One woman was randomly selected from each block within the 32 block area. She was interviewed and asked: "Could you name some women within the neighborhood—say within a mile—that you see most often and with whom

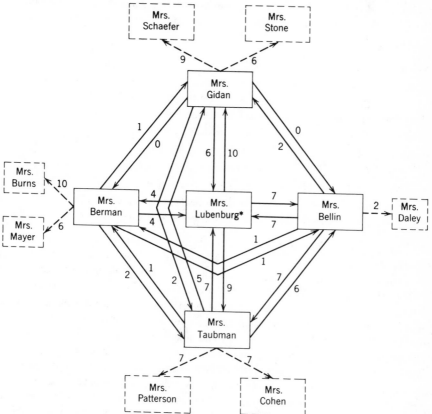

Figure 1. Reported interaction, Group No. 6. The numbers represent the total reported interactions by telephone or in-person per week. The solid-line boxes represent specified group. The dashed-line boxes represent subsidiary friendship mentions.

*Initial respondent who identified group.

you are most friendly?" A minimum of three names was sought and these mentions constituted the preliminary definition of the group.

2. The actual existence of groups was then tested by subsequently interviewing each person mentioned and measuring the level of interaction among group members. A sociogram depicting the flow of interaction for one of the groups obtained is given in Figure 1.

3. The operational definition employed for the existence of a group was that it must include at least three persons, all of whom interacted with one another.

Under these conditions, nonresponse could not be tolerated since the existence of a group could not be determined, nor could group characteristics be completely assessed. An elaborate procedure to insure response was used, consisting of an advance letter requesting cooperation, follow-up telephone calls to arrange appointments, and further letters and calls where necessary. The final sample included 20 groups consisting of 85 members.

DATA COLLECTION AND ANALYSIS

In-home personal interviews were conducted with the 85 group members. Interviews took approximately 90 minutes to complete.

The group characteristics of concern and their forms of measurement are noted in Table 1. These characteristics were measured for each individual and then over-all group means and standard deviations were computed. Basically, three types of measures were involved:

1. reported behavior measures—innovativeness and new product communication;
2. peer evaluations—opinion leadership and group cohesion;
3. attitudinal measures—norms on innovation, social integration and perceived risk.

While the measure of innovativeness used in the presentation of these results is self-report of number of innovations purchased, other measures were also obtained. One such measure was self-perceived innovativeness (Q: "Are you generally among the first to buy new products or do you prefer to wait?"). A zero-order correlation coefficient of .34, significant beyond a .01 level, was obtained between this measure and total number of innovations reported purchased. This is a higher correlation than that reported by Summers[6] between self-perceived innovativeness and fashion ownership, but is considerably lower than might be expected.

Another measure was peer evaluation of each group member's innovativeness (Q: "Indicate for each person mentioned how willing you feel she is to buy new products"). The zero-order correlation coefficient obtained between this measure and actual purchases was .23, significant beyond the .05 level. It appears, therefore, that while these measures are significantly correlated, different results could be forthcoming depending on the measure used.

[6] John O. Summers, "The Identity of the Women's Clothing Fashion Transmitter," unpublished doctoral dissertation, Purdue University, 1967.

TABLE 1 MEASUREMENT

Characteristic	Measure	Questionnaire Component
Activity		
Innovativeness: Food, Clothing, Appliances, Total	Number of new products purchased from a list of 42	"Which of the following items have you purchased?"
Interaction		
New Product Communication: Food, Clothing, Appliances, Total	Discussion with group members about new products	"How often do you talk with the women mentioned above about new (food/clothing/appliance) items on the market?" Often O o . . o O Seldom
Opinion Leadership: Food, Clothing, Appliances, Total	Peer evaluation of member influence	"Mark an *F* next to the woman's name who would be your best source of information about foods." (Repeats for clothing, appliances, and total)
Sentiment		
Norm on Innovation: Food Clothing, Appliances, Total	Attitude toward new products	"How do you feel about buying *new* food items?" (Repeats)
Group Cohesion	Liking of group member for one another	"Indicate how much you like to get together with each person mentioned." Very much O o . . o O Very much like to dislike to
Social Integration	Participation in neighborhood activities	"How do you feel about socializing with the other women in the neighborhood?" "List the organizations, if any, to which you belong."
Perceived Risk: Food, Clothing, Appliances, Total	Scale ranking how "dangerous" or "safe"	"We all know that not all products work as well as others. Please indicate how dangerous or safe you feel it is to buy new products instead of established products." Dangerous O o . . o O Safe

Data were secured, where appropriate, for three product categories—food, clothing, and appliances—and a "total"score was generally based on these three component scores. It is thus possible to identify differences in findings depending upon the product category under consideration. Such differences can be noted initially in Table 2, which shows the total sample mean and standard deviation scores for each characteristic under investigation.

TABLE 2   OVERALL MEANS AND STANDARD DEVIATIONS OF CHARACT-ERISTICS

Characteristic	Mean/Maximum	Standard Deviation
Activity		
Innovativeness:		
Food	8.7/14.0	2.6
Clothing	3.2/14.0	2.0
Appliances	4.2/14.0	1.8
Total	16.0/42.0	4.5
Interaction		
New Product Communication:		
Food	4.0/6.0	1.7
Clothing	4.2/6.0	1.5
Appliances	3.2/6.0	1.4
Total	3.8/6.0	1.3
Opinion Leadership:		
Food	0.5[a]	0.6
Clothing	0.4[a]	0.6
Appliances	0.5[a]	0.7
Total	1.5[a]	1.1
Sentiment		
Norm on Innovation:		
Food	3.9/6.0	1.7
Clothing	3.1/6.0	1.4
Appliances	3.2/6.0	1.5
Total	4.1/6.0	0.9
Group Cohesion	4.8/6.0	0.9
Social Integration	3.4/6.0	1.7
Perceived Risk:		
Food	2.4/6.0	1.2
Clothing	2.6/6.0	1.3
Appliances	2.7/6.0	1.3
Total	2.5/6.0	1.1

[a]Mean score is based on frequency of mentions without a specified range.

Hypothesis testing for the group analysis uses nonparametric techniques, basically the Spearman (r_s) rank correlation coefficient. Hypothesis testing for the individual analysis is in terms of zero-order correlation.

Findings: Group Analysis

INTERACTION

Rank correlation coefficients for each hypothesis are presented in Table 3. Extent of new product communication in and of itself apparently does not lead to high group innovativeness (the summation of member innovativeness) nor to sim-

TABLE 3   HYPOTHESIS TESTING: RANK CORRELATIONS FOR GROUP ANALYSIS

Hypothesis			r_s
Interaction (I)			
I-1.	a)	> communication, > likeness	−.06
	b)	> communication, > innovativeness	
		total	−.19
		food	−.10
		clothing	.31
		appliances	.00
I-2.	a)	> opinion leadership, > likeness	−.03
	b)	> opinion leadership, > innovativeness	−.07
Sentiment (S)			
S-1.		> norm, > innovativeness	
		total	.49[a]
		food	.20
		clothing	.53[b]
		appliances	.34
S-2.		> cohesiveness, > likeness	−.16
S-3.		< perceived risk, > innovativeness	
		total	.56[b]
		food	.53[b]
		clothing	.00
		appliances	.23

[a] r_s significant at or beyond .05 level.
[b] r_s significant at or beyond .01 level.

ilarity in innovative behavior patterns (in terms of the standard deviation for the innovativeness variable within the group) (I-1). This may be due to the facts that both positive and negative information is transferred and that group agreement does not exist on the topic of new product adoption. Arndt has found that women who were exposed to positive word-of-mouth information about a new product were more likely to buy, and women who were exposed to negative information were less likely to buy. To the extent that a mixture of positive and negative information is relayed, a high level of innovative behavior would not be expected.

Festinger has found that group pressure to communicate concerning an "item x" increases with perceived discrepancy in opinion among members of the group concerning that item. Thus, higher communication about new products may not relate to consistency of innovative behavior as much as to perceived inconsistency. This may reflect the fact that members of a group do not have the same probability of buying new products—no matter how much communication occurs. Innovative behavior is very much related to certain predispositions on the part of the person. The innovator has, in fact, been found to be "different" from the later adopter. Within a group are found individuals who may represent several adopter categories, from innovators to early adopters, early majority, late majority, to laggards.

The remaining interaction hypothesis, concerning a posited relationship between opinion leadership and consistency and extent of innovative behavior is not supported (I-2).[7] Again, it would appear that both positive and negative influence transfer can occur; that the exercise of opinion leadership need not change the person's propensity to innovate; and that various underlying needs, which may not relate to consistency and extent of innovativeness, may prompt influence transfer.

In the framing of this hypothesis, opinion leadership was not viewed as a discrete trait which either does or does not exist within the individual. Instead, opinion leadership is a matter of degree. All persons can exercise a certain amount of influence. Also, opinion leadership was not viewed as a one-way occurrence, *i.e.,* a dominant opinion leader influencing others, but as most often a two-way occurrence, whereby in the process of interaction, group members influence and are influenced.

The "opinion leadership" concept is misleading in many ways. The tendency is to think in terms of a dominant influential seeking out influences who never influence the influential. Yet, both source-initiated and recipient-initiated influence occurs; influence is often two-way; and influence is a matter of degree—no one person is exclusively influential. The idea of opinion transfer or *influence transfer* may more accurately reflect the underlying process.

SENTIMENT

Group innovativeness is significantly correlated with favorability of the group norm on innovation (S-1, $r_s = .49, < .05$ level). The extent of this relationship, however, varies for the three product categories. Food ($r_s = .20$) and appliance

---

[7] One of the few researchers to report a similar lack of relationship between these variables is Charles W. King, "Fashion Adoption: A Rebuttal to the 'Trickle Down' Theory." In *Proceedings of the American Marketing Association,* ed. Stephen A. Greyser, Chicago, 1963, pp. 108-125.

(r_s = .34) innovativeness scores, while positively related to group norms, are not significantly so. Clothing innovativeness, on the other hand, is highly related to group norm (r_s = .53, < .01 level).

It would be expected that a greater relationship would exist between an activity (such as innovativeness) and the group norm on that activity to the degree that one or both of the following conditions are met: 1) the more important the activity to the group, the more binding the norm and the more severe the sanction for norm violation; 2) the more likely the observation of norm violation, the greater the risk in deviate behavior. In the present case, the more significant norm-innovativeness correlation for clothing may be due to clothing activity being more meaningful than food and appliance activity and therefore a more rigidly defined norm being present. It may also be due to the greater visibility of clothing leading to greater norm adherence since deviance is readily observable and punishable. The latter explanation appears more likely.

Results for hypothesis S-2 are not supported and, in fact, a somewhat negative (although non-significant) relationship exists between group consistency on innovativeness and group cohesiveness. Greater attractiveness of the members for one another apparently does not mean that they will behave more alike in the purchase of new products. Again, the group seems to provide enough latitude for the performance of numerous innovativeness roles from innovator to laggard.

Innovativeness is found to be associated with lower levels of perceived risk (S-3, r_s = .56, < .01 level). Despite the high association on a total basis, food is the only product category for which innovativeness is significantly correlated with perceived risk (food: r_s = .53 < .01 level; clothing: r_s = .00; appliances: r_s = .23). Yet, slightly less risk is perceived for food than clothing or appliances, although the difference is not statistically meaningful (see Table 2). It has been found previously that innovators are more willing to take risks. The clothing realm may be where women exhibit their capacity for daring activity. If this is so, then a certain amount of risk may be desirable and yield the present finding. The appliance finding may, be due in part, to the fact that appliance purchases are most often joint husband-wife decisions, which spreads the risk and neutralizes the relationship with innovativeness.

Findings: Individual Analysis

INNOVATIVE BEHAVIOR OVERLAP

A question of initial interest is whether innovative behavior is specific to each product category or whether a general innovator exists. Innovators for each product category were therefore defined as the top 10 percent in number of new items purchased, and a test for overlap of innovators by product category was made. While 25 respondents were innovators in one product category, only 4 were innovators in two product categories, and there were no three-product category innovators. Using the Marcus and Bauer method to test the significance of overlap, it was concluded that innovative behavior is bound to specific product categories.[8]

Analysis of the zero-order correlation coefficients reveals that appliance and food innovativeness are significantly related (r = .28, < .01 level), as are appliance and clothing innovativeness (r = .28, < .01 level). Clothing and food innovativeness are not significantly related (r = .18). These coefficients, while statistically significant, are pragmatically low, and seriously dispute much of the discussion in marketing circles of "innovators" and "innovator characteristics" which implicitly assumes that the innovator is a general innovator. If innovativeness is specific to a given product category, then varying innovator characteristics can be the case, necessitating varying marketing strategies.

INTERACTION

Communication about innovation and innovativeness are significantly related in the case of clothing (I-3, r = .31, < .01 level), but not in the case of food or appliances (Table 4). These findings bear some resemblance to group analysis findings in that clothing is again the area where communication and innovativeness are most related and, on the whole, the same general lack of relationship between the two variables is shown.

Opinion leadership and innovativeness correlate for two of the product categories (I-4, appliances: r = .31, < .01 level; clothing: r = .29, < .01 level). These results attest that while a statistically significant overlap of innovativeness and opinion leadership is the case, the overlap is minimal in terms of equating innovators with opinion leaders.

Prior research by Summers and Rossiter and Robertson[9] has also assessed the association between innovativeness and opinion leadership. Both studies focused on women's clothing fashions, a product category under analysis in the present research, and obtained very similar correlation coefficients of .33 and .35, respectively, as compared to the .29 value obtained in the present case.

SENTIMENT

As was true in the group analysis, reflection of a favorable norm on innovativeness is associated with higher levels of new product purchases (S-4). This is especially true for the clothing (r = .41, < .01 level) and food (r = .40, < .01 level) product categories, and not so much so for the appliance (r = .22, < .05 level) product category.

Social integration and innovativeness are not much related, reflecting a fairly comparable lack of relationship as in the group cohesion-innovativeness anlaysis, although for the individual analysis no negative trend is reported (S-5). Acceptance

[8] Alan S. Marcus and Raymond A. Bauer, "Yes: There are Generalized Opinion Leaders," *Public Opinion Quarterly*, Vol. 28, Winter, 1964, 628-632.
[9] John R. Rossiter and Thomas S. Robertson, "A Conceptual Examination of Innovativeness and Opinion Leadership in the College Fashion Context." Working paper, Graduate School of Business Administration, UCLA, 1968.

TABLE 4 ZERO-ORDER CORRELATIONS OF INTERACTION AND SENTI-MENT VARIABLES WITH INNOVATIVENESS: INDIVIDUAL ANALYSIS

Independent Variables	Innovativeness			
	Total	Food	Clothing	Appliances
Interaction				
I-3 Communication about Innovation				
Total	$.22^a$			
Food		.14		
Clothing			$.31^b$	
Appliances				.11
I-4 Opinion Leadership				
Total	.12			
Food		.02		
Clothing			$.29^b$	
Appliances				$.31^b$
Sentiment				
S-4 Norm on Innovation				
Total	$.43^b$			
Food		$.40^b$		
Clothing			$.41^b$	
Appliances				$.22^a$
S-5 Social Integration	.08	−.04	.13	.09
S-6 Perceived Risk				
Total	$.35^b$			
Food		$.31^b$		
Clothing			.06	
Appliances				.18

[a] correlation significant at or beyond .05 level.
[b] correlation significant at or beyond .01 level.
Note: For purposes or individual analysis , N = 91 since data for three two-person groups, excluded in the group analysis, were included.

by the group and participation within the group, therefore, do not seem to relate to the individual's innovative willingness.

The final relationship for analysis is that between perceived risk and innovativeness (S-6). Significant correlations are found on a total basis (r = .35, < .01 level) and for food (r = .31, < .01 level), but not for appliances, and almost no relationship is found for clothing. Thus, earlier findings that perceived risk varied by product may be extendable to product categories. It may be that the perceived risk variable is most meaningful for new food purchases, less meaningful for appliances, and of no meaning for clothing purchases, at least as suggested in this study.

Conclusion

Examination of small, informal neighborhood groups has revealed that certain group variables are correlated with aggregate innovative behavior, and that certain characteristics specifying the individual's relationship to the group are correlated with individual member innovative behavior. Generally, "sentiment" characteristics are more important than "interaction" characteristics in determining innovative "activity," especially in the group analysis.

Variables correlating most highly with innovativeness are group norm on innovation and level of perceived risk. Variables are found to have differential effect depending upon the product category, e.g., food, clothing or appliances. The group has been found to be a meaningful unit of analysis which could lead to improved predictions of an individual's probability of new product adoption for a given product category.

ECONOMIC INFLUENCES

19. Economic Motivation and Behavior

"Determinants of Private Brand Attitude," John G. Myers (Marketing Educator), *Journal of Marketing Research,* Vol. 4 (February, 1967), pp. 73-81.

Although not well understood by most consumers, economic factors are powerful determinants of consumer behavior. One significant example is given in the selection that follows.

19 Economic Motivation and Behavior

Determinants of Private Brand Attitude

JOHN G. MYERS* *(Marketing Educator)*

Differences in price and promotional elasticity are potentially the most useful criteria for market segment identification of low-cost consumer goods. This article presents an approach to segment identification using private brand attitudes.

Various possible determinants are tested on data from a field study of women's attitudes toward private brands.

Economic theory suggests that differential price elasticity, that is, a tendency for one group of consumers to respond to a price change differently from another group of consumers, provides a potentially useful criterion for market segment identification in low cost consumer goods. Although both theory and management practice [20] suggest the desirability of a segmentation strategy, criterion variables have generally shown relatively low discriminatory power. Recent studies have suggested predictability might be increased by first identifying differences in response pattern with respect to price and then searching for possible determinants of those patterns. As stated by Frank and Massy:

Source: John G. Myers, "Determinants of Private Brand Attitude," *Journal of Marketing Research,* Vol. 4 (February, 1967), pp. 73-81.

*John G. Myers is assistant professor of business administration, University of California, Berkeley. The data are from a study of determinants of brand imagery and attitude [18] financed by the Kimberly-Clark Corporation, Inc., and the Ford Foundation Research Program in Marketing at Berkeley. Appreciation is extended to these institutions for financial support and to the Computer Center, University of California, Berkeley, for programming assistance.

What management needs to know is whether or not customers belonging to the upper class have a different set of price and promotional elasticities for the firm's products than do customers in the lower class, or whether customers with a dominant personality tend to have different elasticities than those with different personality profiles [13, p. 188].

This article suggests an attitudinal construct as a measure of consumer price and proportional elasticities and an approach to studying the stability and determinants of the construct. The approach depends on knowledge of differences of promotional strategy in marketing private and national brands.[1] Basic methodological features of the approach are an attitudinal rather than a behavioral criterion, a test of the validity of the criterion through cross-method and cross-trait analysis [3], and a research unit concentrating on classes of brands rather than on individual brands. It is argued that carefully controlled attitude studies can contribute to an understanding of demand elasticity and provide useful criteria for identifying differences in consumer types.

The utility of any construct used to characterize different market segments depends on the degree to which it truly identifies relatively stable attitudinal or behavioral patterns. Panel data and theoretical treatments of consumer decision processes [19] attest to the difficulty of identifying meaningfully stable patterns. There is little question that patterns will only be stable to some degree, and that determinants or correlates will show both low predictive power and inconsistencies varying with the time period or geographic location.

Published research on differential price sensitivity or elasticity supports this conclusion. Studies on price-consciousness, deal-proneness, or private brand choice, which all bear some relationship to differential response to price or promotional appeals, usually identify the phenomenon but reveal many inconsistencies concerning its pattern or determinants. Gabor and Granger [14], for example, suggest that price-consciousness is inversely related to social class, is different among branded and unbranded goods, and seems to decrease as the number of purchases of a commodity increases. Webster [24] finds some tendency for deal-proneness among women to be positively related to age and the number of different brands purchased, and negatively related to brand loyalty and total number of units purchased. Frank and Boyd [12] identify differential attraction to private and national brands, but conclude generally that there are no distinguishing socioeconomic differences between private and national brand buyers. An earlier study by Trier et al. [23] suggests that of a variety of criteria that might differentiate shopper types, sensitivity to price is the most discriminating, but that it is not strongly associated with other consumer characteristics.

[1]The terms private and national are generally accepted trade terms, although they are not as descriptive as some less familiar alternatives. See Cole et al. [7] for a discussion of the definitional problems involved. Some appreciation for the scope of private brand activity can be gained from a report in Sales Management [15]. In 1960, 84 percent of all supermarkets were reputed to be stocking private brands, 71 percent to a considerable extent, and 13 percent to a limited extent. Good synopses of background data on private brands appear in Frank and Boyd [12] and Stern [21].

Segmentation and Private Brand Attitude

Marketing strategies in low cost products are characterized by the interplay between two manager-manipulated conditions—price and promotion.[2] A criterion
for market segmentation can be derived from the identification of differential
consumer response to either one. The segmentation criterion is predictively useful
if differences in response pattern are relatively stable over specified time periods
and within acceptable tolerance limits.

Differences in price and promotional strategies are reflected in basic distinctions
in private and national brands. To some degree each brand type represents
an extreme in price or promotional appeal, private brands tending to be lower
in price and promoted locally, and national brands tending to be higher in price
and promoted nationally. Typically, a manufacturer can supply an unbranded
good to a distributor who adds his own label to it and sells it as a private brand.
Also, a manufacturer may supply the distributor with a branded good to be sold
under a manufacturer label as a national brand. Private brands are usually lower
priced than national brands.[3] It is a simple step to the market segmentation notion that consumers who respond differently to private brands are those more
readily influenced by a price appeal than by a promotion appeal.

Assume that a relatively stable market situation exists in which prices of private
brands in one product class are lower than its comparable national brand prices
and in which the product qualities[4] of the private and national brands are equal.
Now assume that consumers are asked to report their impressions of price-quality
distinctions in the group of national and private brands. Even if the assumption
that private brands have lower prices but the same quality is true, they may not
be reported as having lower prices and the same quality. A consumer group might
easily say that private brands have similar prices but lower quality. If these reactions adequately represent a predisposition, the former group has a higher probability of purchasing private brands than the latter group because brands of lower
price and similar quality are preferred purchases.

Assuming that consumers might judge private brands as being either higher, the
same as, or lower in price, and higher, the same as, or lower in quality than nation-

---

[2] Promotion here is all nonprice activity in which manufacturer or middlemen may engage,
and follows the traditional economic distinction between price and nonprice competition.

[3] The price dynamics of most low cost consumer goods markets make this at best a tenuous
generalization. It has been identified empirically by Cole *et al.* [7], is recognized by Telser
[22], and is an accepted trade opinion stemming from the essential differences in price-promo-
tion strategies described above. See, for example, the discussions in the case of *The Borden
Company* v. *The Federal Trade Commission* [1].

[4] Product quality in a product class is not necessarily the same under comparable national and
private labels. Manufacturers are often reputed to use private labels to dispose of surpluses
or inferior quality products. In agricultural markets in particular where quality variations are
common, private branded products are likely to be of inferior quality compared with nationally
branded products than they are of equal or higher quality.

al brands, the possible combinations can generate a typology. Each of the nine generated types defines a potential market segment. In the case of similar price-quality conditions (lower-lower, same-same, higher-higher), the direction of an attitudinal or behavioral response is indeterminate. It depends on whether price or quality is more significant to the respondent. In the remaining six cases, the responses represent either the tendency to purchase or not to purchase private brands. The terms private brand acceptors and private brand rejectors are used to refer to the several kinds. Figure 1 shows the matrix of acceptors and rejectors represented by each of the alternatives generated.

FIGURE 1   CONSUMER TYPES BASED ON PRICE-QUALITY COMPARISONS OF PRIVATE AND NATIONAL BRANDS

Consumer types	Price-Quality Comparisons[a]
Acceptor/rejector	Lower price–Lower quality
Acceptor	Lower price–Same quality
Acceptor	Lower price–Higher quality
Rejector	Same Price–Lower quality
Acceptor/rejector	Same Price–Same quality
Acceptor	Same price–Higher quality
Rejector	Higher price–Lower quality
Rejector	Higher price–Same quality
Acceptor/rejector	Higher price–Higher quality

[a]Each of the combinations of price and quality shown is a possible response to a question of the type, "In a comparison of private with national brands, private brands would be. . ."

The specification of these varying types of consumer response as potential segments raises questions about the size of each segment and the reasons for its existence. For example, it is very likely that the lower price-lower quality and the lower price-same quality segments would be larger than the higher price-lower quality or the higher price-higher quality segments. The former are closer to reality than the latter, and most consumers react rationally. The rejector group, same price-lower quality, may, however, represent a large segment if for any reason consumers need a rationale for their purchases of national brands. For example, advertising can create an impression of higher quality that serves to induce many people to give this response. This pattern may be typical, considering the large market shares held by most national brands compared with private brands in the same product class.

Many behavior theories could suggest the internal or social forces that might be responsible for each type of response pattern.[5] Differences in role perception [23], differences in persuasibility [8], or differences in achievement-security orientation [2] could contribute to an overall explanation. Explanation may be found

[5]These are discussed in detail in Myers [18], Chapters 3, 4, and 5.

in a recognition of differential learning rates. For example, Demsetz [10] shows that some individuals become acceptors of private brands more quickly than others. Shopper patterns such as loyalty to a particular store [9] or other structural variables [11] may serve as the predominant explanation. The complexities and interrelationships of causal forces that may be involved in any specific purchasing decision are well documented.

This relatively simple paradigm was used as a guide to the empirical investigation of private brand attitude and its determinants now reported.

Methodology

A field study of working and nonworking or housewife groups conducted in the Evanston and Chicago area in Spring, 1964, provided basic data. Respondents were purposively selected from various employing institutions and community groups. Each respondent completed a self-evaluative questionnaire of approximately one hour's length. A total of 347 questionnaires were completed—181 by working women and 166 by housewives.

Ninety-four nurses, 42 high school teachers, and 45 department store sales clerks were represented in the subgroups of working women sampled. Housewife groups were represented by 52 lower middle class, 58 middle class, and 56 upper middle class women. Social class placement was based upon the economic characteristics of the neighborhoods in which the respondents lived. Group administration procedures were used in administering questionnaires. Respondents in each of the six working and housewife groups met together in a central location and completed questionnaires in the presence of other group members under the supervision of the investigator. A small monetary incentive, one dollar, was given for each completed questionnaire.

Private brand attitude was measured by a rating instrument that asked the respondent to rate 29 national and private brands according to the frequency with which each brand would probably be used. The question was framed as an anticipation question to control for effects of store preference and to provide a consistent set of store-sponsored private brand types. Respondents were asked to simulate what they would probably purchase if a new supermarket opened nearby and they decided to shop there. Ratings on a five-point scale were made of each of the 29 brands under these conditions: (a) use regularly, (b) use occasionally, (c) might use, (d) probably never use, and (e) would never use.[6]

---

[6]The brand rating question was phrased as follows: Suppose that a large, new A. & P. has recently opened up in your neighborhood, and you have decided to shop there. Listed below are several brands of products that the store carries. Check in *one* of the spaces beside each brand how you think you might feel about using the brand.

Fourteen of the brands in the list were private brands.[7] A summation of the rating scores for these 14 brands was used as a measure of private brand attitude and cross tabulated with other indicators of price-consciousness, store preference, and open-end replies to a question on price-quality comparisons of national and private brands. Regression analysis tested the degree to which differences in private brand attitude were explained by differences in various socioeconomic and personality characteristics of the sample.

Results

PRIVATE BRAND ATTITUDE

Private brand attitude (P.B.A.) was defined as the summated rating of each respondent for the 14 private brands in the total number of 29 national and private brands rated. Ratings for individual brands could range from 1 to 5 so that summated scores for 14 brands ranged from 14 to 70. Although the distribution of P.B.A. was not centered on the numerical mean 42, but to the rejection side at about 55, it was quite symmetrical around 55. Four nearly equal groups approximating the quartile ranges were generated from the distribution. The ranges of scores and the frequencies in each of the groups were as follows:

Score Range	Frequency
14-49	79
50-54	63
55-59	66
60-70	73

The mean rating of the 14-49 group was 3.10, compared with 4.55 for the 60-70 group. The first was more likely to consist of individuals who might use private brands, and the last of those who would never use them.

Respondents in the lowest (3.10) and highest (4.55) scoring groups were analyzed to determine the various degrees to which they were affected by price and advertising appeals. The first group were called acceptors and the second rejectors.

---

[7]The private brands included in the question were: A. & P. frozen beans, A. & P. instant coffee, A. & P. aspirin, Sweetheart hand soap, Iona canned peaches, Nutley margarine, Formula 20 shampoo, Sunnyfield flour, Lyric lipstick, Mellow Mood nylons, Angel Soft facial tissue, A. & P. frozen orange juice, Cara Nome face powder, and Pacific brassiere. The last brand is a fictitious brand. Because questions were asked as a simulation of possible behavior, it was not considered particularly contaminating to retain this brand in index construction. Although all of these brands are not distributor sponsored, they represent a range of private and low-priced or little-advertised brands against which national, high-priced, and widely-advertised brands can be compared.

Two questions were asked on factors most likely to influence brand choice on regular purchasing occasions and on brand-switching occasions for each of four product types: facial tissue, flour, lipstick, and cigarettes.[8] A relatively strong tendency for acceptors to give price as a primary reason for purchasing a particular brand was shown for facial tissue, flour, and lipstick, but not for cigarettes. This effect appears reasonable since there is generally little price difference among cigarette brands.

In the regular purchasing case for facial tissue, for example, twice as many rejectors as acceptors gave the reply, "I buy one brand regularly which I think is the best brand," and six times as many acceptors as rejectors gave the reply, "I buy the brand with the lowest price." The effect was less noticeable in the switching influence case. About twice as many rejectors gave the reply, "an advertisement," and three times as many acceptors gave the reply, "lower price of another brand." These effects were also apparent in flour purchases for both the regular purchasing and switching influence situations. Chi squares and the levels of significance of the associations for regular and switching influences in each product type were as follows: facial tissue, 21.80 (.01), 11.56 (.05); flour, 11.01 (.05), 17.60 (.01); lipstick, 11.32 (.05), 3.10 (.50); and cigarettes, 1.26 (.90), 1.54 (.80).

Respondents were then reclassified into acceptor and rejector groups on the basis of their replies to open-end questions concerning their opinion of private brands.[9] In each group, rough sub-classifications were made on the basis of the particular responses given. The most frequent acceptor response was interpreted as a belief that the products of the private and national branders were essentially the same and that the prices of the private brands were lower. These respondents appeared to reply much as those who might appear in the consumer-types paradigm of Figure 1 as lower price-same quality. The second most frequent response was interpreted as a reluctance to pay for national brands' higher costs of packaging and advertising. Other acceptors mentioned that they would tend to use private brands regularly but for special occasions or special purposes would use more expensive brands.

---

[8] The format for the regular purchasing occasions question was, "Which one of the following is most nearly like the way you buy facial tissue? (Check one) I buy one brand regularly which I think is the best brand. I buy the brand with the lowest price. I generally buy what my friends buy. I buy the brand my husband likes. I generally buy the same brand each time without thinking much about it. I buy whatever brand is handy; one is as good as the other." The switching question was slightly different although some of the same categories were involved. Its format was, "In trying out a different brand, which of the following do you think is likely to be the most influence on you? (Check one) A friend's recommendation. A desire to try something new. Lower price of another brand. What my group does. An advertisement."

[9] Three open-end questions were asked in this part of the questionnaire, "(1) Do you generally use retailer brands of food products? (Please elaborate explaining how often you use them, any special uses or preferences, etc.), (2) In your opinion, do the retailer brands differ significantly in price or quality from the nationally advertised brands? (3) Please make any other comments concerning retailer brands which will help us to understand how you feel about them."

Contrasting with the acceptors, the rejectors tended to have negative opinions of private brands. The typical rejector believed in the greater utility of value of national brands. The notion, you get what you pay for, was implicit in many replies. Some rejectors gave specific examples of retailer brands being inferior in quality or gave highly moral or ethical reasons for their rejection. A few specifically mentioned that national brands were purchased because of habit, convenience or economy, or advertising influence.

A chi square of 22.27, significant well beyond the .01 level, was derived from a cross tabulation of respondents classified on the basis of these replies and the acceptor-rejector index classification derived earlier.

Further analysis of open-end questions involved classification on the basis of differing perceptions of price-quality comparisons of national and private brands. Four groups were formed on the basis of interpreted replies: lower price-lower quality, lower price-same quality, same price-lower quality, and same price-same quality. These were cross tabulated with the four groups derived from the acceptor-rejector index. All four quartiles of the earlier distribution were included in an attempt to take full advantage of the available data.

The cross tabulation for 140 respondents in Table 1 shows a tendency for respondents who use private brands regularly to believe they have lower prices and

TABLE 1   PRICE-QUALITY COMPARISONS OF PRIVATE AND NATIONAL BRANDS AND REPORTED USE OF PRIVATE BRANDS[a]

Price-Quality Comparison	Reported use of private brands[b]				
	Use Regularly	Use Occasionally	Use Rarely	Use Never	Total
Lower price-lower quality	26%	49%	56%	64%	48%
Lower price-same quality	51	21	13	6	23
Same price-lower quality	—	6	3	6	4
Same price-same quality	23	24	28	24	25
Total	100	100	100	100	100
n	39	33	32	36	140

[a]Rows refer to the classification of respondents on the basis of their replies to the question, "In your opinion, do retailer brands differ significantly in price or quality from the nationally advertised brands?" Columns refer to the classification of respondents on the basis of replies to the question, "Do you generally use retailer brands of food products?" Chi square across all groups is 46.74, significant beyond .01.
[b]Figures in percentages.

the same quality as national brands; whereas those who state they never use private brands believe they are lower in price but also lower in quality. Although almost equal numbers of respondents fall into each of the private brand use groups, the distribution of price-quality comparison groups is much less rectangular. Almost one-half of the respondents indicated that they thought private brands had lower prices and quality than national brands, whereas only four percent stated they were the same price but lower quality. These relationships are reasonably consistent with some of the notions outlined in the matrix of consumer types (Figure 1).

Validity of the measure of private brand attitude was further checked by examining the degree of distortion that results from variations in store preference. The rating index was based largely on brands of one supermarket chain, the A. & P. Company. Summing scores across private brands of this company might simply identify respondents who prefer A. & P. to some other store or are more familiar with A. & P. private brands rather than those who are more willing to purchase private brands. If, on the other hand, rejectors were found in an A. & P. store preference group, and acceptors in a non-A. & P. store preference group, rationale for postulating the existence of a differential private brand reaction independent of store effect would seem to exist.

Table 2 is a cross tabulation of the store preference and private brand preference groups. There is a tendency for the A. & P. store preference group to be classified as private brand acceptors, but many acceptors are also found in other store preference groups and many rejectors in the A. & P. store preference group.

TABLE 2   STORE PREFERENCE AND PRIVATE BRAND PREFERENCE GROUPS[a]

Store Preference Group	Private Brand Preference Group[b]				
	High Acceptor	Medium Acceptor	Medium Rejector	High Rejector	Total
A. & P.	5	3	2	2	12
Jewel	8	9	7	11	35
National	3	2	4	3	12
Other	7	8	10	11	36
None	1	—	2	2	5
Total	24	22	25	29	100
n	57	52	59	69	237

[a]Store preference groups are classified on the basis of replies to the questions, "At what store or stores did you shop the last time you bought food?" and "How do you generally shop for food?" In cases where several stores were mentioned, the first mentioned was used as the criterion for group placement. The "None" group refers to those respondents who indicated no measurable degree of store preference. Private brand preference groups are classified on the basis of summed rating scores over fourteen private brands. The score ranges and frequencies for each group are: High acceptor, 14-49 (79); Medium acceptor, 50-54 (63); Medium rejector, 55-59 (66); and High rejector, 60-70 (73).
[b]Figures in percentages of total sample.

Store preference does seem to affect private brand attitude but not to a degree that destroys the notion that respondents have different private brand attitudes or price sensitivities that are independent of their preferences for a particular store.[10]

SOCIOPSYCHOLOGICAL DETERMINANTS

P.B.A. was used as a criterion or dependent variable in a series of regression analyses in which personality and socioeconomic variables were used as predictors or independents. Eight traits from the original A form of Cattell's 16 Personality Factor Inventory were adapted for the measurement of personality needs [5]. Each trait was measured by 10 questions that were summed to obtain a trait score. These raw trait scores were used as predictor variables. Table 3 shows the results of the step-wise multiple regression analysis of the eight traits regressed against P.B.A.

TABLE 3   BETA COEFFICIENTS FOR CATTELL PERSONALITY TRAITS AND PRIVATE BRAND ATTITUDE[a] (N = 208)

Personality Trait	All Predictors	Best Predictors
Sociable	.088	.086
Stable	.037	
Dominant	$.130^d$	$.132^d$
Enthusiastic	$-.251^b$	$-.248^b$
Sensitive	$-.132^c$	$-.133^c$
Tense	$-.063$	$-.074$
Radical	.007	
Self-sufficient	.092	.092
R	$.197^c$	$.217^c$

[a]Beta coefficients are shown for the case of all predictors included in the regression equation and for the case of the six best predictors included in the equation. The dependent variable is P.B.A. (private brand attitude) derived by summing respondent ratings of 14 private brands in the rating index.
[b]Significant at $\alpha = .01$.
[c]Significant at $\alpha = .05$.
[d]Significant at $\alpha = .10$.

Enthusiasm is the strongest of the eight predictors, having a beta weight of $-.251$, significant well beyond the .01 level. Sensitivity and dominance have betas of $-.133$ and .132, significant at the .06 and .08 levels. The data suggest some tendency for women who are enthusiastic, sensitive, and submissive to be

[10]It is deceptively easy to consider private brand attitude, price-consciousness, and deal-proneness to be similar when in reality they may be associated with much different patterns. Private brand acceptance, for example, may follow the development of a preferential pattern for a particular store and be associated with a relatively loyal or committed brand-store individual. Deal-proneness, on the other hand, may effectively characterize a person with very little store or brand loyalty.

more prone to purchase private brands than their counterparts. As indicated by the multiple regression coefficient of .217, R^2 = .047, however, the predictive power of the personality variables, even in the best combination, is very low. Less than five percent of the total variance in the criterion is explained by the personality predictors in either the all-predictor or best-predictor case.[11]

A wide range of socioeconomic variables were substituted for the personality traits in the regression analysis and P.B.A. retained as the criterion. Socioeconomic variables included measures of age, income, occupation, and reading habits. Perceptual indicators of social position or aspiration were also included, such as social class perception and satisfaction with general living conditions or occupation. The lower middle class group was dropped because sufficient brand rating data were not available for an adequate measure of P.B.A. Several of the variables were classificatory. A multiple classification routine enabled the analyst to examine both continuous and classificatory variables without conversion to dummy variables. The multiple classification analysis program treats both types of variables, considering each subgroup of each predictor separately, and shows the direction and degree of its association with the criterion [4].

Of 15 socioeconomic and perceptual variables used in multiple classification analysis, socio-occupational group had the highest degree of association with P.B.A. Figure 2 shows a plot of the deviations for each of the occupational and social class groups involved. Deviations show both the strength and direction of each relationship. Positive deviations indicate a tendency to be associated with low P.B.A. or private brand rejection, and negative with high P.B.A. or private brand acceptance.

Figure 2 suggests that a woman's occupational status, working or not working, seems to affect her attitude toward private brands. Of five socio-occupational groups tested, housewives are more likely to accept private brands and working women to reject them. Although differences in the housewife group and in the working women group are not significant, the direction of the deviations suggests that nurses are the strongest rejectors and middle class wives the strongest acceptors. Of greater significance is the tendency for working women, regardless of occupation, to fall into the rejector category, and the housewives, regardless of social class, to fall into the acceptor category. Although some of the other predictors showed significant relationships (ideal occupation, magazine type read, social class perception, and occupational satisfaction), none showed beta coefficients greater than .202.

[11] In a subsequent analysis, the 80 questions in the personality inventory were factor analyzed. Twelve factors were generated and their factor scores used as measures of the predictor variables. Two factors identified as enthusiasm and sensitivity produced beta coefficients of .193 and −.132. The R coefficient improved slightly to .224 but the improvement was not sufficient to suggest a strong association between the refactored personality indicators and P.B.A., although the factor results did show the same direction of association in each case.

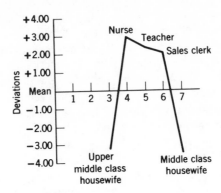

Figure 2. Socio-occupational group and private brand attitude: multiple class-ification analysis.

Each of the classifactory variables was converted to a dummy variable and used in a step-wise regression analysis in which both personality and socioeconomic variables were combined. Table 4 shows the results of the best predictive combination. Variables of relatively low significance are included because they contributed something to the overall association, and because those such as income and self-sufficiency have a particular interest as potential predictors.

The degree of association between combined predictors and criterion P.B.A. is higher than when either the personality or socioeconomic variables are treated separately[12] ($R^2 = .154$). Although the socioeconomic predictors are generally consistent with those relationships identified in multiple classification analysis, a religious factor appears to be more significant in multiple regression analysis. Both Protestants and Catholics are shown to be more likely to accept private brands. Upon further analysis, however, the apparent strength of the religious factor was discounted because of the small numbers of respondents represented in each of the remaining religious groups, only 10 respondents were Jewish, and only eight were in the other groups.

The variables upper middle class wife and middle class wife are among the strong-est of the predictors. Social class perception, occupational aspirations to be either writers or artist-singers, readership of *Woman's Day*, and education, all show signifi-

[12] Many other combinations of both predictor and criterion variables were tested in an attempt to find improved relationships. For example, the number of predictors was reduced to test if the inclusion of a large number of predictors in the regression served in any way to suppress the associations of the major predictors. In none of these trials, however, did the associations improve beyond those reported above.

TABLE 4   BETA COEFFICIENTS FOR COMBINED PERSONALITY AND SOCIOECONOMIC VARIABLES AND PRIVATE BRAND ATTITUDE (N = 208)

Personality Traits and Socioeconomic Variables[a]	Beta Coefficients
Social class perception	.211[b]
I.O.: Artist-singer (D)	−.203[b]
Protestant (D)	−.325[b]
I.O.: writer (D)	−.205[b]
Middle class wife (D)	−.241[b]
Woman's Day (D)	−.185[b]
Enthusiasm (P)	−.194[b]
Upper middle wife (D)	−.192[c]
Education	−.181[c]
Catholic (D)	−.244[c]
General satisfaction	−.131[d]
Sensitive (P)	−.104
I.O.: Businesswoman-doctor (D)	−.097
Occupational satisfaction	.099
Self-sufficient (P)	.089
Father's occupation	−.082
Income	.102
Dominant (P)	.085
R	.393[b]

[a]I.O. before a variable indicates that the variable is derived from a question on ideal occupation. A (P) or (D) following a variable indicates a Cattell personality trait or a dummy variable. The dependent variable in this regression is private brand attitude derived from summed respondent ratings of 14 private brands.
[b]Significant at α = .01.
[c]Significant at α = .05.
[d]Significant at α = .10.

cant relationships. The personality trait of enthusiasm also shows a relatively strong association. The step-wise multiple regression routine rejected the three working woman groups from the analysis because of their strong intercorrelation with the housewife groups. In a subsequent regression run in which the housewife groups were omitted, betas of .229, .209, and .209 were obtained for the teacher, sales clerk, and nurse groups. As in multiple classification analysis, there appears to be a relatively strong association between a woman's working status and her attitude toward private brands. Each of the working woman groups showed a positive association, and each of the housewife groups a negative association with the criterion.

Discussion

PRIVATE BRAND ATTITUDE

Several assumptions are implicit in the term private brand attitude used to characterize the criterion variable. The term attitude implies a pro or con predisposition about a class of brands. It may be quite unrealistic to conclude that such attitudes exist, particularly when the respondent must identify a class of brands as private brands. On the other hand, there is significant evidence to suggest that respondents do treat private or lower priced brands differently from national brands, even though they do not give explicit labels to them. Factor analysis of other ranking and rating data strongly suggests a tendency for respondents to lump together the private and lower priced brands and to treat them differently from nationals.

Assuming a certain minimum validity of construct, it is relatively easy to argue that advertising, pricing, or some other combination of factors succeeds in creating highly meaningful distinctions in the two classes of brands, but that these distinctions are recognized and treated in the same way by everyone. The utility of the construct as a segmentation criterion under these circumstances would be negligible If special uses in isolated situations are predominant patterns, there is little or no basis for proposing predictive segments. Alternately, differential consumer response to price or promotional influences may be identified, but may be so inconsistent or complicated that prediction is meaningless. Interpretations made on the basis of cross-sectional data, particularly where attitudes or opinions are criterion variables, are restricted to one time period, adding yet another source of bias or error.

On the other hand, there is a significant amount of published research evidence to suggest that consumers do respond to price and advertising appeals in predictively identifiable patterns, and that price-sensitivity in particular is a criterion well worth further study. Whether the research unit is private brands in panel data [6, 12], some direct indicator of deal- or price-sensitivity [24], or attitude evidence, such as that presented in these results, the conclusion that different consumer responses to these stimuli occur in predictively meaningful patterns appears warranted. In this sample, respondents expressed degrees of acceptance and rejection of private brands that were relatively consistent with tendencies to be influenced by price and advertising, with perceptions of price-quality differences in brand types, and with manifest rationale for using or not using private brands.

DETERMINANTS OF PRIVATE BRAND ATTITUDE

The emphasis of the empirical work was on testing the degree to which psychological and sociological characteristics might explain differences in private brand attitude. The conclusion, that these variables do not explain or predict large amounts of attitude variance, appears consistent with the findings of related studies of private brand choice previously mentioned. Respondents classified as private brand acceptors showed some tendency to be more enthusiastic, sensitive, and submissive, but the best association shown, that for enthusiasm ($\beta = -.251$), could not be considered a strong predictor of the criterion. Whether treated as raw or factored scores, personality differences in respondents explained less than five percent of the total variance in P.B.A.

Socioeconomic or perceptual variables were also not strong predictors of differences in private brand attitude, although as a group they were superior to personality variables. Housewives showed a greater acceptance of private brands than working women, the direction of the association supported by the direction of the association of each subgroup within the working-nonworking women classifications. A relatively simple explanation for this effect may be found in the reply of one working woman who reported that she had little time to concern herself with brand differences. National brands were chosen because, not being willing or able to invest much time in brand comparisons, she found it more convenient to purchase well-known, popular brands. The explanation that working women have more disposable income and thus have less need to be price-conscious was not supported by the data. Income was generally found to be a poor predictor of the attitude. Two of the working women groups, nurses and salesclerks, reported lower average incomes than the other groups tested.

The apparent inconsistency between the identification of a pattern of differential private brand attitude and the low predictive power of social, psychological, or economic determinants suggests the need for further theoretical and empirical investigation of this and related price-sensitivity constructs. Specific attention to the behavioral determinants of price-consciousness within the context of existing complex consumer models appears warranted.[13] Empirical designs which depend on attitudinal indicators should pay particular attention to reliability and validity and where possible should utilize logitudinal or time series data. In a recent article, Massy [17] proposes the use of stochastic rather than deterministic models in studies of brand choice, pointing out the prohibitive complexity of the latter. When research interest concerns an attempt at deterministic explanation rather than pattern identification, schemes such as those presented in this article provide useful guides to design and analysis.

References

1. "The Borden Company versus The Federal Trade Commission," 339, F.2d133 (1964).
2. Elise Boulding, "Orientation Toward Achievement or Security in Relation to Consumer Behavior," *Human Relations,* 13 (1960), 365-83.

[13] One investigator, for example, has recently defined price-consciousness as "the awareness of the role of price in the process of maximizing satisfaction derived from a purchasing act [16]." The author points out the significance of the time factor in studies of price-consciousness (daily, weekly, monthly, and even yearly or seasonal effects can probably be identified), and several potentially useful classifications of price-conscious types. Cultural determinants are also explored as having some potential utility for predictive purposes.

3. Donald T. Campbell and Donald W. Fiske, "Convergent and Discriminant Validation by the MultiTrait-MultiMethod Matrix," *Psychological Bulletin,* 56 (March 1959), 81-105.

4. James M. Carman, *The Application of Social Class in Market Segmentation,* Berkeley, Calif.: Institute of Business and Economic Research, University of California, 1965.

5. Raymond B. Cattell and Glen F. Stice, *Handbook for the Sixteen Personality Factor Questionnaire, The 16 P.F. Test,* Forms A, B, and C, Champaign, Ill.: The Institute for Personality and Ability Testing, 1957.

6. Lee Chaden, *An Empirical Test of Differential Consumer Response to Private Brands,* Master's thesis, University of California, Berkeley, February, 1966.

7. Robert H. Cole, *et al., Manufacturer and Distributor Brands, Some Facts and Issues,* Urbana, Ill.: University of Illinois Press, 1955.

8. Donald F. Cox and Raymond A. Bauer, "Self Confidence and Persuasibility in Women, " *Public Opinion Quarterly,* 28 (Fall 1964), 453-66.

9. Ross M. Cunningham, "Consumer Loyalty to Store and Brand," *Harvard Business Review,* 39 (November-December 1961), 127-37.

10. Harold Demsetz, "The Effect of Consumer Experience on Brand Loyalty and the Structure of Market Demand," *Econometrica,* 30 (January 1962), 22-33.

11. John U. Farley, "Why Does Brand Loyalty Vary Over Products?" *Journal of Marketing Research,* 1 (November 1964), 9-14.

12. Ronald E. Frank and Harper W. Boyd, "Are Private-Brand-Prone Grocery Consumers Really Different?" *Journal of Advertising Research,* 5 (December 1965), 27-35.

13. ———— and William F. Massy, "Market Segmentation and the Effectiveness of a Brand's Price and Dealing Policies," *Journal of Business,* 38 (April 1965), 186-200.

14. Andre Gabor and G. W. J. Granger, "On the Price Consciousness of Consumers," *Applied Statistics,* 9 (November 1961), 170-88.

15. Lawrence M. Hughes, "The 'Secret' Hand of Private Brands," *Sales Management,* 85 (September 16, 1960), 35-9.

16. Gerhard C. Hamm, *Price-Consciousness, The Antithesis to Pricing Decisions or A Demographic, Socio-Economic or Psychological Variable,* Unpublished working paper, Univeristy of California, Berkeley.

17. William F. Massy, "Order and Homogeneity of Family Specific Brand-Switching Processes," *Journal of Marketing Research,* 3 (February 1966), 48-54.

18. John G. Myers, *Determinants of Brand Imagery and Attitude with Special Reference to Private Brands,* Unpublished Ph.D. dissertation, Northwestern University, 1966.

19. Francesco M. Nicosia, *Consumer Decision Processes,* Englewood Cliffs, N.J.: Prentice-Hall, Inc., 1966.

20. Wendell R. Smith, "Product Differentiation and Market Segmentation as Alternative Marketing Strategies," *Journal of Marketing,* 21 (July 1956), 3-8.

21. Louis W. Stern, "The New World of Private Brands," *California Management Review,* 8 (Spring 1966), 43-50.

22. Lester G. Telser, "Advertising and Competition," *The Journal of Political Economy,* 72 (December 1964), 537-62.

23. Howard Trier, Henry Clay Smith, and James Shaffer, "Differences in Food Buying Attitudes of Housewives," *Journal of Marketing,* 25 (July 1960), 66-9.
24. F. E. Webster, Jr., "The 'Deal-Prone' Consumer," *Journal of Marketing Research,* 2 (May 1965), 186-9.

THE BUSINESS FIRM
AND THE CONSUMER

20. The Business Firm

"Consumer Purchasing Patterns as a Guide to Market Potential," Stephan Buck (Marketing Executive), *Admap,* Vol. 4 (May, 1968), pp. 214-218.

21. Interactions in the Marketplace

"Direct Observation of Purchasing Behavior," William D. Wells (Psychologist) and Leonard A. Lo Sciuto (Psychologist), *Journal of Marketing Research,* Vol. 3 (August, 1966), pp. 227-233.

There are significant differences between how a consumer sees his role in the market place and how a marketer perceives this same individual and his behavior. Often depending on judgment, the businessman must predict how consumers will react to his products and services.

In the two selections in Part VI we have reports of experimental studies that provide some insights into the relationships between the business firm and the consumer.

20 The Business Firm

Consumer Purchasing Patterns as a Guide to Market Potential

STEPHAN BUCK *(Marketing Executive)*

This article presents a new procedure for examining the repeat-buying and brand-switching that occurs in a frequently bought, nondurable consumer-product field. This method, supported by statistical theory, overcomes the main practical difficulties usually associated with this type of examination, and, in addition, indicates a useful method of market segmentation as a guide to market potential.

The value of purchasing patterns is first discussed. The basic concepts of loyalty and switching as applied in the conventional approach, together with the practical difficulties thereby encountered, are then described. The new procedure in practice and the way in which the main difficulties are overcome follow, together with practical applications of the method, including market segmentation and brand prediction.

The Value of Purchasing Pattern Data

The regular reports that are produced from purchasing data collected on a continuous panel of households, fulfil an important marketing requirement in that brand shares, absolute market levels and other basic statistics are monitored on a regular basis over time.

In addition, purchasing histories for individual households, usually held in the form of computer records, provide a rich source of the amount of loyalty and switching that normally exists in a market and the changes brought about by mar-

Source: Stephan Buck, "Consumer Purchasing Patterns as a Guide to Market Potential," *Admap,* Vol. 4 (May, 1968), pp. 214-218.

keting activities. Such records, for example, are extremely useful in measuring the effect of a free sample or the launch of a new brand.

Much of the previous literature on brand switching models has been concerned primarily with brand switching analyses employed to predict eventual 'steady state' or equilibrium brand shares, given the assumption that switching continues as currently measured. This assumption can obviously be challenged in the dynamic marketing situation that very often exists. Experience has shown that either the switching does not remain constant, in which case the prediction no longer holds, or if it is constant then this product field has already achieved its 'equilibrium' and the prediction is in fact the current market share.

Such predictions are perhaps best viewed as a standard of what would be achieved if present conditions continue; the extent to which actual events differ from the predicted position is a measure of market movement as affected by marketing policy. However, I consider the prediction capabilities of the analysis as less important than:

(1) Determining the degree of loyalty and switching that occurs among the brands and sizes in the product field.

(2) Examining the extent to which this behaviour is affected by marketing activity.

The Concept of Loyalty and Switching

The simple idea behind the construction of a brand switching table (or matrix) is the comparison of purchases made in one time period with purchases made in the next period.

As a simple example consider the hypothetical results of a sample of 1,000 homes in a two-brand market over two time periods (Table 1).

TABLE 1   HYPOTHETICAL EXAMPLE OF SWITCHING IN A TWO-BRAND MARKET

Purchasing Activity	Brand Purchased		No. of Households
	Period 1	Period 2	
Purchase Brand A in both periods	A	A	300
Purchase A in Period 1 and B in Period 2	A	B	100
Purchase B in Period 1 and A in Period 2	B	A	200
Purchase B in both periods	B	B	400

The data can be summarised by the following brand switching matrix (Table 2).

TABLE 2   BRAND SWITCHING MATRIX (USING TABLE 1 DATA)

Period 1	Period 2		Total Period 1 Purchases
	Brand A	Brand B	
Brand A	300	100	400
Brand B	200	400	600
Total Period 2 Purchases	500	500	

The numbers of households in Table 2 can be converted into proportions based on purchasing in the first period (Table 3).

TABLE 3   BRAND SWITCHING AND REPEAT BUYING PROPORTIONS

Period 1	Period 2		Total Period 1
	Brand A	Brand B	
Brand A	0.75	0.25	1.00
Brand B	0.33	0.67	1.00

From this we can conclude that the loyalty factor or habit index for Brand A is 75 per cent since 75 per cent of households who buy 'A' in Period one, also buy 'A' in Period two. Similarly, the habit index for Brand B is 67 per cent.

It is this probability matrix which, if assumed constant over time, can lead to predictions of equilibrium brand shares. Briefly, the switching matrix in Table 3 can be applied to the level of buyers in Period 2 to estimate the Period 3 shares and so on. By repeating the operation a number of times, the equilibrium brand shares are reached, i.e., brand share which are not changed by further multiplication by the switching matrix. This procedure is described more fully in the literature Ehrenberg (1), Howard (2), Styan & Smith (7), Longton & Warner (4).

Practical Difficulties

The method of constructing a brand-switching matrix applied in the over-simplified example above, meets with a number of difficulties in the practical situation. In the main, this is because households do not conveniently make one purchase of a single brand in each of two successive time periods. In practice, households can make multiple purchases of different brands in a time period, or alternatively make no purchase at all, (ie the inter-purchase time is not constant). Also taking into account different pack sizes can be a problem. These difficulties are discussed more fully by Howard (2) and Ehrenberg (1).

Attempts have often been made to overcome these difficulties by, for example:

(1) working with combinations of brands, i.e., purchasing both Brand A and B in a time period is considered as a buying category.

(2) defining a nil purchase as a mythical brand.

(3) working in unit sizes to overcome pack size problems.

These methods lead to unwieldy and unsatisfactory solutions in all but a few product fields. Howard (2) describes a 'semi-Markov' process to overcome the difficulty of irregular purchasing over time, but Ehrenberg (1) criticises the underlying assumptions of this approach.

The New Procedure

This section deals almost exclusively with the practical steps of the new method. I wish to acknowledge here Mr. K. Dennis for the extremely valuable help he gave in developing these models.

One of these approaches shows that purchasing activity should be examined separately for groups of households with different purchasing intensity; for example, heavy purchasers should be distinguished from light purchasers. This approach is followed in the practical methods below.

In practice, the method considers purchasing activity that occurs during a single period of time only. The choice of period length is dependent on the amount of information that it is sensible to consider and will vary between product fields. Also, as the example below will show, the purchasing activity is considered separately according to the time that elapses between one purchase and another.

Consider then, as an example, the purchasing pattern for a household over an eight weeks period (Table 4). The switching that occurs between successive purchases, indicated by the arrows, can be summarised (Table 5), and this type of summary can be made for all households in the sample.

TABLE 4   PURCHASING HISTORY FROM ONE HOUSEHOLD

Week	1	2	3	4	5	6	7	8
Purchase	Brand B	Brand A	Brand B	Nil	Brand B	Nil	Nil	Brand A
	$\longrightarrow$	$\longrightarrow$		$\longrightarrow$			$\longrightarrow$	
		1	2		3		4	

TABLE 5   SUMMARY OF SWITCHING (FROM TABLE 4)

Switch	Switching Activity			
	1st Purchase		2nd Purchase	Interval Between Purchases
1	Brand B	to	Brand A	1 week
2	Brand A	to	Brand B	1 week
3	Brand B	to	Brand B	2 weeks
4	Brand B	to	Brand A	3 weeks

The information for all cases where the interval is one week is then accumulated to form a 'brand switching' matrix for one week intervals. Similar matrices are formed separately for intervals of two weeks, three weeks, etc.

If the switching is constant (except for sampling error) for all 'intervals,' then the matrices can be combined into one brand switching table regardless of the interval between purchases. If, however, the switching varies according to the interval between purchases, then the matrices should be considered separately. This leads to an interesting method of market segmentation which will be developed in section six. If the data is to be used for predicting the equilibrium brand shares, then this can be done for each of the matrices separately and the results aggregated for an overall prediction.

In practice, it may not be necessary to deal with a large number of different matrices since these can often be grouped into a smaller number. As an alternative to calculating separate matrices for each interval, the decision as to the number of matrices to be used can be based on an examination of the brand shares for each of the intervals between purchasing. If brand shares are constant for different intervals, then it is a reasonable assumption that the matrices will be constant.

The method will cope with different pack sizes in that each size within a brand is considered as a separate classification in the tabulation process. Thus, the two main difficulties of the conventional approach, i.e., the varying inter-purchase time and the need to take into account different pack sizes, are solved in the new method.

Certain limitations, however, that do exist with the new method are now considered. Continuous household panels usually report on a weekly basis. Certain simple assumptions are necessary to deal with multiple purchases made during a single week since it is not possible to know the order in which the purchases were made. The incidence of multiple purchases of this sort is very low in the majority of product fields. See the example in Table 6.

Households purchasing only once in the whole time period considered cannot be tabulated in a switching matrix. However, they can contribute to an examination of the stability of brand share according to interval between purchases, and can be allowed for in the prediction of equilibrium brand share. The overall time period for study is chosen so as to ensure that 'once only' purchasers are relatively unimportant.

TABLE 6   OVERCOMING THE DIFFICULTY OF MULTIPLE PURCHASES
WITHIN A WEEK

Week	1	2	3
Purchase	Brand A, Brand B	Nil	Brand A

Switching Activity	Interval	No. of Switches
Brand B to Brand A	Less than 1 week	$\frac{1}{2}$
Brand A to Brand B	Less than 1 week	$\frac{1}{2}$
Brand B to Brand A	2 weeks	$\frac{1}{2}$
Brand A to Brand A	2 weeks	$\frac{1}{2}$

The method will not deal adequately in those fields where 'parallel' buying occurs, i.e., where multiple brand purchasing occurs on behalf of different members of the family. Gains/loss analysis as in Rohloff (6) and Kuehn (3) may be the method to use in these cases, but this type of purchasing does not occur to any marked extent in most product fields.

An Application of the Method

The results given in the example below are typical of those obtained from actual cases to which the techniques have been applied in the recent past. The figures have been rounded to whole numbers for convenience, since the object is to illustrate as clearly as possible how the techniques are applied.

Consider a product field with three main brands, A, B, and C, accounting for some 80 per cent of the market with a number of smaller brands making up the remainder; these 'other brands' are grouped together under the code OB. Using the Television Consumer Audit panel it was decided to study the purchasing patterns of 1,000 households in one ITV region. An eight-week period was used since 'once only' buyers who cannot be included in the switching analysis accounted for only five per cent of total purchases during that period.

The first step is to determine whether the brand switching matrices are different for the different intervals between purchases. As an alternative to the calculation of separate matrices for all possible intervals (one week, two weeks . . . . seven weeks) it is reasonable to examine only the brand shares according to the interval between purchases (Table 7).

Inspection of Table 7 indicates that there is a difference in brand shares and thus probably in brand switching for purchase intervals of three weeks or less compared to more than three weeks. It will then be necessary to tabulate switching for these two sets of purchases separately. Had we found that, except for sampling

TABLE 7   EXAMINATION OF BRAND SHARES ACCORDING TO INTERVAL
BETWEEN PURCHASES IN AN EIGHT-WEEK PERIOD

% Brand Shares

Interval between successive purchases	Brand A	Brand B	Brand C	OB	Total
Not more than 1 week	40	25	17	18	100%
2 weeks	42	24	17	17	100%
3 "	38	25	19	18	100%
4 "	30	33	18	19	100%
5 "	31	33	19	17	100%
6+ "	27	36	17	20	100%
Households who buy once in 8-week period	28	36	18	18	100%

error, the brand shares were similar for all intervals, then only one switching matrix
would need to be calculated and the interval between purchases would have been
ignored.

Before considering the switching matrices themselves, it is of interest to follow
up the indication in Table 7 that Brand A is the brand leader for short intervals,
whilst Brand B has the largest share for longer intervals. Short intervals between
purchases usually, though not necessarily, emanate from households who have
purchased frequently during the eight-week period, whilst the longer intervals occur
amongst the infrequently purchasing households. The brand shares were retabulated
according to frequency of purchase and the groupings below are informative (Table
8).

TABLE 8   BRAND SHARES ACCORDING TO FREQUENCY OF PURCHASE
IN AN EIGHT-WEEK PERIOD

| | No. of H/Holds | No. of Purchases | Brand Shares | | | | |
			Brand A	Brand B	Brand C	OB	Total
Frequent Purchasers (4 or more purchases)	320	1,960	40	25	17	18	100%
Infrequent purchasers	430	1,200	29	34	18	19	100%

Large differences in brand shares between the two groups of households can be seen. The frequent (or heavy) purchasers, who account for about 60 per cent of total purchases, buy significantly more of Brand A and less of Brand B than the infrequent (or light) buyers. This segmentation of the market by frequency of purchase has exhibited differences in brand share which are rarely seen when the sample is segmented by the usual classifications like social class or age of house-wife. These results lead to interesting marketing considerations and are well worth further investigation into the reasons behind the brand share differences.

We can now return to the calculation of the two switching matrices. These should be calculated separately for intervals of three weeks or less and intervals of four weeks or more (Tables 9 and 10).

TABLE 9   BRAND SWITCHING FOR INTERVALS OF THREE WEEKS OF LESS*

First Purchase	Second Purchase				Total No. of 1st Purchases
	Brand A	Brand B	Brand C	OB	
Brand A	420(80%)	70	20	20	530
Brand B	80	240(70%)	15	5	340
Brand C	30	20	180(72%)	20	250
OB	40	20	15	205(70%)	280
Total No. of 2nd Purchases	570	350	230	250	1,400

*Contains the purchases made mainly by the infrequently purchasing households.

TABLE 10   BRAND SWITCHING FOR PURCHASING INTERVAL OF FOUR WEEKS OR MORE*

First Purchase	Second Purchase				Total No. of 1st Purchases
	Brand A	Brand B	Brand C	OB	
Brand A	200(70%)	30	30	30	290
Brand B	20	240(73%)	30	40	330
Brand C	30	30	120(63%)	10	190
OB	40	60	—	100(50%)	200
Total No. of 2nd Purchases	290	360	180	180	1,010

*Contains the purchases made mainly by the infrequently purchasing households.

Table 9, containing the purchasing behaviour mainly exhibited by the frequently purchasing households, shows that Brand A has a higher loyalty factor than the other brands in the market. The figure of 80 per cent in parenthesis indicates that four out of every five purchases of Brand A is followed by another purchase of Brand A. Comparison of the off-diagonal terms in the table shows that A is gaining slightly from B (80 switches from B to A, compared with 70 from A to B) and also from C, and to a greater extent from other brands. Brand B is gaining slightly from Brand C and to a greater extent from other brands. Brand C and particularly other brands are losing share quite markedly. This can be seen from a comparison of the total numbers of first and second purchases given in the table.

Table 10, containing the behaviour of the infrequently purchasing households, shows that Brand A and B have similar loyalty factors of about 70 per cent compared with just over 60 per cent from Brand C and only 50 per cent from other brands. Brand A is holding its position, whilst Brand B is gaining mainly at the expense of other brands. Brand C appears to be losing a little share, whilst other brands are again doing poorly. A lot of switching occurs between Brand B and other brands whilst little occurs between C and other brands.

These tabulations are thus useful for measuring the degree of loyalty and competition that exists among the different brands in the market. Equilibrium brand shares are then calculated separately from Tables 9 and 10 and combined using the number of switches as a weight; the brand shares of the 'once-only' buyers are also taken into account. These predictions are shown in Table 11, compared to the current share.

TABLE 11   CURRENT AND PREDICTED EQUILIBRIUM BRAND SHARES

	Frequent Purchasing		Infrequent Purchasing		Combined Total	
	Current %	Equil. %	Current %	Equil. %	Current %	Equil. %
Brand A	39.3	47.2	29.0	27.5	34.7	38.5
Brand B	24.6	27.7	33.5	38.1	29.4	32.2
Brand C	17.1	13.0	18.5	17.4	17.5	15.0
OB	19.0	12.1	19.0	17.0	18.4	14.3
Total	100	100	100	100	100	100

From this it can be seen that a continuation of the current purchasing behaviour will result in gains for Brands A and B at the expense of C and the other brands. A study of the equilibrium shares for the frequent and infrequent purchases separately shows that different marketing action may need to be taken in the two segments of the market.

Summary

(a) The new method presented in this paper overcomes the main practical difficulties which previously existed for this type of brand switching analysis.

(b) It is a useful descriptive tool for examining the loyalty and switching activity that exists in a product field, In addition, it provides predictions of future brand shares that can be valuable if used sensibly.

(c) Examples have shown how the procedure exposes large differences in brand share between different market segments.

(d) Further work to be carried out on this subject will use the Television Consumer Audit data to examine the stability of the loyalty and switching that occurs for different product fields and for different time periods for the same product field. In particular the effect of marketing promotions and new brand launches will be examined.

References

1. A. S. C. Ehrenberg, "An Appraisal of Markov Brand Switching Models," Journal of Marketing Research, Vol. II (November 1965) pp. 347-62.

2. R. A. Howard, "Stochastic Process Models of Consumer Behaviour," Journal of Advertising Research, 1963, Vol. 3, pp. 35-42.

3. A. A. Kuehn, "Gains-Loss Analysis of New and Established Brands," Paper given to the AGB Seminar at the London Hilton, February 8th, 1968.

4. P. A. Longton and B. T. Warner, "A Mathematical Model for Marketing," METRA Offprint, Vol. I, No. 3 1962.

5. D. G. Morrison, "Interpurchase Time and Brand Loyalty," Journal of Marketing Research, Vol. III (August 1966) pp. 289-91.

6. Albert C. Rohloff, "New Ways of Analyze Brand-to-Brand Competition," Proceedings of the Winter Conference of the American Marketing Association: Toward Scientific Marketing, Chicago 1963. The American Marketing Association 1963, pp. 224-40.

7. G. P. H. Styan and H. Smith Jr., "Markov Chains Applied to Marketing," Journal of Marketing Research, Vol. 1 (February 1964) pp. 50-5.

21 Interactions in the Marketplace

Direct Observation of Purchasing Behavior

WILLIAM D. WELLS *(Psychologist)* AND LEONARD A. LO SCIUTO* *(Psychologist)*

Much marketing research relies on consumers' retrospective reports of purchasing behavior.

This article shows that it is possible to supplement and enrich questionnaire results by making direct observations of purchasing. It describes the observation technique, discusses advantages and limitations, and presents some specimen results.

The time is 7:30 on a Thursday evening. The location is the Good Deal supermarket in Totowa, New Jersey. The following episode takes place:

A school age boy and his parents enter the aisle.

The parents hurry down the aisle, looking straight ahead and not even glancing at the cereals.

Source: William D. Wells and Leonard A. Lo Sciuto, "Direct Observation of Purchasing Behavior," *Journal of Marketing Research,* Vol. 3 (August, 1966), pp. 227-233.

*William D. Wells is professor of psychology and marketing, Graduate School of Business, University of Chicago, and a consultant to Leo Burnett, Inc. Leonard A. Lo Sciuto is assistant professor of psychology, Newark College, Rutgers University, where he teaches research methodology in the Consumer Psychology Graduate Program. The observations at the cereal counter were made by Carol Astuni and Judy DiLallo, research students at Rutgers. The observations at the candy and detergent counters were made by Amy Tamburi, a graduate student at Queens College. Miss Tamburi's observations were the data for her master's thesis, "Controlled Direct Observations of Shoppers in Supermarkets," Queens College 1965. The authors would also like to thank Larry Strassman, Benton & Bowles Research Fellow at Rugers, who contributed greatly to the data analysis. The study was sponsored by Benton & Bowles, Inc.

"Can't I have some cereal?" asks the boy very winningly.

"No," answers the father very sternly, and quickly continues up the aisle.

"You dirty crumb," is the boy's reply as he walks up the aisle with his head lowered.

This episode is one of 1,500 observations of shopping behavior made in supermarkets in Northern New Jersey. The observations were collected to find out what information this method might yield and what problems might arise if it were to be used routinely on a larger scale.

The idea of making detailed on-the-spot observations of purchasing behavior was suggested by the work of Iowa psychologist Roger Barker [1]. In studying the behavior of children, Barker and his colleagues trailed their subjects with pad and pencil in hand, making detailed records of how the children dealt with the environment. Their findings suggested that direct observations of consumer purchasing behavior might provide information which cannot be obtained from experiments or questionnaires.

This article begins with some observations about the art of making observations. It continues with a discussion of the advantages and disadvantages of using direct observations in marketing research and concludes with a presentation of some specimen results.

Making Observations

In the pilot study reported here, the process of collecting observations proved tedious but not especially difficult. The supermarket managers agreed to cooperate as soon as they were sure that the observers were not going to interfere with normal business, were not trying to discover something that would discredit the store, and were not shoplifting! The shoppers seldom noticed the observers. When they did, they usually regarded the observers as part of the scenery.

The observers stood by the counters with pad and pencil recording "episodes." An episode began when a shopper appeared in the aisle with the apparent intention of buying something, and it ended when the shopper left the aisle. If the shopper appeared to be interested only in the counter across the aisle, or seemed to be just passing through, no record was made. Collecting 1,500 episodes required about 600 hours, including travel and write-up time.

The only real data collection problem was persuading the observers to include sufficient detail in their records. In practice trials the observers were inclined to record only the bare bones of each transaction, omitting the detail which is the essence of the method. This problem was solved after repeated use of explicit examples.

A second, comparatively minor data collection problem, was persuading the observers to prepare permanent records immediately after a day's observations were made. It became important to transfer the observations from notes to permanent record cards before the notes got cold. Again, the problem was solved by repeated instruction and use of examples.

Advantages of the Method

WHAT PEOPLE DO, NOT WHAT THEY SAY

The principal advantage of direct observation is that when it is done well it produces a highly detailed, nearly complete record of what people actually do. It does not depend on the respondent's ability to interpret a questionnaire question correctly, or on the respondent's memory of a not very important and perhaps not very recent event. It is not influenced by any tendency to rationalize behavior to make it appear in the best light.

SERENDIPITY

A secondary but sometimes important advantage of this method is that it occasionally produces an idea that can be tested later. In this investigation, for example, the candy counter watcher noticed that shoppers seemed to be rejecting candy packaged in grayish, semitransparent material in favor of candy packaged in clear, transparent plastic. The evidence from the observations was not conclusive, but the hypothesis would be easy to test by experiment. If confirmed, the finding would be important.

Despite these apparent advantages, few studies involving direct observation of consumer behavior have been reported. Lorie and Roberts [5] mentioned a study which employed direct observations, but they gave only the briefest account of the results. Hicks and Kohl [4] used a motion picture camera to photograph purchasing activities but did not report results in much detail. More recently, large scale, well-reported observations of shopping behavior were combined with survey methods in a series of studies for Colonial Supermarkets [2]. Generally, however, purchasing behavior has been studied by means of retrospective reports, as in the recent study sponsored by *Life* [3].

Disadvantages of the Method

WHAT, BUT NOT WHY

One disadvantage of direct observation is that it provides information on behavior only, and behavior cannot always be interpreted easily. Take this episode for example:

A man with his arms full of cans throws the armful into a cart at the beginning of the aisle. He pulls the cart by the front along with him down the aisle. He turns around a Rinso Blue box and reads the front for a moment. Then he walks back to the beginning of the aisle and looks at Oxydol, regular size. He hesitates and picks up a large package of All with the rose bush offer. He leaves this box and walks up the rest of the aisle. He then reads an All box (in a display with the rest of the All's) and puts it back. He backs down the aisle halfway and reads the Dreft box then further up he reads the Ivory Snow box. He then takes a box of Instant Fels and puts it in the cart.

What was the man looking for? In this particular instance it was possible to ask him what he was doing. He explained:

"I am allergic and was looking for one with 'soap' marked on it. I have a terrible reaction to detergents." He pointed to Salvo and said, "That kills me." He went on to discuss septic tanks, saying that people with septic tanks are told not to use detergents, that it is against the law in some places, etc. and related an army experience. The observer commented that the shopper had a hard time choosing, and asked, "Haven't you found one that you like?" The shopper said, "Every once in a while I get allergic to the one I am using so I have to switch." The observer asked, "Do you think this Instant Fels will do it?" He answered, "I haven't tried it. I hope so."

But it is not always possible to get an explanation because stopping one shopper may interfere with observing the next. Unanswered questions remain to tantalize the analyst, and sometimes must be resolved by a best guess.

SAMPLING PROBLEM

A second disadvantage of the direct observation method is that the results can be biased by when and where the observations are made. Shopping behavior varies with the kind of store because different shopping environments give the shopper different problems. It is one thing to shop in a small, crowded, urban market which offers limited selection, and something else again to fill a cart in a large highway store or spacious modern market in suburbia. Since all three kinds of markets sell large amounts of groceries, it is essential that all three be included *in their proper proportions* if the observations are to provide a true picture of shopping behavior.

In addition to differences in shopping environment among stores, shopping environment varies within the same store at different hours of the day and on different days. Stores are much more crowded at some times and on some days than others, and the probability that a shopper will be buying a lot of items at once is much higher on weekends and in the evenings [2].

Still another reason shopping behavior is different in different time periods is that the shopper population shifts from time to time. Employed men and women are seldom in stores during the business day. School children are usually not in the stores during school hours, but they appear in droves after school and on weekends.

These population shifts are not trivial. One can see their importance by trying to answer a simple question like, "What proportion of shoppers use a shopping list when buying cereal?" In the present observation shopping lists were used by 34 percent of the males, 20 percent of the females, and 12 percent of the couples. Since the relative proportions of males, females and couples change from time to time, the answer to the question will depend on when the observations are made.

The direct observation method creates two other problems. Both are important, but because they are shared with other research methods they will be only briefly noted.

NO EXPERIMENTAL CONTROL

One problem is that since the observer has no control over important variables, cause and effect are sometimes indistinguishable. If a difference is observed between behavior in urban stores and behavior in suburban stores, for instance, it is hard to tell whether the difference is caused by the different shopping environments, by the fact that urban shoppers tend to be of lower economic class and of different ethnic groups, or by some combination of these and other factors. Sometimes it is possible to partial out confounding variables by multivariate analysis, but the basic problem always remains.

QUALITATIVE DATA

The other problem this method shares with some other research methods is that the reports are narrative rather than quantitative. This means that analysis of the data will be time-consuming and that the results will be subject to the questions and reservations always associated with results based on interpretation and judgment.

Sometimes, of course, the interpretation problem is minor. To answer the question sequence:

What proportion of cereal shoppers had children with them?
In what proportion of the episodes did children attempt to influence cereal purchases?
And in what proportion of the episodes did they succeed?

it is merely necessary to count accurately if the observations were made correctly in the first place. But, to answer the question, "What proportion of the shoppers knew what they wanted when they approached the cereal counter?" it is necessary to infer a state of mind. When the shopper marches right up to a specific spot in the display, grabs a box and goes, the evidence in favor of a preformed choice is all but conclusive. But when a shopper hesitates, searches, picks things up and puts things down, it is hard to guess whether the shopper doesn't know what he wants, or knows what he wants but can't find it. In cases such as this a judgment must be made.

These disadvantages are important, but they are not necessarily negative. All research methods have their limitations, and some of the most popular and widely accepted methods have limitations which the direct observation method eliminates. The question is, can the limitations of the method be accepted considering the information it yields?

Some Results

COMPOSITION OF THE SHOPPER POPULATION

Because most marketing research consists of interviews with housewives, one can easily get the impression that most supermarket shopping is done by housewives acting on their own. Table 1 shows that this is not the case. A housewive alone

TABLE 1   COMPOSITION OF THE SHOPPER POPULATION

Shopper	Cereal	Candy	Detergent	Total
Housewife alone	36%	44%	46%	39%
With child or children	16	11	7	13
With husband	16	9	12	14
With other adult	6	5	4	5
Adult male alone, with other adult male, or with children	22	23	27	24
Child or children alone	4	8	4	5
Base (Number of episodes)	1000	250	250	1500

was the shopper in 39 percent of the episodes, but in 32 percent of the episodes the housewife was accompanied by someone else who often participated in shopping decisions, and in 29 percent of the cases the housewife was not present.

The finding that housewives are not the only shoppers is supported by other studies, when the other studies include other groups. For instance, the *Life* study of family shopping behavior [3] indicated that men had done the shopping exclusively in one out of six recent shopping trips and had participated in a large proportion of the other trips. The Colonial Supermarket study [2] produced percentages of nonhousewife shoppers similar to the percentages reported above. It seems clear that marketers who pay exclusive attention to housewives are making a mistake.

INFLUENCE OF CHILDREN

Table 2 shows the influence of children when present. As might be expected, this influence was strongest at the cereal counter, but at the candy counter it was distinct, and it was even present to some degree at the detergent display.

Table 2 also confirms an impression, reported by the observers early in the study, that suburban parents are more indulgent than urban parents, except when it comes to the purchase of candy. Suburban children made more influence attempts, and, except at the candy counter, they succeeded in a higher proportion of attempts.

TABLE 2   INFLUENCE OF URBAN AND SUBURBAN CHILDREN ON
ADULTS' SHOPPING BEHAVIOR

Item	Cereal	Candy	Detergent
All Children			
Influence attempted	59%	55%	24%
Influence successful	36	29	20
Base (Episodes with children present)	338	84	46
Urban			
Influence attempted	57%	58%	13%
Influence successful	31	33	6
Base (Episodes with children present)	260	40	16
Suburban			
Influence attempted	68%	52%	30%
Influence successful	50	25	27
Base (Episodes with children present)	78	44	30

INFLUENCE OF ADULT MALES

As indicated earlier, adult males do a significant amount of grocery shopping by themselves or with children, and at other times they accompany wives. They are important because when they make a serious attempt to influence a purchase, they almost always succeed. Almost, but not always:

A young couple in their twenties enters the aisle. First they look at the tuna fish across the aisle. After choosing some, they turn to the cereal.

"Get a special flavor," says the wife. Her husband then looks and grabs a package of Variety.

"No, no," says the wife quickly. "You don't like them."

"Yes I do," protests the husband. "I like Corn Flakes and stuff," he says as he reads the cereals in the package.

"No you don't," replies the wife. The husband continues to look. "How about these?" he says as he grabs a Shop-Rite Variety Pak.

"That's the same thing," answers the wife.

"How about Corn Flakes?" he then suggests.

"No get something different."

Her husband looks again. 'How about Rice Krispies?"

"No," answers the wife. She looks and says, "Get Special K." He then looks and reaches for a box of Special K Handi-Pak. He puts it in the cart and they then turn to look at the soup across the aisle.

Milquetoast episodes such as this are rare. In the present observations adult males were the sole purchasers or were present and exercised decisive influence in 20 percent of the cereal purchases, 14 percent of the candy purchases and 24 percent of the detergent purchases.

THE ROLE OF ATTITUDES

One of the perennial questions in attitude research is "Do attitudes predict behavior?" The traditional approach to this question has been to measure attitudes, usually by some paper-and-pencil test, and then to measure behavior at some later date, usually by means of a retrospective interview. The relations found by this approach have never been perfect. Sometimes they have been so low that the investigators have concluded that attitudes influence behavior little if at all.

Direct observation provides a different point of view. Since it records behavior, the task is to infer the degree to which some preformed attitude or intention played a guiding role. Sometimes the evidence is clear.

Two women in their forties enter the aisle. They have no cart. They stop and look at cereal. They seem to be looking for a certain kind. They stand back and look at all the cereal.

"I want a small box. I got it here before," says the first woman.

"What kind is it?" asks the second woman.

"Bran and Prune Flakes," answers the first. The woman then looks around and glances down the aisle.

"I see it," calls out the second woman.

"I see it," calls out the first woman who also looks down the aisle.

"I think I see it," adds the second woman. They both begin to walk down the aisle.

"Here it is," says the second woman as she points to it.

"Yes."

"How are we going to get it?" asks the second woman. (It is located on the top shelf and the first row is gone.) The second woman then grabs the bottom box and lifts three boxes together. The first woman then takes the top box and the other woman puts the others back.

"There," she says as she turns around. She has a big smile on her face. They both then leave.

In other cases the evidence for clear intention is weaker, but nevertheless it is there. For example:

A woman walks slowly up the aisle while her husband follows pushing the cart. She pauses halfway past the display and looks at the detergent. Meanwhile her husband passes her and picks up a giant size All, reaching forward. He places it directly in his cart. He steps back a few steps, reaches up and slides out the top boxes of Ivory Snow, and places them in his cart.

The wife asks, "Did you get All?" while looking at her list.

He says, "Yes."

Then they walk on.

Evidence on the influence of attitudes is summarized in Table 3.

TABLE 3   INFLUENCE OF ATTITUDES ON PURCHASES

Item	Cereal	Candy	Detergent
Clear evidence of intention to buy specific brand	55%	38%	72%
Purchase or brand undecided; Purchase made	30	18	12
No purchase	15	44	16
Base (Number of episodes)	1000	250	250

Of the people who approached the cereal counter, 55 percent seemed to have had what they wanted either written down or in mind. An attitude or intention of some sort was obviously involved.

The figure 55 percent, representing clear intention to purchase a specific brand, is interesting for several reasons. First, even though it may not be absolutely correct because of sampling and interpretation problems, it shows why attitude measures often do not predict accurately. Slightly more than half of the people who showed up at the cereal counter knew exactly what they wanted and were able to find it. Others, about 30 percent, had a difficult time deciding or had difficulty finding what they wanted, and about 15 percent finally went away without buying anything. It is not surprising that attitude measures taken some time in the past are not perfect predictors of what the shopper is going to do some time in the future.

The 55 percent "knew-what-they-wanted" figure for cereal is interesting also because it differs from the corresponding figures for candy and for detergent which are 38 percent and 72 percent, respectively. The low figure for candy probably resulted because a surprisingly large proportion (44 percent) of those who approached the candy counter went away without buying anything. Just why this should be true is not clear, but the no sale proportion for candy was higher than the corresponding proportions for cereal and detergents in both urban and suburban stores, and in urban stores the difference was particularly great. This finding is supported by the Colonial study observations. There, the proportion of candy no sales was twice that of cereal and detergents [5, p. C90]. Perhaps the candy counter lures people who have no real intention of buying and who manage to resist temptation—this time.

This study revealed the following information about attitudes. Attitudes and behavior are only loosely related. Much shopping takes places without a fixed predisposition as a guide. Furthermore, the degree of relation appears to be different from product to product, and there is some evidence that it is different in different types of stores. This explains why measures of predisposition are rough indicators at best.

IN-STORE INFLUENCE OF PRICE

Knowing that price-cutting can and does move large amounts of merchandise, one might assume that most grocery shoppers are highly price-conscious most of the time. Indeed, most grocery store advertisements speak of price and little else.

But how much attention do shoppers pay to prices as they shop? The observer cannot always tell, when a shopper picks up a package, whether he or she is looking at the price. But if the observer watches closely, he can usually be reasonably sure; if he is in doubt, he can often stop the shopper and ask.

In the present observations, 13 percent of the cereal shoppers showed concern for price, while as far as the observers could tell the remaining 87 percent did not look at the price at all. The corresponding figures for candy and detergent were 17 percent and 25 percent, respectively. Even though these figures may not be absolutely accurate, both because of uncertainties in interpreting the observations and because of the sampling problem, it is clear that a great many shoppers do not check the price of what they buy. These figures also suggest that concern with price differs from product category to product category. The figure for detergents is almost twice as high as the figure for cereal.

Only small differences are found when the price data are broken down according to composition of the shopper population (Table 4). Females shopping alone appear to be a bit more price conscious than females shopping with others. As one might expect, children appear to be least price conscious of all.

Urban shoppers showed more concern with the prices of candy and detergents than did suburban shoppers (Table 4). This is also to be expected since the urban shoppers in this study were at generally lower income levels than the suburban shoppers. For cereal, very few urban or suburban shoppers (11 percent and 13 percent, respectively) paid any attention to the price.

The data on price, then, suggest four main conclusions. First, concern with price is far from universal. It was present in some degree for all three products, but many shoppers just grabbed the box and left. Second, concern with price differs from product to product; in this case it was high for detergents, low for cereals. Third, when price is important, it is more important in urban than in suburban stores. Finally, sex differences in price consciousness are surprisingly small—much smaller than differences attributable to type of product or type of store.

INSPECTING THE PACKAGE

An elderly woman walks down the cereal aisle.

When she sees the cereals, she immediately stops and picks up a large box of H.O. Quick Oats.

She looks the box over entirely (apparently looking at the price and weight content).

While still holding this box in her hand, she picks up a box of Mother Oats.

TABLE 4   CONCERN WITH PRICE AMONG URBAN AND SUBURBAN SHOPPERS

Shopper	Cereal		Candy		Detergent		Total
	Urban	Suburban	Urban	Suburban	Urban	Suburban	
Adult male	11%	17%	17%*	16%*	30%*	11%*	15%
Adult female	11	19	21	14	33	22	17
Couple (with or without children)	12	8	25*	14*	14*	26*	13
Children (without adults)	7*	11*	0*	14*	22*	0*	10
Total	11	13	24	14	30	20	16

*Base less than 50.

She then looks this box over entirely and compares the two boxes.

She looks at the H.O. Quick Oats and then at the Mother Oats (apparently comparing their prices).

After comparing the two, she puts the box of Mother Oats back on the shelf and puts the other box in the cart.

After making this decision she remains where she is and continues to look at the cereals.

She then notices the smaller box of H.O. Quick Oats, which is on the upper shelf.

She picks up this box and looks at it, again reading the panels.

She puts the box down and turns around to her carriage.

She then stops, turns around, picks up the box again, and places it in her cart.

She replaces the larger box on the shelf, in the wrong place, and continues down the aisle not looking at the rest of the cereals.

This illustrates behavior which was first noted by Lorie and Roberts [5] and which appeared in the observations to an unexpectedly high degree. People spend a lot of time handling packages—picking them up, putting them down, fondling them, reading them, dropping them, picking them up and putting them back in the wrong place, etc. Sometimes they are looking at the weight and price, sometimes to see what premiums are being offered on the package back, and sometimes just reading the fine print.

Twenty-two percent—more than one in five—of the cereal shoppers and the detergent shoppers spent enough time inspecting the package to cause the observer to make note of the fact. The figure for candy was lower—16 percent. These figures suggest that it is worth paying close attention to what the package looks like, *how it feels,* and what it says since people look them over carefully.

Table 5 indicates that women shopping alone paid the most attention to packages, while the least was by couples. However the differences among the shopper groups, and between urban and suburban shoppers were generally small.

Summary and Conclusions

When questions arise about consumer behavior at the point of purchase, the traditional practice has been to rely on retrospective reports from questionnaires. This pilot study shows that it is possible, and, in fact, easy to collect direct observations of purchasing behavior instead. As a marketing research method, direct observation has some drawbacks:

It shows what, not why.
It requires adequate sampling of both points in space and points in time.
It does not permit control over important variables.
It produces qualitative, not quantitative data.

TABLE 5   PACKAGE INSPECTION BY URBAN AND SUBURBAN SHOPPERS

Shopper	Cereal		Candy		Detergent		Total
	Urban	Suburban	Urban	Suburban	Urban	Suburban	
Adult male	23%	20%	3%*	11%*	24%*	21%*	20%
Adult female	25	28	25	16	30	17	24
Couple (with or without children)	15	13	13*	7*	14*	16*	14
Children (without adults)	17*	25*	29*	0*	22*	0*	17
Total	22	23	19	13	27	18	21

*Base less than 50.

267

On the other hand, direct observation has the advantage of revealing what people actually do, as distinguished from what people say. It can yield the correct answer when faulty memory, desire to impress the interviewer, or simple inattention to details would cause an interview answer to be wrong.

What kinds of answers can direct observation yield? In addition to an occasional lucky insight—like the observation that the candy shoppers were rejecting gray plastic packages—direct observation can provide answers to questions like these:

Who actually buys the product, and who influences the choice?

To what extent are brand choices made before the shopper enters the store, and to what extent are they made at the point of purchase?

How many people check the price?

Do shoppers study the package before purchase?

Within the limitations described in the body of this report, the following conclusions may be made:

1. Women do more of the family shopping than men, but men do enough of it to warrant the marketer's attention.

2. Husbands accompanying wives almost always influence purchase decisions when they try.

3. Children, especially suburban children, are also quite influential, although the amount of influence varies from product to product.

4. Plenty of shopping behavior takes place without fixed intention to buy specific brands. Attitude measures can, therefore, never be more than rough indicators of purchases.

5. Urban shoppers show somewhat greater concern with price than suburban shoppers, but many in both groups pay no attention at all to prices marked on packages.

6. Price consciousness varies according to type of product.

7. Price consciousness seems to be slightly more characteristic of women than of men.

8. Many shoppers of all types inspect packages carefully before they buy. The tactile dimension therefore deserves more attention than it usually receives in package research.

References

1. Roger G. Barker, "Explorations in Ecological Psychology," *American Psychologist,* 20 (January 1965), 1-14.

2. "Colonial Study—A Report on Supermarket Operations and Customer Habits," *Progressive Grocer,* (Undated, probably 1965).

3. "Family Participation and Influence in Shopping and Brand Selection—Phase II," Nowland & Co., Inc., May 1965 (A study sponsored by *Life*).

4. J. W. Hicks and R. L. Kohl, "Memomotion Study as a Method of Measuring Consumer Behavior," *Journal of Marketing,* 20 (October 1955), 168-70.

5. James H. Lorie and Harry V. Roberts, *Basic Methods of Marketing Research,* New York: McGraw Hill, Inc., 1951.

PRODUCT ATTRIBUTES
AND THE CONSUMER

22. The Product

"Can New Product Buyers Be Identified?" Edgar A. Pessemier (Marketing Educator), Philip C. Burger (Marketing Educator) and Douglas J. Tigert (Marketing Educator), *Journal of Marketing Research,* Vol. 4 (November 1967), pp. 349-354.

23. Imagery and Symbolism

"Product Symbolism and the Perception of Social Strata," Montrose S. Sommers (Marketing Educator), in Stephen A. Greyser, Editor, *Toward Scientific Marketing* (Chicago: American Marketing Association, 1963), pp. 200-216.

24. The Package and the Label

"Wrapper Influence on the Perception of Freshness in Bread," Robert L. Brown (Psychologist), *Journal of Applied Psychology,* Vol. 42 (August, 1958), pp. 257-260.

25. The Price

"The Price-Quality Relationship in an Experimental Setting," J. Douglas McConnell (Economist), *Journal of Marketing Research,* Vol. 5 (August, 1968), pp. 300-303.

26. The Buying Environment

"Price Perception and Store Patronage," F. E. Brown (Marketing Educator), in Robert L. King, Editor, *Marketing and the New Science of Planning* (Chicago: American Marketing Association, 1968), pp. 371-376.

Any product, no matter how seemingly simple, is a combination of many factors as perceived by consumers. Among the most important of these factors are the product itself, its imagery, and the buying environment.

The interaction among these variables differs for every product and for every consumer, as exemplified by the five selections in Part VII.

22 The Product

Can New Product Buyers Be Identified?

EDGAR A. PESSEMIER *(Marketing Educator)*, PHILIP C. BURGER *(Marketing Educator)*, AND DOUGLAS J. TIGERT* *(Marketing Educator)*

Insights into the characteristics of buyers and nonbuyers of a new branded detergent are given. These are based on measures obtained both before and after the product's introduction.

Primarily because of the paucity of relevant data, few empirical studies have appeared on the characteristics of early, late, and nonbuyers of new products. This article discusses data collected for the "Lafayette Consumer Behavior Research Project" [9]. For the project, a great deal of information was gathered about introduction of a new heavy duty detergent. The branded detergent used was promoted as having a new fluorescent ingredient with unusual brightening power. Data were obtained from diary records and two questionnaires. One questionnaire was given before the product introduction and the other after a seven-month period during which purchase diaries were kept by 265 housewives.

The theoretical basis for this study was largely derived from the literature on adoption and diffusion. Studies by rural sociologists [11], Katz and Lazarsfeld [6], C. W. King [7], Coleman, Katz, and Menzel [3] and others led to the following hypotheses about variables that would discriminate among early, late, and non-buyers of the new laundry detergent:

Source: Edgar A. Pessemier, Philip C. Burger, and Douglas J. Tigert, "Can New Product Buyers Be Identified?" *Journal of Marketing Research,* Vol. 4 (November, 1967), pp. 349-354.

*Edgar A. Pessemier is professor of industrial administration, Purdue University; Philip C. Burger is assistant professor of marketing, Northwestern University; and Douglas J. Tigert is assistant professor of marketing, University of Chicago.

The project was supported by the Ford Foundation; Batten, Barton, Durstine, and Osborn, and Krannert Graduate School of Industrial Administration, Purdue University. Dr. David Learner, vice president of reserach, B.B.D. & O., and Professor Charles W. King, Purdue University both provided valuable assistance.

1. Early buyers would be more trial-prone toward brands in the product class and be heavier users of the product class (high salience) than late or nonbuyers.

2. Early buyers would actively transmit information about their experience with the brand and class; late buyers would be information receivers.

3. Early, late, and nonbuyers could be identified on the basis of demographic characteristics, mass media exposure factor scores, activity, interest, and opinion factor scores, and several product variables.

Because of the sample size (265) subjects could not be assigned to the five classifications described by Rogers [10]: innovators, early adopters, early majority, late majority, and laggards. Only the trial stage of the adoption process was investigated. The time to trial, if any, may be influenced by the level of current satisfaction, the perceived risk of trial as modified by advertising and feedback from earlier buyers, the available stock, and the rate of usage of the product class (subjects who purchase infrequently may fall by chance into the late buyer category). Subjects may develop brand preference leading to adoption after receiving information about the product and after using the product. Nonbuyers may have a poor opinion of the new brand or no opinion. A great many consumer attributes could be related to these elements, for example, the independent variables that will be examined. In addition, laboratory research indicates that experimental data on buyer preferences for existing brands, and possibly for a new brand, may materially aid in predicting brand switching and market behavior for the new brand [8].

Data and Definitions

A buyer of the new detergent was anyone who bought the product at least once in the seven-month period of diary keeping. An early buyer was one who purchased the product in the first 70 days after introduction. All remaining subjects who bought were late buyers. The 70-day period was a cutoff because the number of first-time buyers per 10-day period reached a peak in the seventh 10-day period.[1] Of the 265 subjects in the sample, 52 were in the early buyer category, 62 the late buyer category, and 151 the nonbuyer category.

Fifty-seven variables (Table 1) were used to examine differences between subjects in the three buyer categories. Each variable was either a "before" or an "after" measure. The before measures were obtained by questionnaire prior to the product introduction and the after measures were gathered from questionnaire at the end of the diary period.

Some comments may clarify the variable groupings. The activity, interest, and opinion factor scores (AIO) and the media factor scores were from two sets of

---

[1] A plot of time to first purchase was made on Weibull probability paper. It indicated a change in the forces influencing first purchase occurred at the 70-day point on the time axis. This result parallels the effect of catastrophic and wearout failures found in the electron tube life-testing investigations of J. H. K. Kao [5].

TABLE 1   LIST OF VARIABLES CROSS-TABULATED AGAINST EARLY,
LATE, NONBUYER CLASSIFICATIONS

Socioeconomic variables (before measures)
1. Number of children 18 years and under living in the home
2. Number of rooms in residence
3. Number of different residences lived in during past 15 years
4. Rent or own residence
5. Present credit buying behavior for durables, including automobiles
6. Wife's age
7. Wife's education[a]
8. Wife's employment status
9. Husband's age
10. Number of different employers husband has had since completing formal education[a]
11. Wife's religion
12. Husband's occupation
13. Husband's education
14. Total family income
15. Socioeconomic status score
16. Status consistency score

Trial-Proneness variables
17. Certainty about current brand versus other brands (before)[a]
18. Willingness to try known but untried brands (before)[a]
19. Perceived seriousness of product failure for detergents (before)
20. Willingness to shop for preferred brand (before)
21. Feelings about experimenting with new detergents (after)[a]
22. Likelihood of trying new detergents early (after)[a]

Activity, interest, and opinions factor scores (before measures)
23. Health and social conformity
24. Price conscious
25. Compulsive, orderly housekeeper
26. Fashion conscious
27. Careless or irresponsible behavior in personal, financial, and shopping affairs
28. Negative attitudes towards the value of advertising
29. Conservative middle class attitudes, sociable, mature
30. Weight watcher, dieter
31. Risk avoidance
32. Outdoor, casual, activist
33. Nonparticipating sports enthusiast[a]
34. Active information seeker
35. Do-it-yourself homemaker
36. Husband-oriented, interested in husband's activities

Product variables (after measures)
37. Total usage rates for all detergents for period (by total weight purchased)
38. Whether housewive received a free sample of the new detergent[a]
39. For those who received the sample, how much was used[a]

TABLE 1   LIST OF VARIABLES CROSS-TABULATED AGAINST EARLY, LATE, NONBUYER CLASSIFICATIONS (Continued)

---

40.   New product preference[a]

Informational variables (after measures)

   41.   Information transmission habits for detergents[a]

   42.   Information receiving habits for detergents[a]

   43.   Awareness score for new detergent[a]

   44.   Advertising slogan recognition score for new detergent[a]

   45.   Opinion leadership

Media exposure factor scores (before measures)

   46.   Factor score, cultural, intellectual magazines (*Atlantic Monthly, New York Times*, etc.)

   47.   Factor score, light reading magazines (*Life, Look, Readers' Digest*, etc.)

   48.   Factor score, fashion magazines (*Vogue, Mademoiselle, Glamour*, etc.)

   49.   Factor score, homemaker magazines (*Family Circle, Woman's Day*, etc.)

Judged importance of information sources on new detergents (after measures)

   50.   Importance of actual trial

   51.   Store display

   52.   Television advertising

   53.   Magazine advertising

   54.   Friends and relatives

   55.   Package label

Social activities (after measures)

   56.   Membership in church groups

   57.   Membership in informal groups

---

[a]Significant at .05 level when cross-classified against the early, late, nonbuyer variable.

questions. In each case, the response sets were obliquely rotated after principal component factor analysis [12]. The product preference variable (Variable 40) was constructed as follows: Each respondent rated 16 general product characteristics for detergents on a five-point scale, from "not important" to "extremely important." She then rated each of the top ten brands that she knew about on the same set of characteristics. These two ratings were vector multiplied giving a number for each brand defined as brand preference. Only the preference score for the new detergent was used in this analysis.

The awareness score (Variable 43) resulted from summing individual responses to four questions about the new detergent. One question asked subjects to write down all brands they knew that were not already listed. A second requested names of brands introduced in the area in the past year. A third requested names of brands for which samples had been given in the area in the past year and the fourth, advertising copy points for new brands recently introduced.

The accurate information score was obtained by scoring responses from a list of true-false questions on product characterisitcs and advertising slogans for several brands. Finally, the opinion leadership measure represented the standard question from the literature: "Would you say you are more likely, about as likely, or less likely than any of your friends to be asked your advice about laundry detergents?"

The purchase data on the new product were taken from diaries for the seven-month period. For each of ten product categories, including detergents, data about date of purchase, price, brand, total weight, deal amount, and place of purchase were collected.

Techniques of Analysis

Three kinds of statistical analysis were done. First, the 57 variables in Table 1 were cross-classified against the early, late, and nonbuyers category. Second, the variables that proved significant from the cross-classification were used in a step-wise multiple regression analysis. The regression involved prediction of number of days to first purchase for the subgroup of 114 respondents who had purchased the new detergent at least once in the seven-month period. Finally, the same set of variables was used in a discriminant analysis to try to classify subjects as triers or non-triers.

Results

CROSS-CLASSIFICATION

Fourteen variables were significantly ($p < .05$) related to the kind of buyer in the cross-classification analysis. These variables (starred in Table 1) were in four distinct categories: socioeconomic, trial-proneness, product-related, and informational. Though all were significant, only those relating to specific hypotheses are examined. The opinion leadership question, the AIO factor scores on information seeking and risk avoidance, and the media factor scores were conspicuous for their inability to distinguish the kind of buyer. Also, usage rate for the product class did not differentiate among early, late, and nonbuyers.

Table 2 shows the relationship between new product brand preference and kind

TABLE 2   DEGREE OF NEW BRAND PREFERENCE VERSUS KIND OF BUYER OF NEW DETERGENT

Preference	Early Buyer	Late Buyer	Non-Buyer
High (250-400)	55%	39%	19%
High Medium (200-249)	25	31	21
Low Medium (50-199)	12	12	17
Low (0-49)	8	18	43
Total	100%	100%	100%
Base	52	62	151

of buyer. Nonbuyers had the least preference for the new brand, and the early buyers the greatest.[2] Also, 19 percent of the nonbuyers indicated a high preference for the new brand. These subjects could eventually become late buyers of the new product.

Table 3 shows that early buyers were significantly less confident about their past brand purchases than late buyers, and that late buyers were less confident than nonbuyers, indicating a predisposition by early and late buyers to try new brands.

TABLE 3   FEELINGS ABOUT PRESENT BRAND OF DETERGENT AND
KIND OF BUYER FOR NEW DETERGENT

Degree of Certainty	Early Buyer	Late Buyer	Non-buyer
Very certain	17%	31%	48%
Usually certain	67	48	37
Sometimes certain or almost never certain	16	21	15
Total	100%	100%	100%
Base	52	62	151

Question: How certain are you that the brand of heavy duty detergent you are using will work as well as or better than any other brand you know of but have not tried?

Table 4 supports the predisposition to try the new brand. When asked about willingness to buy known, but untried brands, early and late buyers indicated a greater willingness than nonbuyers. This result suggests that an advertising campaign

TABLE 4   WILLINGNESS TO TRY NEW BRANDS AND KIND OF BUYER
FOR NEW DETERGENT

Feelings	Early Buyer	Late Buyer	Non-buyer
Very anxious or willing to try it	40%	36%	20%
Hesitant about trying it	52	53	49
Very unwilling to try it	8	11	31
Total	100%	100%	100%
Base	52	62	151

Question: When I am shopping and see a brand of heavy duty detergent that I know of but have never used, I am . . .

[2]Note that the early buyers would have a longer period for evaluating the product and to develop stronger likes or dislikes for this new brand.

aimed at shaking confidence in current brand offerings may be an effective strategy.
Two slightly different questions about innovativeness, reported in Tables 5 and 6, were part of the follow-up questionnaire. Early buyers clearly see themselves as experimenters to a significantly greater degree than late or nonbuyers (Table 5).

TABLE 5   FEELINGS ABOUT TRYING NEW DETERGENTS AND KIND OF BUYER FOR NEW DETERGENT

Feelings	Early Buyer	Late Buyer	Non-buyer
Enjoy experimenting with new detergents	42%	29%	13%
Prefer to wait until others have tried it	33	29	22
Prefer to wait until product has been established for some time	17	27	45
Don't know	8	15	20
Total	100%	100%	100%
Base	52	62	151

Question: (an "after test") Check the one statement that best describes your feelings about trying new detergent products.

TABLE 6   TRYING NEW DETERGENTS AND KIND OF BUYER FOR NEW DETERGENT

Likely to Try New Detergents	Early Buyer	Late Buyer	Non-buyer
Earlier than most people	8%	8%	1%
About the same time as most people	54	39	25
Later than most people	27	34	46
Don't know	11	19	28
Total	100%	100%	100%
Base	52	62	151

Question: In general, are you more likely to try new laundry detergents earlier, about the same time, or later than most people?

However, early buyers *did not* perceive themselves as innovators (Table 6). It seems that early buyers view their buying time for new detergents as concurrent with others. That is, there seems to be a perceived difference between experimentation and innovation. Other consumers that the early buyers had in mind might include other innovators. Literature on adoption indicates that innovative people with high interest tend to maintain active communication with one another. In this context the hypothesis seems tenable. Finally, in Tables 5 and 6, a significantly greater percentage of nonbuyers are in the "don't know" category.

Table 7 confirms an additional finding of adoption researchers about information transmission and reception. Compared with late and nonbuyers, the early buyers exhibited a higher degree of transmission of product information. However, a greater percentage of the late buyers were information receivers.

TABLE 7   INFORMATION TRANSMISSION AND RECEIVING ABOUT DETER-GENTS AND KIND OF BUYER

Information	Early Buyer	Late Buyer	Non-buyer
Kind of buyer—transmitting[a]			
Yes	40%	32%	22%
No	52	65	69
Don't know	8	3	9
Total	100%	100%	100%
Base	52	62	151
Kind of buyer—receiving[b]			
Yes	29%	43%	27%
No	65	57	65
Don't know	6	—	8
Total	100%	100%	100%
Base	52	62	151

[a]Question: Have you recently been asked your opinion on detergents or have you volunteered any information on detergents to anyone?
[b]Question: Have you recently asked or has anyone volunteered information on detergents to you?

Two demographic variables were significant in the cross-classification analysis. Late buyers, compared with early and nonbuyers, had a significantly higher education. The other significant demographic variable, the number of different employers of the husband for the past 15 years, is a partial indicator of mobility. Here 43 percent of the husbands of early buyers had four or more employers; comparable figures for late and nonbuyers were 25 and 19 percent. High mobility might create the capability to easily adjust to new elements in one's environment or might reflect dissatisfaction with present conditions.

The effect of the free sampling campaign is shown in Table 8. Sixty-five percent of all subjects reported receiving a free sample; however, in the late buyer group, 77 percent reported receiving the sample. When only those who received the sample are used as a base for studying the relationship between usage of the sample and kind of buyer, the nonbuyers do not give the sample a fair test. (Instructions on the package told housewives that several washings were needed to fully demonstrate the cumulative effects of the brightening agent in the product. Nonbuyers may have rejected the sample before trying it or after incomplete testing.)

TABLE 8   RECEIVING AND USING FREE SAMPLE AND KIND OF BUYER

Free Sample	Early Buyer	Late Buyer	Non-buyer
Receiving free sample			
Did receive a free sample	67%	77%	59%
Did not receive a free sample	33	23	41
Total	100%	100%	100%
Base	52	62	151
Using free sample			
Used all of the free sample	100%	98%	73%
Used some of the free sample	—	—	16
Used none of the free sample	—	2	11
Total	100%	100%	100%
Base	35	48	89

REGRESSION ANALYSIS

To further examine differences between triers of the new product, a stepwise regression analysis was done on the early and late buyers. The dependent variable was the number of days to first purchase, and the independent variables were all variables which were significant in the cross-classification analysis as well as several additional variables from Table 1. The results are as follows:

Significant independent variables	Increase in R?
Number of rooms in the house	7.3%
Total family income	5.7
Number of husband's employers	6.6
Buying on credit	4.4
Feelings about trying known but unused detergents	3.7
Media FS; movie, crime	3.4
New product preference score	1.8
Total	32.9%

The demographic variables dominated the analysis. Early buyers lived in smaller houses, were in higher income groups, had husbands who had worked for more employers, and were less likely to buy large items on credit. In addition, early buyers expressed willingness to try new detergents, were relatively heavier readers of movie-crime magazines, and developed a higher preference for the new product. Remember, on the basis of the cross-classification analysis, early buyers were in relatively lower education groups. Thus, except for the income relationship, early buyers compared with late buyers appear to be typical of the lower socioeconomic classes. No convincing explanation for the income relationship appeared.

Several of the demographic variables, significant in the regression analysis, were not significant in the cross-classification analysis. The cross-classification analysis involved three groups: early, late and nonbuyers, whereas the regression analysis treated only early and late buyers. Many variables that were significant in the cross-classification analysis reflected differences between triers and non-triers rather than between early and late buyers. The latter differences are reported in the discussion of the discriminant analysis. Conversely, several demographic variables, significant in the regression analysis, were not significant in the cross-classification analysis because their power to discriminate between early and late buyers was reduced after adding the third group (nonbuyers) to the cross-classification analysis.

Although the stepwise regression analysis explained only 33 percent of the variance in number of days before the first purchase, the results are highly significant and suggestive of the market segment at which advertising should be aimed. For those people who made at least one purchase of the new product, one must accept the hypothesis that there were significant differences between the early and late buyers.

MULTIPLE DISCRIMINANT ANALYSIS

Also, the data can be examined for differences between triers and non-triers of the product. A two-group discriminant analysis was done on the buyer, nonbuyer classification, using the Cooley and Lohnes [4] program and then the BIMD 07M stepwise discriminant program [1]. The BIMD program was run to examine the multicollinearity among variables in the analysis. The analysis using the Cooley and Lohnes program resulted in eight significant variables not reported here. Table 9 gives the results of the stepwise discriminant analysis resulting in four significant variables, a subset of the eight variables from the Cooley and Lohnes analysis. The stepwise discriminant analysis gave the same "hit and miss" classification as the Cooley and Lohnes program with only four rather than the original eight variables.

The buyer and nonbuyer samples were split into an analysis and validation group, and the results are shown in Table 9. For the validation sample, 72 percent of subjects were correctly classified compared with 54 percent if all subjects had been assigned to the largest group. A 72 percent classification was also achieved for the analysis group of subjects. Early buyers were more aware of the product, had a higher preference, were more willing to try new brands, and scored higher on likelihood of trying new brands early.

TABLE 9   STEPWISE MULTIPLE DISCRIMINANT ANALYSIS OF BUYERS
VERSUS NONBUYERS

Discriminatory Variable	F Value Contribution
Awareness of the new product (after measure)	50.1[a]
Willingness to try unused brands (before measure)	20.9[a]
Preference for new product (after measure)	10.0[a]
Likelihood of early new brand trial (after measure)	5.0[b]

| Actual category | Classified as | |
	Buyer	Nonbuyer
	Analysis Sample	
Buyer	57	23
Nonbuyer	31	79
	Validation Sample	
Buyer	24	10
Nonbuyer	12	29

[a]Significant at .01 level.
[b]Significant at .05 level.

Conclusions

Cross-classification, regression and discriminant analysis of differences between early, late, and nonbuyers for a new brand detergent gave significant results that tended to support several hypotheses on new-product trial. Triers and non-triers of the new detergent were significantly different for product specific and trial minded variables. But given that the consumer made at least one purchase, differences between early and late trial tended to relate to socioeconomic factors.

Several important variables differentiating between buyers and nonbuyers may be interesting but impractical because they were measured after purchase. That is, are buyers more aware of the product because they purchased it, or did they purchase it because they were more aware? Similarly, did brand preference develop after buying and using, or vice versa? For some subjects a high awareness and a strong brand preference developed, which might account for the eventual wide market acceptance of the new detergent. Future research should be aimed at measuring brand preference before purchase, maybe by laboratory experiments or test marketing.

How much these findings can be generalized to other product categories or brands in this product category was not tested. The particular brand studied was heavily promoted and also free sampled, undoubtedly contributing to the high product awareness in the community. The free-sample strategy may have added to the heavy level of trial purchases. However, the findings are generally applicable. In particular, it is likely that early and late buyers are qualitatively different and that the variables that most strongly separate these groups will be different from the ones that separate buyers from nonbuyers.

References

1. *Biochemical Computer Programs,* Health Sciences Computing Facility, Department of Preventive Medicine and Public Health, School of Medicine, University of California, Los Angeles, September 1965, 587-98.

2. Philip C. Burger, Charles W. King, and Edgar A. Pessemier, "A Large Scale Systems View of Consumer Behavior Research," University of Texas Symposium, *Exploration in Consumer Behavior,* April 1966.

3. James Coleman, Elihu Katz, and Herbert Menzel, "The Diffusion of an Innovation Among Physicians," *Sociometry,* 20 (December 1957), 253-70.

4. William W. Cooley and Paul R. Lohnes, *Multivariate Procedures for the Behavioral Sciences,* New York: John Wiley & Sons, Inc., 1962, 116-133.

5. John H. K. Kao, "A Graphic Estimation of the Mixed Weibull Parameters in Life Testing of Electron Tubes," *Technometrics,* 1 (November 1959), 389-407.

6. Elihu Katz and Paul F. Lazarsfeld, *Personal Influence,* Glencoe, Ill.: The Free Press, 1955.

7. Charles W. King, "Adoption and Diffusion Research in Marketing: An Overview," *Science Technology and Marketing,* fall conference proceedings, American Marketing Association, August 1966, 665-84.

8. ———, Edgar A. Pessemier, *Experimental Methods of Analyzing Demand for Branded Consumer Goods with Application to Problems in Marketing Strategy,* Pullman, Wash.: Washington State University, June 1963.

9. Richard Teach, and Douglas J. Tigert, *The Consumer Behavior Research Project,* Herman C. Kranner Graduate School of Industrial Administration, Purdue University, 1965.

10. Everett M. Rogers, *Diffusion of Innovations,* Glencoe, Ill.: The Free Press, 1962.

11. Bryce Ryan and Neal C. Gross, "The Diffusion of Hybrid Seed Corn in Two Iowa Communities," *Rural Sociology,* 8 (March 1943), 115-24.

12. Douglas J. Tigert, "Consumer Typologies and Market Behavior," Unpublished doctoral dissertation, Herman C. Krannert Graduate School of Industrial Administration, Purdue University, 1966.

23 Imagery and Symbolism

Product Symbolism and the Perception of Social Strata

MONTROSE S. SOMMERS* *(Marketing Educator)*

The meaning that a product has varies from group to group within our society. And the more marketers can learn about the various product meanings or the various symbolisms that exist, as well as the way in which different social groups perceive different products, the more effective can be their strategies in defining markets and making product presentations.

This article illustrates the application of an easily manageable research method, the Q-Technique, to provide information on product symbolism, in terms of the descriptive value of products and the way in which different groups perceive the same products.

The results are reported in terms of how the members of two social strata describe "Self" in terms of products, and how they describe typical members of the opposite stratum.

The question: "Why do people buy?" is constantly being answered in innumerable ways. One approach to answering it is to focus on what people buy and their perceptions of products. Newman views a product as

a symbol by virtue of its form, size, color, and functions. Its significance as a symbol varies according to how much it is associated with individual needs and

Source: Montrose S. Sommers, "Product Symbolism and Perception of Social Strata" in Stephen A. Greyser, Editor, *Toward Scientific Marketing* (Chicago: American Marketing Association, 1963), pp. 200-216.

*Montrose S. Sommers was Assistant Professor, Faculty of Commerce and Business Administration, The University of British Columbia, at the time he wrote this article.

and social interaction. A product, then, is the sum of the meanings it communicates, often unconsciously, to others when they look at it or use it.[1]

If such a concept of a product has merit, if products do have symbolic values and these are perceived differently by individuals and groups, it should be possible to relate differential product perception to those who hold these perceptions. As far as a marketer is concerned, if a product is the sum of the meanings it communicates, and these meanings may be many, a basic problem he faces would be ascertaining the different perceptions of his products which are taken by actual and potential consumers. Insofar as he can do this, he is better able to develop effective marketing strategy and achieve a more efficient allocation of his resources.

In order for marketers to make use of this concept of perception of product symbolism, a suitable research technique and instrument that can be handled with ease must be available. It was the basic objective of my research *to design a research instrument for studying perceived product symbolism* so that this concept could be more easily applied to practical marketing problems.

DESIGN OF THE RESEARCH

The project was undertaken on an exploratory basis and designed so that products became the vehicle for expression for housewives. Product symbolism was investigated within two frames of reference, the Self (S) and the described Other (O). Basically, housewives were asked to describe themselves in terms of a set of products and then to describe a particular other housewive using the same products as descriptive symbols.

- When a subject adopts the frame of reference of the Self, she is saying: "What kind of a person am I? How do I see myself? What is my image of myself?" The answers elicited are in very specialized terms, in terms of products as they embody and stand for role components.

- When the housewive adopts the frame of reference of the described Other, she is role playing and acting as if she were this person. From this position she is saying: "If I were she, how would I answer the same questions; what kind of a person am I? How do I see myself? What is my image of myself?"

By having subjects describe themselves and another person, it is possible to get an indication of the different descriptive symbolic values of the products used. The Self description provides an indication of perceived product symbolism and the nature of the Self perception; that is, through the relationship of product and role, which of the feminine role components are most important and their order of importance. The description of the Other provides an indication of how a subject perceives the descriptive product symbolism of another person. This descrip-

[1] Joseph W. Newman, "New Insights, New Progress, for Marketing," *Harvard Business Review*, November-December 1957, p. 100.

tion illustrates something of the perceived nature and importance of product symbols and related roles which are attributed, possible inaccurately, to Others.

OPERATIONAL HYPOTHESES TESTED

The operational hypotheses which were tested were designed to determine whether or not a product test of the type designed could actually differentiate between members of two different social strata; the nature of the perceptions of Other and the solidarity of perception of Self and Other that exists within strata. The statement of the major hypothesis is: *members of a high stratum (H) describe Self and Other significantly differently from members of a low stratum (L).*

The theoretical basis of this hypothesis is the sociological theory of symbolic interaction. The expectation that social strata will demonstrate unique stereotypes is based on the communication process used to transmit symbolic meaning and value. "The basis of symbolic interaction is the communication process, for society exists in and through it. Shared perspectives are the products of common communication channels."[2] The variations which arise in the modes of life of different social groups and the group perspectives which develop results "not because of anything inherent in economic position but because similarity of occupations and limitations set by income level dispose them to certain restricted communication channels."[3] Each social world is a culture area with its boundaries set neither by territory nor formal group membership, but by the limits of effective communication.

Our view of a social stratum is that while individuals within one certainly do not form a reference group in terms of formal associations, as long as there are mutual understandings and common presuppositions which are shared, as a result of a basic similarity in communication channels, there can be a common pattern of behavior. The concept of the reference group is maximized when it signifies "that group whose presumed perspective is used by an actor as the frame of reference in the organization of his perceptual field."[4] The broad category used here is not an organized group or a voluntary association but an unorganized informal group which offers a common frame of reference.

The research which is pertinent to this hypothesis is that which focused basically on the solidarity of meaning and value within a social stratum. The early work of Chapin in 1933 in developing a Social Status Scale commonly called the "living-room scale" was a pioneering effort in this area.[5] A similar type of scale was constructed by Sewell for use in measuring the status of farmers.[6] While both of

[2]Tamotsu Shibutani, "Reference Groups and Social Control," in Rose (ed.), *Human Behavior and Social Processes* (Boston: Houghton Mifflin Co., 1960), p. 134.
[3]*Ibid.*
[4]*Ibid,* p. 132.
[5]F. Stuart Chapin, *Contemporary American Institutions* (New York: Harper and Bros., 1935), pp. 373-397.
[6]William H. Sewell, "A Short Form of the Farm Family Socio-Economic Status Scale," *Rural Sociology,* Vol. 8 (June, 1943), pp. 161-170.

these scales were criticized, their basic contributions stand as the first systematic attempts at making use of products as indicators of social strata.

The well-known community studies of Warner, Hollingshead, and Kaufman, while they also raised methodological problems still result in the conclusions that a rank order or hierarchy of social strata exists and that the criteria which people use in perceiving of the hierarchy is expressed in the vague term "the way they live." The most conspicuous aspect of the "way they live" is, of course, consumption behavior. Warner summarizes his view on this by saying "it is certain that the use and meaning of most objects sold on the American market shift from class to class."[7]

The work of Centers exemplified the objective approach to this type of research in that, rather than using placement in a stratum based on objective factors or community judges, he relied on self-awareness and self-placement.[8] This subjective approach of Centers' comes closer to our theoretical position that a stratum can be viewed as a reference group in that there is a basic degree of subjective solidarity within the stratum. Support for this approach also comes from the work of Bott which was concerned with class ideology and which illustrates that strata or classes are constructed reference groups which are psychologically real even if they do not appear to be objectively real.[9] The Bott research aids in explaining some of the inconsistencies which are found when the data from objectively and subjectively oriented research projects on social class are compared.

The above research findings not only suggest the major hypothesis but also the supporting ones below.

The second hypothesis, that *members of H are more accurate in perceiving members of L than are members of L in perceiving those of H* is suggested by the tradition of upward mobility in American society and the idea that people in higher social strata not only have had experience in reference groups in lower strata but also are more articulate regarding prestige differences and make more divisions into groups than those in lower strata.

The third hypothesis, that *members of L demonstrate greater agreement in describing Self than members of H* is based on the idea that individuals within a stratum generally have access to similar communication channels but that members of a lower stratum have fewer alternatives in terms of roles and communication channels than those of a higher stratum. Because of the smaller numbers of alternatives available to those in the lower stratum, it is expected that there will be a greater degree of homogeneity of Self descriptions in the lower stratum than in the higher one.

[7]W. Lloyd Warner, Marchia Meeker and Kenneth Eells, *Social Class in America* (New York: Harper and Bros., 1960), p. 31.
[8]Richard Centers, *The Psychology of Social Classes* (Princeton: Princeton University Press, 1949).
[9]Elizabeth Bott, "The Concept of Class as a Reference Group," *Human Relations,* Vol. 7 (August, 1954), No. 2, pp. 259-283.

Hypothesis four, that *members of H demonstrate greater agreement in describing an Other than members of L* relies on the same basic position as those that preceded. Members of a higher stratum can be expected to demonstrate greater agreement in Other description than those of a lower one for the same reasons that they are expected to be more accurate in their perceptions. The better the persons and occupations are known, the more agreement concerning them.

Members of the lower stratum can be expected to have diverse concepts of Other because of their lack of actual reference group knowledge and relationships with members of groups like those in the higher stratum. In addition, the multiplicity of reference points presented by radio, television, newspapers, magazines, and other media is also expected to result in a diversity of descriptions of Other. The fifth hypothesis, that *members of H demonstrate greater agreement in describing an Other than in describing Self* develops naturally from the previous hypotheses dealing with accuracy of perception and agreement on Self descriptions for a higher stratum.

The sixth hypothesis is based on the same type of logic. Because *members of a lower stratum (L)* have fewer role alternatives, they *demonstrate greater agreement in Self description than members of H.* Because they have not had actual reference group contact with members of a higher stratum and receive much conflicting information through the mass media, their perceptions of Other are diverse and relatively inaccurate.

Measuring Perceptions of Self and Other

The basis for measuring the perceptions of products and their use lies in Q-methodology as propounded by William Stephenson.[10] Stephenson's intent was to deal with the total personality in action, with "wholes" and "descriptions" rather than traits or characteristics. The evidence of the total personality in action would be represented in the recorded reactions a person had with reference to a large number of test items. What is important in the approach is the form in which recorded reactions appear. It is the distribution of reactions, a forced normal distribution, which allows for the use of correlation and factor analysis techniques.

The test that an individual takes, under Q-methodology, is composed of items drawn from some type of population, in this case, a population of products. The methodology does not concern itself with the populations as such but with the statistical universes which are derived from them. In the product test designed for this project, the concern is not with the representativeness of the products selected, but with the manner in which an individual, when she is asked to grade products on a scale, from those which best describe her to those which least describe her, arrays these products. The procedure for evaluating each item and placing it in some kind of an array is called Q-sort. The method of evaluating such arrays and

[10]William Stephenson, *The Study of Behavior* (Chicago: University of Chicago Press, 1953).

and the position of items within them requires the establishment of a number of classes, each with a different score, and with each class containing an appropriate number of test items so that the array takes the shape of a quasi-normal frequency distribution. The quasi-normal frequency distribution for a sample of 50 products is shown in Table 1.

TABLE 1   FREQUENCY DISTRIBUTION AND SCORES FOR PRODUCTS
(N = 50)

	Best Describes					Least Describes			
Score	9	8	7	6	5	4	3	2	1
Frequency	2	3	6	9	10	9	6	3	2

Those two items which a subject places in the class on the extreme left receive a score of 9 for each. These would be the two products in the group available which best describe Self or Other. The second class contains the next three items which best describe Self or Other and each receives a score of 7. The score for items in each subsequent class is reduced to the point where the last two items, those which least describe Self or Other, receive a score of 1. From the frequency distribution it can be seen that those classes at the extremes of the distribution can be considered to be highly discriminating and have few items falling within them while those classes in the central positions could be less discriminating and have a greater number of items falling within them. The scores which the different items receive, under the two conditions of sorting, Self and Other, become the basis for analysis and comparisons.

Comparisons and analysis of arrays resulting from Q-sorting operations can be made using product moment correlation (Pearson r). The array which results from the Q-sort technique can also be scored on a rank order basis with the first item placed (that one being most descriptive) scored 1 and all the other items placed (in succeeding order to least descriptive) so numbered that the last item receives lowest ranking or 50. The technique is therefore flexible from the point of view of analysis.

In determining what kinds of items are to be used for Q-sorting operations, two basic considerations are to be heeded. Care must be taken to see that none of the items included are so apparently similar as to make distinctions between them extremely difficult. In addition, a basic type of homogeneity of class of items is important so that a subject can make decisions about how the items are related and what their relative values might be. For the Q-sorting operations of this project, the items included in the test are products which can be and are used in the fulfillment of feminine role components either in the home environment, with members of the family or as a representative of the family.

Five classes of products were selected for inclusion in the product test: (1) clothing; (2) toiletries and cosmetics; (3) food; (4) household appliances; and (5) leisure products. Each class was divided into 5 products defined as standard and 5 defined as specialty; in the case of leisure products the dichotomy was made for items which have a non-participative individual or participative group orientation in use. The complete listing of products which comprised the test is shown in Table 2.

TABLE 2   TEST ITEMS BY CATEGORIES AND SUB-GROUPS

Category	Standard Sub-group	Specialty Sub-group
1. Clothing	shoes skirts dresses blouses suits	hat gloves lingerie hosiery slacks
2. Toiletries and Cosmetics	toothpaste hand soap deodorant facial tissue hair shampoo	hair spray permanent waves eye shadow lipstick nail polish
3. Food	catsup flour shortening potatoes bread	frozen orange juice instant coffee frozen sea food cake mix refrigerator biscuits
4. Household Appliances	refrigerator iron toaster stove washing machine	electric can opener automatic dish washer rotisserie food blender automatic clothes dryer
5. Leisure Products	Non-Participative—Individual television books magazines records Hi-Fi set	Participative—Group sports equipment playing cards camping equipment boating equipment cocktail set

IMPLEMENTATION OF THE INSTRUMENT

The instrument, the product test, was used to test the product perceptions of housewives who represented two social strata. Fifty subjects were selected from each of two census tracts using a sampling design termed area sample with quota controls. One census tract (designated Low or L) was generally equivalent to a combination of the Warner classifications upper lower-lower middle. The second tract (designated High or H) was generally equivalent to the Warner classification upper-middle.

Each subject, using the product test which was presented as a deck of 50 cards with a product name on each card, sorted the cards to describe Self. The Self sorts for both strata (LS and HS) were recorded and then subjects assumed the role of a member of the opposite stratum. This was done by presenting subjects with a "cue" card which characterized a typical member of H for members of L and a typical member of L for members of H. Assuming the appropriate roles and again making the descriptions of Self and Other ("as if I were this person") resulted in Other sorts for both strata; the Low stratum descriptions of H (LO) and the High stratum descriptions of L (HO).

The implementation of the test resulted in the four basic sorts; LS, LO, HS, and HO, which provided the measurements necessary for hypothesis testing. The four basic sorts were obtained by developing a mean array for Self and Other for each stratum.

TEST RESULTS

The hypotheses were tested with the results shown in Table 3. Two statistics

TABLE 3   RESULTS OF TESTS OF THE HYPOTHESES

Hypothesis	Operational Statement	Measurement	Finding
H I	r_1 (LS:HS)$\neq$1.0 and r_2 (LO:HO)$\neq$ 1.0	r_1 = .669 r_2 = .185	Accept
H II	r_1 (LS:HO) $>$ r_2 (LO:HS)	r_1 = .919 r_2 = .601	Accept
H III	W(LS) $>$ W(HS)	W(LS) = .481 W(HS)= .303	Accept
H IV	W(LO) $<$ W(HO)	W(LO)= .181 W(HO)= .541	Accept
H V	W(HS) $<$ W(HO)	W(HS) = .303 W(HO)= .541	Accept
H VI	W(LS) $>$ W(LO)	W(LS) = .481 W(LO)= .181	Accept

were used in demonstrating the relationships between the sorts: (1) Pearsonian r; (2) the coefficient of concordance W. Product movement correlation was used to correlate the basic product arrays, and the coefficient of concordance was used as a measure of the level of agreement to be found in each of the basic arrays.

Being able to accept the first research hypothesis, that members of different strata have different Self and Other perceptions, was a major objective of the study. This is not because the finding is significant, *per se*, but because of the method used. The support of this operational position demonstrates the ability of the Q-sort procedure, given a selection of items to be arrayed, to yield results which distinguish between members of two social strata.

An analysis of the four basic arrays LS, HS, LO, and HO (shown in Table 4), resulted in information demonstrating which products were most and least descriptive and how members of both strata viewed each other.

1. The basic product categories of Clothing, Toiletries and Cosmetics, Food, Appliances, and Leisure Products were too broad and too mixed in order to demonstrate the descriptive properties of products in terms of their item scores. By breaking the basic categories into Standard and Specialty Sub-groups, much more accurate and descriptive information was obtained on which types of groups of products best describe Self and Other. Virtually all the Standard Sub-group items were found to best describe with higher descriptive scores than the Specialty Sub-group items.

2. The product categories were also found to be not accurate enough in demonstrating which types of items were responsible for differences between pairs of basic arrays. The Standard and Specialty Group sub-group breakdown showed that the largest differences between LS and HS were accounted for by the different scores given to Specialty Appliances and Standard Clothing items. The largest differences between LS and HO were accounted for by H's inaccurate perception of how members of L would score Specialty Appliances and Standard Toiletries and Cosmetics. The largest differences between HS and LO were accounted for by L's inaccuracy in perceiving how members of H would score Specialty Appliances.

3. In the analysis of descriptive ability of Sub-groups related to accuracy of description, it was found that members of L were generally accurate in best describing members of H but they were inaccurate in being able to select items which were least descriptive of members of H. On the other hand, members of H were generally accurate in being able to select those items which both best and least describe members of L.

4. The analysis of the scores which individual items received for the descriptions of Other (LO and HO) compared to the descriptions of Self demonstrated that members of L generally focused on the differences which actually existed between LS and HS and tended to magnify them or overestimate scores. Members of H, on the other hand, tended to minimize differences between LS and HS by tending to project their own descriptions to members of L.

Marketing Implications

The marketing implications of this exploratory study flow from two bases: the characteristics of a Q-array of products and the implications of an item's position

TABLE 4 PRODUCT ARRAYS FOR LS, HS, LO, AND HO WITH ITEMS FROM MOST DESCRIPTIVE TO LEAST DESCRIPTIVE

Scores	LS	HS	LO	HO
9 (n=2)	washing machine stove	washing machine dresses	dresses automatic clothes dryer	refrigerator stove
8 (n=3)	refrigerator electric iron hand soap	refrigerator books shoes	shoes hosiery automatic dishwasher	electric iron bread washing machine
7 (n=6)	toothpaste hair shampoo potatoes bread toaster television	skirts blouses lingerie lipstick stove automatic dishwasher	television refrigerator lingerie hats washing machine skirt	blouses television dresses flour electric toaster potatoes
6 (n=9)	dresses blouses lingerie shoes deodorant facial tissues books flour shortening	hand soap toothpaste deodorant hair shampoo toaster electric iron clothes dryer records television	suits blouses deodorant gloves electric toaster lipstick electric rotisserie hi-fi stove	frozen orange juice shoes deodorant toothpaste shortening hair shampoo hand soap lipstick skirts

5 (n=10)			
skirts	slacks	hair spray	suits
slacks	hosiery	slacks	slacks
hosiery	suits	toothpaste	catsup
lipstick	gloves	hair shampoo	hosiery
hair spray	facial tissues	electric can opener	permanent waves
catsup	bread	hand soap	books
magazines	potatoes	electric iron	lingerie
cake mix	playing cards	facial tissues	facial tissues
frozen orange juice	hi-fi	nail polish	cake mix
refrigerated biscuits	frozen orange juice	record	magazines
4 (n=9)			
frozen seafood	hats	frozen orange juice	instant coffee
suits	hair spray	sports equipment	hair spray
gloves	nail polish	playing cards	playing cards
permanent waves	catsup	permanent waves	gloves
nail polish	flour	books	frozen seafood
camping equipment	shortening	eye shadow	hats
records	magazines	cocktail set	nail polish
clothes dryer	cake mix	bread	refrigerated biscuits
sports equipment	sports equipment	blender	records
3 (n=6)			
instant coffee	instant coffee	instant coffee	sports equipment
playing cards	camping equipment	shortening	camping equipment
electric can opener	frozen seafood	boating equipment	automatic dishwasher
blender	eye shadow	frozen seafood	eye shadow
hi-fi	blender	magazines	automatic clothes dryer
hats	refrigerated biscuits	refrigerated biscuits	hi-fi

TABLE 4   PRODUCT ARRAYS FOR LS, HS, LO, AND HO WITH ITEMS FROM MOST DESCRIPTIVE TO LEAST DESCRIPTIVE (CONTINUED)

Scores	LS	HS	LO	HO
2 (n=3)	automatic dishwasher eye shadow electric rotisserie	permanent waves electric can opener cocktail set	flour potatoes cake mix	cocktail set blender electric rotisserie
1 (n=2)	boating equipment coctail set	boating equipment electric rotisserie	catsup camping equipment	electric can opener boating equipment

in an array, and the differential perception of products and the accuracy of perception demonstrated by L and H.

This discussion of the marketing applications is based, in part, on two assumptions.

1. That product appeals and presentations are most effective when they are meaningful to consumers in terms of portraying roles and symbols which are perceived as being accurate and realistic in their own terms.

2. That product presentations may also be effective when a product or idea is presented to consumers without any role relationship. The absence of a structured role allows a consumer to structure the role which she feels is properly related to the product.

SIGNIFICANCE OF ITEM SCORES

The position of individual items in a Q-array has marketing implications insofar as the placement aids marketers in determining how their products are viewed. The scores which each of the 50 products in the test received, both in the Self and Other sorts, are indicative of the potential sensitivity of the item in a product appeal. The items which appear in the tails of the Q-array are those most easily discriminated. Items with high scores (9, 8, 7. . .) best describe while those with low scores (1, 2, 3. . .) least describe. A marketer who deals in products which appear in the tails of a product array must be aware that he is dealing with highly descriptive and easily discriminated items. Items which appear in the central scoring classes of an array are not as easily discriminated nor are they highly descriptive. The items appearing in the tails would be most sensitive in product presentations in terms of obviously attracting attention. Inaccuracies and errors in the presentation of easily discriminated items would be more easily discerned than in the presentation of less easily discriminated items. The amount or degree of error which would be accepted in a presentation before it would be rejected as unrealistic or too inaccurate is something upon which we have no information.

Products which receive high scores in LS and HS are, in general, most appropriate in presentations to members of L and H. These are items which are not only highly descriptive but are perceived of accurately by members of L and H when they view each Other. If a marketer feels that perceived reality is most effective in product appeals, the inclusion of items with high scores should increase the probability of acceptance. On the other hand, products with low scores may be scored as least descriptive because they are related to "improper" roles or because they are unobtainable although related to desirable role components. High scoring products, because they are so descriptive, can stand on their own in a presentation and may be acceptable to large audiences. Low scoring products, because they are not descriptive in a positive sense when presented by themselves, may be acceptable to only a small audience. One way for a marketer to deal with low scoring items would be to avoid role presentations and allow the consumer to relate the item to roles as she sees fit. Another approach may be to relate a low scoring item to a high scoring one and thus attempt to identify it with a highly descriptive role component.

IMPLICATIONS OF THE HYPOTHESES

The implications of differential and accurate product perception concern the marketing strategies of product differentiation and market segmentation. The fact that a Q-sort of products successfully distinguishes between strata (Hypothesis I) aid in the determination of strategies for items which are viewed as common to both strata and which distinguish between them.

When members of the two strata agree on the Self descriptive ability of an item, the marketer knows that the item and its related role is viewed with the same amount of importance when it comes to describing members of these strata. On this basis, he faces a potentially broad unsegmented market composed of both L and H insofar as he can make one product presentation to both. His appeals to this broad market should be based on symbols and roles which are common to both strata. He always has the alternative of product differentiation or segmentation if he so chooses.

When the members of two strata disagree on the Self descriptive ability of an item, the marketer is faced with a different set of alternatives. He can always make product presentations which do not rely on role portrayals and allow members of each stratum to construct their own frame of reference. Using this approach, he need make but one presentation. If he feels that role portrayals are more effective, he can attempt differentiation or segmentation or both. The fact that members of each stratum view the same product with a different amount of descriptive importance indicates the differential value it has. This is particularly true with items which are easily discriminated (with scores of 9, 8, 7. . . 3, 2, 1) but it also applies to items which are more difficult to discriminate (with scores of 6, 5, and 4). As long as members of L and H disagree on the descriptive ability of an item different product presentations should be made to each stratum, for if a common one is made, it may be rejected by either or both strata because of its perceived inaccuracy.

The support of the second hypothesis, that members of a high stratum have a better perception of members of a low stratum than those in the low have of the high, helps clarify when differentiation and segmentation strategies are suitable. Consumers who are very adept at discerning the differential meaning and value of symbols are likely to view and reaction to their presentation in a much clearer manner than those who are not as adept. Thus, when roles are portrayed, members of H should be presented with appropriate (in this case, quite accurate) symbols in product appeals. If this is not done, the appeals may be rejected because they do not coincide with the perceived evaluation of product symbols. The fact that members of H are more adept at perceiving symbols which both best and least describe does not allow too much room for error in terms of presenting products with mixed symbolic meanings and values. If a specific "class" or group market segment is important, and this segment is accurate in perception, accuracy in presentation is important. The accuracy of perception demonstrated by members of H shows that differentiation of product appeals is important. Segmentation strategy would perhaps be an even more effective approach because variations of a product, supported by different appeals, could be presented to each stratum instead of just differentiated appeals.

When a marketer deals with a stratum, like L, which does not have accurate perceptions of higher strata or groups, he faces a different problem. He must concern himself with the possible rejection of symbols which are in fact accurately descriptive of a higher stratum. This means he must be aware of any discrepancy in scores between symbols which are Self descriptive and the perception which Others have of them. If he is not aware of such discrepancies, his appeals may be rejected because, while they are accurate, they are perceived as being inaccurate.

Because of lesser accuracy of perception, as well as the possibility of emulation, the problems a marketer faces in dealing with L are more complex than those which exist in dealing with H. In dealing with H, a marketer must, if he relies on role presentations, be able to present accurate symbols in product appeals. The problem of H emulating L is not considered to be present. In dealing with L, the marketer must, if he relies on role presentations, generally be able to present symbols which are both perceived as being accurate (although they may not be) and those which are accurate (for L is not always inaccurate). In addition, the predisposition of L to emulate H further complicates presentation problems. Either the strategy of differentiation or the use of presentations without role portrayals would both be appropriate where members of L inaccurately perceive differences between themselves and H are not prepared to emulate H. Where they inaccurately perceive similarities, differentiation of presentations or presentations without role portrayals would also be necessary as accurate presentations may be rejected. Where they inaccurately or accurately perceive differences and are prepared to emulate H as well as when they accurately perceive similarities, differentiated product presentations without role portrayals are not necessary.

The testing of the four hypotheses (III, IV, V, and VI) dealing with the solidarity of perception of Self and Other within the strata have further implications for marketers. The level of solidarity of perception exhibited by a stratum will influence the need for differentiated appeals, the presentation of appeals which do not rely on role portrayals and the usefulness of segmentation strategy.

The fact that members of L demonstrate greater agreement in making Self descriptions than members of H (Hypothesis III) indicates that a marketer may make product presentations, using roles, to L as if it were a single market segment. The need for further differentiation is not as pressing as it would be if there were a great deal of variation in Self descriptions. It can be expected, of course, that a single presentation will be rejected by some. Segmentation may prove to be a worthwhile strategy but it is not necessary because of the homogeneity of perceptions.

On the other hand, the lack of agreement or solidarity of Self description exhibited by members of H points out the need for presentations which either do not rely on roles or differentiated presentations, using roles, in dealing with this stratum. If a marketer wishes to deal with all members of the stratum, then either presentations without role portrayls or differentiation of products appeals are essential. The diversity of Self descriptions indicates that segmentation strategy may be feasible.

Hypothesis IV, that members of H demonstrate greater agreement in describing an Other than members of L is a reinforcement of Hypothesis II which finds H more perceptive of the Other than L. This finding also reflects on the problems of using emulative appeals directed at members of L. The low level of agreement demonstrated by L in describing H implies a great diversity of perceived Others. If members of L perceive a number of Others, product presentations which rely upon emulation must present the correct Other. If the marketer can define those groups within L which emulate a particular Other, it may be possible to both differentiate and segment the stratum.

The marketing implications of Hypotheses V and VI, that members of H demonstrate greater agreement in describing an Other than in describing Self and that members of L demonstrate greater agreement in describing Self than in describing an Other, have already been amplified above.

While it has been demonstrated in general terms what the implications of Q-sort can be for marketing much more intensive investigation of different types of sorts for different purposes is required in order to apply the approach to specific marketing problems. Further exploration is warranted in the areas of the structuring of product tests, product perception amongst other strata and groups, stability and change through time in item arrays as well as the implications of the positions of items in arrays.

24 The Package and the Label

Wrapper Influence on the Perception of Freshness in Bread

ROBERT L. BROWN *(Psychologist)*

How much influence does a product's package or wrapper have on consumers' perceptions of that product? Is it possible that among identical products consumers consistently prefer one on the basis of the package? Answers to these kinds of questions are given in this article on the perception of freshness in bread.

In previous consumer research (1) it has been found that the two properties looked for in bread by the majority of people are freshness and flavor. Freshness is determined largely by "feeling" of the loaves of bread and flavor is determined by taste. At the present time, breads are being wrapped in a number of different type wrappers ranging from a cellophane to a heavy wax or plastic. There are perhaps both advantages and disadvantages to each type of wrapper. Persons engaged in the marketing of bread have often reported the opinion that some breads sell better in one wrapper than in another. Many hypotheses have been made with reference to this difference, but little has been done in the way of controlled research. This is the second in a series of proposed studies on the influence of the wrapper on the perception of freshness in bread.

In the original study conducted at Purdue University, 1955 (2), it was hypothesized that the tactual sensations aroused by the wrapper influence the perception of freshness in bread. More specifically, it was hypothesized that two loaves of equal freshness, but with different type wrappers, would be judged to have differential degrees of freshness.

Source: Robert L. Brown, "Wrapper Influence on the Perception of Freshness in Bread," *Journal of Applied Psychology,* Vo. 42 (August, 1958), pp. 257-260.

In testing the above stated hypothesis, four different type wrappers were selected. These were: cellophane; Saran; regular wax; and a special wax with a subwrapper. The experiment was performed in a laboratory situation in which 16 male and 16 female students were used as Ss. Sixteen loaves of fresh bread, all baked together during the night before the experiment, were rewrapped in the various wrappers by the experimenters. The Ss were seated parallel with the side of a table with their right arm around behind a screen. The S was instructed that this was an experiment to determine whether or not people can tell how fresh bread is by feeling it; that one loaf and then another would be presented under the S's hand; that he should feel the one and then the other and tell the experimenter which of the two was fresher. No equal judgments were allowed.

A full paired-comparison design was used and the pairs were randomly presented. The responses of the Ss were recorded on individual record sheets for the purpose of subsequent analysis.

From the analysis of the data, no significant differences were found between sex, between sequence of presentation, between first and second halves of groups feeling the same set of loaves; or between the first and second halves of the total group during the experimental day. The difference between the observed and expected frequencies of judgments for the four wrappers gave a chi-square value of 26.38 which is significant beyond the 1% level with 3 degrees of freedom. The percentage of judgments of "fresher" made by these 32 Ss were as follows: Cellophane, 68%; Saran, 56%; regular wax, 42%; and the special wax with subwrapper, 34%. The percentages were determined on the basis of the number of judgments in favor of a particular wrapper over the total number of times that wrapper appeared in the judgment pairs. Since a full paired-comparison design was employed for the four wrappers, the percentages add up to 200%.

The original study left a number of questions unanswered and raised some other questions. The purpose of this second study is to determine the answers to two of these questions: (*a*) Will the same differential influence of wrappers on the perception of freshness in bread also be found among the primary consumer group—housewives—as with university students? and (*b*) Will the same differential influence of the wrappers on the perception of freshness in bread hold for one- and two- day-old bread as it does for fresh bread?

Procedure

In order to answer these questions, three conventional type wrappers were selected: cellophane; cellophane with a five-inch waxed paper insert band; and wax. The cellophane wrappers were the commonly used .001-inch thick and weighed approximately one pound per 21,000 square inches. The waxed paper for the wrapper and for the insert band was of base paper weighing 25 pounds per ream and waxed up to 37 pounds per ream. All wrappers were unprinted.

Eighteen regular, one-pound, round-top, sliced loaves of white bread were used. Six of these were fresh, having been baked at the same time on the afternoon before the experiment; six were one day older; and six were two days older. All of the loaves were stored in their original wrappers until a few hours before the experiment when they were rewrapped in the various wrappers for the experiment. The wrappers were adjusted to a degree of tightness (or looseness) judged to be comparable.

The experiment was performed in a laboratory type situation set up in the foyer of a large supermarket. Fifty of the housewives coming to the market to shop volunteered to serve as Ss.

The Ss were tested under blinded conditions made possible by seating each S parallel with the side of a table and close enough to place her right forearm and hand behind a screen which was mounted to the table. This arrangement made it possible to place the loaves, one at a time, under the Ss hand and prevented the S from seeing the loaves being judged.

Each S was instructed that this was an experiment to determine whether or not people can tell how fresh bread is by feeling it; that one loaf and then another would be presented under the S's hand; that she should feel one and then the other and tell the experimenter which of the two was fresher. No equal judgments were allowed.

A full paired-comparison design was used and the pairs were randomly presented according to a system previously worked out for each S. The responses of the Ss were recorded on the individual record sheets for subsequent analysis.

Results

The numbers and percentages of judgments of "fresher" made for each of the three wrappers when presented in a full paired-comparison design to the 50 housewives under blinded conditions are presented in Table 1. The percentages are de-

TABLE 1   JUDGMENTS OF "FRESHER" MADE FOR EACH OF THREE WRAPPERS AND THREE AGES OF BREAD WHEN PRESENTED IN A PAIRED-COMPARISON DESIGN TO 50 HOUSEWIVES

Wrapper	Age of Bread			Total
	Fresh	One-day	Two-day	
Cellophane	(125)	(122)	(126)	(373)
	62.5%	61.0%	63.0%	62.2%
Cellophane with waxed band insert	(118)	(97)	(94)	(309)
	59.0%	48.5%	47.0%	44.1%
Wax	(57)	(81)	(80)	(218)
	28.5%	40.5%	40.0%	36.3%

termined on the basis of the number of judgments in favor of a particular wrapper over the total number of times that wrapper appeared in the judgment pairs. Since a full paired-comparison design was employed for the three wrappers, the percentages add up to 150%.

A full analysis of the data was made by the chi-square technique. The results of these analyses are to be found in Table 2. No significant differences were found

TABLE 2   CHI-SQUARE VALUES BETWEEN OBSERVED AND EXPECTED FREQUENCIES OF JUDGMENTS OF "FRESHER" MADE FOR EACH OF THREE WRAPPERS AND THREE AGES OF BREAD

Variables	df	x^2 Value
Between first and second halves of sets of loaves used	8	10.84
Between sets of loaves used in the first and second halves of the experimental day	8	11.89
Between fresh and one-day-old bread	2	6.26*
Between fresh and two-day-old bread	2	6.58*
Between one- and two-day-old bread	2	0.12
Between observed and expected frequencies of judgments for three wrappers for:		
Fresh bread	2	27.98**
One-day-old bread	2	8.54*
Two-day-old bread	2	11.12**
All three ages of bread	2	40.45**

*Significant at the 5% level.
**Significant at the 1% level.

between the frequencies of judgments as "fresher" for the first and second halves of Ss tested on a set of loaves in the various wrappers. Fearing that some differences might be found between the sets of loaves used in the first half and those used in the second half of the experimental day, a x^2 test was made on these data. No significant differences were found. With S degrees of freedom and an alpha equal to .05, a single x^2 value of 15.5 or more would be necessary to indicate a difference that was not due to chance variations in 95 out of 100 cases. It will be noted from Table 2 that the x^2 values obtained are clearly below this value for significant differences. For an interpretation of the remainder of the tests reported in Table 2, at the 95% confidence level a x^2 of 5.99 or greater is required, and at the 99% confidence level a x^2 of 9.21 or greater is required. These values are for two degrees of freedom.

Discussion

The purpose of this study was to ascertain the answers to two questions. The first question was: Will the same differential influence of wrappers on the perception of freshness in bread be found among the primary consumer group—housewives—as with university students? The plain cellophane and the plain waxed wrappers were identical in the two studies. The percentages of judgments of "fresher" for the cellophane wrappers on fresh bread were 68.0% and 62.5%, respectively, for students and housewives. The judgments for the plain wax wrappers on fresh bread by students was 42% and by housewives it was 28.5%. These percentages are not strictly comparable because the percentage for a given wrapper depends upon the other wrappers in the group. All the wrappers were not the same in the two studies. However, it will be noted that the order or ranking is the same for cellophane and wax in both studies. Therefore, for cellophane and wax, it can be concluded that the primary consumer group—housewives—responded in the same way as did university students. It may also be concluded with a very high degree of confidence that fresh bread (of equal freshness) feels fresher when it is wrapped in cellophane than when it is wrapped in a wax wrapper.

The second question was: Will the same differential influence of the wrappers on the perception of freshness in bread hold for one- and two-day-old bread as it does for fresh bread? An examination of the percentages of "fresher" in Table 1 shows some change in the magnitude of the judgments of "fresher" for the wax wrapper and for the cellophane wrapper with the wax band insert with one- and two-day-old bread. Although the orders remain the same, there is a significant difference between the percentages on fresh bread and those for one-day-old bread. Likewise, there is a significant difference between fresh bread judgments and two-day-old bread judgments for the various wrappers. The chi-square values are given in Table 2 and were found to be significant at the 95% level of confidence. No significant differences were found between the one- and two-day-old bread in percentages of judgments. All three ages of bread showed significant deviations from chance expectancies for the three wrappers. It may be concluded, therefore, that, like fresh bread, one- and two-day-old bread also feels fresher when wrapped in a plain cellophane wrapper than when wrapped in wax or cellophane with a wax band insert.

Summary and Conclusions

The purpose of this experiment was to answer two questions with reference to the influence of tactual sensations supplied by the wrapper on the perception of freshness in bread. Previous research by the author had revealed that for fresh bread, loaves of equal freshness were perceived by university students to be fresher when wrapped in cellophane than when wrapped in wax. In this study the following questions were asked: (*a*) Will the same differential influence of wrappers on the perception of freshness in bread be found among the primary consumer groups—housewives—as with university students? (b) Will the same differential influence of the wrappers on the perception of freshness in bread hold for one- and two-day-old bread as it does for fresh bread.

In order to answer these questions, three conventional type wrappers and three ages of bread in a paired-comparison design were presented to 50 housewives under blinded conditions. The results warrant the following conclusions:

1. Housewives, the primary consumer group, responded to the test situation in the same way the university students responded. They perceived fresh bread of equal freshness to be fresher when wrapped in cellophane than when wrapped in wax.

2. The same differential influence of the wrappers on the perception of freshness in bread applies to one- and two-day-old bread as it does to fresh bread. The magnitude of the judgments was not as great for one- and two-day-old bread, but the order remained the same and judgments still differed significantly from expected frequencies.

Received October 7, 1957.

References

1. Brown, R. L. *A consumer research study of bread.* Greenville, S. C.: Henderson Advertising Agency, 1953.
2. Brown, R. L., Brune, R. L., Thackray, R., & Kephart, N. C. Wrapper influence on the perception of freshness in bread, I. Unpublished manuscript, Furman Univer., 1955.

25 The Price

The Price-Quality Relationship in an Experimental Setting

J. DOUGLAS McCONNELL* *(Economist)*

Although management assumes a relationship between price and quality when making decisions about pricing and when acting against price-cutting within distribution channels, little research on this relationship has been done. Earlier price-quality studies have not involved consumers actually using products over time.

This article reports a study in which price was the *only* variable; and over 24 trials, quality differences for three brands were perceived by when no quality difference existed. The relationship between price and perception of quality was positive but not linear.

Introduction

The price-quality relationship suggested in [5, 7, 9] forms the basis of many marketing decisions. Similar grade and quality for national brands and private labels produced by one processor largely depend on consumer perception of the price-quality relationship. For example, national brands of gasoline command a two or three cent-per-gallon premium over identical independent brands. Manufacturers seeking resale price maintenance have argued that price cutting cheapens the product's perceived quality. This concept also has relevance for pricing new products. Management must decide whether to introduce a brand at a higher price than, a

Source: J. Douglas McConnell, "The Price-Quality Relationship in an Experimental Setting," *Journal of Marketing Research,* Vol. 5 (August, 1968), pp. 300-303.

*J. Douglas McConnell is marketing economist, Stanford Research Institute. This article is based on research conducted by the author for his doctoral dissertation.

price competitive with, or a lower price than substitute products. The decision is often considered to be a choice between skim pricing and penetration pricing [2]. Although the price-quality concept has been a basis of argument, the empirical support for such an hypothesis has been meager.

This study examines the relationship between price and quality for a frequently purchased consumer product, beer, in an experimental and considerably realistic setting.

Methodology

The basic methodology was previously reported [4, 6]. In essence, subjects made 24 selections (purchase trials) among three brands of beer, identical except for price and brand identification.

For each of the three brands, subjects were shown the prices in two ways. First, the price per six-pack was on a card because this is how most consumers see beer prices in stores. Second, because the beer was being given away, some realism was added to the selection process by taping a nickel to each bottle of the least expensive Brand P ($0.99 per six-pack), and two cents to each bottle of the medium-priced Brand L ($1.20 per six-pack). Nothing was added to the most expensive Brand M ($1.30 per six-pack).

After their final selection in Trial 24, subjects were given a questionnaire asking them to select from a list of words, commonly used to describe beer, the three that best described each brand. The words in the list, which follows, have generally favorable or unfavorable connotations for beer.

Favorable (implied high quality)	Unfavorable (implied low quality)
Tangy	Flat
Rich-flavored	Biting
Smooth	Acidy
Malty	Watery
Full-bodied	Bitter
Light	Sour
Dry	

Three analyses were used to test the hypothesis that price and perceived quality are related. First, a simple contingency table analysis was performed to test the relationship between the ratings obtained and the three price levels of the brands. It was assumed that points on a five-point scale: "undrinkable," "poor," "fair," "good" and "very pleasant" increased monotonically, and values were assigned to the respective points. Second, differences between mean scale values were tested using the Student "t" distribution and the method for correlated observations [10]. Third, the price-quality relationship was also tested by a one-way analysis of variance [10].

Test Results

Table 1 produced significant findings: the chi-square value being significant at the $p < .005$ level, indicating a price-quality relationship. The "t" tests of differences among mean rating values of the three brands indicated that the high- and low-priced brands were perceived to be of significantly different quality at the $p < .01$ level. The high- and medium-priced brands were perceived to have different quality at the $p < .06$ level. However, the medium-priced brand was not thought to have significantly higher quality than the low-priced brand. The perceptual space between the high- and the middle-priced brands was greater than between the middle-and low-price brands, although the actual price differential would have led one to suspect the reverse.

TABLE 1   DATA FOR CONTINGENCY TABLE ANALYSIS*

Rating	Price Level		
	High	Medium	Low
Undrinkable (0)	4	1	4
Poor (1)	8	21	20
Fair (2)	26	22	23
Good (3)	15	12	9
Very pleasant (4)	7	4	4
Total score	133	117	109
Mean score	2.23	1.93	1.80

*Ratings for Likert-type scale.

The third test used subjects' selection of words describing the beer for a one-way variance analysis. The overall direction of respondents' selections is readily apparent in the tabulation. The differences were significant at the $p < .05$ level. (Figures in the tabulation are number of words.)

Type of words chosen	Brand and price per six-pack		
	M ($1.30)	L ($1.20)	P ($0.99)
Favorable	93	73	57
Unfavorable	71	82	101

Discussion

FINDINGS

Subjects used price as an indicator of product quality. With a physically homogeneous product and unknown brand names (having so little meaning that many subjects never used them), subjects perceived the highest priced brand to have better quality than the other two brands. The medium-priced brand was perceived to be marginally better than the lowest priced brand. If knowledge had been complete, the truly economic subject would have tried each brand once and then chosen the lowest priced for the remaining trials. In this way, informed subjects would have maximized their utility, receiving the same beer and five cents at each trial instead of getting less. Subjects, however, selected the high-priced brand in over 41 percent of all trials, and the middle-priced brand in 25 percent of all trials. Price, without other cues, was an effective factor in determining how brands were perceived.

There was a high correlation between ratings and preferred brands. Only 9 of the 60 rated all three brands as having the same quality, and 6 of the 9 were regular purchasers of the low-priced beer.

By the end of Trial 3, about 50 of the 60 subjects had tried all three brands. Fifty-nine had tried all brands by the end of Trial 6. The one remaining subject finally switched and tried the third brand at Trial 13.

All three brands were physically identical. In this respect, the study was similar to Tucker's [8] in which identical loaves of bread had different brand names. Both studies indicated that consumers differentiate between homogeneous products by cues supplied by the marketer. For Tucker's consumers, the variable was brand name. Here, it was price. The statistical data are supported by comments similar to those made at Trial 20 by a male subject,

"I've just realized that I've been behaving as the marketing people say I would. I tried them all, then settled on the one I liked best (brand M), and occasionally try the cheap one to check my judgment."

A female subject observed at Trial 20 that "L and M are very similar; I can't see a difference worth the price. We didn't like P at all."

A possible explanation for this price-quality phenomenon can be drawn from dissonance theory [1,3]. The consumer seeks to maintain consonance between his cognitive structure and his perception of the real world. In this experiment, the subjects' cognitive set was that you pay for what you get, and the quality beer was, therefore, high priced and the cheap beer was low priced, with the medium-priced brand somewhere between. Actual tasting of all three brands revealed no real difference for many subjects. This was dissonant with their set that quality costs more. Because there was no way of altering prices to reduce cognitive dissonance, these subjects had to alter their perception of the products, which they did by imputing different qualities to the three brands. This varied with subjects; some said certain brands had always been undrinkable. Subject 14 said after the study, "I never could finish a bottle of L (medium price). It was like the T.C.P. they put in Shell, only not so pure." The subject selected that brand on Trials 1, 7, and 22 only. On each occasion, he said he could not finish the 12-ounce bottle and had to pour most of it down the sink. This subject developed a preference for the low-priced brand, which he rated very pleasant and described as "full bodied, appeared to have a good high alcohol content, coming close to European beers." He rated the high-priced beer as good but the medium beer was rated poor. In the initial questionnaire, he described himself as an occasional beer drinker, a buyer of Waldech, Heineken, and Miller High Life who "goes for quality rather than quantity in beer drinking."

This distortion to achieve consonance is again evident in number 17's comment after Trial 24,

"I have a confession to make. When my father-in-law was here (Trials 14 and 15), I had an L (medium price) I hadn't drunk and took an M (high price) on the next trial, and we tested them. I thought L was terrible but he didn't think it was too bad. But we both liked the M much better."

The medium-priced brand chosen at Trial 14 had been chosen only once previously (at Trial 2) by this subject. She switched from the high-priced beer to the medium-priced product at Trial 14 for a two-cent offer, then reverted to the high-priced beer, stayed loyal for the remaining trials and only agreed to take another of the medium-priced brand when the offer reached 18 cents.

Perceived quality did not vary linearly with price. The greater price disparity was a three-cent difference between the middle and lower priced brands, compared with a two-cent difference between the medium- and high-priced brands. However, the middle- and low-priced brands were perceived to be much closer than the middle- and high-priced brands. No causal explanation was found for this phenomenon. A first-order Markov brand-switching analysis revealed that the medium-priced brand lost to those both higher and lower in price, with the greatest movement to the high price. This analysis tended to confirm the significance of the quality rating.

I examined the scales for the ratings and the selections of descriptive words indicated that they were consistent measures of perceived quality. One possible explanation may be that subjects used the high-priced brand as a benchmark again which to test the two lower-priced brands. There is some evidence in brand selection patterns and subjects' comments to support this. Thus, subjects would tend to increase the perceptual distance between the high-priced (benchmark) brand and the others, and to reduce the perceptual distance between the two other brands since it was regarded as less important.

External validity has primary importance in any study, particularly a small artificial experiment using atypical consumers as subjects. It is believed that our results have some external validity for the following reasons. Subjects could drink their beer in a normal setting and at usual times. By continuing the experiment for two months, the "beer man" was accepted as much a caller as a milkman. Subjects' comments on brands were spontaneous and indicated that they were involved in the project as consumers and not simply as students helping a fellow student complete his research. At the end of the study, several subjects were reluctant to accept the fact that the three brands of beer had identical quality.

It could be argued that for reasons of pride subjects were reluctant to take the brands with money attached, but this was not so. For many subjects, the nickel on the lowest priced brand was the main reason for selecting it; and when the money (at Trial 8) was moved from the label to the opposite side of the bottle, several subjects had to reassure themselves that the money was still there. Further support for external validity was provided by comparing the repurchase probability states, given various combinations of past selections, with those obtained by Kuehn pertaining to frozen orange juice purchases by 600 housewives from 1950 through 1953 [4]. The correlation coefficients obtained from this comparison were all above .89 and ranged to .98. Finally, one would expect the community's more intelligent sector to be more aware of product differences and values than those less intelligent and less educated.

IMPLICATIONS FOR BUSINESS

Price is one attribute used by consumers to cue quality, and marketing management should be aware that the price of their brand or product is as significant as many of its physical characteristics. For new products or brands, this is even more likely. Because a new product or brand has no traditional price, no reputation other than the company name, its quality is likely to be appraised largely by its price.

With price perceived as a cue to quality when differences in products are not readily apparent, the marketer can often segment his market effectively. Profit maximization from segmenting the market by brand name and price has been applied generally by many corporations for several years, despite legal complications of the Robinson-Patman Act.

Although the price-quality relationship has now been shown several times, little is known about the relative importance of price to the other variables, such as product characterisitcs, brand features, corporate name, advertising, and distribution channels, which also contribute to a brand's image. This is an area for further research. Also, several studies cannot fully reveal the nature of a construct; replication with different products, different time periods, different populations, and different circumstances are essential for greater knowledge. The study reported here strongly supports earlier research and management thinking about the relationship between price and quality.

References

1. Jack W. Brehm, and A. R. Cohen, *Explorations in Cognitive Dissonance,* New York: John Wiley and Sons, Inc., 1962.

2. Joel Dean, "Pricing a New Product," *The Controller,* 23 (April 1955), 163-5.

3. Leon Festinger, *A Theory of Cognitive Dissonance,* New York: Harper and Row, 1957.

4. Alfred A. Kuehn, "Consumer Brand Choice—A Learning Process," *Journal of Advertising Research,* 2 (December 1962), 10-7.

5. Harold J. Leavitt, "A Note on Some Experimental Findings About the Meaning of Price," *Journal of Business*, 27 (July 1954), 205-10.

6. J. Douglas McConnell, "An Experimental Study of the Development of Brand Loyalty," *Journal of Marketing Research*, 5 (February 1968), 13-9.

7. Tibor Scitovsky, "Some Consequences of the Habit of Judging Quality by Price," *The Review of Economic Studies*, 12 (1944-45) 100-5.

8. William T. Tucker, "The Development of Brand Loyalty," *Journal of Marketing Research*, 1 (August 1964), 32-5.

9. D. S. Tull, R. A. Boring, and M. H. Gonsior, "A Note on the Relationship of Price and Imputed Quality," *Journal of Business*, 38 (April 1964), 186-91.

10. B. J. Winer, *Statistical Principles in Experimental Design*, New York: McGraw-Hill Book Company, Inc., 1962, 29-32.

26 The Buying Environment

Price Perception and Store Patronage

F. E. BROWN* (Marketing Educator)

Is there a relationship between the supermarket patronized and the validity of perceptions formed by shoppers? Do price conscious shoppers perceive price differences among competing stores more validly than non-price conscious shoppers?

These questions were investigated in five different neighborhoods, each in a different state. A dual-data base of shelf-pricing in 27 supermarkets and with over 1000 consumer interviews provided empirical evidence for the study.

The image of a supermarket may make or break the store. The perceptual process is the crux of image, and the choice of a particular supermarket depends on the differences the customer *perceives* among alternative offerings. The perceptions formed need not coincide with the reality of the offerings. Given the possibility of misperception, questions arise concerning differences among customers in the validity of perceptions formed and the explanations of these differences.

The interaction between misperception and patronage work in both directions. A misperception may lead a customer to patronize a store that is less than optimal for her. It is also possible that patronage of a given store may distort the perceptions formed both of that store and of competitors. The resulting misperception may be a case of cognitive dissonance, or it may be much less subtle. The customer may be comparing data from two different time periods; she may have current information from her favorite store, but the data for competitors may pertain to former periods. The distortion may also result from inferences based on small

Source: F. E. Brown, "Price Perception and Store Patronage," in Robert L. King, Editor, *Marketing and the New Science of Planning* (Chicago: American Marketing Association, 1968), pp. 371-347.

*J. E. Brown is associate professor of marketing and statistics, Wharton School, University of Pennsylvania.

samples, comparisons of specials from one store with regular prices at another store, and many other possibilities.

This paper considers only price perceptions, but the method would be equally appropriate for other characteristics. It is concerned primarily with differences among supermarket customers in the validity of price perceptions formed and the explanations for these differences. The number of potential explanatory variables is infinite. The present paper investigates (a) the relationship between perceptual validity and differences in the stores patronized and (b) the relationship between perceptual validity and the stress placed upon price by respondents.[1] The two specific hypotheses to be tested are:

Hypothesis 1: Patrons of the lowest priced stores have the most valid price perceptions.

Hypothesis 2: The validity of price perceptions is no better for persons who stress price than for those who do not stress price.

Taken together, these two hypotheses yield the view that shopping behavior is a better indicator of the ability to perceive price differences than is stated concern for price.

Data Base and Method of Analysis

This study is based upon four different types of data: (1) market basket price indices for each supermarket, (2) price perceptions of the supermarkets reported by the customers, (3) store patronage information for each customer, and (4) reasons for shopping at particular stores or avoiding particular stores. The price information for each store was collected by on-site shelf pricing of 80 items; all data with respect to consumer behavior, attitude, and perception were collected by personal interviews.

The study was conducted in five different cities: St. Louis, Missouri; San Francisco, California; New York, New York; Havertown, Pennsylvania; and Greensboro, North Carolina. A total of 27 different supermarkets were studied in the five different cities, and over 1000 shoppers were interviewed.

The sampling plan was somewhat unique. In each neighborhood a group of competing supermarkets lying on the circumference of a circle was chosen. The consumers located at the center of such a circle were then interviewed. This plan minimized the importance of convenience which is typically quite large in supermarket shopping. The individual doing most of the shopping for each dwelling unit was chosen as the appropriate respondent.

A market basket price index was computed for each store by the weighted arithmetic mean of relatives method. The weights correspond to the importance of each

---

[1] Analysis of other explanatory variables is currently in process.

item as determined by the Bureau of Labor Statistics for each city.[2]   A figure of
100 represents the average for each city. Thus all price comparisons refer to a
specific city, and comparisons of stores in different cities or comparisons of the
cities cannot be made with the data in the present form.

Each respondent was asked to name the highest priced store, the second highest
priced store, the lowest priced store, and the second lowest priced store.[3]   For
those cities in which there were four or five stores, this procedure resulted in a
complete ranking for all stores. Where more than five stores were studied only a
partial ranking was obtained.

Each shopper was asked to name the store at which she usually did her main
food shopping. She was also asked if there were any stores in the neighborhood
she would not patronize for reasons other than price. She was asked to name
those stores and the reasons she would not patronize them. Finally, she was asked
to give the principal reasons she patronized her main stores. Any shopper who did
not shop in the immediate area was excluded from the present analysis.

The relationship between various characteristics and perceptual validity scores
was tested by either a "t" test or an analysis of variance. Perceptual validity was
measured on a scale developed in this research project and is illustrated in the
Appendix. A zero on the scale corresponds to a perfect perception, and the highest
scores indicate the least valid perceptions. All tests were made for each question
separately and each city separately. Since the perceptual validity scores were
based upon specific stores in specific communities, it was deemed inappropriate
to attempt an analysis based upon combined scores for all cities. It was also possible that variables which differentiated valid from invalid perceivers in one community were not appropriate in another community.

Patronage and Motives for Patronage

The lowest priced store did not consistently receive the largest market share. In
both St. Louis and San Francisco, the lowest priced store had less than 10% of
the market (see Table 1). In both of these neighborhoods, and also in New York,
the largest market share was captured by the store with the next to highest prices.
In contrast, the lowest priced store in Greensboro had captured over 50% of the
market. In Havertown, both the lowest priced store and the highest priced store
received market shares of almost 40%.

Customers do not consistently gravitate to the low priced stores. Factors other
than price may dominate the decision making process in either of two ways. Consumers may insist that thresholds for various non-price factors be met before a

[2]The author wishes to express his appreciation to the Bureau of Labor Statistics for providing
city specific weights.
[3]Questions involving complete ordinal or complete interval scales were tried in pre-tests, but
the results were unsatisfactory. In order to maintain rapport for the rest of the questionnaire,
only the ranking of four stores was requested.

TABLE 1   PERCENTAGE OF RESPONDENTS SHOPPING REGULARLY AT
EACH STORE, STORES CLASSIFIED BY RANK IN PRICE

Store Rank*	New York	Haver-town	Greensboro	St. Louis	San Francisco
1	22	38	53	5	8
2	16	1	21	25	20
3	56	21	5	8	25
4	6	3	2	6	0
5		37	19	30	0
6				25	42
7					4

*Stores ranked from lowest to highest, *i.e.,* rank 1 is the lowest in price.

store is even considered, or the choice of a regular supermarket may be a complex
decision involving many factors with little weight given to price.

Respondents were asked to name any stores that they eliminated from consideration on non-price bases. Over 30% of the respondents indicated they had eliminated at least one of the stores being studied; the percentage differed from one community to another, varying from a low of 26% in St. Louis and San Francisco to
a high of 52% in Havertown. The percentage of shoppers eliminating any one
store was too small to justify firm conclusions, but the data suggested that the
high priced stores and the low priced stores were equally likely to be eliminated.[4]

The reasons given for eliminating stores from consideration were quite similar
from city to city. Poor quality was mentioned more often than any other reason,
ranking first in two cities and among the top three in each of the other cities.
Lack of cleanliness, inadequate service, and crowded conditions were also cited
frequently. Despite the study design, some stores were eliminated as inconveniently
located. Although these stores were relatively near in distance, the respondents
routine travel patterns were in another direction.

Convenience was the number one reason for selecting a particular store (see
Table 2). This again underlines the importance of traffic patterns and location
even when attempts have been made to neutralize them. Price ranked second as
a patronage motive, slightly lower in St. Louis and San Francisco. This high rating
for price attaches additional significance to the validity of price perceptions which
is investigated in the next section.

Differences between reasons for choosing stores and reasons for eliminating stores
were striking. Cleanliness and uncrowded conditions were expected of all stores;
if they were lacking, the store was not even considered. Quality, a good meat de-

[4]Only one store in the entire study was eliminated by as many as 10% of the respondents;
that store ranked third in price in Havertown. The highest priced or lowest priced store was
the one most frequently eliminated in only New York where 7% of the respondents eliminated
the highest priced store.

TABLE 2   PRINCIPAL REASONS FOR SELECTING REGULAR SUPERMARKET (PERCENTAGE OF RESPONDENTS GIVING REASON)

Reason	New York	Haver-town	Greensboro	St. Louis	San Francisco
Convenience	68	49	57	55	63
Price	45	36	41	31	30
Good Values	43	18	30	20	34
Overall Quality	34	26	23	38	23
Meat Department	25	24	24	40	20
Friendliness	23	8	26	24	36
Assortment	24	16	9	18	27
Service	20	14	21	14	32
Produce Department	19	14	5	14	20

partment, and other characterisitcs which depend on the local clientele were then introduced as bases for choosing among the remaining stores.

Patronage and the Validity of Price Perception

Shoppers who regularly patronized the lowest priced stores were the most valid perceivers of price. Those who patronized the highest priced stores were the least valid perceivers. As shown in Table 3, patrons of the lowest priced store recorded

TABLE 3   MEAN PERCEPTUAL VALIDITY[a] SCORES BY PRICE LEVEL OF STORE SHOPPED REGULARLY

Store Rank	New York	Haver-town	Greensboro	St. Louis	San Francisco
1	.060	.026	.058	.112	.059
2	.045	c	.074	.115	.085
3	.116	.035	c	.104	.078
4	.144	c	.086	.121	c
5		.044	.092	.121	c
6				.139	.081
7					c
F Ratio	20.15[b]	3.12	2.57	2.76	1.28

[a]The lower the score, the more valid the perception. Each mean was computed for the respondents who shopped at the indicated store regularly.
[b]Significant at .01 level.
[c]Less than 10 respondents.

the lowest mean (most valid perception) in three cities and next to the lowest mean in a fourth city. Regular customers of the highest priced store recorded the highest mean (least valid perception) in four cities and next to the highest in the fifth.

The observed differences among shoppers of the various stores were statistically significant in only one city, but the consistency in the validity rankings compensated for the lack of statistical significance.[5] In both Havertown and Greensboro, the sequence in perceptual validity corresponded precisely to the sequence in price level; *i.e.,* customers of the lowest priced stores were the best perceivers, customers of the second lowest priced store were the next best perceivers, etc. In both New York and San Francisco, only one store was out of sequence. The St. Louis results did not support the general pattern found elsewhere, except for the customers of the highest priced stores who recorded the least valid perceptions.

It was not clear that patrons of low priced stores had the *ability* to perceive prices more validly than patrons of the high priced stores. They did perceive better in the existing environment, but this need not have been the result of superior ability. Many respondents showed a tendency to rank their regular stores lower in price than the price index warranted.[6] This downward bias produced misperception for all customers except those who patronized the lowest priced store. These respondents could not rank their store lower than it was; *viz.,* the lowest rank.

If the price indices had showed Store N rather than Store O was the lowest priced store, patrons of Store N would have been rated as more valid perceivers and patrons of Store O would have recorded less valid perceptions. Did superior perceptual ability produce the more valid scores by the customers of Store O, or were their more valid scores the result of a prevailing downward bias in favor of one's own store, a bias which acted against all respondents except them?

Regular patrons of the lowest priced stores did perceive prices with the greatest validity. But the existing data did not indicate whether these individuals had a higher level of perceptual ability or whether their superior scores were produced by the fact that the store they patronized happened to be the lowest priced store.

Perceptual Validity of Price Conscious Shoppers

Price conscious shoppers were more valid perceivers of price than shoppers who were not price conscious. Respondents had an opportunity to classify themselves

[5]The analysis of variance yielded statistically significant differences at .01 level for only New York. The results of paired comparisons between the low priced store and all others showed statistically significant differences (.01 level) in 6 of 16 comparisons—three in San Francisco, two in New York, and one in Havertown.

[6]For example, 57% of the patrons of the second lowest priced store in Havertown ranked their store as lowest in price. The remaining 43% correctly identified the lowest priced store, but over 60% of the customers of every other store made the proper identification. Patrons of the highest priced store did not usually claim their store was the lowest in price, but they did show a tendency to rank it below the highest.

with respect to price consciousness on three different questions. They were asked 1) whether they looked harder for low prices than most shoppers in their area, 2) how often they compared advertised prices, and 3) their reasons for selecting their regular supermarket. The last was an open end question; some respondents indicated that price was a reason and some did not name price. Table 4 summarizes the results to these questions for the five cities.

The most price conscious respondents recorded better perceptual scores than the least price conscious respondents in thirteen of fifteen comparisons. In every city at least two of the three questions showed the most price conscious respondents to be better perceivers. The evidence was much less conclusive when a middle group in price consciousness was introduced into the analysis. This group occupied an intermediate position with respect to perceptual validity in only two of ten instances. In some cases this middle group perceived more validity than the price conscious respondents; in others they were even less valid perceivers than the non-price conscious respondents. For example, in San Francisco those who compared advertised prices "sometimes" recorded the lowest perceptual validity of all three groups; in St. Louis, on this same question, those who compared "sometimes" recorded the most valid perceptual scores.

Price consciousness was a better discriminator of perceptual validity than was the price level of the store patronized. This was true despite the fact that the range in perceptual validity scores was larger when based upon store patronage. The results based upon price consciousness were more consistent, and statistically significant differences were observed more frequently.[7] Six tests yielded significant differences at the .01 level, and three others were significant at the .05 level. At least one comparison in each city showed a significantly more valid perception by price conscious shoppers.

The most consistent results were found in New York where 45% of the respondents gave price as a reason for choosing their regular store. The sequence of perceptual scores for the self-classification questions proceeded from price conscious to intermediate to non-price conscious, and all three questions yielded significant differences at the .05 level. Neither of these conditions existed in the other four communities.

The smallest differences among respondents were in Havertown, the community with the most valid overall price perceptions. In this environment, shoppers found it particularly difficult to classify themselves in price-consciousness. Differences in perceptual validity appeared between those who stated "price" was a reason for selecting their regular store and those who did not, but the self-evaluation questions did not discriminate very well.

Taking all of the results together, the evidence that price conscious shoppers were the most valid perceivers of price was overwhelming. Six of fifteen tests were significant was the .01 level and another three were significant at the .05 level. On a

[7]The tests were more powerful for the price conscious analysis because the sample was more evenly divided among the groups. In the store shopped analysis, some of the groups were quite small.

TABLE 4   STRESS ON PRICES VS. PERCEPTUAL VALIDITY

Question	New York	Havertown	Greensboro	St. Louis	San Francisco
Look Hard for Low Prices					
Harder than Others	.092	.024	.073	.126	.067
Same as Others	.109	.024	.069	.120	.090
Not as Hard	.117	.027	.105	.128	.079
F Ratio	5.90[a]	0.25	4.85	1.09	2.22
Compare Advertised Prices					
Usually	.093	.024	.074	.117	.073
Sometimes	.107	.023	.093	.115	.098
Hardly Ever	.120	.028	.069	.137	.087
F Ratio	3.29	0.56	2.06	7.48[a]	7.36[a]
Price as a Reason For Choosing Store					
Yes	.094	.028	.059	.124	.071
No	.111	.041	.086	.124	.086
"t"	1.85	2.93[a]	2.69[a]	0.00	2.34[a]

[a] Significant at .01 level.

non-parametric basis, the most price conscious shoppers were more valid perceivers than the least price conscious in thirteen of the fifteen comparisons.

Conclusions

Hypothesis 1: Patrons of the lowest priced stores have
the most valid price perceptions.

This hypothesis was accepted. Those individuals who shopped at the lowest priced stores were more valid price perceivers, but this result may have been produced by chance patronage of low priced stores rather than perceptual ability. A type of cognitive dissonance was evident for all shoppers, *i.e.*, they showed a downward bias in the rating of their regular store's price level. This bias rather than perceptual ability may have produced the more valid ratings. Not to be overlooked are the unique opportunities created for the stores by this downward bias. They should capitalize on existing favorable dispositions by offering selected price reductions, even if the number is kept to a minimum. This procedure will permit the retention of the favorable disposition via cognitive dissonance and selective perception.

Hypothesis 2: The validity of price perceptions is no
better for persons who stress price than for those who do not stress price.

This hypothesis was rejected. Shoppers who were very price conscious, *i.e.*, who placed a lot of stress on price, were more valid perceivers of price than those who were not at all price conscious. Generalizations with respect to intermediate groups in price consciousness were not warranted.

The combination of conclusions based on the testing of these two hypotheses indicated that a stated concern for price was a better predictor of perceptual ability than was the price level of the store shopped. The price conscious shoppers constitute a distinct market segment. They have not fooled themselves or idealized their own actions. They perceived price levels validly and were not easily misled.

Appendix

THE MEASUREMENT OF PERCEPTUAL VALIDITY

A zero on the scale for perceptual validity indicates that the complete or incomplete ordinal scale provided by the respondent corresponded perfectly to the market basket rankings. The higher the score assigned to the respondent, the more disagreement between his ranking and the market basket ranking. The scale is constructed in such a way that the respondent is penalized more for a shift in rankings between stores that have large differences in price indices than for a shift in rankings for stores that have small differences in price indices.

Table A-1 illustrates the calculation of perceptual validity scores for four different respondents in a city with four stores. Respondent I was assigned a perfect

TABLE A-1   EXAMPLES OF CALCULATION OF PERCEPTUAL VALIDITY
SCORES, 4 STORES*

Store	Price Index	Respondents' Rankings			
		I	II	III	IV
A	.975	1	1	2	1
B	.990	2	3	1	4
C	1.015	3	4	3	3
D	1.020	4	2	4	2

*Scorings:

I. No errors		Score	.000
II. Incorrect Paired Comparisons		BD	.030
		CD	.005
		Score	.035
III.		AB	.015
		Score	.015
IV.		BC	.025
		BD	.030
		CD	.005
		Score	.060

score of 0 because her ranking corresponded perfectly with the ranking of the price indices. Respondent II placed Store D as next to the lowest priced store when in fact it was the highest priced store. Consequently, she was wrong in two of six paired comparions: B versus D and C versus D. The difference in price indices between B and D was .030; that between C and D was only .005. The total of the two errors was assigned as the score (.035). Respondent III was incorrect with respect to only one paired comparison: that between A and B. Her score was .015—the difference between the market basket indices of these two stores. Respondent IV was incorrect in three of the paired comparisons; Table A-1 shows the calculation of the score for this respondent.

For those cities for which more than five stores were priced, the respondent was not asked for a complete ordinal ranking. In these cities the score was based upon the number of paired comparisons requested; *e.g.,* with six stores there were 15 possible paired comparisons but only 14 were implicit in the selection of four ranks. The respondent's score was based upon those 14 comparisons.

In certain instances respondents did not supply the four ranks requested. For example, a few respondents identified the lowest priced store and the highest priced store but did not differentiate among any of the other stores. The score assigned to such an individual assumed that the ranks not specified by the respondent would be determined by chance. Therefore, one half the difference associated with the omitted paired comparisons was scored against the respondent. This process was even more complicated in the case of incomplete rankings for cities with six or more stores.

Table A-2 illustrates the scoring method for a city in which there were six stores. The first three respondents supplied the four ranks requested, but the fourth respondent did not. Implicitly this respondent made twelve of the fourteen comparisons

TABLE A-2   EXAMPLES OF CALCULATION OF PERCEPTUAL VALIDITY SCORES, 6 STORES*

Store	Price Index	Respondents' Rankings			
		I	II	III	IV
A	.950	1	1		1
B	.970	2		1	2
C	.995		2		
D	1.010			2	
E	1.035	5	5	6	6
F	1.040	6	6	5	

*Scorings:

Number of Possible Paired Comparisons = 15
Number of Paired Comparisons Requested = 14

I. Number Comparisons Made = 14

Incorrect · · · · · · · · · · None
Score · · · · · · · · · · · · .000

II. Number Comparisons Made = 14

Incorrect BC · · · · · · · · · .025
Score · · · · · · · · · · · · .025

III. Number Comparisons Made = 14

Incorrect AB · · · · · · · · · .020
            AD · · · · · · · · · .060
            CD · · · · · · · · · .015
            EF · · · · · · · · · .005
Score · · · · · · · · · · · · .100

IV. Number Comparisons Made = 12

Incorrect EF · · · · · · · · · .005

Comparisons Not Made CD .015
                      CF .045
                      DF .030
                      Σ.090
Adjusted Penalty 2/3 $\times$ 1/2 $\times$ .090 · .030
                              Score · · · · · · · · · · · · .035

requested. Only one was incorrect, and the difference between these two stores (E and F) was .005. It would be improper to penalize her for all of the three comparisons she did not make since no respondent was asked to make the total of fifteen comparisons. It was assumed that chance would have dictated which two of the remaining three comparisons she would have made had she completed the assignment. The appropriate adjustment then was two-thirds of the usual figure for missing comparisons. As shown in Table A-2, there were two factors here: 1/2 corresponding to the assumption that she would have missed half of these comparisons and 2/3 corresponding to the proportion of missing comparisons requested.

PROMOTION AND THE CONSUMER

27. Communication

"An Experimental Study of the Effects of Information on Consumer Product Evaluations," Donald J. Hempel (Marketing Educator) in Raymond M. Haas, Editor, *Science, Technology, and Marketing* (Chicago: American Marketing Association, 1966), pp. 589-597.

28. Advertising

"The Measurement of Advertising Involvement," Herbert E. Krugman (Sociologist) *Public Opinion Quarterly,* Vol. 30 (Winter, 1966-1967), pp. 583-596.

29. Selling and Sales Promotion

"Customer and Salesman: The Anatomy of Choice and Influence in a Retail Setting," Ronald P. Willett (Marketing Educator) and Allan L. Pennington (Marketing Educator), in Raymond M. Haas, Editor, *Science, Technology, and Marketing* (Chicago: American Marketing Association, 1966), pp. 598-616.

The processes by which the buying public is informed of what products and services are being offered is highly complex, and can be examined from a number of angles. That is why we need to investigate the overall process of communication — and of persuasion — as a background for an examination of advertising, and of selling and sales promotion. Three different research studies of *promotion* are reported in Part VIII.

27 Communication

An Experimental Study of the Effects of Information on Consumer Product Evaluations

DONALD J. HEMPEL* *(Marketing Educator)*

The development of a conceptual framework for explaining and predicting consumer decisions must give consideration to the relative importance of environmental factors influencing consumer behavior, the effects of their interaction, and the role of the individual's predispositions as mediating forces in the decision process.

This article presents the findings of an experiment which studied the effects of two communication variables on consumer product evaluations and brand choice, as they operated through the mediating influences of brand preference and judgment difficulty.

Are consumer decisions regarding the relative merits of a product influenced by informational cues associated with a consumer product-rating publication and a salesman? Which of these information sources has the greater influence on product evaluations and brand choice? Does the influence of a communication from one source interact with the effects of the information obtained from the other source? How are the effects of these communications modified by the consumer's prior attitudes toward the brand names identifying product alternatives? What is the relationship between communication influence and the consumer's perceived difficulty of judging the product? These questions were the topics of investigation for the study described in this paper.

Source: Donald J. Hempel, "An Experimental Study of the Effects of Information on Consumer Product Evaluations," in Raymond M. Haas, Editor, *Science, Technology, and Marketing* (Chicago: American Marketing Association, 1966), pp. 589-597.

*Donald J. Hempel is assistant professor of Marketing at the University of Connecticut. This paper is based on his doctoral dissertation at the University of Minnesota.

329

Every purchase made by a consumer represents a decision which has been influenced by a vast number of factors. From the viewpoint of the seller, the most relevant factors are those over which he has some direct control—price, advertising, communications from the salesman, and other elements of the marketing mix. To explain and predict consumer behavior, however, it is necessary to also consider two sets of influencing variables over which the firm has little or no direct control: (1) other environmental influences such as advice given by friends or relatives and recommendations appearing in a product-rating publication; and (2) individual or psychological variables such as attitudes, cognitions, values, and other predispositions which incorporate past experiences. Although the importance of these three sets of factors is frequently mentioned in the literature of marketing, there is very little empirical evidence to illustrate their interrelationships in a setting involving consumer behavior. The laboratory experiment described below was undertaken to provide such evidence.

Research Plan

The primary purpose of this study was to explore the relationships among the effects of two communication factors and consumer predispositions in a decision-making situation. Communications from two consumer information sources—a product rating publication and a salesman—incorporated the environmental cues expected to influence the decision process. Brand preferences and difficulty of product judgment were considered as predispositions which might modify the effects of the communications on the decision process. The basic objective of the research design was to determine the relative influence of these variables upon product evaluations under controlled conditions.

HYPOTHESES

Several hypotheses about the relationships among these variables were tested:

(1) A communication from the product rating publication will have greater influence upon product evaluations than a similar cue from the salesman.

(2) The influence of a communication will be greater when it confirms the consumer's prior attitudes toward the brand than when it disconfirms these predispositions.

(3) The influence of a communication from one source will depend upon the other cues to which the individual is exposed. In other words, there will be significant interaction between the effects of the two communication factors.

(4) The influence of informational cues upon product evaluations will be greater among those who find the product difficult to judge.

PROCEDURE

These hypotheses were tested in an experimental situation involving the evaluation of two brands of men's white dress shirts. One hundred and thirty-five male college students from a marketing course at the University of Minnesota were employed as subjects. Most of the subjects were experienced buyers and consumers of the experimental product.

Measures of each subject's attitudes toward various brands of shirts and anticipated difficulty of judging several products were taken in the classroom three weeks prior to the experiment under the guise of another study.

In the experiment two similar but not identical white shirts with brand labels (Van Heusen and Truval) intact were presented to each subject in clear plastic packages marked with $5.00 price tickets. While the subject was examining the shirts, he was exposed to the information appropriate for the treatment combination to which he was assigned. Exposure to *Consumer Reports* communications consisted of having the subject read a copy of a page of product ratings appearing in *Consumer Reports* magazine. Subjects exposed to Salesman communications listened to a tape recorded simulation of a salesman's comments regarding the relative merits of each brand of shirt. Extensive preparations were made to create communications which would be considered genuine by the subjects. Interviews conducted with the subjects after the experiment was completed indicate that this objective was accomplished.

Subjects were randomly assigned to receive one of the nine communication treatments formulated by considering three variations in the information from each communication source. The three-by-three factorial experiment representing these treatment combinations is shown below:

CONSUMER REPORTS COMMUNICATION	SALESMAN COMMUNICATION		
	No Exposure	Confirms	Disconfirms
No Exposure	RnSn	RnSc	RnSd
Confirms	RcSn	RcSc	RcSd
Disconfirms	RdSn	RdSc	RdSd

The three variations in the information from each communication source reflect the alternative states of information to which a consumer might be exposed. No exposure treatment presented a situation in which the subject was not exposed to information from the communication source. Confirming communications favored the brand (Van Heusen) of shirts that pre-experiment measures indicated the subjects preferred. Disconfirming communications advocated the superiority of the brand (Truval), least preferred by the group of students used as subjects. For example, an individual assigned to the RdSc treatment received information from *Consumer Reports* favoring Truval (disconfirming communication) followed by information from the Salesman which supported Van Heusen (confirming communication). The content of the confirming and disconfirming communications was identical except for the brand name mentioned.

Following exposure to the informational cues, each subject completed a questionnaire designed to measure his opinions regarding various characteristics of the shirts. The main dependent variables of the study were the subject's product evaluations recorded on graphic rating scales such as the one reproduced below:

Q3: If you were purchasing one of these shirts for your own use, which would you buy?

:						:
3	2	1	0	1	2	3
definitely buy the Van Heusen brand		probably buy the Van Heusen brand		probably buy the Truval brand		definitely buy the Truval brand

These questions were scored by measuring the distance in millimeters between the subjects rating (recorded as an "X") of the product and the midpoint of the scale. Since the length of the rating scale was 128 millimeters, these scores could range from +64 (extremely favorable to Van Heusen) to −64 (extremely favorable to Truval).

Results and Discussion

The results indicated that the experimental manipulations did produce differences in expressed product evaluations which were consistent with the communications received by the subjects in each treatment group. Table 1 shows the analysis of variance results for the influence of the communication variables on responses to two important product evaluation questions.

TABLE 1   ANALYSIS OF VARIANCE FOR THE INFLUENCE OF COMMUNICATION VARIABLES

		Q3: Which brand would you buy?		Q4: Which brand provides better quality?	
	d.f.	Mean Square	F Ratio	Mean Square	F Ratio
Consumer Reports	2	7,594	8.31**	9,282	15.71**
Salesman	2	5,916	6.47**	5,465	9.25**
Interaction: CRxS	4	1,441	1.58	315	0.53
Error	126	914		591	

** Significant at .01 level: $F_{.99}(2,126) = 4.78$; $F_{.99}(4,126) = 3.47$

The pattern of variation in response across the nine treatment conditions is revealed in the profile of mean scores presented in Figure 1.

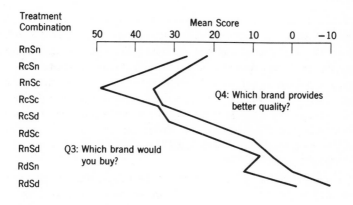

Figure 1. Profile of mean scores for the subjects exposed to each treatment.

HYPOTHESIS 1

The results did not provide consistent support for the first hypothesis. Comparisons among the mean scores for each treatment group indicated that *Consumer Reports* effects were greater than those of the Salesman only when the communications presented disconfirming information. When the communications favored the preferred brand (confirming cues), the influence of the Salesman was either equal to or slightly greater than that of *Consumer Reports.*

The predicted difference in the effects of the two sources was based upon the presumption that *Consumer Reports* would be perceived as a more credible source of information. This presumption was confirmed by measures of the subject's attitude toward the communication source. The apparent inconsistency between the findings of this study and existing evidence indicating that communication influence is a positive function of source credibility can be explained by the mediating effects of the subject's attitudes toward the brand alternatives. Source credibility is likely to become a more significant determinant of communication influence as suspicion of the communication's validity increases. This suspicion was probably greater when the information confronting the subject was inconsistent with his prior attitudes toward the product. Therefore, it is not surprising that the influence of a high credibility source such as *Consumer Reports* was more apparent when the content of the communication was disconfirming. Conversely, the differences in communication effects attributable to source credibility probably diminish when the information does not challenge existing attitudes. This proposition would explain the observed tendency toward equality of *Consumer Reports* and Salesman effects for confirming communication conditions.

HYPOTHESIS 2

Contrary to expectations, confirming communications from either source tended to exert less influence on expressed evaluations of the shirts than disconfirming communications. Comparisons among the main effects indicated that most of the product ratings of those exposed to disconfirming communications from *Consumer Reports* were significantly (at the .01 level) more favorable to Truval. Similar comparisons among the average effects of the Salesman variable indicate the same pattern of influence but only a few of the effects were statistically significant. Product evaluations of those exposed to confirming cues from either source were consistently more favorable to Van Heusen but most of the effects were not significant at the .05 level.

Existing research findings generally support the notion that people are more likely to be persuaded by communications which are consistent with their predispositions. Thus, it was reasonable to anticipate that communications favoring the brand most preferred by the subjects (Van Heusen) would have greater influence on product evaluations than those favoring the least preferred brand (Truval).

The discrepancy between the predicted pattern of influence and the experimental results might be accounted for in terms of assimilation and contrast effects.[1] Those subjects who perceived the confirming communications as advocating a position quite similar to their own (assimilation effect) would be less likely to reconsider their prior attitudes toward the brand. Confirming cues may have been considered rather superfluous since they supported a belief to which the subject already subscribed. Consequently, the product ratings recorded by those who disregarded the confirming communications would tend to be similar to the evaluations of subjects not exposed to information from either source. Subjects exposed to disconfirming information would experience greater motivation to review their own stand if they exaggerated the difference between their own position and that advocated by the communication (contrast effect). Unsettled by the possiblity that

[1] Sherif contends that perception and interpretation of a communication are significantly affected by the distance between the position advocated in a communication and the individual's own stand. When this distance is slight, the positions are perceived to be closer than they actually are (an assimilation effect). When the positions are more discrepant, there may be a tendency for the individual to perceive the position advocated to be further removed than it actually is (a contrast effect). In other words, the recipient of a communication may tend to minimize or positively distort (assimilate) information which is similar to his own predispositions and exaggerate or negatively distort (contrast) information which is inconsistent with his own position.
M. Sherif and C. I. Hovland, *Social Judgment* (New Haven: Yale University Press, 1961), p. 11 ff and p. 182 ff.

their prior beliefs are inaccurate, they may have been more receptive to any new information which would assist accurate evaluation of the product. Thus, the influence of disconfirming communications may have been greater not because the content was inherently more persuasive, but because the cues created a more receptive environment in which the subject was willing to reconsider his opinions toward the product alternatives.

This reasoning may appear somewhat inconsistent with dissonance theory until the role of ego-involvement is considered. When ego-involvement is low, the dissonance created by disconfirming information would tend to be minimal. Consumer decision processes concerning the purchase of a white shirt (and many other products characterized by low saliency) are not likely to be very ego-involving even in a natural environment. It is presumed that the equality of prices, the physical similarities of the product alternatives, and other characteristics of the research design tended to further reduce the saliency of the decision for the subjects. There is evidence from other studies which indicates that advocacy of positions quite discrepant from the individual's own position has a marked effect on opinions when the judgment issues are relatively uninvolving.[2]

HYPOTHESIS 3

The influence of a communication from either source was not significantly affected by the information received from the other source. As Table 1 shows, the test of interaction effects by the analysis of variance indicated that there was no reliable basis for the hypothesis that the influence of *Consumer Reports* and Salesman communications were interdependent. However, there were several consistent (but not signifciant at the .05 level) departures from an additive relationship among the effects of the communication variables: (1) the influence of the Salesman communications were greater when subjects were not exposed to *Consumer Reports* cues; and (2) the joint influence of confirming communications from both sources (the RcSc treatment) was less than the separate effects of a confirming cue from either source (the RcSn or RnSc treatments).

Empirical observations suggest that consumers are less susceptible to a salesman's influence when they have been forearmed with information from a source which they believe to be trustworthy and authoritative. The reduction in the Salesman's influence resulting from prior exposure to *Consumer Reports* is presumed to reflect a comparable reaction in the experimental situation. The apparent interaction effects resulting from exposure to confirming communications from both sources may reflect a defensive reaction to retain independence in the presence of rather intense persuasive pressures.

[2]C. I. Hovland, "Reconciling Conflicting Results Derived From Experimental and Survey Studies on Attitude Change," *The American Psychologist,* Volume 14 (1959), pp. 8-17.

HYPOTHESIS 4

Correlation between product evaluations and judgment difficulty was generally inconsistent but there was some evidence of an inverse relationship between these variables. High difficulty subjects appeared more responsive to communication exposure only in the condition involving disconfirming cues from the Salesman (the RnSd treatment). A pattern of relationships opposite that postulated was observed more frequently and attained a higher level of significance. This pattern was most apparent in the treatments consisting of confirming communications where subjects reporting low judgment difficulty tended to evaluate Van Heusen more favorably.

Previous studies of social influence have usually indicated that the perceived difficulty of the judgment issue is directly related to the individual's compliance with the position advocated by others.[3] A key to reconciling the contradiction between the results and existing evidence from conformity studies may be the subject's ego-involvement in the decision process. Subjects encountering greater judgment difficulty were more likely to become ego-involved because of their concern with the shortcomings of their product evaluations. Frustrated by their perceived inability to judge the alternatives, these subjects may have reacted defensively in order to maintain their self-esteem and avoid anxiety. Defensive reactions such as discounting the value of the information presented or rendering more cautious judgments would produce results similar to those observed. Those encountering less judgment difficulty may have been more willing to consider the advice of others because they had confidence in their ability to evaluate the product alternatives. Consequently, they would be more receptive to relevant informational cues and more susceptible to communication influence.

Conclusions

The findings indicate that the influence of informational cues is a function of both the source and content of communications presented in a controlled product judgment situation. The research evidence also suggests that the successful prediction and explanation of communications effects require consideration of factors such as brand preference and perceived difficulty of judging product alternatives. Finally, it is apparent from the discussion of the results that generalizations drawn from studies of social influence and communications effects in other fields are not always strictly applicable to a situation involving product evaluations.

Considering the multiplicity and complexity of variables influencing consumer behavior, it is unlikely that there will be many generalizations from any field which can be applied to all consumers or to all consumer decision-making situations. The conditions under which general findings from the behavioral sciences are transferable to the explanation of consumer behavior invite further exploration by students of marketing.

[3] See D. Krech, R. S. Crutchfield and B. L. Ballachey, *Individual in Society,* (New York: McGraw-Hill, 1962), pp. 504-522, for a review of this evidence.

28 Advertising

The Measurement of
Advertising Involvement

HERBERT E. KRUGMAN* *(Sociologist)*

In an earlier article** the author suggested that the processes of attitude change underlying mass communication impact are of two kinds. With low involvement to persuasive stimuli, one might look for gradual shifts in perceptual structure, aided by repetition, activated by behavioral choice situations, and followed at some time by attitude change. But with high involvement, one could look instead for the classic and familiar conflict of ideas at the level of conscious opinion and attitude that precedes changes in behavior.

The present article described the development and application of a workable tool to measure this involvement, a necessary step if the study of communication impact along these lines is to proceed intelligently.

The study of involvement has a long and impressive history culminating in the recent classic by the Sherifs and Nebergall.[1] However, all the recent history concerns involvement with issues or topics, and not with particular and specific persuasive stimuli. While topic or issue involvement does hold implications for the level of stimulus involvement that a subject is predisposed to bring into the stimu-

---

Source: Herbert E. Krugman, "The Measurement of Advertising Involvement," *Public Opinion Quarterly,* Vol. 30 (Winter, 1966-1967), pp. 583-596.

*Dr. Krugman is vice president of MARPLAN, a division of Communications Affiliates, Inc., New York City, and a member of the Editorial Board of the *Quarterly.*

**Herbert E. Krugman, "The Impact of Television Advertising: Learning Without Involvement," *Public Opinion Quarterly,* Vol. 29 (Fall, 1965), pp. 349-356.

[1] Carolyn W. Sherif, Muzafer Sherif, and Roger E. Nebergall, *Attitude and Attitude Change: The Social Judgment-Involvement Approach,* Philadelphia, Saunders, 1965.

lus situation, it is demonstrably inadequate as a measure of stimulus (e.g. advertising) differences on the same topic (e.g. product or brand).

The main difference between involvement predispositions associated with topics and the actual involvement in exposure to persuasive stimuli concerns the factor of *direct personal experience*. In the United States the study of experience, or what is usually called "subjective" experience, has had a peculiar history. Since the death of Edward Titchener in 1927, and the ultimate triumph of the then rising tide of behaviorism, there has been little concern with introspection or with immediate experience. Titchener and other students of Wundt declined in prestige to such an extent that by the middle thirties no major department of psychology in the United States was visibly active in this area of study. Then came Freudian psychology, without competition then and without competition today. That is, only the psychoanalysts seem interested specifically in what went through one's mind, what one thought at a given moment in time, what was one's immediate subjective experience of some particular event or stimulus.

Our definition of involvement is the number of "connections," conscious bridging experiences or personal references per minute, that the subject makes between the content of the persuasive stimulus and the content of his own life. This definition necessitates a report of immediate experience or conscious reaction to a stimulus. "Connection" must be identified and counted in the protocols. Manuals must be prepared for coders. The requirements take us back, therefore, to Titchener to pick up what he learned of the errors of objective reference and to carry on from there.[2] This paper will report three small studies which applied the measurement of connections to various mass media stimuli.[3]

Comparisons Across Media

In the earlier development of the model,[4] only the television medium was discussed, because it was in the attempt to understand the impact of television that the low involvement model was developed. In the present paper, we hypothesize that the special quality of television advertising impact is low involvement, as compared with higher involvement for magazine advertising.[5] Therefore, to illustrate differences between the low and high involvement models we propose here to formally compare the television and magazine media.

[2]Summaries of Titchener's relevant methodological contributions appear in Robert S. Woodworth, *Contemporary Schools of Psychology,* New York, Ronald, 1931, pp. 40-41, and in Edna Heidbreder, *Seven Psychologies,* New York, Appleton-Century, 1933, p. 129.
[3]The studies reported here were sponsored by Time Magazine. For those who may be interested, a manual that discusses rules for scoring of connections is available from the author.
[4]Krugman, *op. cit.*
[5]It is relevant that the Sherifs did find that highly involved and less involved persons appraise communications differently (*op. cit.* Chap. V).

TELEVISION VERSION OF LOW INVOLVEMENT MODEL

1. The quality of the stimulus is animate while the observer is inanimate. With the pace of the experience or rate of stimulation out of the individual's control, there is relatively low opportunity for connections, for dwelling upon a point of advertising.

2. The change processes require:

a. Stimulus repetition to build a potential for alteration in perceptual structure of advertised brands, i.e. a gradual development of the ability to see the brand differently without being specifically aware of any change.

b. A behavioral opportunity, such as in-store shopping, to trigger the potential for shift in perceptual structure, i.e. suddenly to see the brand in the new manner when confronted by it on the supermarket shelf.

c. Behavioral completion to release appropriate attitudes supportive and consistent with the shift in perceptual structure, i.e. if the brand is then purchased the new way of seeing it may then for the first time be expressed in words, for example, to "explain" why it was selected.

3. The role of behavior is as part of the change process, which continues beyond the store. Unless behavior completion, or purchase, occurs, there ensues an unstable condition characterized by a shift in perceptual structure without a corresponding shift in attitudinal structure. Without behavioral completion, therefore, the impact of a behavior opportunity is temporary only and perceptual structure reverts to its initial condition, though still carrying the potential for shift on other occasions. For example, a housewife may be repeatedly struck by some new (advertised) brand attribute each time she confronts it on the store shelf, and yet never retain this impression long enough to put into words, until one day the actual purchase is made.

MAGAZINE VERSION OF HIGH INVOLVEMENT MODEL

1. The quality of the stimulus is inanimate, while the observer is animate. With the pace of the experience, or rate of stimulation, under the individual's control, there is relatively high opportunity for connections, for dwelling upon a point of advertising.

2. The change processes require transmission of specific news, new information, or new ideas which represent a way of looking at a topic that is in conflict with or different from that represented in older information or ideas, and which may lead to resolution of the difference through new decision making.[6]

[6]The concept of motivation is excluded from the model because its arousal is often so general as to permit a large and unpredictable number of resolutions, including, commercially, the purchase of a competitor's brand.

3. The role of behavior is as a consequence of new decisions, and is not part of the change process itself, i.e. the change process may be over before the subject enters the store.[7]

Before field studies, we wanted to create various degrees and conditions of involvement with advertising in order to become familiar with whatever problems of measurement might arise. To this end, an experimental laboratory exercise was conducted.

1. To create variety of involvement with advertising it was decided to manipulate (a) medium, (b) expensiveness of product or service advertised, (c) interest value of editorial environment of ad, and (d) instructional "set" given to respondents.

   a. Medium

      Magazine—A.M.O. portfolio[8]

      Television—Fairchild #400 rear projector, 8 X 10 inch screen

   b. Product or service advertised

      Airline   { Similar television and print versions of brand and ad theme;
      Margarine { airline roughly similar but margarine almost identical

   c. Editorial environment

      Magazine:

         "Personalities":

            Two-page article, "England's Firebrand Princess," with five photos of Princess Anne

         ADVERTISEMENT

            Two-page article, "Some Poignant and Memorable Personal Reflections, What Prayer Means to Me," with nine photos of various entertainment and political personalities and their comments about prayer

         "Dollars":

            Two-page article, "Stanching the Dollar Outflow," with one illustration, no photos

         ADVERTISEMENT

            Two-page article, "Riches for a New Region—Harnessing the Arkansas River," with three photos, one map

---

[7]The point here is that the magazine itself is a store (like a catalogue) where "browsing," shopping, and purchase decisions may occur.

[8]The *Appareil à Mesure d'Observation* (Instrument for Measuring Observation) designed at the Marplan Perception Laboratory in Paris, France, is a fourteen-page hard-cover portfolio that contains seven stop watches within the back cover of the portfolio. A complex of unseen pulleys permits the opening and closing of seven of the pages to be precisely timed.

Television:

"Variety show":

2'25" of a visit with James Bond (Sean Connery) sequence from a popular variety show

COMMERCIAL

2'2" of an Edie Gorme song from same variety show

"Press interview":

1'06" of a translated interview between a group of reporters and a Dominican political leader

COMMERCIAL

3'00" of same interview

d. Instructions

Editorial set: "We're doing a study of magazine topics and I'd like you to spend a few minutes looking at some stories that appeared recently."

Advertising set: "We're doing a study of magazine advertising and I'd like you to spend a few minutes looking at a particular ad and also the stories that appeared next to it."

2. Combinations of the above four variables provided sixteen experimental conditions for observation:

	Magazine		Television	
Editorial	P$P	P¢P	V$V	V¢V
set	D$D	D¢D	I$I	I¢I
Advertising	P$P	P¢P	V$V	V¢V
set	D$D	D¢D	I$I	I¢I

NOTE: P = personalities and D = dollars; V = variety show and I = press interview; $ = airline and ¢ = margarine.

Testing was conducted at various times during the day with a variety of women recruited at a regional shopping center in New Jersey. Respondents were unpaid. The test environment was a rented store which has been regularly used as a research center within the shopping center area.

The definition of involvement required that conscious connections occur between the persuasive stimulus and something in the respondent's life. This differs from the more general definition of involvement phrased in terms of the importance of issues or of opinions or positions taken about issues, i.e. definitions oriented to topic rather than to stimulus *material*. The interview situation is also somewhat different in that, rather than information, opinions, or attitudes, respondents are asked to recall and report what they were thinking at the (earlier) time they viewed an advertisement, i.e. they are asked to report mental incidents.

The method of questioning included a few questions on likes and dislikes of the editorial material followed by, "What about the advertisement—what thoughts came to mind while you looked at it?" with such probes as, "Can you remember all your thoughts about the ad?" and "Try to think back to everything that went through your mind as you looked at it." The major problem in this type of interview is that the respondent may occasionally switch from past to present tense in reporting, suggesting that she may be reporting a connection of the moment rather than one that occurred while viewing the ad. This was checked with, "I'm going to read back to you each of the thoughts you have mentioned. For each one I'd like you to tell me whether you had this thought *while* you were looking at the advertisement or *while* you were talking to me." This probe finally became shortened to the vernacular "Then or now?"

Some examples of single connections per protocol:

"It made me think of traveling there myself."
"It made me feel as if I would like to go on my vacation."

Some examples of double connections per protocol:

"My husband flies all the time. . . . I think wouldn't it be great to go."
"I thought I'd like to go. . . . you'll think I'm crazy [in response to probe] my niece is getting married and going to Europe to live."

When connections go above three or four, they may require the careful checking of inconsistencies in tense.

"I recognized the brand name though I don't really use margarine. My husband is a strict believer in butter or oil. I have tried using it but they prefer the flavor of butter. . . . It's interesting to know that you can buy margarine which doesn't burn. With butter you have to be careful. I may even try this. . . . The main thing is the burnt egg [in ad illustration]. If there's anything I detest it's burnt egg. We like our eggs soft and juicy. . . . I was just thinking I bought some [brand] oil this morning. I had a recipe for fruit bread. It turned out so nice. I made two fruit breads. I'm not interested in margarine. . . I may try it now that I know it doesn't burn at high heat. . . . I had one thought here. This was the main thought I don't cook with high heat unless I'm searing. Particularly I cook eggs on a low heat. . . . The margarine is either good or bad. Some people like to cook with less heat; that has nothing to do with margarine."

The checking question on connections during exposure vs. connections during interview suggested a fifty-fifty split. Thus, if half are spontaneous in response to test stimuli and half are liberated by the interview, we have here a crude and quite tentative indication that some pre-test research procedures may double the apparent involvement of respondents with the advertising copy being tested.

A structured scale administered at the end of the interview was pre-tested to see if respondents themselves could differentiate between those of their responses which were only stimulus-oriented and those which made a connection to their own lives.[9] Results indicated that they could not do this reliably (i.e. in agreement with the taped interview protocol) on the scale in question, and that coding of unstructured interview response was essential. The major problem in coding individual protocols was to identify separate thought sequences, usually in terms of temporally different incidents or interpersonal situations mentioned. There are, however, some types of connections that deserve special comment. These appeared in response to the advertising "set," and concern connections to the interview or to other occasions when the ad was seen.

"I thought you would want to know what attracted me."

"I was wondering if this was the ad you wanted my opinion on."

"I thought, here's another ad. I hope it doesn't take too long."

"I've seen this on TV."

"I've seen the ad before. It's not convincing."

It may be noted, as in the last above, that a few connections are unfavorable and are so tallied. It may also be noted that, while connections to other advertising could reasonably be expected to occur quite often, they appeared in the experiment only in response to the advertising set. Again, therefore, one must indicate concern about conventional pre-test research procedures; in this case because of their apparent tendency to create irrelevant connections.

Use of the experimental materials produced two surprises. One was that Princess Anne and the prayers of famous personalities were less interesting than the dollar gap and hydroelectric resources. Most seemed obliged to read the "serious" material more carefully. A second surpise was that the airline advertisement was only slightly more involving than the margarine advertisement. The largest difference in involvement was produced by the variation in instructions, or perceptual set.

Twenty-nine female respondents spent an average of 21.0 seconds per page on the seven pages over all, and an average of 19.4 seconds on the advertising page itself. To the advertisement they produced an average of 1.55 connections. While ten respondents "read" the material and spent over 150 seconds over all, and

[9]Please check those statements that best describe the kinds of thoughts that came to mind while you looked at the advertisement.

———The advertisement didn't hold my attention.

———The advertisement held my attention but no particular thought came to mind.

———I had at least one thought but it had nothing to do with the main idea of the advertisement.

———I had at least one thought about the advertisement but it had nothing to do with me personally.

———I had at least one thought which tied in something about the main idea of the advertisement to something about me personally.

nineteen respondents "browsed" over the material in less than 150 seconds over all, each of these groups produced an average of 1.5 connections per advertisement.

Table 1 suggests that direction attention to advertising material produces fewer and slower connections than when attention is focused on something else, in this case the more natural focus on editorial matter.[10] One may reappreciate the psychoanalyst's persistent view that peripheral thoughts obtained under real-life conditions or under conditions of relaxed association may have as much value for the understanding and prediction of behavior as do responses to direct questions.[11]

In the television materials, the more serious press interview unexpectedly aroused much closer attention and interest than the variety-show material. Another surprise was the frequency of unfavorable remarks about television commercials, occurring in a third of all television interviews.

Forty-one female respondents produced an average of .59 connections in response to the commercials, contrasting markedly with the 1.55 for print advertisements.[12] In other respects, the results paralleled the print data. That is, there were more connections in response to an editorial than to an advertising set, more connections when the editorial matter was serious, more connections to airline than to margarine advertising.

Within the context of the laboratory exercise, it would seem that the magazine advertising was indeed more involving than the television advertising. A 2 or 3 to 1 ratio is suggested by the contrast between one and a half connections in twenty seconds and a half connection in sixty seconds. Of course, these figures are products of a small piece of research and one that has itself provided fresh grounds for questioning the predictive ability of laboratory evaluations of advertising.[13]

[10]In terms of distraction theory, these data are consistent with earlier findings by L. Festinger and N. Maccoby, "On Resistance to Persuasive Communications," *Journal of Abnormal and Social Psychology,* Vol. 68, No. 4, 1964, pp. 359-366.

[11]The quality of relaxation in viewing assumed unexpected importance when an attempt was made to interrupt and terminate the viewing procedure immediately after the third, or advertising, page, without removing the following two pages. This unsuccessful experiment in interview economy was attempted with an additional twenty-four respondents, almost all of whom indicated some degree of suspicion or complaint about not being allowed to finish the "book" and then showed what seemed like a constricted response. Thus, the average number of reported connections dropped to .6, and the average number of words of comment about the *advertising* dropped from 120 to 86.

[12]It should be noted, however, that the transmission quality of the commercials seemed inferior to that on home television receivers. This should be corrected in future tests.

[13]One implication here for modifcation of laboratory research procedures is to *depersonalize* the researcher and his influence on the respondent. At the least, he might be out of the room when copy is viewed and questionnaires completed; "obviously" recorded (voice) instructions might represent a further step; one ultimate procedural goal might be described as self-service research. For a broader discussion of this problem, see M. T. Orne, "On the Social Psychology of the Psychological Experiment: With Particular Reference to Demand Characteristics and Their Implications," *American Psychologist,* Vol. 17, 1962, pp. 776-783.

TABLE 1 NUMBER OF CONNECTIONS PER SECOND AND EXPOSURE TIME FOR MAGAZINE AND TV COMMERCIALS, BY EDITORIAL OR ADVERTISING SET, EDITORIAL ENVIRONMENT, AND PRODUCT ADVERTISED

	Magazine				TV	
	(N)	Seconds Per Ad	Number Conn.	Seconds Per Conn.	(N)	Average Conn.
Set:						
Editorial	(14)	17.6	1.9	9.14	20	.75
Advertising	(15)	24.3	1.2	20.25	21	.43
Editorial environment:						
Serious/news	(15)	21.9	1.8	12.14	26	.65
Light/entertainment	(14)	19.6	1.3	15.23	15	.47
Product advertised:						
Airline	(15)	24.2	1.8	13.48	9	.67
Margarine	(14)	16.6	1.3	12.90	32	.56

345

Comparisons Across Testing Situations

The field work of the laboratory study was conducted with women respondents in a rented store in Paramus, New Jersey, in July 1965. A second study was conducted in Cleveland, Ohio, in November of the same year, but on a home-interview basis, and with a fresh selection of materials. This time 156 women were tested, 53 on print, 56 on a sixty-second television version of the same ad, and 47 on a twenty-second version. The subject of the advertising was an electric broiler that cooked both sides of a steak simultaneously.

During the same period, 144 men were tested, 44 on print, 56 on a sixty-second television version of the same ad, and 44 on a twenty-second version. The subject of the advertising was a small cigar currently in competition with cigarettes.

Editorial matter for both men and women consisted of the following:

Magazine:

Cover plus one page of article "Modern Living—The Best Resorts," with one photograph

ADVERTISEMENT

Two pages of continued article with two photographs

Television (Same for 60″ and 20″ commercials):

6′ 19″ of an Alan King comedy sequence from a popular variety show

COMMERCIAL

2′ 01″ of continued King sequence

Only an editorial set was used in the instructions to the respondent, since this seemed more "natural" as well as more involving. The average number of connections per female respondent was 1.00 for print, .86 for 60″ TV, and .72 for 20″ TV. Connections per male respondent were .34 for print, .37 for 60″ TV, and .30 for 20″ TV. The low level of male involvement was a surprise. Apparently, the "entertaining" aspects of the advertisement were responded to more than those related to smoking or to the product. An over-all comparison with results of the first study is presented in Table 2.

The evidence presented in Table 2 of a decrease in print connections from about 1.8 for airlines to less than parity for cigars suggested that an "advantage" in involvement for magazines may hold true only with higher involvement topics, products, or advertisements. It should be emphasized, however, that the data in this report are presented only as suggestive aids in the refinement of hypotheses.

Comparisons Across Advertisements

Fifteen pairs of print ads were selected for study. Each pair contained a high and a low Starch ("Noting") advertisement for the same products and brand (H and L

TABLE 2 NUMBER OF CONNECTIONS PER SECOND AND EXPOSURE TIME FOR MAGAZINE AND TV COMMER-
CIALS, LABORATORY AND HOME SETTINGS COMPARED

	20" TV		60" TV		Print		
	No. Conn.	(N)	No. Conn.	(N)	No. Conn.	Seconds per Ad	(N)
Laboratory (half editorial set, half advertising set):							
Airline			.67	(9)	1.8	24.2	(15)
Margarine			.56	(32)	1.3	16.6	(14)
Home (editorial set):							
Range	.72	(47)	.86	(56)	1.0	18.9	(53)
Cigar	.30	(44)	.37	(56)	.3	14.7	(44)

FIGURE 1

For February 1966 Testing with Women		For March Testing with Men and Women			For April Testing with Managers	
Women H/L	Product Advertised	Men H/L	Women H/L	Product Advertised	Men H/L	Product Advertised
67/41	Hair coloring	47/22	45/20	Cigarette	62/43	Automobile
54/26	Canned corn	57/27	43/23	Organ	59/30	Industrial glass
65/41	Refrigerator	52/25	47/39	Insurance	30/19	Insurance
68/33	Carpeting	59/30	57/30	Travel	57/25	Business machines
37/27	Analgesic	39/22	60/45	Scotch	61/14	Corporate (fuel)

in the table below).[14] The fifteen pairs were then separated into three groups. Within each group each respondent was exposed to one ad from each pair. Half the respondents saw three high- and two low-Starch ads (HLHLH) and half saw two high- and three low-Starch ads (LHLHL). Each of the two sequences was rotated through five subgroups of six respondents each. Presentation of the ads was made in the A.M.O. book with exposure time recorded. Respondents for the February and March groups were again recruited at the Paramus, New Jersey, shopping center, while the April group was recruited at a shopping center in Ridgewood, New Jersey, and screened for management or technical positions earning over $10,000. No editorial matter was used in testing the three groups in Fig. 1.

The results of the February test of connections to the first group of advertisements are shown in Table 3.

TABLE 3   AVERAGE NUMBER OF CONNECTIONS AND EXPOSURE TIME TO HIGH- AND LOW-STARCH WOMEN'S PRINT ADS, WOMEN ONLY

	Average No. Connections			Average No. Seconds		
Product Advertised	Total (60)	High Starch (30)	Low Starch (30)	Total (60)	High Starch (30)	Low Starch (30)
Refrigerator	.35	.43	.30	17.5	12.3	22.7
Hair coloring	.28	.13	.43	12.7	13.5	11.8
Carpeting	.27	.20	.33	14.5	16.4	12.6
Analgesic	.25	.13	.37	14.7	17.4	12.1
Canned corn	.22	.30	.13	12.8	10.5	15.0

Several observations can be made from Table 3. (1) The general level of involvement (i.e. under .5) is significantly less than under previous conditions of testing, presumably because of concentration of ads without editorial relief. (2) The range of involvement across categories (.35/.22) is less than 2 to 1 and frequently less than the range within categories (.43/.13, .37/.13, .30/.13), which over all tends to be more than 2 to 1. (3) There appears to be no relationship between involvement and Starch Noting, and no relationship between involvement and exposure time. (4) The + 2 to 1 range of involvement within categories is greater than the Starch range within categories, which over all tends to be slightly under 2 to 1. (5) The + 2 to 1 range of involvement within categories is greater than the range of exposure time within categories, which tends over all to be less than 2 to 1.

---

[14] Starch Noting scores are the percentage of readers of magazine issues who at least noticed high- and low-scoring advertisements, as reported by the Daniel Starch organization.

In short, the involvement variable seemed more sensitive than Starch "Noting" or exposure (dwell) time, and is independent of them. Most important, it needed to be examined on a specific stimulus basis and not solely in terms of categories. These observations were then reconsidered in the light of the next group of ads.

It is apparent from Table 4, which gives the results of the March test, that the

TABLE 4   AVERAGE NUMBER OF CONNECTIONS IN RESPONSE TO HIGH- AND LOW-STARCH GENERAL PRINT ADS, MEN AND WOMEN SEPARATELY

Product Advertised	Men			Women		
	Total (30)	High Starch (15)	Low Starch (15)	Total (30)	High Starch (15)	Low Starch (15)
Travel	.33	.53	.13	.70	.60	.80
Organ	.37	.20	.53	.57	.33	.80
Insurance	.17	.27	.07	.33	.33	.33
Cigarette	.13–[a]	.00	.27–	.30–	.33–	.27–
Scotch	.20	.20	.20	.20	.20	.20

[a] Minus signs indicate unfavorable connections.

over-all level of involvement of men is about half that of women. Furthermore, the sensitivity of the involvement variable among the relatively less involved men is consistent with the findings of the February group, i.e. the more than 2 to 1 range of involvement within categories is greater than across categories and greater than the variation of Starch "Noting" (or exposure time, not shown) within categories.

It had been noted earlier (Table 2) that the level of involvement of men was half or less than that of women. At the time it was considered to be a reflection of the particular ads used, rather than a possibly general difference between men and women. It should also be noted that the lowered stimulus sensitivity of the involvement variable among the relatively more involved women in the March group should be seen along with the greater stimulus sensitivity and lower involvement of the women of the February group. Thus, apart from questions of differences between the sexes, we have here two cases where stimulus sensitivy varied with the general level of topic involvement. This suggests a possible postscript to the work of Gutman, Hovland, Sherif, *et al.,* which treats issue or topic involvement but tends to ignore stimulus involvement as an important variable in attitude change. It is suggested that at some point of (decreasing) involvement, the stimulus involvement within issues or topics may be just as varied and important, if not more so, than involvement across issues or topics. Coupled with this suggestion is the observation that for women this "point" is represented in the present data, i.e. the women of the February group represent a level of involvement in which stimulus supersedes topic, whereas the women of the March group represent a higher level of involvement in which topic involvement (especially travel) supersedes stimulus involvement.

The final group of ads, tested on male managers, tended to cast some doubt on the generality of a sex difference in involvement (Table 5). While the average

TABLE 5   AVERAGE NUMBER OF CONNECTIONS AND EXPOSURE TIME TO HIGH- AND LOW-STARCH MEN'S PRINT ADS, MALE MANAGERS ONLY

Product Advertised	Average No. Connections			Average No. Seconds		
	Total (60)	High Starch (30)	Low Starch (30)	Total (60)	High Starch (30)	Low Starch (30)
Automobile	.38	.33	.43±[a]	12.0	11.6	12.4
Insurance	.30	.30±[b]	.30	12.4	12.2	12.6
Industrial glass	.28	.30	.27	14.5	12.9	16.0
Business machines	.28	.27	.30	11.6	10.7	12.6
Corporate (fuel)	.18	.30	.27	13.3	12.1	14.4

[a]Six of thirteen connections unfavorable.
[b]Four of nine connections unfavorable.

number of connections is not high, it is not lower than that of the women responding to women's ads (Table 3). It does, however, include a higher number of unfavorable connections, and it does include such interesting topics as automobiles and dogs (glass advertisement).

Table 5 shows more variation across topics than within. The data were then split into lower vs. higher income (age-related) subgroups. In Table 6 it is shown

TABLE 6   AVERAGE NUMBER OF CONNECTIONS IN RESPONSE TO HIGH- AND LOW-STARCH MEN'S PRINT ADS' MALE MANAGERS BY LOW AND HIGH INCOME

Product Advertised	Incomes $10,000-14,999[a]			Incomes $15,000 and Up		
	Total (22)	High Starch (11)	Low Starch (11)	Total (38)	High Starch (19)	Low Starch (19)
Automobile	.64±	.64±[b]	.64±[b]	.24	.16	.32
Industrial glass	.45	.55	.36	.18	.16	.21
Insurance	.36	.27	.45	.26	.32	.21
Business machines	.27	.36	.18	.29	.21	.37
Corporate (fuel)	.14	.18	.09	.21	.10	.32

[a]Average age of lower income respondents = 40.0; higher income 45.3
[b]Three of seven connections unfavorable.

that the less affluent but younger respondents are much more involved, especially with automobiles and the glass advertisement (showing the head of a strikingly handsome collie dog), than the more affluent older respondents. While variation in stimulus involvement increases to 2 to 1 as topical involvement declines, this is evident only within the younger group.

Conclusions

The series of small studies described in this report point to certain hypotheses about the nature of involvement with advertising, and to some degree with media messages in general. These hypotheses are as follows:

1. Involvement with advertising in magazines or television tends to be highest when attention is directed to the editorial environment, less when it is directed to the advertising, and least when advertising is presented alone.

2. Involvement with advertising tends to be consistent with interests in the editorial environment, i.e. greater interest "carries over" to produce higher involvement.

3. Involvement with advertising tends to be higher for magazines than for television with high involvement products, but no different with low involvement products.

4. Involvement, as measured by number of "connections" per minute, tends to be more sensitive than, and independent of, two other measures (a) Starch Noting scores, and (b) seconds of stimulus exposure.

5. Involvement with specific stimuli tends to be more varied and consequently less predictable with products of intrinsically low involvement, while stimuli representing a high involvement product more often tend to share the same level of involvement.

A final and equally tentative hypothesis may apply only to advertising and not to media messages in general. This is the hypothesis that women tend toward higher or more favorable involvement than man. The difference may be viewed in terms of the woman's role as family "purchasing agent" in American society. Moreover, in terms of our general theory of involvement, which relates low involvement impact to conditions in which behavioral changes precede attitude changes, it supposes that the less highly involved men are more likely to be "impulse" buyers, while the more highly involved women are more likely to be "planful" buyers of advertised goods and services.

A next step in research will be to attempt to relate involvement measures to the purchasing consequences of advertising exposure.

29 Selling and Sales Promotion

Customer and Salesman: The Anatomy of Choice and Influence in a Retail Setting

RONALD P. WILLETT *(Marketing Educator)* AND
ALLAN L. PENNINGTON* *(Marketing Educator)*

The encounter between customer and salesman in retail appliance transactions can be viewed as a process of social interaction, in which both buyer and seller must participate if personal selling is to be effective.

The hypothesis here is that customer-salesman interaction in appliance transactions takes the form of problem-solving. A study of actual behavior on retail appliance floors indicates that problem-solving is a central part of selling, and that the content of customer-salesman interaction can be used to predict successful transactions.

There is a paradox of heroic proportions in the low esteem accorded personal selling as an area of inquiry by the academic researcher in marketing. Few visible marketing phenomena would appear to offer as rich a setting for the study of choice and influence processes as the interaction of a buyer and seller in the pursuit of a completed transaction. To add to the paradox there has been extensive investigation of selling by researchers of a different bent, for as Miner suggests, the salesman has been one of the most extensively studied men in the business world.[1] But the great strength of this stream of research—its singleness of pur-

Source: Ronald P. Willett and Allan L. Pennington, "Customer and Salesman: The Anatomy of Choice and Influence in a Retail Setting," in Raymond M. Haas, Editor, *Science, Technology, and Marketing* (Chicago: American Marketing Association, 1966), pp. 598-616.

*Ronald P. Willett, Associate Professor of Marketing in the Graduate School of Business at Indiana University, and Allan L. Pennington, Assistant Professor of Marketing in the School of Business Administration at the University of Minnesota.

[1] J. B. Miner, "Personality and Ability Factors in Sales Performance," *Journal of Applied Psychology*, Vol. XLVI, No. 1 (February, 1962), p. 6.

pose in seeking predictors of occupational performance—also limits its applicability in explaining transactional behavior and differentiating the successful from unsuccessful transaction. An endorsement of this latter focus is implied in an articulate critique of research in personal selling by Hauk.[2] Viewing personal selling as a central part of certain types of marketing transactions, the question becomes the causation for a successful transaction.

A Process Approach

The central thesis of this paper is that personal selling of consumer durables—specifically household appliances—can be viewed usefully as a problem-solving process, requiring the joint participation and interaction of customer and salesman for a successful outcome. Components of this conceptualization of personal selling include: 1) The actors (customer shopping party and salesman) and a stage (retail appliance selling floors) for the action that is to be played out; 2) An organizing scheme that determines the roles of the participants, 3) The mechanisms for maintenance and mediation of the process implicit in buyer-seller interaction; and 4) Assumed starting positions for the players. The first and last components are in a sense not functional, and their existence and configuration must be specified. Normally, these givens will not change appreciably during the transaction itself.

THE SETTING FOR THE TRANSACTION

Assumptions about the starting positions of the two parties to the transaction are most meaningfully presented in terms of latent predispositions for action. For example, on the salesman's side in a retail appliance setting there is little basis for predicting from one potential transaction to the next exactly what customer intent or action will prevail. The retail floor salesman is confronted by a continuous stream of customers, with little consistency in the order of their appearance or the characteristics of those who do appear. Floor salesmen normally will have little opportunity—unless a particular customer has been a prior patron of that salesman—to form any extensive set of expectations about specific customers prior to contact. On the other hand, on the customer's side, a significant selection process has been exercised. The customer's choice of retail store, and perhaps even his selection of a salesman, may be quite deliberate.

Another assumption relating to the customer concerns his predisposition to purchase at the time of customer-salesman contact. It is contended, and was documented in the present study, that the decision to purchase as a generic choice in most appliance transactions is no longer an issue at the time that customer-salesman contact is made. If this is true one might infer that the substance of a potential transaction is more likely to revolve around the specific offer alternatives from

[2]James G. Hauk, "Research in Personal Selling," in George Schwartz, ed. *Science in Marketing* (New York: John Wiley & Sons, Inc., 1965), p. 217.

which choice can be made, and the conditions under which execution of the purchase decision might be possible.

BUYER AND SELLER AS A GROUP

At the very heart of the interaction approach to personal selling is the view that, since buyer and seller share participation in the marketing transaction, they might meaningfully be considered as a group, specifically, a dyad. Admittedly this is an attractive point of view. Viewing buyer and seller as a dyad allows one to bring a great number of variables and a great deal of insight from social psychology into the explanations for transactional behavior. If this is an attractive strategy, it is also a risky strategy, for although certain kinds of buyer-seller relationships—especially those in the industrial area—may last over time, the occasional contact that accompanies the great majority of retail transactions raises serious doubts as to the true presence of a dyad. Becker and Useem define a dyad in terms of the length of time of relations of members of the pair, pointing out that the relationship must have persisted over a length of time sufficient for the establishment of a discernible pattern of interacting personalities.[3] It is assumed that the dyad will continue to exist and will form the basis for future relationships. This does not appear to be the case in the large portion of typical retail transactions.

Goffman offers a very persuasive alternative to automatic classification of a two person relationship as a group. He suggests that the designation "encounter" or "focused gathering" may be much more appropriate, allowing one to explore what is uniquely characteristic of the less formal relationship. He points out that some of the properties important to encounters are much less important to groups as such. For example, embarrassment, maintenace of poise, capacity for verbal communication, exchange of speaker role, and in particular, maintenance of continuous focus on the official activity of the encounter are not properties of social groups in general.[4]

Use of the encounter as a potential frame of reference for the analysis of buyer-seller behavior has both strengths and limitations. Highly situational properties of the transaction assume additional significance, and this orientation seems to match more closely the reality of the retail marketing transaction. Additionally, enough is known about durable goods purchasing to infer that it would be difficult to maintain a true dyad given the spacing of durable goods purchases and their dispersion across sellers. With its principal focus on the immediate interaction between participants an "encounters" approach offers a better chance of supplying inductive explanation. Conversely, it would be more difficult to draw inferences from this concentration on social interaction without the benefit of the additional conceptual insight that accompanies viewing buyer and seller as a true group. Sources of explanatory variables are drastically reduced. Despite these limitations

[3]Howard Becker and Ruth Hill Useem, "Sociological Analysis of the Dyad," *American Sociological Review,* Vol. 7, January, 1942, p. 13.
[4]Erving Goffman, *Encounters* (Indianapolis: The Bobbs-Merrill Company, Inc., 1961), pp. 9-14.

it was concluded that this approach offered the greatest possibility of generating defensible and useful findings.

THE PROCESS MECHANISMS

To define the exchange between buyer and seller in the transaction as interaction is, in and of itself, of only limited usefulness. Interaction takes place by definition when the parties to the transaction emit behavior in each other's presence.[5] But if behavior can take on various forms it can be argued that highly subtle forms of behavior might not be perceptible to even a careful observer. Interaction, nevertheless, serves, in communications parlance, as the carrier for the modulating effects of both parties' purposeful behaviors.

Of all the possible process orientations that could be adopted to guide investigation of buyer-seller interaction, the problem-solving or decision process perspective seemed the most cogent. There has been a virtual explosion of work dealing with problem-solving behavior, and meaningful inductive evidence has begun to stack up in support of this kind of explanatory model.[6] The problem-solving approach adopted implies that a continuous problem-solving role be exercised by the buyer. Extending this logic, customer and salesman might be expected to specialize in the performance of the phases of the problem-solving process. Further, the exclusion of one or more phases of the problem-solving process would seem to reduce the likelihood of a successful outcome to the transaction. Finally, the problem-solving approach supplies in its internal structure the guidelines for detecting its presence, given longitudinal measurements of customer-salesman interaction.

To implement a process approach required that some method be devised that would permit a systematic analysis of the content of customer-salesman interaction. Although the possibilities here are legion the more conservative strategy—using an extant classification system—was employed. Bales has developed and recorded substantial experience with a method for interaction analysis which he refers to as Interaction Process Analysis. As defined by Bales, the heart of the method is a way of classifying behavior in face-to-face groups on an act by act basis, permitting one to obtain indices that provide description of group process.[7] A simplified statement of categories employed by Bales appears in Figure 1.

It should be noted that the indicated categories are not only pragmatic definitional units. As Bales points out, therterms are related to a conception of an over-arching problem-solving sequence of interaction between two or more persons. He postulates six interlocking functional problems applicable to any concrete type of interaction system. These conform in part to the previously noted stages of

[5]John W. Thibaut and Harold H. Kelly, *The Social Psychology of Groups* (New York: John Wiley & Sons, Inc., 1959), p. 10.
[6]See, for example, Barry E. Collins and Harold Guetzkow, *A Social Psychology of Group Processes for Decision-Making* (New York: John Wiley & Sons, Inc., 1964).
[7]Robert F. Bales, "A Set of Categories for the Analysis of Small Group Interaction," *American Sociological Review,* Vol. 15, April, 1950, p. 258.

Figure 1   Definition of Social Interaction Categories

Social-Emotional
Area: Positive Reactions

1. Shows solidarity, raises other's status, gives help, reward[f]

2. Shows tension release, jokes, laughs, shows satisfaction[e]

3. Agrees, shows passive acceptance, understands, concurs, complies[d]

Task Area:
Attempted Answers

4. Gives suggestion, direction, implying autonomy for other[c]

5. Gives opinion, evaluation, analysis, expresses feeling, wish[b]

6. Gives orientation, information, repeats, clarifies, confirms[a]

Task Area:
Questions

7. Asks for orientation, information, repeats, clarifies, confirms[a]

8. Asks for opinion, evaluation, analysis, expression of feeling[b]

9. Asks for suggestion, direction, possible ways of action[c]

Social-Emotional
Area: Negative Reactions

10. Disagrees, shows passive rejection, formality, withholds help[d]

11. Shows tension, asks for help, withdraws out of field[e]

12. Shows antagonisms, deflates other's status defends or asserts self[f]

a. Problems of orientation
b. Problems of evaluation
c. Problems of control

d. Problems of decision
e. Problems of tension-management
f. Problems of integration

Source: Robert F. Bales, "A Set of Categories for the Analysis of Small Group Interaction," *American Sociological Review*, April, 1950, p. 258.

decision-making. Bales describes the early stages of interaction in terms of emphasis on problems of orientation, that is, describing or deciding what the situation is like. Problems of evaluation, involving decisions about what attitude should be taken toward the situation, occur next. As interaction continues, and behavior ideally moves closer and closer to some ultimate agreement or solution, problems of control become paramount. This phase of interaction takes the form of decisions about the solutions to the problem. During this entire process it is possible that members of the group can contribute positively or negatively toward the maintenance of group rapport.[8] Each of the Interaction Process categories, then, permits the classification of individual acts, but also maintains these acts in a system of coding that retains the underlying problem-solving context for the interaction. This analytical scheme was adopted and forms the basis for subsequent findings.

The Study

A multidimensional research approach—involving both direct observation of retail appliance customers and salesmen, and consumer survey—was required to carry out the study objectives. Because the methodology employed is complex, a brief review of the techniques used may be helpful in understanding and interpreting specific findings.

STUDY'S DESIGN AND SETTING

Research operations in the study started on the retail sales floor and ended with consumer survey work. First, selected appliance shoppers were identified as they entered retail appliance stores. Second, provision was made to observe and record the exchange between customer and salesman while the customer was on the floor. Prior to the time that the customer exited the store, he was given the opportunity to win a door prize. The customer's name, address and phone number were secured in this fashion.

The second phase of the data gathering involved two waves of follow-up interviews with the appliance customers identified in the stores. Within three days after the customer had been observed shopping, he was contacted to determine: a) Whether or not he had purchased a major appliance; b) His intentions to purchase an appliance; and c) The extent of deliberation and shopping associated with the purchase or potential purchase. All customers who had not purchased by the time of the first interview were reinterviewed in approximately two weeks. In this terminal interview, it was determined whether the customer had purchased since the first interview, and whether he had conducted additional shopping during that period.

Customers included in the study came from eleven appliance stores, located in seven midwestern metropolitan areas. Three types of appliance floors were included in the study. They were: a) Department store major appliance departments; b) The multi-line appliance store, that is, the appliance store that handled more than one major full line brand; and c) The brand specialist, or retailer that handled

[8]Robert F. Bales, "A Set of Categories for the Analysis of Small Group Interaction," *American Sociological Review*, Vol. 15, April, 1950, pp. 259-261.

the full line of only one major appliance manufacturer. A total of fourteen sales-men were included in the study, and study observations are based on a sample of each of these salesman's customers over a period of time.

RESPONDENT SELECTION

Fifteen of each salesman's customers, or a total of 210 appliance shoppers, were included in the study. Participating customers were selected systematically at store entry. As the customer was not aware of his participation in the study at this time, observations were obtained for every customer selected. To further avoid systematic bias, salesmen were given no latitude to select customers to be included. Consequently, every selected shopper, no matter how poor a prospect he appeared to be, was covered in the analysis. Specific exclusions in the selection process were made for service calls—where there was no potential for a sale—and for customers shopping for appliances tagged at less than $100. Both brown goods (electronics) and white goods (kitchen appliances) were included in the study in approximately equal proportions.

MEASUREMENT OF INTERACTION

The most critical part of the study involved the record of customer-salesman interaction. This was accomplished by equipping the salesman with a wireless microphone, a combination of microphone and miniature FM transmitter. This device was carried by the salesman in a convenient pocket. The transaction was picked up on a remote FM receiver and tape recorded for later analysis. This aural record of the transaction was supplemented by visual observations made by one member of the research team. From a distance this observer systematically timed and noted physical actions or gestures, facial expression, and other events that would not be identifiable from the taped record. These observations were later synchronized with the taped record, and this evidence of interaction was analyzed using Interaction Process Analysis.

Customer-Salesman Interaction

Appliance shoppers, no matter how disinterested they appeared to be in immediate purchase, by an overwhelming majority had definite intentions to purchase. Over 53 per cent of the 210 customer subjects indicated definite plans to purchase an appliance and could articulate that they intended to carry out that decision soon. An additional 35 per cent of all respondents indicated definite plans to purchase accompanied by some uncertainty as to the time of purchase. Further, the major-ity of these high intentions shoppers quickly implemented their intentions to pur-chase. A total of 132 or 63 per cent of all appliance shoppers completed their major appliance purchase either at the time they were observed on the retail floor or within two weeks of that time. These findings help validate the earlier assump-tion that the decision to purchase is generally concluded by the time serious shopping starts, and pinpoints a customer group, homogeneous in intentions, that can serve as a basis for accumulating interaction data. Accordingly, subsequent data on interaction are confined to the transactions associated with the 132 respondents who completed purchase.

SOME PARAMETERS OF APPLIANCE TRANSACTIONS

The average retail appliance transaction observed lasted approximately 23 minutes from the point of customer-salesman contact to the point where the interaction was either terminated or a sale had been consummated. As one might expect, the length of time of transactions differed markedly in individual cases, and ranged from approximately one minute to nearly two hours. A distribution of lengths of time for transactions appears in Table 1. Noteworthy is the 75 per cent

TABLE 1   TEMPORAL LENGTH OF RETAIL APPLIANCE CUSTOMER-SALESMAN TRANSACTIONS

Length of Time from Customer-Salesman Contact to Close or Termination of Transaction	Per Cent of Transactions
0-7.5 minutes	17.4
7.6-15.0 minutes	31.1
15.1-30.0 minutes	26.5
Over 30.0 minutes	25.0
All Transactions*	100.00

*N = 132

of all transactions that lasted less than 30 minutes. Potential for true dyad information can, of course, not be based merely on time alone; however, the findings would seem to support the proposition that true group formation in this kind of personal selling situation is highly tenuous, if not unlikely.

The 132 instances of customer-salesman interaction produced a total of over 26,000 interaction acts, with a mean number of acts per transaction of 198. Again, as in the case of the lengths of transactions, there was high dispersion, and in individual cases the total number of acts per transaction was as low as seven and as high as 920. While these data indicate enormous variability, a more stable pattern develops when the effect of length of transaction is netted out, and gross interaction is converted into interaction per minute. The distribution of interaction rates appears in Table 2. It is apparent that transactions show a much higher degree of consistency than would be suggested by either time spent in the transaction or the gross interaction alone. Over 50 per cent of all transactions generated rates of between six and eleven acts per minute, and the mean interaction rate for all transactions was approximately ten acts per minute. Bales has ordinarily

TABLE 2   RATE OF CUSTOMER-SALESMAN INTERACTION DURING
RETAIL APPLIANCE TRANSACTIONS

Interaction Acts per Minute	Per Cent of Transactions
0-6.0/ minute	12.1
6.1-11.0/ minute	50.8
11.1-16.0/ minute	30.3
Over 16.0/ minute	6.8
All Transactions*	100.0

*N = 132

recorded interaction rates of from 15 to 20 acts per minute in problem-solving
groups, although he is dealing with substantially different groups.[9]

CONTENT OF CUSTOMER-SALESMAN INTERACTION

Table 3 presents the pattern of customer-salesman interaction, showing the mean

TABLE 3   COMPOSITION OF RETAIL APPLIANCE CUSTOMER-SALESMAN
SOCIAL INTERACTION

Interaction Process Categories		Mean Number of Acts per Transaction	Per Cent Distribution
Social-Emotional Area: Positive Reactions	1. Shows Solidarity	.08	.04
	2. Shows Tension Release	5.64	2.84
	3. Agrees	7.60	3.83
Task Area: Attempted Answers	4. Gives Suggestion	4.07	2.05
	5. Gives Opinion	74.56	37.61
	6. Gives Orientation	76.74	38.71
Task Area: Questions	7. Asks for Orientation	22.84	11.52
	8. Asks for Opinion	6.15	3.10
	9. Asks for Suggestion	.24	.12
Social-Emotional Area: Negative Reactions	10. Disagrees	.31	.16
	11. Shows Tension	.01	.01
	12. Shows Antagonism	.02	.01
All Transactions*		198.26	100.00

*The distributions encompass 26,170 "acts" in 132 customer-salesman encounters.

[9] Robert F. Bales, "Task Roles and Social Roles in Problem-Solving Groups," in Eleanor E.
Maccoby, Theodore M. Newcomb, and Eugene L. Hartley, eds., Readings in Social Psychology
(New York: Holt, Rinehart and Winston, Inc., 1958), p. 438.

number of acts per transaction and per cent distribution of acts across each of the interaction categories. Category 6, gives orientation, was the most frequent type of exchange recorded, representing on the average over 38 per cent of total interaction acts. Following closely in terms of volume of acts is Category 5, gives opinion, and together these two categories of acts account for, on the average, over 75 per cent of the total interaction between customer and salesman. These categories of interaction denote attempted answers, specifically, attempts to define problems or issues and to evaluate problems or issues. Thus, three-quarters of total customer-salesman interaction was concentrated on efforts to simply lay the groundwork for effective communication.

Low volumes of acts in the functional problem area of control and decision should not be construed as indicating a lack of importance, for despite low frequency of occurrence, these acts become instrumental in predicting the outcome of the transaction.

Some preliminary evaluation of the problem-solving hypothesis is possible at this point by comparing the pattern of customer-salesman interaction with the pattern of interaction that Bales has recorded for groups facing a standard task.[10] Despite the differences in setting, amount of control over the situation, and kind of task facing the participants, it might be argued that if the sales situation does represent problem-solving, the common thread of a decision process running through even such diverse situations would generate at least roughly comparable kinds of behavior. In fact, the parallel between findings recorded by Bales and the present study is encouraging. There are, of course, differences in the percentage concentrations in specific categories, but the structural patterns of interaction are congruent. Customer-salesman interaction was characterized by lower proportions of categories 3 and 10 (involving problems of decision), lower proportions of categories 4 and 9 (involving problems of control), and a higher proportion of requests for information than has generally been recorded by Bales.

Customer and Salesman Interaction Roles

The overall pattern of interaction, while useful, fails to provide any insight about the roles played by customer and salesman. Consequently, a further stage of analysis was initiated to trace the origin of interaction, and the source of control of interaction. The origin of interaction is a measurable property of customer-salesman behavior, and was evaluated by separately analyzing the customer and salesman interaction acts. Questions of control, however, constitute a separate problem, in that here an attempt is being made to infer the source of power over the course of interaction. This latter question was tested through the use of analysis of variance. Essentially, the total variation of each interaction category across the customers of each salesman was compared with the variation among salesmen's cus-

[10]*Loc. cit.*

tomer groups. If a particular variable was consistent for all transactions of a given salesman, but varied greatly among salesmen, the inference would be that this variable was subject to control by the salesman. On the other hand, if a given variable fluctuated widely for each salesman's cutomers, but there were few differences in the behavior of that variable averaged and compared across salesmen, the variable would appear to be controlled by the customer. Note that this analysis does not imply that either party consciously exercises his power in controlling the course of interaction.

CUSTOMER-SALESMAN INTERACTION SEGMENTATION

Comparisons of the interaction contributions of customer and salesman appear in Table 4. Data reflect the ratios of customer to salesman acts in each transaction

TABLE 4   RELATIVE CONTRIBUTIONS OF CUSTOMER AND SALESMAN TO INTERACTION IN THE TRANSACTION

Interaction Process Categories	Mean of Ratios of Customer to Salesman Acts (Number of Ratios Equals 132 for Each Category Set)
Total Interaction Acts	.56
Task Area:	
Attempted Answers (Categories 4 to 6)	.36
Questions (Categories 7 to 9)	3.86
Social-Emotional Area:	
Positive Reactions (Categories 1 to 3)	1.41
Negative Reactions (Categories 10 to 12)	.12

averaged across all transactions. In general, the customer performed half as many interaction acts as the salesman. However, there is wide variation in the customer to salesman ratios across the interaction categories. As the table indicates, attempted answers were primarily the prerogative of the salesman, while in the question categories customer acts outnumbered salesman acts nearly four to one. One jarring finding concerned customers' and salesmen's contributions to the social-emotional area. Customers were more frequently responsible for positive reactions (embracing categories 1 to 3), while salesmen were almost uniquely responsible for disagreement, tension, and antagonism in the transaction.

SOURCES OF CONTROL OF INTERACTION

A second test, to determine the inferred source of control over interaction, was applied to two dimensions of total interaction—the relative contributions of each interaction category and the ratio of customer to salesman participation by interaction category. The analysis of relative contributions of each interaction category to total interaction appears in Table 5. Without exception, salesmen acting

TABLE 5   ANALYSIS OF VARIANCE OF CUSTOMER-SALESMAN INTERACTION ACROSS SALESMEN

Variable: Per Cent Contribution of Interaction Process Category to Total Interaction	F Ratio	Inferred Source of Control of Relative Occurrence of Interaction Category
Categories 1 to 3: Shows Solidarity; Shows Tension Release; and Agrees	3.62*	Salesman
Category 4: Gives Suggestion	3.43*	Salesman
Category 5: Gives Opinion	7.38*	Salesman
Category 6: Gives Orientation	3.26*	Salesman
Category 7: Asks for Orientation	4.29*	Salesman
Category 8: Asks for Opinion	3.67*	Salesman
Category 9: Asks for Suggestion	3.29*	Salesman
Categories 10 to 12: Disagrees; Shows Tension; and Shows Antagonism	3.05**	Salesman

*Significant at .01
**Significant at .05

in concert with their selling environment appear to control customer-salesman interaction. Whether he is aware of it or not, by virtue of his patterning of interaction and his response to customer interaction, the salesman does exercise the power to shape the content of interaction.

If it would appear that the influence of salesmen is almost complete, the analysis appearing in Table 6 will help to build a more balanced perspective. This table

TABLE 6   ANALYSIS OF VARIANCE OF RELATIVE CUSTOMER TO SALES-MAN INTERACTION CONTRIBUTIONS ACROSS SALESMEN

Variable: Ratio of Customer to Salesman Contributions of Interaction Process Categories	F Ratio	Inferred Source of Control of Ratio of Customer to Sales-man Interaction
Total Interaction Acts	3.81*	Salesman
Task Area:		
Attempted Answers (Categories 4 to 6)	1.56	Customer
Questions (Categories 7 to 9)	2.29**	Salesman
Social-Emotional Area:		
Positive Reactions (Categories 1 to 3)	1.70	Customer
Negative Reactions (Categories 10 to 12)	1.01	Customer

*Significant at .01
**Just Significant at .05

contains the products of a comparable analysis applied to the relative contributions of customer and salesman to the transaction by Interaction Process category. The salesman is truly in control of total interaction, as evidenced by the significant F Ratio in the case of customer to salesman total interaction. However, when inter-action is examined by category it is revealed that the customer is influential in determining the parties' relative contributions in the case of attempted answers, positive social-emotional reactions, and negative social-emotional reactions. Con-versely, the salesman appears to hold the key to the relative contributions made by both parties to the question categories.

Additional insight is provided if one compares the findings in Tables 4 and 6. It will be recalled that Table 4 shows the relative contributions of interaction by customer and salesman, while Table 6 supplies inferences as to the source of influ-ence. The salesman is the major contributor to interaction and also the source of influence in affecting total interaction. In contrast, attempted answers, represent-ing possible problem-solving attempts, are contributed most heavily by the sales-man, but as evidenced by Table 6, can be inferred to be controlled by the custom-er. Conversely, the question categories are contributed heavily by the customer, yet appear to be influenced predominantly by the salesman. While this evidence is hardly conclusive it is exciting. In this pattern of reciprocal question and answer control there is a suggestion of a true problem-solving process in operation.

Interaction Determinants of Successful Transactions

Thus far, the data presented have served to clarify the structure of customer-salesman interaction in the appliance transaction and portray the roles played by customer and salesman in contributing and influencing interaction. Some indication of the hypothesized problem-solving orientation has appeared, but this evidence is, of course, merely suggestive. Additionally, there is no indication from the foregoing data that the interaction is in any definitive way related to some success criterion. Consequently, a more discrete test was conducted, relating interaction to transactional outcomes. The basis for such a test exists in the potential discrepancies between interaction in transactions where purchase occurred at the time customer and salesman were observed, as opposed to transactions where purchase occurred at a later time and not necessarily in the same store. Out of the 132 customers who had purchased within two weeks of the time observed, 58 of these transactions were closed at the time the shopper was observed on the floor.

INTERACTION COMPONENT PREDICTORS

Mean interaction acts per transaction for transactions producing spontaneous purchase and transactions not closed were virtually identical. However, significant differences appeared in the structure of interaction. Table 7 presents the ratios of the mean per cents of acts by category for transactions closed at the time observed to the mean per cents of acts for transactions that were not closed. Significant differences occurred in two categories, category 4 (attempted answers in the form of suggestions) and category 8 (requests for opinions). More importantly, the categories that registered significant differences are the evaluation and control categories.

Another significant indicator of the successful transaction, not contained explicitly in Table 7, was the relationship between customer and salesman contributions of task-question acts; successful transactions were likely to involve a significantly higher proportion of instances where the ratios of customer to salesman task-question acts were low. Interpreting this, the lower the ratio the greater the contribution of the salesman to the task-question categories. Task-question categories are customer contributed; consequently, a small ratio means that the salesman has participated more heavily in asking for information, asking for opinions, and asking for suggestions. Overall, then, interaction in that group of transactions associated with spontaneous purchase was marked by significantly higher rates of offerings of attempted solutions, accompanied by significantly greater amounts of search for evaluation (attempts to determine what attitude should be taken toward the situations represented in the transaction).

TABLE 7   DIFFERENCES IN THE COMPOSITION OF CUSTOMER-SALES-
MAN INTERACTION ASSOCIATED WITH CUSTOMERS PUR-
CHASING AT TIME OBSERVED VERSUS CUSTOMERS PUR-
CHASING LATER

Interaction Process Category	Ratio, Mean Per Cent of Acts for Transactions Closed at Time Observed to Mean Per Cent of Acts for Transactions Not Closed
Categories 1 to 3: Shows Solidarity; Shows Tension Release; and Agrees	.96
Category 4: Gives Suggestion	1.97*
Category 5: Gives Opinion	.98
Category 6: Gives Orientation	.99
Category 7: Asks for Orientation	.96
Category 8: Asks for Opinion	1.28**
Category 9: Asks for Suggestion	1.33
Categories 10 to 12: Disagrees; Shows Tension; and Shows Antagonism	.80

*Differences significant at .02
**Differences significant at .09

The Time Path to Purchase

Significant differences in interaction between the spontaneous purchase group and the group representing transactions that were not closed, while consistent and seemingly meaningful, were not great in number. There is, of course, a chance—given that problem-solving does constitute a meaningful explanation for transactional behavior—that differences between the two groups could have been cancelled out over the time path of the transaction. A final stage of analysis—involving an examination of the longitudinal change in components of interaction during the transaction—served a dual purpose, supplying clarification of the differences between the two purchase groups and also providing a more definitive test of the problem-solving hypothesis. Analyses of change during the transaction were conducted in the following fashion. Interaction associated with each transaction was first divided into thirds on the basis of total number of interaction acts. The composition of interaction by category was then reconstructed.

LONGITUDINAL CHANGE IN INTERACTION COMPONENTS

Table 8 presents the pattern of longitudinal change in the components of cus-

TABLE 8   PATTERN OF LONGITUDINAL CHANGE IN THE COMPONENTS OF CUSTOMER-SALESMAN INTERACTION DURING THE TRANSACTION

Interaction Process Category	Index of Change First Third Acts = 100		
	First Third	Second Third	Last Third
Transactions Closed at Time Observed:			
Categories 1 to 3: Shows Solidarity; Shows Tension; Agrees	100	127	165
Category 4: Gives Suggestion	100	156	346
Category 5: Gives Opinion	100	107	118
Category 6: Gives Orientation	100	89	74
Category 7: Asks for Orientation	100	100	85
Category 8: Asks for Opinion	100	107	124
Category 9: Asks for Suggestion	100	137	262
Categories 10 to 12: Disagrees; Shows Tension; Shows Antagonism	100	72	45
Transactions Not Closed:			
Categories 1 to 3: Shows Solidarity; Shows Tension; Agrees	100	116	165
Category 4: Gives Suggestion	100	142	262
Category 5: Gives Opinion	100	117	113
Category 6: Gives Orientation	100	85	91
Category 7: Asks for Orientation	100	99	68
Category 8: Asks for Opinion	100	119	68
Category 9: Asks for Suggestion	100	137	62
Categories 10 to 12: Disagrees; Shows Tension; Shows Antagonism	100	225	575

tomer-salesman interaction during the transaction. Using the proportion of inter-action acts in each category during the first third of the transaction as a base, the index values for the second third and last third of the transaction were calculated. Viewing Table 8 and the index values for transactions that were closed at the time they were observed, a pattern of movement toward purchase appears to emerge. Problems of orientation (problem definition) decline as the transaction moves toward a conclusion. The evaluative and control areas experienced rather sharp increases in acts. Finally, there was a noticeable increase in positive social-emotional content as the transaction moved toward a conclusion, accompanied by a parallel decline in the amounts of negative social-emotional interaction.

In contrast, in transactions that were not closed somewhat different patterns of change emerged. Categories 8 and 9, representing search for solutions decline sharply in the last third of the transaction, despite the fact that attempted solutions increase through the last third of the transaction, although not as much as in transactions that resulted in spontaneous purchase. Transactions that were not closed also experienced substantial increases in the amount of disagreement, tension and antagonism, although interestingly, this is accompanied by a seemingly paradoxical increase in positive social-emotional acts. This latter finding may be explained in part by customers' efforts to detach themselves from the transaction, in effect, to "cool-out" the salesman but to do so amicably. Another interesting feature of transactions that were not closed was an indication of regression in problem-solving attempts beginning in the second third of the transaction. Attempts to supply evaluation as manifested by category 5 decline from the second third to the last third of the transaction, while attempts to supply orientation, as evidenced by category 6, actually show a modest increase.

Conclusions

Taken together, results from this study seem uniformly consonant with a problem-solving conceptualization of selling behavior in major appliance transactions. Longitudinal changes in interaction during successful transactions show discernible parallels with descriptions by Bales of interaction in groups created specifically for purposes of generating problem-solving behavior. Indeed, one abstract by Bales of the act sequencing observed in his groups could have been applied almost without modification to the pattern of change in interaction in successful customer-salesman transactions.[11]

On a more cautious note, it is highly unlikely that problem-solving as a process constitutes a sufficient explanation for successful outcomes in these transactions. Full study findings demonstrated to be significant indicators of purchase included, in addition to interaction, specific customer shopping behaviors and elements of a

[11] Robert F. Bales, "How People Interact in Conferences," *Scientific American, CXCII,* March, 1955, pp. 31-35.

formal bargaining process. It would also be presumptuous to rule out the possibility that more durable psychological traits of customer and salesman are affective, operating through the mediating processes of social interaction and communication.

DECISION-MAKING
BY CONSUMERS

30. Believability

"The Influence of Source Credibility on Communication Effectiveness," Carl I. Hovland (Psychologist) and Walter Weiss, (Psychologist) *Public Opinion Quarterly,* Vol. 15 (Winter, 1951-1952, pp. 635-650.

31. Making Consumer Decisions

"The Measurement of Information Value: A Study in Consumer Decision-Making," Donald F. Cox (Marketing Educator) in William S. Decker, Editor, *Emerging Concepts in Marketing* (Chicago: American Marketing Association, 1963), pp. 413-421.

32. Evaluating and Predicting Consumer Decisions

"Simulation, Scaling and Predicting Brand Purchasing Behavior," Edgar A. Pessemier (Marketing Educator) and Richard D. Teach (Marketing Educator) in Robert L. King, Editor, *Marketing and the New Science of Planning* (Chicago: American Marketing Association, 1968), pp. 206-212.

This final section is concerned with actual *decision-making* by consumers. Three empirical reports are included on believability, on decision-making by consumers, and on predicting and evaluating decisions by consumers.

30 Believability

The Influence of Source Credibility
on Communication Effectiveness*

CARL I. HOVLAND *(Psychologist)* AND WALTER WEISS† *(Psychologist)*

In a new test of the process of forgetting, the authors found that subjects, at the time of exposure, discounted material from "untrustworthy" sources.

In time, however, the subjects tended to disassociate the content and the source—with the result that the original skepticism faded and the "untrustworthy" material was accepted. Lies, in fact, seemed to be remembered better than truths.

An important but little-studied factor in the effectiveness of communication is the attitude of the audience toward the communicator. Indirect data on this problem come from studies of "prestige" in which subjects are asked to indicate their agreement or disagreement with statements which are attributed to different individuals.[1] The extent of agreement is usually higher when the statements are attrib-

Source: Carl I. Hovland and Walter Weiss, "The Influence of Source Credibility on Communication Effectiveness," *Public Opinion Quarterly,* Vol. 15 (Winter, 1954-1955), pp. 635-650.

†Carl I. Hovland is professor of psychology at Yale University. Walter Weiss is at the same school.

*This study was done as part of a coordinated research project on factors influencing changes in attitude and opinion being conducted at Yale University under a grant from the Rockefeller Foundation. (See Hovland, C. I., "Changes in Attitude Through Communication," *Journal of Abnormal and Social Psychology,* Vol. 46 (1951), pp. 424-437.) The writers wish to thank Prof. Ralph E. Turner for making his class available for the study.

[1]See e.g. Sherif, M., "An Experimental Study of Stereotypes," *Journal of Abnormal and Social Psychology,* Vol. 29 (1935), pp. 371-375; Lewis, H. B., "Studies in the Principles of Judgments and Attitudes": IV. The Operation of "Prestige Suggestion." *Journal of Social Psychology,* Vol. 14 (1941), pp. 229-256; Asch, S. E., "The Doctrine of Suggestion, Prestige, and Imitation in Social Psychology." *Psychological Review,* Vol. 55 (1948), pp. 250-276.

uted to "high prestige" sources. There are few studies in which an identical communication is presented by different communicators and the relative effects on opinion subsequently measured without explicit reference to the position taken by the communicator. Yet the latter research setting may be a closer approximation of the real-life situation to which the results of research are to be applied.

In one of the studies reported by Hovland, Lumsdaine and Sheffield, the effects of a communication were studied without reference to the source of the items comprising the opinion questionnaire. They found that opinion changes following the showing of an Army orientation film were smaller among the members of the audience who believed the purpose of the film was "propagandistic" than among those who believed its purpose "informational."[2] But such a study does not rule out the possibility that the results could be explained by general predispositional factors; that is, individuals who are "suspicious" of mass-media sources may be generally less responsive to such communications. The present study was designed to minimize the aforementioned methodological difficulties by experimentally controlling the source and by checking the effects of the source in a situation in which the subject's own opinion was obtained without reference to the source.

A second objective of the present study was to investigate the extent to which opinions derived from high and low credibility sources are maintained over a period of time. Hovland, Lumsdaine and Sheffield showed that some opinion changes in the direction of the communicator's position are larger after a lapse of time than immediately after the communication. This they refer to as the "sleeper effect." One hypothesis which they advanced for their results is that individuals may be suspicious of the motives of the communicator and initially discount his position, and thus may evidence little or no immediate change in opinion. With the passage of time, however, they may remember and accept *what* was communicated but not remember *who* communicated it. As a result, they may then be more inclined to agree with the position which had been presented by the communicator. In the study referred to, only a single source was used, so no test was available of the differential effects when the source was suspected of having a propagandistic motive and when it was not. The present experiment was designed to test differences in the retention, as well as the acquisition, of identical communications when presented by "trustworthy" and by "untrustworthy" sources.

Procedure

The overall design of the study was to present an identical communication to two groups, one in which a communicator of a generally "trustworthy" character was

[2]Hovland, C. I., A. A. Lumsdaine and F. D. Sheffield, *Experiments on Mass Communication.* Princeton: Princeton University Press, 1949, pp. 101f.

used, and the other in which the communicator was generally regarded as "untrustworthy." Opinion questionnaires were administered before the communication.

Because of the possibility of specific factors affecting the relationship between communicator and content on a single topic, four different topics (with eight different communicators) were used. On each topic two alternative versions were prepared, one presenting the "affirmative" and one the "negative" position on the issue. For each version one "trustworthy" and one "untrustworthy" source was used. The topics chosen were of current interest and of a controversial type so that a fairly even division of opinion among members of the audience was obtained.

The four topics and the communicators chosen to represent "high credibility" and "low credibility" sources were as follows:

	"High Credibility" Source	"Low Credibility" Source
A. *Anti-Histamine Drugs:* Should the anti-histamine drugs continue to be sold without a doctor's prescription?	*New England Journal of Biology and Medicine*	Magazine A* [A mass circulation monthly pictorial magazine]
B. *Atomic Submarines:* Can a practicable atomic-powered submarine be built at the present time?	Robert J. Oppenheimer	*Pravda*
C. *The Steel Shortage:* Is the steel industry to blame for the current shortage of steel?	*Bulletin of National Resources Planning Board*	Writer A* [A widely syndicated anti-labor, anti-New Deal, "rightist" newspaper columnist]
D. *The Future of Movie Theaters:* As a result of TV, will there be a decrease in the number of movie theaters in operation by 1955?	*Fortune* magazine	Writer B* [An extensively syndicated woman movie-gossip columnist]

In some cases the sources were individual writers and in others periodical publications, and some were fictitious (but plausible) and others actual authors or publications.

*The names of one of the magazines and two of the writers used in the study have to be withheld to avoid any possible embarrassment to them. These sources will be referred to hereafter only by the letter designations given.

The "affirmative" and "negative" versions of each article presented an equal number of facts on the topic and made use of essentially the same material. They differed in the emphasis given the material and in the conclusion drawn from the facts. Since there were two versions for each topic and these were prepared in such a way that either of the sources might have written either version, four possible combinations of content and source were available on each topic.

The communication consisted of a booklet containing one article on each of the four different topics, with the name of the author or periodical given at the end of each article. The order of the topics within the booklets was kept constant. Two trustworthy and two untrustworthy sources were included in each booklet. Twenty-four different booklets covered the various combinations used. An example of one such booklet-combination would be:

Topic	Version	Source
The Future of Movie Theaters	Affirmative	Fortune
Atomic Submarines	Negative	Pravda
The Steel Shortage	Affirmative	Writer A
Anti-Histamine Drugs	Negative	New England Journal of Biology and Medicine

The questionnaires were designed to obtain data on the amount of factual information acquired from the commmunication and the extent to which opinion was changed in the direction of the position advocated by the communicator. Information was also obtained on the subject's evaluation of the general trustworthiness of each source, and, in the after-questionnaires, on the recall of the author of each article.

The subjects were college students in an advanced undergraduate course in history at Yale University. The first questionnaire, given five days before the communication, was represented to the students as a general opinion survey being conducted by a "National Opinion Survey Council." The key opinion questions bearing on the topics selected for the communication were scattered through many other unrelated ones. There were also questions asking for the subjects' evaluations of the general trustworthiness of a long list of sources, which included the critical ones used in the communications. This evaluation was based on a 5-point scale ranging from "very trustworthy" to "very untrustworthy."

Since it was desired that the subjects not associate the experiment with the "before" questionnaire, the following arrangement was devised: The senior experimenter was invited to give a guest lecture to the class during the absence of the regular instructor, five days after the initial questionnaire. His remarks constituted the instructions for the experiment:

Several weeks ago Professor [the regular instructor] asked me to meet with you this morning to discuss some phase of Contemporary Problems. He suggested that one interesting topic would be The Psychology of Communications. This is certainly an important problem, since so many of our attitudes and opinions are based not on direct experience but on what we hear over the radio or read in the newspaper. I finally agreed to take this topic but on the condition that I have some interesting live data on which to base my comments. We therefore agreed to use this period to make a survey of the role of newspaper and magazine reading as a vehicle of communication and then to report on the results and discuss their implications at a later session.

Today, therefore, I am asking you to read a number of excerpts from recent magazine and newspaper articles on controversial topics. The authors have attempted to summarize the best information available, duly taking into account the various sides of the issues. I have chosen up-to-date issues which are currently being widely discussed and ones which are being studied by Gallup, Roper and others interested in public opinion.

Will you please read each article carefully the way you would if you were reading it in your favorite newspaper or magazine. When you finish each article write your name in the lower right hand corner to indicate that you have read it through and then go on to the next. When you finish there will be a short quiz on your reaction to the readings.

Any questions before we begin?

The second questionnaire, handed out immediately after the booklets were collected, differed completely in format from the earlier one. It contained a series of general questions on the subjects' reactions to the articles, gradually moving toward opinion questions bearing on the content discussed in the articles. At the end of the questionnaire there was a series of fact-quiz items. Sixteen multiple choice questions, four on each content area, were used together with a question calling for the recall of the author of each of the articles.

An identical questionnaire was administered four weeks after the communication. At no prior time had the subjects been forewarned that they would be given this second post-test questionnaire.

A total of 223 subjects provided information which was used in some phase of the analysis. Attendance in the history course was not mandatory and there was considerable shrinkage in the number of students present at all three time periods. For the portions of the analysis requiring before-and-after information, the data derived from 61 students who were present on all three occasions were used. Thus, for the main analysis a sample of 244 communications (four for each student) was available. Since different analyses permitted the use of differing numbers of cases, the exact number of instances used in each phase of the analysis is given in each table.

Results

Before proceeding to the main analyses it is important to state the extent to which the sources selected on *a priori* grounds by the experimenters as being of differing credibility were actually reacted to in this manner by the subjects. One item on the questionnaire given before the communication asked the subjects to rate the trustworthiness of each of a series of authors and publications. Figure 1 gives the percentages of subjects who rated each of the sources "trustworthy."

Figure 1   Credibility of Sources

Topic	Source	N	Per Cent Rating Source as Trustworthy
Anti-Histamines	*New Engl. J. Biol. & Med.*	208	94.7%
	Magazine A	222	← 5.9%
Atomic Submarines	Oppenheimer	221	93.7%
	Pravda	223	← 1.3%
Steel Shortage	*Bull. Nat. Res. Plan. Bd.*	220	80.9%
	Writer A	223	17.0%
Future of Movies	*Fortune*	222	89.2%
	Writer B	222	21.2%

The first source named under each topic had been picked by the experimenters as being of high credibility and the second of low. It will be observed that there is a clear differentiation of the credibility in the direction of the initial selection by the experimenters. The differences between members of each pair are all highly significant (*t*'s range from 13 to 20). The results in Figure 1 are based on all the subjects present when the preliminary questionnaire was administered. The percentages for the smaller sample of subjects present at all three sessions do not differ significantly from those for the group as a whole.

Differences in perception of communication of various audience sub-groups. Following the communication, subjects were asked their opinion about the fairness of the presenation of each topic and the extent to which each communicator was justified in his conclusion. Although the communications being judged were *identical*, there was a marked difference in the way the subjects responded to the "high credibility" and "low credibility" sources. Their evaluations were also affected by their personal opinions on the topic before the communication was ever presented. Audience evaluations of the four communications are presented in Table 1. In 14 of the 16 possible comparisons the "low-credibility" sources are considered

TABLE 1   EVALUATION OF "FAIRNESS" AND "JUSTIFIABILITY" OF IDENTICAL COMMUNICATIONS WHEN PRESENTED BY "HIGH CREDIBILITY" AND "LOW CREDIBILITY" SOURCES AMONG INDIVIDUALS WHO INITIALLY AGREED AND INDIVIDUALS WHO INITIALLY DISAGREED WITH POSITION ADVOCATED BY BY COMMUNICATOR

A. PER CENT CONSIDERING AUTHOR "FAIR" IN HIS PRESENTATION*

Topic	High Credibility Source		Low Credibility Source	
	Initially Agree	Initially Disagree (or Don't Know)	Initially Agree	Initially Disagree (or (Don't Know)
Anti-Histamines	76.5%	50.0%	64.3%	62.5%
Atomic Submarines	100.0	93.7	75.0	66.7
Steel Shortage	44.4	15.4	12.5	22.2
Future of Movies	90.9	90.0	77.8	52.4
Mean	78.3%	57.9%	60.5%	51.9%
N=	46	76	43	79

B. PER CENT CONSIDERING AUTHOR'S CONCLUSION "JUSTIFIED" BY THE FACTS**

Topic	High Credibility Source		Low Credibility Source	
	Initially Agree	Initially Disagree (or Don't Know)	Initially Agree	Initially Disagree (or Don't Know)
Anti-Histamines	82.4%	57.1%	57.1%	50.0%
Atomic Submarines	77.8	81.2	50.0	41.2
Steel Shortage	55.6	23.1	37.5	22.2
Future of Movies	63.6	55.0	55.6	33.3
Mean	71.7%	50.0%	51.2%	36.7%
N=	46	76	43	79

*Question: Do you think that the author of each article was fair in his presentation of the facts on both sides of the question or did he write a one-sided report?
**Question: Do you think that the opinion expressed by the author in his conclusion *was* justified by the facts he presented or do you think his opinion *was not* justified by the facts?

less fair or less justified than the corresponding high credibility sources. The differences for the low credibility sources for the individuals initially holding an opinion different from that advocated by the communicator and those for the high credibility sources for individuals who initially held the same position as that advocated by the communicator are significant at less than the .004 level.[3]

Effect of Credibility of Source on Acquisition of Information and on Change in Opinion

Information. There is no significant difference in the amount of factual information acquired by the subjects when the material is attributed to a high credibility source as compared to the amount learned when the same material is attributed to a low credibility source. Table 2 shows the mean number of items correct

TABLE 2   MEAN NUMBER OF ITEMS CORRECT ON FOUR-ITEM INFORMATION QUIZZES ON EACH OF FOUR TOPICS WHEN PRESENTED BY "HIGH CREDIBILITY" AND "LOW CREDIBILITY" SOURCES' (TEST IMMEDIATELY AFTER COMMUNICATION)

Topic	Mean Number of Items Correct			
	High Credibility Source		Low Credibility Source	
Anti-Histamines	(N=31)	3.42	(N=30)	3.17
Atomic Submarines	(N=25)	3.48	(N=36)	3.72
Steel Shortage	(N=35)	3.34	(N=26)	2.73
Future of Movies	(N=31)	3.23	(N=30)	3.27
Average	(N=122)	3.36	(N=122)	3.26
Per cent of items correct		84.0		81.5
Pdiff. M.			.35	

on the information quiz when material is presented by "high credibility" and "low credibility" sources.

Opinion. Significant differences were obtained in the extent to which opinion on an issue was changed by the attribution of the material to different sources. These results are presented in Table 3. Subjects changed their opinion in the direction advocated by the communicator in a significantly greater number of cases when the material was attributed to a "high credibility" source than when attributed to a "low credibility" source. The difference is significant at less than the .01 level.

[3]The probability values given in the table, while adequately significant, are calculated conservatively. The two-tailed test of significance is used throughout, even though in the case of some of the tables it could be contended that the direction of the differences is in line with theoretical predictions, and hence might justify the use of the one-tail test. When analysis is made of *changes,* the significance test takes into account the internal correlation (Hovland, Sheffield and Lumsdaine, *op. cit.,* pp. 318ff.), but the analyses of cases of post-communication agreement and disagreement are calculated on the conservative assumption of independence of the separate communications.

TABLE 3 NET CHANGES OF OPINION IN DIRECTION OF COMMUNICA-
TION FOR SOURCES CLASSIFIED BY EXPERIMENTERS AS
"HIGH CREDIBILITY" OR "LOW CREDIBILITY" SOURCES*

| Topic | Net Percentage of Cases in Which Subjects Changed Opinion in Direction of Communication | | | |
	High Credibility Sources		Low Credibility Sources	
Anti-Histamines	(N=31)	22.6%	(N=30)	13.3%
Atomic Submarines	(N=25)	36.0	(N=36)	0.0
Steel Shortage	(N=35)	22.9	(N=26)	−3.8
Future of Movies	(N=31)	12.9	(N=30)	16.7
Average	(N=122)	23.0%	(N=122)	6.6%
Diff.		16.4%		
$p_{diff.}$		<.01		

*Net changes = positive changes *minus* negative changes.

From Figure 1 it will be recalled that less than 100 per cent of the subjects were in agreement with the group consensus concerning the trustworthiness of each source. The results presented in Table 3 were reanalyzed using the individual subject's own evaluation of the source as the independent variable. The effects on opinion were studied for those instances where the source was rated as "very trustworthy" or "moderately trustworthy" and for those where it was rated as "untrustworthy" or "inconsistently trustworthy." Results from this analysis are given in Table 4. The results, using the subject's own evaluation of the trustworthi-

TABLE 4 NET CHANGES OF OPINION IN DIRECTION OF COMMUNICA-
TION FOR SOURCES JUDGED "TRUSTWORTHY" OR "UN-
TRUSTWORTHY" BY INDIVIDUAL SUBJECTS

| Topic | Net Percentage of Cases in Which Subjects Changed Opinion in Direction of Communication | | | |
	"Trustworthy" Sources		"Untrustworthy" Sources	
Anti-Histamines	(N=31)	25.5%	(N=27)	11.1%
Atomic Submarines	(N=25)	36.0	(N=36)	0.0
Steel Shortage	(N=33)	18.2	(N=27)	7.4
Future of Movies	(N=31)	12.9	(N=29)	17.2
Average	(N=120)	22.5%	(N=119)	8.4%
Diff.		14.1%		
$p_{diff.}$		<.03		

382   Decision-Making by Consumers

ness of the source, are substantially the same as those obtained when analyzed in terms of the experimenters' *a priori* classification (presented in Table 3). Only minor shifts were obtained. It appears that while the variable is made somewhat "purer" with this analysis this advantage is offset by possible increased variability attributable to unreliability in making individual judgments of the trustworthiness of the source.

Retention of Information and Opinion in Relation to Source

Information. As was the case with the immediate post-communication results (Table 2), there is no difference between the retention of factual information after four weeks when presented by high credibility sources and low credibility sources. Results in Table 5 show the mean retention scores for each of the four topics four weeks after the communication.

TABLE 5   MEAN NUMBER OF ITEMS CORRECT ON FOUR-ITEM INFOR-
MATION QUIZZES ON EACH OF FOUR TOPICS WHEN PRE-
SENTED BY "HIGH CREDIBILITY" AND "LOW CREDIBILITY"
SOURCES (RECALL FOUR WEEKS AFTER COMMUNICATION)

	Mean Number of Items Correct			
Topic	High Credibility Source		Low Credibility Source	
Anti-Histamines	(N=31)	2.32	(N=30)	2.90
Atomic Submarines	(N=25)	3.08	(N=36)	3.06
Steel Shortage	(N=35)	2.51	(N=26)	2.27
Future of Movies	(N=31)	2.52	(N=30)	2.33
Average	(N=122)	2.58	(N=122)	2.67
Per cent of items correct		64.5		66.7
$p_{diff.}$			.46	

Opinion. Extremely interesting results were obtained for the retention of opinion changes. Table 6 shows the changes in opinion from immediately after the communication to those obtained after the four-week interval. It will be seen that compared with the changes immediately after the communication, there is a *decrease* in the extent of agreement with the high credibility source, but an *increase* in the case of the low credibility source. This result, then, is similar to the "sleeper effect" found by Hovland, Lumsdaine and Sheffield.[4] The results derived from Tables 3 and 6 are compared in Figure 2, which shows the changes in opinion from before the communication to immediately afterwards and from before to four weeks afterwards.

[4] *Op. cit.*

TABLE 6   NET CHANGES OF OPINION FROM IMMEDIATELY AFTER
COMMUNICATION TO FOUR WEEKS LATER IN DIRECTION
OF "HIGH CREDIBILITY" AND "LOW CREDIBILITY" SOURCES

Topic	High Credibility Source (A)		Low Credibility Source (B)		Difference (B-A)
Anti-Histamines	(N=31)	−6.5%	(N=30)	+6.7%	+13.2%
Atomic Submarines	(N=25)	−16.0	(N=36)	+13.9	+29.9
Steel Shortage	(N=35)	−11.4	(N=26)	+15.4	+26.8
Future of Movies	(N=31)	−9.7	(N=30)	−6.7	+3.0
Average	(N=122)	−10.7%	(N=122)	+7.4%	+18.1%
$P_{diff.}$					.001

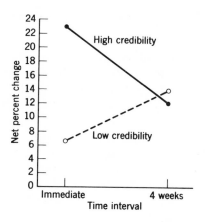

Figure 2. "Retention" of opinion. Changes in extent of agreement with position
advocated by "high credibility" and "low credibility" sources.

The loss with the "trustworthy" source and the gain with the "untrustworthy"
source are clearly indicated. A parallel analysis using the individual's own evaluation of the source credibility (similar to the method of Table 4) showed substantially the same results.

Retention of Name of Source. One hypothesis advanced for the "sleeper effect"
involved the assumption that forgetting of the source would be more rapid than
that of the content. This is a most difficult point to test experimentally because
it is almost impossible to equate retention tests for source and for content. It is,
however, possible to make a comparison of the retention of the name of the source
where the subjects initially agreed with the source's position and considered the
source "untrustworthy." Data on this point are presented in Table 7.

TABLE 7   RECALL OF SOURCE IMMEDIATELY AFTER COMMUNICATION
AND AFTER FOUR WEEKS

Recall	Trustworthy Source		Untrustworthy Source	
	Individuals Initially Holding Position Advocated by Communicator	Individuals Not Initially Holding Position Advocated by Communicator	Individuals Initially Holding Position Advocated by Communicator	Individuals Not Initially Holding Position Advocated by Communicator
Immediately after communication	93.0% (N=43)	85.7% (N=77)	93.0% (N=43)	93.4% (N=76)
Four weeks after communication	60.5 (N=43)	63.6 (N=77)	76.7 (N=43)	55.3 (N=76)

No clear differences are obtained immediately after the communication, indicating comparable initial learning of the names of the different sources. At the time of the delayed test, however, there appears to be a clear difference in the retention of the names of "untrustworthy" sources for the group initially agreeing with the communicator's position as compared with that for the group disagreeing with the communicator's position ($p = .02$). Since the "sleeper effect" occurs among the group which initially disagrees with an unreliable source (but subsequently comes to agree with it), it is interesting to note that among this group the retention of the source name is poorest of all. Too few subjects were available to check whether retention was poorer among the very subjects who showed the "sleeper effect," but no clear-cut difference could be seen from the analysis of the small sample.

Discussion

Under the conditions of this experiment, neither the acquisition nor the retention of factual information appears to be affected by the trustworthiness of the source. But changes in opinion are significantly related to the trustworthiness of the source used in the communication. This difference is in line with the results of Hovland, Lumsdaine and Sheffield, who found a clear distinction between the effects of films on information and opinion.[5] In the case of factual information they found that differences in acquisition and retention were primarily related to differences in learning ability. But in the case of opinion, the most important

[5]*Ibid.*

factor was the degree of "acceptance" of the material. In the present experiment, this variable was probably involved as a consequent of the variation in source credibility.

The present results add considerable detail to the Hovland-Lumsdaine-Sheffield findings concerning the nature of the "sleeper effect." While they were forced to make inferences concerning possible suspicion of the source, this factor was under experimental control in the present experiment and was shown to be a significant determinant of subsequent changes in opinion. In terms of their distinction between "learning" and "acceptance," one could explain the present results by saying that the content of the communication (premises, arguments, etc.) is learned and forgotten to the same extent regardless of the communicator. But the extent of opinion change is influenced by both learning and acceptance, and the effect of an untrustworthy communicator is to interfere with the acceptance of the material ("I know what he is saying, but I don't believe it"). The aforementioned authors suggest that this interference is decreased with the passage of time, and at a more rapid rate than the forgetting of the content which provides the basis for the opinion. This could result in substantially the same extent of agreement with the position advocated by trustworthy and by untrustworthy sources at the time of the second post-test questionnaire. In the case of the trustworthy source, the forgetting of the content would be the main factor in the decrease in the extent of opinion change. But with an untrustworthy source the reduction due to forgetting would be more than offset by the removal of the interference associated with "nonacceptance." The net effect would be an increase in the extent of agreement with the position advocated by the source at the time of the second post-communication questionnaire. The present results are in complete agreement with this hypothesis; there is a large difference in extent of agreement with trustworthy and untrustworthy sources immediately after the communication, but the extent of agreement with the two types of source is almost identical four weeks later.

The Hovland-Lumsdaine-Sheffield formulation makes forgetting of the source a critical condition for the "sleeper" phenomenon. In the present analysis the critical requirement is a decreased tendency over time to reject the material presented by an untrustworthy source.[6]   This may or may not require that the source be forgotten. But the individual must be less likely with the passage of time to asso-

---

[6]In the present analysis the difference in effects of trustworthy and untrustworthy sources is attributed primarily to the *negative* effects of rejection of the untrustworthy source. On the other hand, in prestige studies the effects are usually attributed to the *positive* enhancement of effects by a high "prestige" source. In both types of study only a difference in effect of the two kinds of influence is obtained. Future research must establish an effective "neutral" baseline to answer the question as to the absolute direction of the effects.

ciate spontaneously the content with the source. Thus the passage of time serves to remove recall of the source as a mediating cue that leads to rejection.[7]

It is in this connection that the methodological distinction mentioned earlier between the procedure used in this experiment and that customarily employed in "prestige" studies becomes of significance. In the present analysis, the untrustworthy source is regarded as a cue which is reacted to by rejection. When an individual is asked for his opinion at the later time he may not spontaneously remember the position held by the source. Hence the source does not then constitute a cue producing rejection of his position. In the usual "prestige" technique, the attachment of the name of the source to the statement would serve to reinstate the source as a cue; consequently the differential effects obtained with the present design would not be expected to obtain. An experiment is now under way to determine whether the "sleeper effect" disappears when the source cue is reinstated by the experimenter at the time of the delayed test of opinion change.

Finally, the question of the generalizability of the results should be discussed briefly. In the present study the subjects were all college students. Other groups of subjects varying in age and in education will be needed in future research. Four topics and eight different sources were used to increase the generality of the "source" variable. No attempt, however, was made to analyze the differences in effects for different topics. Throughout, the effects of the "Atomic Submarine" and "Steel Shortage" communications were larger and more closely related to the trustworthiness of source variable than those of the "Future of Movies" topic. An analysis of the factors responsible for the differential effects constitutes an interesting problem for future research. A repetition of the study with a single after-test for each time interval rather than double testing after the communication would be desirable, although this variation is probably much less significant with opinion than with information questions. The generality of the present results is limited to the situation where individuals are experimentally exposed to the communication; i.e. a "captive audience" situation. An interesting further research problem would be a repetition of the experiment under naturalistic conditions where the individual himself controls his exposure to communications. Finally for the present study it was important to use sources which could plausibly advocate either side of an issue. There are other combinations of position and source where the communicator and his stand are so intimately associated that one spontaneously recalls the source when he thinks about the issue. Under these conditions, the forgetting of the source may not occur and consequently no "sleeper effect" would be obtained.

---

[7]In rare instances there may also occur a change with time in the attitude toward the source, such that one remembers the source but no longer has such a strong tendency to discount and reject the material. No evidence for the operation of this factor in the present experiment was obtained; our data indicate no significant changes in the evaluation of the trustworthiness of the sources from before to after the communications.

Summary

1. The effects of credibility of source on acquisition and retention of communication material were studied by presenting identical content but attributing the material to sources considered by the audience to be of "high trustworthiness" or of "low trustworthiness." The effects of source on factual information and on opinion were measured by the use of questionnaires administered before, immediately after, and four weeks after the communication.

2. The immediate reaction to the "fairness" of the presentation and the "justifiability" of the conclusions drawn by the communication is significantly affected by both the subject's initial position on the issue and by his evaluation of the trustworthiness of the source. Identical communications were regarded as being "justified" in their conclusions in 71.7 per cent of the cases when presented by a high credibility source to subjects who initially held the same opinion as advocated by the communicator, but were considered "justified" in only 36.7 per cent of the cases when presented by a low credibility source to subjects who initially held an opinion at variance with that advocated by the communicator.

3. No difference was found in the amount of factual information learned from the "high credibility" and "low credibility" sources, and none in the amount retained over a four week period.

4. Opinions were changed immediately after the communication in the direction advocated by the communicator to a significantly greater degree when the material was presented by a trustworthy source than when presented by an untrustworthy source.

5. There was a *decrease* after a time interval in the extent to which subjects agreed with the position advocated by the communication when the material was presented by trustworthy sources, but an *increase* when it was presented by untrustworthy sources.

6. Forgetting the name of the source is less rapid among individuals who initially agreed with the untrustworthy source than among those who disagreed with it.

7. Theoretical implications of the results are discussed. The data on post-communication changes in opinion (the "sleeper effect") can be explained by assuming equal *learning* of the content whether presented by a trustworthy or an untrustworthy source but an initial resistance to the *acceptance* of the material presented by an untrustworthy source. If this resistance to acceptance diminishes with time while the content which itself provides the basis for the opinion is forgotten more slowly, there will be an increase after the communication in the extent of agreement with an untrustworthy source.

31 Making Consumer Decisions

The Measurement of Information Value: A Study in Consumer Decision-Making

DONALD F. COX* *(Marketing Educator)*

In order to evaluate a product, consumers must utilize information of some kind. For a number of reasons, the consumer probably uses only a small portion of the many pieces of information available to her about a product. How does she discriminate between information she will use and information she will discard?

In this reading, the idea is developed that consumers assign value to information about a product, and tend to use high-value information in evaluating the product.

An experiment is reported that attempts to isolate the dimensions on which consumers evaluate information, measure the value assigned to information in a particular situation, and relate information value to the probability of information utilization in evaluating a particular product.

How does a consumer evaluate a product? On what bases does the suburban housewife distinguish between high and low quality electric hand mixers, dishwashing detergents, or stereo amplifiers? Clearly the consumer must base her judgment on some type of information about the product. But what is the nature of the information she uses? Does she pick at random from the many pieces of information available to her? Or is she selective in using information? If she is selective, does she base her evaluation only on high value information?

Source: Donald F. Cox, "The Measurement of Information Value: A Study in Consumer Decision-Making," in William S. Decker, Editor, *Emerging Concepts in Marketing* (Chicago: American Marketing Association, 1963), pp. 413-421.

*Donald F. Cox, Assistant Professor, Harvard Graduate School of Business Administration.

A product can be conceived of as an *array of cues*. The array can include information such as price, color, scent, friends' opinions, taste, feel, salesmen's opinions, and so on. The consumer's task in evaluating a product is to use cues (information) from the array as the basis for making judgments about the product.

My thesis is that when presented with an array of cues, consumers will value some cues more than others. Furthermore, the higher the value a consumer places on a cue, the higher the probability that she will utilize that cue as the primary basis for evaluating the product.

In other words, the consumer is selective in her use of information about a product, and tends to base her evaluation primarily on high value information or cues. This remains to be demonstrated. But even if this were the case, in order to predict which cues a consumer would use in a given situation, it would be necessary to know how she assigns value to the various cues. That is, how does the consumer distinguish high value information from low value information?

Some Examples of Product Evaluations

For some time, sophisticated marketers have been aware that consumers may judge a product on the basis of a few cues or bits of information. Consider the following examples of product evaluations.

In 1932, Laird[1] conducted an experiment in which housewives were asked to examine and evaluate four pairs of silk stockings which were as identicial as possible in manufacture, but differed in scent. The scents were so faint, however, that only six of the 250 housewives tested noticed them. Nevertheless, one pair of stockings (with a 'narcissus' scent) was judged to be the best hosiery—on the basis of such attributes as texture, weave, feel, wearing qualities, lack of sheen, and weight—by 50% of the housewives. Another pair (with a 'natural' scent) was judged best by only 8%.

In a recent sales test[2], two piles of nylons were placed on a counter in a retail store. The stockings in both piles were identical in price and manufacture, but differed in that one pile had been scented (with an 'orange' aroma), the other pile was left with the natural (from the factory) scent. About 90% of the women who purchased stockings from this counter selected the orange-scented stockings. When asked why, many replied that they seemed to be better quality stockings and would probably wear better and longer than the other brand.

An experiment conducted by a large dairy found that consumers considered a cream colored, 14% butterfat ice cream to be richer in flavor than white colored, 16% butterfat ice cream.

[1]Donald A. Laird, "How the Consumer Estimates Quality by Subconscious Sensory Impressions," *Journal of Applied Psychology*, June, 1932, p. 241.
[2]*Women's Wear Daily*, January 28, 1961, p. 15.

Detergent manufacturers have found that housewives tend to judge the cleaning power of a detergent on the basis of suds level and smell. Similarly, the color of a detergent and its package is a cue often used to judge mildness. (Thus it is neither accident nor chemical necessity which leads manufacturers of liquid dishwashing detergents to color their products pink.)

However, even given this awareness that consumers may base their evaluation of a product on a very small number of cues, it still would be highly useful to be able to predict, for a given product, which cues are most likely to influence consumer evaluations. Given this ability, problems such as the case of the noiseless mixer might be avoided. (A noiseless electric hand mixer was developed and marketed but did not sell. Why? Consumers thought it had insufficient power).[3]

In order to make such predictions it is necessary to measure the value consumers assign to various bits of information or cues. This is turn implies two requirements:

(1) Isolating the dimensions on which consumers evaluate information; and
(2) Developing measures of the value a consumer assigns to information on each of the value dimensions she uses.

The Dimensions of Information Value

The first question to be resolved is the determination of the dimensions of information value. How many dimensions are used, and what is the nature of each?

Previous work in psychology[4] has been based on the assumption that people tend to evaluate information on only one dimension. We might call this dimension the *predictive value* of a cue. Predictive value is a measure of the probability with which a cue seems associated with (i.e., predicts) a specific product attribute. For example, if I knew for certain that a stereo amplifier contained high quality internal components, I would say that there was a high probability that the amplifier was of good quality. Internal components, then, would be a high predictive value cue. On the other hand, the knobs on the front of the amplifier would be a low predictive value cue as far as I am concerned. That is, if I only knew for certain that the knobs were of good quality, the probability that the amplifier itself was good is not high.

The measurement of information value on the basis of predictive value seems like a sensible procedure. Maybe it is too sensible. In any event, it has been found that people don't always behave as if this were the procedure they followed. A number of studies have shown that consumers may base their evaluation of a

[3]Robert Froman, "Marketing Research, You Get What You Want," pp. 231-238, in Westing, J. H. (ed.), *Readings in Marketing*, (New York, Prentice-Hall, 1953).
[4]For example, see Jerome S. Bruner, Jacqueline J. Goodnow, and George A. Austing, *A Study of Thinking*, (New York, Wiley, 1956), and Leo Postman and Edward Tolman, "Brunswick's Probabilistic Functionalism," pp. 502-564, in Sigmund Koch, (ed.), *Psychology: A Study of Science, Study I, Vol. 1, Sensory, Perceptual, and Physiological Foundations*, (New York, McGraw-Hill, 1959).

product on low predictive value information (e.g., scent can affect evaluations of the wearing qualities of nylon stockings.)

There are two possible explanations for this behavior. Either consumers do not always use high value information, *or* they do use high value information, but they measure information on some other dimension in addition to predictive value.

Hunch led me to reject the first alternative and to try to find an additional dimension on which consumers might assign value to information. I finally hit upon another dimension, and will call it the *confidence value* of a cue. Confidence value is a measure of how *certain* the consumer is that the *cue* is what she thinks it is. For example, consider an audiophile and a suburban housewife, both of whom were trying to form independent judgments of the quality of a stereo amplifier. Both might share the belief, that the internal components represent a high predictive value cue. That is, if they knew for certain that the components were good, they would also feel that in all probability the amplifier itself was good. In addition, the audiophile presumably could tell with a high degree of confidence whether or not the components *were* of good quality. Thus the internal components would, for this audiophile, be both a high predictive value cue, and a high confidence value cue. The housewife, on the other hand, may be unable to discriminate with confidence between good and bad innards. For her, this is a low confidence value cue, even though it is high in predictive value.

Hypotheses

The first hypothesis established was that consumers assign value to information or cues on *two* independent dimensions—predictive value and confidence value. A further hypothesis was that when confidence value was held constant, the higher the predictive value of a cue, the higher the probability that it would be utilized as the primary basis for evaluating a product or product attribute. On the other hand, when predictive value was held constant, it was hypothesized that the cue highest in confidence value was most likely to be used. In the case where consumers were faced with a choice between a cue high in predictive value but low in confidence value, and a cue low in predictive value, but high in confidence value, the hypothesis was that they would tend to favor the latter cue, that is, the low predictive value—high confidence value cue.

The Experiment

The following experiment was designed to test these hypotheses.

Three separate groups, totaling 414 lower and middle class housewives were asked to evaluate "two brands" of nylon stockings and to indicate how confident they were about their evaluation. The stockings were in fact identical, except for the identifying letters R and N. After making the evaluations (on 18 attributes) subjects heard a tape-recorded salesgirl's opinion that Brand R stockings were better on six attributes (feel, weight, texture, fit, weave, and versatility). The subjects then re-evaluated the nylons, evaluated the salesgirl, and indicated how confident they were about their evaluations of the salesgirl.

Subjects' ratings of the salesgirl on experience, reliability, etc., were taken as a measure of the predictive value of the salesgirl cue, on the assumption that an apparently experienced salesgirl is more likely to know the difference between good and bad quality nylons than an inexperienced salesgirl. Thus if a subject rated the salesgirl high, she was assumed to have assigned a high predictive value to this cue. If she was also very certain that the salesgirl *was* experienced and reliable, the subject was also assumed to have assigned a high confidence value to the salesgirl cue. The confidence value assigned to the other "cue" (the stockings themselves) was measured according to how confident subjects were about their evaluations of the nylons.

Results

The results of the experiment, shown below in Table 1, supported the hypotheses.

TABLE 1   CHANGE IN EVALUATION IN RELATION TO SALESGIRL RATING AND RELATIVE DEGREE OF CONFIDENCE IN RATING THE SALESGIRL VS. THE NYLONS

Salesgirl Was Rated:	Subject had Greater Confidence Evaluating the:	Positive	None	Negative	Base
1. High	Salesgirl	68%	18%	14%	119
2. High	Stockings	46	35	19	69
3. Low	Salesgirl	56	19	25	64
4. Low	Stockings	30	44	26	87
5. High	Equal confidence	46	42	12	41
6. Low	Equal confidence	18	64	18	34

diff (1,2) $P < .003$ diff (5,6) $P < .009$**
diff (3,4) $P < .001$ diff (2,3) $P < .16$

*e.g., Of 119 subjects who rated the salesgirl high, *and* who were more confident in evaluating the salesgirl than the stockings, 68% changed their evaluation of the nylons in the direction advocated by the salesgirl.
**e.g., Among those equally confident in evaluating the salesgirl and the stockings, the difference between 5), the proportion of those rating the salesgirl *high* who showed positive change in evaluation, and 6), the proportion of those rating the salesgirl low who showed positive change is statistically significant beyond the .009 level.

Among subjects who were equally confident in their evaluations of the nylons and of the salesgirl, (i.e., when confidence value was held constant) those who rated the salesgirl high on experience, etc. (i.e., who assigned a high predictive value to the salesgirl cue) were significantly more likely to utilize the salesgirl cue and hence to change their evaluations of the nylons in the direction advocated by the salesgirl.

When predictive value was held constant, as for example, among subjects who rated the salesgirl high, those who were more confident in evaluating the salesgirl than in evaluating the nylons were most likely to change.

Finally, as hypothesized, subjects who rated the salesgirl low but who held the rating with a high degree of confidence were more likely to change than subjects who rated the salesgirl high, but who held the rating with a relatively low degree of confidence. In other words, a low predictive value-high confidence value cue was more likely to be utilized than a high predictive value-low confidence value cue.

Discussion of Results

In sum, it was found that consumers use at least two dimensions in assigning value to information, and that the value assigned to one dimension can vary independently of the value assigned to the other. In other words, the same cue may be high in predictive value and low in confidence value, or vice versa. Furthermore, each dimension of information value has quite different operating characteristics as far as the utilization of information is concerned. If a person wanted to identify an object on a dark night, and had a choice between a high candlepower light and one low in candlepower, he would most likely choose the former. But only if he could turn the light on. If for some reason, possibly because of a faulty switch, he couldn't turn the high power light on, he would then use the low candlepower light. Predictive value seems to work much like candlepower in the process of cue utilization. Predictive value seems to be the basic force in determining information value, and hence cue utilization. We have seen that when confidence value is held constant, the higher the predictive value of the cue, the higher the probability that the cue will be utilized as the basis for evaluating the product. But confidence value, like the light switch, acts as a qualifying variable and carries a strong veto. Unless a consumer feels sufficiently confident about evaluating a cue she is not as likely to use it—no matter how high its predictive value.

The procedure makes good sense, even though it may violate "common sense." If I have to evaluate the quality of a stereo amplifier, and if I can't tell a condenser from a scratch filter, it would be foolhardy to try to base my evaluation on an assessment of the internal components. If no other information were available, I'd feel more confident about estimating the quality of the set on the basis of its external features, such as the knobs.

One of the consequences of the fact that information is valued on two different and independent dimensions and that information value is not a simple additive or multiplicative function of predictive value and confidence value, is that a good deal of high value information—when measured by predictive value—is never used, or at best is underutilized.

On the other side of the coin, low value information (again when measured by predictive value) is often overutilized because its confidence value is high. The consumer who estimates the quality of a stereo amplifier on the basis of its external appearance rather than its internal components is basing his evaluation on low (predictive) value information.

It is not surprising, then, that consumers make many errors in evaluating products. We have seen that they can be persuaded (or can persuade themselves) that one of two identical stockings is better than the other; that a noiseless mixer is powerless; that a cream colored, low butterfat ice cream is rich in flavor; that a detergent packaged in a violently colored box is harsh, while the same detergent packed in pleasing colors is mild.

Lest anyone think I have a low opinion of the consumer, I should point out that the same type of behavior has been exhibited by college admission boards—presumably learned men and women. The boards, according to one study[5] consistently (though unintentionally) underutilized all information about candidates except for their scores on scholastic aptitude tests.

The problem lies not in the consumer as much as in the enormous difficulty of evaluating a product. Faced with a bewildering array of information, a need to economize (her time if nothing else) and a desire for certainty, the consumer has little choice but to be selective in her use of information.

Implications for Marketing Action

If the results of this study are valid, we can conclude that the information value of a cue is a function (but not a simple function) of the predictive value and the confidence value assigned to the cue.

According to the concepts developed in this study, in order to change the image of a product or brand, the marketer has a choice between two main types of strategies. He may alter the characteristics of dominant cues, and/or he may alter the information value of the cues in the array in order to make some cues more (or less) dominant or to alter the nature of cue-attribute associations. To the extent that he can: a) identify dominant cues, and b) specify the factors which will alter the information value of a cue, his job will be that much easier, and his efforts that much more effective.

For a number of reasons, these tasks are very difficult, and it is likely to be some time before they can be accomplished in a precise manner in many practical situa-

[5]See David C. McClelland, "Encouraging Excellence," *Daedalus*, 1961, 90, pp. 711-725.

tions. First among these reasons is the great difficulty of measuring the predictive value and confidence value of various cues.

The present study involved (not by accident) much easier and simpler measurement problems than one is likely to meet in the real world. In addition, the information value of a cue is by no means fixed. It may vary considerably for different consumers; hence an influential cue for one type of consumer may be unimportant to another. Furthermore, the array of cues associated with a product is rarely static. And a cue which is dominant in one array may become less important as new (higher information value) cues are added to the array. For example, many consumers formerly used size as a guide to the quality of high fidelity speakers, until a new cue—*Consumer Reports*—was added. This higher value cue then became the dominant cue for many people.

Another complicating factor, evident in the above example, is that not all of the cues associated with a product are controllable by the marketer. Outside sources of information such as word of mouth advertising, *Consumer Reports,* and competitors' advertising must also be taken into consideration, even though they cannot be controlled.

Finally, it should be pointed out that identification of dominant cues only indicates which cues are influential in affecting consumers' images of a product. It does not tell us whether the effect will be beneficial or detrimental to the product's image.

All of these complications add to the problems of measuring or estimating the information value of cues. But to the extent that these problems can be overcome, and information value and the factors which alter information value can be estimated, the payoff for marketing strategy could be quite handsome.

32 Evaluating and Predicting Consumer Decisions

Simulation, Scaling and Predicting Brand Purchasing Behavior*

EDGAR A. PESSEMIER *(Marketing Educator)*
AND RICHARD D. TEACH *(Marketing Educator)*

The focus of this selection is on consumer behavior recorded in an experimental environment, and transforming the experimental results to predict real market behavior.

The problems discussed involve developing an appropriate degree of psychological equivalence between the laboratory and the real marketplace.

The data were collected in a study of 230 housewives and cover 3 multibrand convenience goods commonly found in supermarkets. The predictive power of laboratory-based models was compared to demographic and nondemographic variables such as attitude, interest and opinion factor scores, media exposure factor scores, and risk-taking propensities using stepwise regression.

The subject matter of this paper is narrower than the title may imply. Rather than cover the full spectrum of buying decisions, industrial and consumer goods, durable and non-durable, discussion will be confined to consumer convenience goods. Also, the range of formal structures which can be used to represent the communication, learning, and decision-making models employed by consumers is

Source: Edgar A. Pessemier and Richard D. Teach, "Simulation, Scaling, and Predicting Brand Purchasing Behavior," in Robert L. King, Editor, *Marketing and the New Science of Planning* (Chicago: American Marketing Association, 1968), pp. 206-212.

*This work was financed in part from grants from the Batten, Barton, Durstine and Osborn, the Ford Foundation, the Herman C. Krannert Graduate School of Industrial Administration, and the State University of New York at Buffalo.
396

very large. In this area, work by Nicosia [10] and Amstutz [1] in complex model building, the research of Bush and Mosteller [4] in learning, Luce [8] in choice behavior, and work by Raiffa [9], Fouraker [6], and Smith [18] in utility and decision theory are representative of notable contributions to the understanding of buying and market behavior. Here these efforts are of indirect interest. Our focus will be on consumer behavior in an experimental environment, and on transforming experimental results to predict market behavior.

In terms of research strategy, an experimental environment should have face validity, measuring consumer characteristics that appear to be related to market behavior. Reference is made to the author's statement in an earlier paper which may clarify the general spirit of this type of simulation [12].

Just how to design experiments with an appropriate degree of psychological equivalence is a matter of practical as well as theoretical concern. Therefore, it may be of some interest to review briefly the evolution of the techniques which one or both of the authors have employed.

An early, if not original, effort to use laboratory-oriented simulated shopping experiments was completed in 1959 [11]. It was largely a pilot study employing price-marked lists of brands. Each subject's normal brand preferences were noted. These controlled the price changes which were made in the four assortments used during the series of simulated shopping trips. By raising the price of a subject's preferred brand or lowering the prices of nonpreferred brands, buying behavior of interest could be observed. For example, the subject's degree of brand loyalty and his brand switching patterns were easily derived. Also, "demand schedules" based on behavior in the experimental environment could be computed for aggregates of subjects. Subjects received the products and change from a given sum of money. Their purchase decision on one of the shopping trips determined the particular product and amount of change. One expanded version of the study was completed in 1960 [12].

Several difficulties were associated with this work. First, setting up the assortment sheets required prior knowledge of the subject's brand preferences. Hence, two contacts were called for. Second, the mechanics of the set-up proper were difficult. Third, lists of brands were hardly suitable substitutes for visual displays. Fourth, little or no data about the consumers' personal characteristics or his judgments about brand characteristics had been gathered during the pilot studies. Furthermore, a record of actual purchases by subjects had not been maintained. To one degree or another, all but the latter problem were dealt with in a new expanded research program conducted during 1961 [13, 14]. In this case, colored photographs of price-market assortments were used. The prices were attached in a manner that permitted easy price changes to allow for each subject's pattern of preferences.

The expanded full-assortment experiments noted above uncovered another limitation in the experimental design. For some product categories and customers, it was difficult for a consumer to indicate a brand preference unambiguously. Two important reasons were observed: some consumers bought for multiple users in the household, or regularly bought from a set of brands. In the latter case, relative indifference, the desire for variety, and buying specially priced merchandise were important. Therefore, a new design was developed which employed special-purpose similarity data. It permitted scaling the degree of preference for each brand. As part of the new design, the authors arranged to collect purchase diary data from the same subjects. Each subject's diaries recorded seven month's purchases for the same product categories used in the experiments.

Before looking at the analysis growing out of the new design and data, a brief note on the literature related to experimentation in marketing may be useful. The easiest way for an interested reader to cover the subject is to read the two excellent review articles by Peters and Holloway [16, 7]. Also, reference is made to papers by Broome and Smith [17] and Barnett [2].

Laboratory Brand Preference Data

The research reported here exploits many of the advantages of laboratory experiments, and relates the results to actual consumer brand purchase decisions. For each subject, scaled brand preference variables from the laboratory were used to predict the relative frequency of brand purchase during a seven month period following the experiment.

THE DATA BASE

The basic data source was the 1965-1966 Purdue Consumer Behavior Research Project, a study using 540 housewives in the Greater Lafayette, Indiana, area. The overall characteristics of the project and the sample have been described elsewhere [19]. Brand purchase predictions in this study were made for a non-student wife subsample of 230 subjects who purchased from all three product classifications, and who completed all relevant phases of the research: a self-administered questionnaire, a series of laboratory experiments, and a diary record covering seven months' purchases.

The laboratory experiments included eight brands of toothpaste, six brands of liquid household cleaner, and five brands of cake mix. For each of the product categories, the housewife was presented with a series of all possible pairs of brands. The brands in each pair were marked with their "regular" prices. In each case the subject selected the brand she would "buy" in a forced choice purchase by circling the most preferred brand in the pair. Next, she indicated the price to which the preferred brand must rise to induce her to switch her original preference. This price was circled in a series of prices shown below the pair of brands. Every subject was paid off on one pair, receiving the brand circled and the change from 75¢ called for by the brand's regular price.

The pay-off was selected at random.

BASIC DATA REDUCTION

By gathering data in this form, a preferred brand k, non-preferred brand j, and the strength of preference in terms of a price increase d_{jk} were obtained for each pair. These data are the basic entries in the subject's skew-symmetric preference matrix. Zeroes were recorded along the diagonal and the columns of the matrix were summed.

Dividing each column sum by n, the number of brands, yields estimated scale locations for each brand. Differences between these estimated scale locations, yield a least squares fit of the estimated distances δ_{jk} to the subject's revealed preference distances, d_{jk}. Detailed development of the mathematics can be found in David [4]. Here, it is sufficient to recall that former distances are always additive, but latter distances are generally nonadditive.[1]

To obtain scale values on the interval (0, 1), and Adjusted Scale Value for each of the j brands was computed from

$$ASV_j = 1.0 - (\Sigma d_{jk}/\max_K \Sigma\, d_{jk})$$

To complete the basic calculations, it is useful to compute a standardized measure of the degree of intransitivity in the subjects' data. Here we use RI as a measure of Relative Intransitivity.

$$RI = [_j\Sigma_{<k}|\, d_{jk} - \delta_{jk}| / (\,_j\Sigma_{<k}|\, d_{jk}|/M)\,]\,, M = \frac{N\,(N-1)}{2}$$

When compared to the Random Intransitivity, that which would result from a random assignment of distances, RI is a measure of the consistency of the data which produced the transitive estimated distances. Since our model for predicting the relative frequency of brand purchase employs the observed relative intransitivity and the expected random relative intransitivy, more will be said about these matters at another point.

PREDICTIVE MODELS – CHARACTERISTICS AND PARAMETER SELECTION

The problem of converting a subject's responses in the experiment to predictions of brand purchases over time has two aspects. One concerns the ability to measure the subject's preferences during the experiment as they aid prediction. Here the issue is experimental bias. The second concerns the movement of preferences and market conditions over time, as well as recording error in diary records. These latter elements concern the lack of control over conditions in which market observations were made. What is needed is a simple link between revealed preferences in the laboratory experiments and revealed preferences (purchases) in the market. Because of the noise, bias and passage of time, building a satisfactory link is an emposing task.

---

[1]Additivity means that the distances between any pairs of brands are not perfectly additive or subtractive; scale values cannot always be obtained as the sums of differences of other scale values.

The scale values which have been developed can be converted to probability of purchase statements for each subject and brand. A model is developed for this purpose which is sufficiently flexible to admit scale transformations which can modify the ratios of the subject's probabilities of brand purchase. The need to do so is dictated by the movement from an experimental to a real-world environment. In the laboratory, the ease of inducing brand switching may be greatly overemphasized, especially as it applies to less preferred brands. Certainly, subjects are far more conscious of their acts and less distracted than they would be in the market. Therefore, the relative separation between brands needed to predict market behavior may be greater than that found in the laboratory. Although this proved to be the case, the degree could not be easily prejudged, and it was likely to vary among product categories.

Adjusted Scale Values of the type which have been described can be converted to simple predictors of the relative frequency of brand purchase by normalizing ASV_j, dividing by the sum of the scale values over j. The most preferred brand is assigned the highest relative frequency of purchase, and the least preferred brand is assigned a value of zero. The remaining brands are located appropriately between these limits. In the model that will be described, a flexible procedure that includes the above simple predictor as a special case is adopted.

The model we will employ uses all the experimental data to produce the predictions. The data include:

1. The Adjusted Scale Value for subject i and brand j, $ASV_{i,j}$.
2. The observed Relative Intransitivity for subject i, RI_i.
3. The Expect Error or the expected relative random intransitivity EE.[2]
4. The relative First Choice Frequency, across all subjects, with which each brand was a first choice selection, FCF_j, an experimental measure of brand preference analogous to market share data.

Modifying the Scale Values: "Complete" Model

To develop relative frequency of purchase predictions, the ith subject's Adjusted Scale Values $ASV_{i,j}$, are raised to a power beta. Then their values over j brands are normalized. The operations yield the expected Relative Frequency of Purchase.

$$RFP_{i,j} = (ASV_{i,j})\ \beta / \sum_j (ASV_{i,j})\beta$$

By adjusting beta, the fit of the expected relative frequency of purchase to the observed relative purchase frequency can be improved. Increasing beta increases the relative distance of the less preferred brands as compared to the more preferred brands. Similarly, as the distance of a brand from the more preferred brand in-

[2]The level of intransitivities if brands were randomly assigned to the line segment bounded by the subjects ASV scale.

creases, the more effect a given beta power will have on reducing the probability of purchase for the less preferred brand. Across all subjects, the extent of the effect on the probability of purchase for each subject and brand is controlled by the degree of preference for the brands recorded in the subject's laboratory experiment.

If inconsistent judgments are interpreted as unstable preferences and noise, less dependence should be placed on the derived scales as the observed intransitivities' rise. At some point, a subject's $RFP_{i,j}$ should be disregarded. One index of the weight in subject's scales should be given is the ratio of the subject's Relative Intransitivity, RI, to EE, the level of Expected Error with random assignments only. It is convenient to raise the ratio to a power γ, and to constrain it to lie in the interval (0,1). Therefore, let the Error Ratio be

$$ER = (R/EE)\gamma \qquad 0 \leq RI \leq EE$$

The Error Ratio is used to weigh $RFP_{i,j}$ with some other forecast source to predict the relative frequency of purchase. When ER approaches one, the scales from the experiment are unlikely to be useful predictors. On the other hand, a ratio close to zero indicates maximum reliance may be placed in this data source. The most natural substitute predictor is the laboratory measure, aggregate Frequency of First Choice. This is a laboratory proxy for market share.

Combining the elements of interest, the final model produces a Predicted Relative Frequency of Purchase for brand i by subject j.

$$PRFP, = (ER_i) \cdot (FFC_j) + (1.0 - ER_i): RFP_{i,j}$$

= the weighted prediction allowing for both the subject's scale data and aggregate frequency of first choice data.

In passing, also observe that EE could be converted to a free parameter, thereby introducing three parameters: β, γ, and EE.

In studying the market behavior of subjects, a frequently observed situation involved purchases concentrated among two or three brands. In the toothpaste category, purchase behavior of this type might be due to different preferences among various members of the family, cents-off label, and coupon buying among a set of relatively acceptable brands, a desire for variety, and so on. In the cake mix category, buying specialty flavors and new mix types assume importance. In addition, heavy promotion, cents-off label, coupons, and special prices could be important influences in purchasing liquid cleaner. Here, no attempt will be made to account for these various influences. Since we assume that the effects of these and other uncontrolled variables are substantial, the task of predicting the relative frequency of purchase over seven months is a difficult one. Furthermore, the frequency of purchase by some subjects was low enough to make the observed frequency a weak proxy for the general purchase pattern of interest.

In addition to the above predictive model, we have studied a variety of alternatives. Predicting that all purchases will go to the first choice or most preferred brand represents the ultimate simplification based on experimental laboratory data. The model uses the same data base, but many data manipulation and parameter selection operations are avoided.

Although they will not be discussed here, other data gathered outside the laboratory and market place can be used to predict market purchase. Two important indicators which can be gathered by survey methods have been examined. The first was unaided recall of the last brand purchased, and the second was the inventory of brands in the home. Although both display significant predictive power, they share an important weakness with most simple predictive models, regardless of their data base. It concerns the concentration of all of the model's predictive power on one brand or a very limited set of brands. As a result, they are mute about each subject's relative preference for the remaining brands. And in the cases where experimental data are used, a great deal of information which can be of value in predicting the results of attempts to modify preferences is lost.

PARAMETER SELECTION FOR THE COMPLETE MODEL

In the absence of an analytical procedure for locating efficient parameter values for each model, the efficiency of various sets of parameter values was examined. We examined the effect of each combination of parameter values on the average absolute error of the prediction. Forty combinations of β and γ were examined for toothpaste and liquid cleaner. For the cake mix classification, 56 combinations of variables were investigated.[3] In each case, the mean absolute error across subjects and brands, and the variance of these errors were computed for each product category and each split-half sample. These same summary statistics were computed when uniform-predicted relative purchase frequencies were assigned to each brand.

Since no clear-cut *a priori* grounds were available for determining the importance of errors associated with a brand of their magnitude, no weighting procedures by brand such as market share, or errors by a criteria such as least squares, were employed in the search for efficient parameters.

As the average absolute error goes down, the variance of the forecast error tends to go up. In the case of all three classifications, the lowest observed variance occurred at $\beta = \gamma = 2$. For cake mix, the minimum absolute error appears to be an interior point. For toothpaste and liquid cleaner, it decreases as β increases, but at the expense of increased variance. This implies that the least error would be found in the Frequency of First Choice model, except when inconsistencies in laboratory data are high. Then FFC would be substituted. The results also point out that raw probability of purchase scales $\beta = 1$, would be inferior predictors, since they overassign purchase frequencies to less preferred brands. This

---

[3]The values were computed using the formula EE = $(2n^2 - 3n)/4$ estimated by Monte Carlo methods.

effect was expected due to the laboratory conditions under which the preference data were collected.

Since high beta values are costly in terms of information loss about less preferred brands, a compromise solution is required. We selected $\beta = 4.0$, $\gamma = 8.0$ for tooth paste and liquid cleaner, and $\beta = 4.0$, $\gamma = 4.0$ for cake mix. Because of the conflicting mean-variance condition, no set of parameters can be judged "best."

The sample size used to obtain parameter values for the model was roughly double the size of the sample for which complete data was available across all product classes and ancillary data sets. Since a reduced sample were employed in the prediction of market behavior, some uncertainty remained concerning the model's ultimate predictive ability under any selected set of parameters. Finally, due to the information loss encountered in the simple First Choice Model, the Complex Model will be preferred if it performs as well as the former models in terms of predicting a subject's relative frequency of purchase of a single brand. To obtain the desired predictions, the scale values from each model were used as independent variables in a series of step-wise multiple regression analyses.

Predicting Market Behavior

PREDICTING THE INDIVIDUAL CONSUMER'S RELATIVE FREQUENCY OF PURCHASE FOR A SINGLE BRAND

In predicting the relative frequency of brand purchase, it was not clear how much the predictive power of scaled probability of purchase variables served as proxies for the predictive effectiveness of demographic and nondemographic variables such as attitude, interest and opinion factor scores, media exposure factor scores, and risk taking propensity. Although we will not report the detailed results here, our analysis offers little hope that large sets of demographic and/or nondemographic measures of the type noted can be analyzed by straightforward regression methods to obtain strong predictors of brand purchase behavior by *individual* consumers. Applying variable-stacking cross classification procedures to convenience goods' brands would doubtless produce more positive findings, but the required sample size may be prohibitive for more practical purposes.

Table 1 presents results of the stepwise regression analyses in which the predicted relative frequency of brand purchase was included in the large, diffuse set of independent variables mentioned above. It is particularly instructive to compare the contribution to the R^2 made by single scale variables obtained from transformed laboratory data to the R^2 in Table 2 derived from the entire set of scale and non-scale variables.

A number of conclusions can be drawn from comparing the summary data displayed in Table 1. For some product classes and brands, the predictive power of the probability of brand purchase scales produced from laboratory data are very strong predictors of market behavior. In the case of the tooth paste classification,

TABLE 1   PREDICTING THE RELATIVE FREQUENCY OF BRAND PUR-
CHASES DURING SEVEN MONTHS USING SCALE VARIABLES
MODIFIED BY THE COMPLEX MODEL AND NONSCALE VARI-
ABLES OF DIFFUSE TYPES

Classification and Brand	N = 230 Total R^2	Contribution to R^2 From Significance Scale Variables
Tooth Paste		
Colgate	.685	.660
Crest	.502	.468
Gleem	.606	.533
Ipana	.535	.517
Liquid Cleaner		
Ajax	.297	.246
Handy Andy	.180	.075
Mr. Clean	.107	.089
Top Job	.321	.292
Cake Mix		
Betty Crocker	.172	.138
Duncan Hines	.445	.359
Jiffy	.386	.317
Pillsbury	.233	.196

TABLE 2   COMPARISON OF THE POWER OF THE TWO SCALING MODELS
IN PREDICTING RELATIVE FREQUENCY OF PURCHASE DUR-
ING SEVEN MONTHS

Classification and Brand	Contribution to R^2 by Scale Variables in predicting Relative Frequency of Purchase	
	Complex Model	First Choice Model
Tooth Paste		
Colgate	.660	.490
Crest	.468	.399
Gleem	.533	.452
Ipana	.517	.444
Liquid Cleaner		
Ajax	.246	.163
Handy Andy	.075	..
Mr. Clean	.089	.047
Top Job	.292	.223
Cake Mix		
Betty Crocker	.138	.085
Duncan Hines	.359	.375
Jiffy	.317	.239
Pillsbury	.196	.131

the results are surprisingly uniform and powerful, R^2 values generally exceeding .5. This is particularly interesting in light of the assumed tendency of subjects to express personal preferences in the laboratory, but actually to satisfy the brand preferences of several individuals when purchasing for the family. The weaker performance in cake mix may be explained by somewhat lower product class salience, and a tendency to have flavor preferences which may override brand preferences. Similarly, the relatively poor showing among liquid cleaner brands may be explained by the heavy promotion of Top Job in comparison to Mr. Clean. Both products were produced and sold by the same firm, creating a tendency to take effect away relatively from the second brand.

Nonscale variables are notable in their inability to predict brand purchase behavior. On the other hand, there is little evidence to suggest that they should be strong predictors of consumers' relative frequency of brand purchases. At best, the nonscale variables are loosely or indirectly associated with brand purchase behavior. Also, the very modest predictive capabilities of these variables are reduced by the degree to which they correlate with the probability of brand purchase scale variables. Again, the relationships which do exist between nonscale variables and purchase behavior are likely to be nonlinear, and probably more amenable to analysis by cross classification routines where sample size permits.

Next, it is interesting to compare the relative predictive power of the two scale models. In Table 2 note that the Complex Model yields the best results except in the case of Duncan Hines cake mix. It is important to recall, however, that the latter model is not only inferior in predictive power, but is also informationless with respect to the degree of the consumer's preferences for the less preferred brands. This point is reemphasized because of the strategic importance of assessing the similarity or substitutability of one brand as compared to another.

THE EFFECTS OF AGGREGATION

Before proceeding, it is useful to recall several characteristics of the data gathering process and the research findings. In the case of individual brands and buyers, the predictive power of scale variables was not high. Across a large sample of buyers, however, reliability would be greatly improved. The only adjustment of consequence which is required to predict market shares would be to allow for the fact that scale predictions tend to overstate the probabilities for purchase for the limited laboratory assortment, compared to the same brands in the market where a wider range of active competitors are present.[4] In the Complex Model, the proportion of purchases going to the four brands of tooth paste discussed was only 91 per cent (.768/.843) of that indicated by the estimates produced by the Model. In the liquid cleaner and cake mix categories, the actual shares were 92 per cent and 93 per cent, respectively, of the predicted figures. Naturally, if prior data are available for converting laboratory scales to predictions of market shares,

[4] Eight brands of tooth paste, six brands of liquid cleaner, and five brands of cake mix were included in the laboratory experiments.

these would be used. In the absence of this knowledge, percentage adjustments to allow for the limited size of the laboratory assortment would be an appropriate substitute.

When estimates are based on samples of at least several hundred subjects, and when allowance is made for the assortment bias, relatively small differences in the mean of the predicted compared to the actual market shares should be expected. In other words, prediction of market shares—based on predicted probabilities of purchase, derived from laboratory data and the Complex Model—are sufficiently precise to permit useful inferences about market behavior. It is only necessary to have a sample of adequate size and knowledge of the share of the market that will go to brands not represented in the assortment used in the laboratory.

Two points are noteworthy concerning aggregate scale values for M subjects.

$$\sum_i^M ((\sum_j d_{jk}/n)_i/M).$$

First, these scales appear to be linearly related to the scale values developed from categorical judgments made by the same subjects about the same brands.[5] In the latter instance, brands were judged on a six point scale ranging from strongly prefer to strongly reject. These judgments formed the basis for aggregate estimates of the brand's scale values. Therefore, when point estimates for groups of consumers are required, transformed categorical judgments may prove adequate.

Second, the aggregate raw scales from the paired preference judgments also appear to be related in a roughly linear manner to aggregate brand market shares. On the whole, however, the slope changes in a piece-wise fashion as the curve moves from positive to negative raw scale values. In other words, a single linear relationship may be satisfactory for those brands having more than a very modest share of the market.[6]

USE OF LABORATORY AND RELATED DATA FOR PLANNING PRODUCT AND MARKETING STRATEGIES

The research reported here does not provide direct evidence about the problems and opportunities associated with applying the laboratory data. It does, however, suggest several approaches.

1. The regular price at which brands were offered in the laboratory can be modified to see the effect which price changes are likely to produce in each subject's predicted frequency of brand purchase. From this evidence the expected effect on market shares could be computed.

2. The degree to which brands appear to be close substitutes can be judged by their proximity along the preference scale. If brands are far apart on a subject's preference scale, typically it will be difficult or costly to induce

[5]For a discussion of the scaling methods that apply to categorical judgment, see Torgerson [21].
[6]For further details, see Teach [19], pp. 182-224.

substitution. On the other hand if they are close, substitution may be obtained with little effort. The marketing strategist wants to differentiate his offering in a manner which will efficiently attract new buyers and retain present buyers. Profiling preference structures for major competing brands and the consumers who appear readily susceptible to influence should suggest fruitful approaches. In turn, these may be tested for relative effectiveness by exposing separate groups of laboratory subjects to each one, and then scaling the probability of brand purchases. For a more complex approach using multidimensional scaling methods, see Barnett and Stefflre [2,19].

3. The same type of profiling and controlled experimentation may permit the examination of alternative product characteristics and assortments.

4. Modest adaptation of the methodology would permit gathering data in the field with standard survey instruments. The ability to do so would further extend the range of problems which could be studied and reduce the cost of study execution.

Summary

A modest group of techniques and findings have been outlined. The requirements of brevity have precluded discussion of the predictive power of variables such as last brand purchased, the brand's share of consumer's home inventory, and other potential predictors of brand purchase behavior. Although in many cases they are not powerful predictors of brand purchasing, various demographic, activity, interest and opinion, media, and risk-taking characteristics of consumers related to brand purchase behavior should be analyzed with care. Again, the need for brevity foreclosed the possibility of exploring this field. However, the more intriguing questions concern future tests applied to other product classifications, and to variables measured across several product classes.

Finally, the application of the procedures to applied problems offers real challenge to the marketing researcher. In particular, it will be important to find meaningful ways to classify buyers who display various types of brand purchase behavior. A separate paper discusses one promising procedure that uses media exposure patterns as the basis for clustering consumers [15]. The work reported here leads one to suspect that clustering consumers by measures of brand purchase behavior and media exposure will have further utility. However, the number of clusters needed to achieve satisfactory homogeneity may be excessive. These questions and others must be left to future research programs.

1. Amstutz, Arnold E., *Computer Simulation of Competitive Market Response* (Cambridge, Mass.: The MIT Press, 1967).

2. Barnett, Norman, Unpublished Doctoral Dissertation, Harvard University.

3. Burger, Philip C., Charles W. King and Edgar A. Pessemier, "A Large Scale Systems View of Consumer Behavioral Research," *Proceedings of the 1966 Symposium on Consumer Behavior* (Austin, Texas: University of Texas, In Press).

4. Bush, Robert R. and Frederick Mosteller, *Stochastic Models of Learning* (New York: John Wiley and Sons, 1955).

5. David, H. D., *The Method of Paired Comparisons* (New York: Hafner Publishing Co., 1963), pp. 44-45.

6. Fouraker, Lawrence E. and Sidney Siegel, *Bargaining and Group Decision Making* (New York: McGraw-Hill Book Company, 1960).

7. Holloway, Robert J., "Experimental Work in Marketing: Current Research and Developments," pp. 383-430, in Frank M. Bass, Charles W. King and Edgar A. Pessemier, eds. *Application of the Sciences to Marketing Management,* (New York: John Wiley and Sons, 1968). In the near future, an annotated bibliography on experimental methods in marketing by the same author will be published by the American Marketing Association.

8. Luce, R. Duncan, *Individual Choice Behavior* (New York: John Wiley and Sons, 1959).

9. Luce, R. Duncan and Howard Raiffa, *Games and Decisions* (New York: John Wiley and Sons, 1957).

10. Nicosia, Francisco M., *Consumer Decision Processes* (Englewood Cliff, N.J.: Prentice Hall, Inc. 1966).

11. Pessemier, Edgar A., "A New Way to Determine Buying Decisions," *Journal of Marketing,* October 1959, pp. 41-46.

12. —————— "An Experimental Method for Estimating Demand." *Journal of Business,* October 1960; pp. 373-383.

13. ——————, *Experimental Methods of Analyzing Demand for Branded Consumer Goods,* Economic and Business Study, No. 39 (Pullman, Wash.: Washington State University Press, 1963).

14. ——————, "Forecasting Brand Performance Through Simulation Experiments," *Journal of Marketing,* April, 1964, pp. 41-46.

15. Pessemier, Edgar A. and Douglas J. Tigert, "A Taxonomy of Magazine Readership Applied to Problems in Marketing Strategy and Media Selection," Institute Paper No. 195, Institute for Research in the Behavioral, Economic, and Management Sciences, Krannert Graduate School of Industrial Administration, Purdue University, Lafayette, Indiana, August, 1967.

16. Peters, William S., "Experimental Reserach in Marketing: Historical Perspective," pp. 357-382, in Bass, King and Pessemier [7].

17. Smith, Edward M. and Charles L. Broome, "A Laboratory Experiment for Establishing Indifference Points Between Brands of Consumer Goods," and "Experimental Determination of the Effects of Price and Market-Standing Information on Consumers' Brand Preferences, *Proceedings of the Fall Conference of the American Marketing Association,* Bloomington, Indiana, August-September 1966 (Chicago, Ill.: American Marketing Association, 1966).

18. Smith, Vernon L., "Bidding Theory and the Treasure Bill Auction: Does Price Discrimination Increase Bill Prices?" *The Review of Economics and Statistics*, Volume XLVIII, No. 2, May 1966.

19. Stefflre, Volney, "Market Structure Studies: . . . ," pp. 251-268, in Bass, King and Pessemier [7].

20. Teach, Richard, *Laboratory Experiments for Measuring Demand for Consumer Goods*, Unpublished Doctoral Dissertation, Purdue University, 1967.

21. Torgerson, Warren S., *Theory and Methods of Scaling* (New York: John Wiley and Sons, 1962), p. 205.

Index